FRANKENSTEIN
AGENT OF S.H.A.D.E.

VOLUME 1 · WAR OF THE MONSTERS

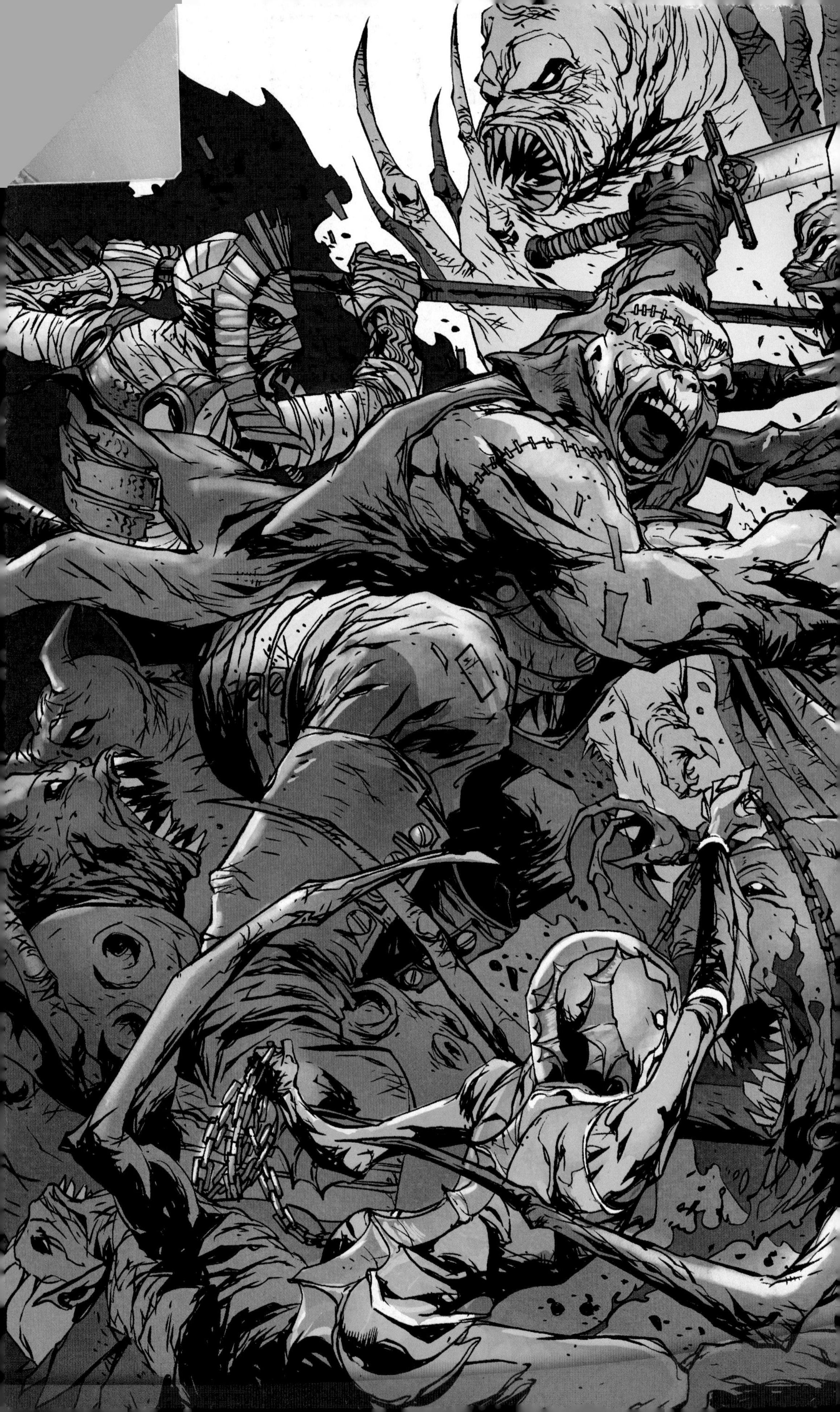

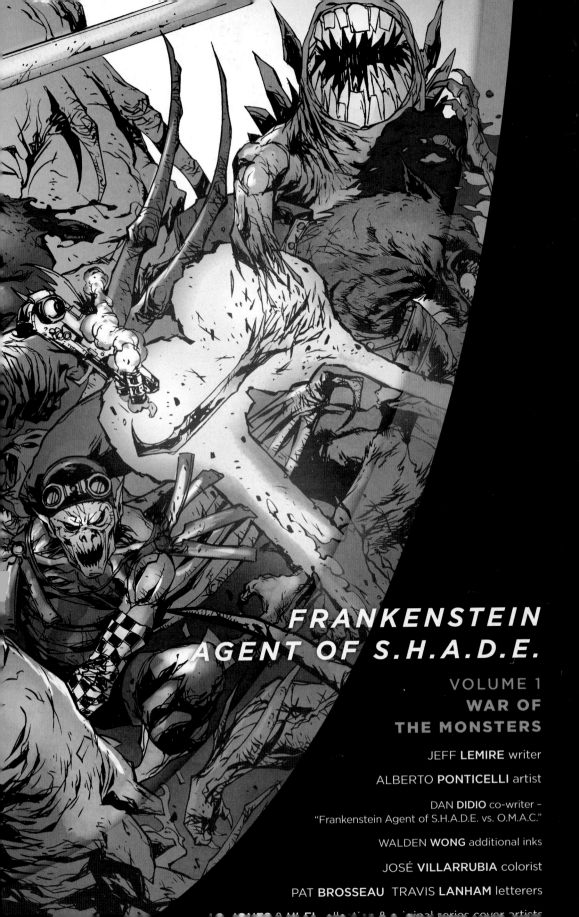

FRANKENSTEIN AGENT OF S.H.A.D.E.

VOLUME 1
WAR OF THE MONSTERS

JEFF **LEMIRE** writer

ALBERTO **PONTICELLI** artist

DAN **DIDIO** co-writer –
"Frankenstein Agent of S.H.A.D.E. vs. O.M.A.C."

WALDEN **WONG** additional inks

JOSÉ **VILLARRUBIA** colorist

PAT **BROSSEAU**   TRAVIS **LANHAM** letterers

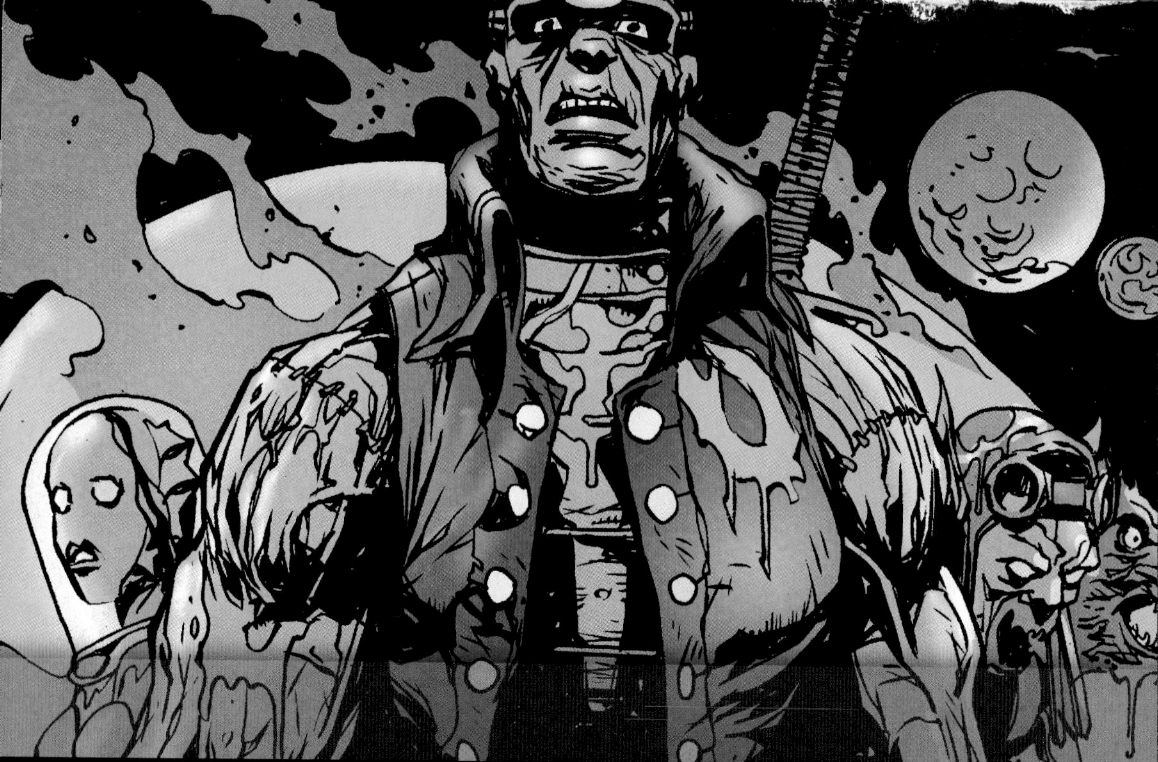

JOEY CAVALIERI Editor - Original Series KATE STEWART Assistant Editor - Original Series
ROBIN WILDMAN Editor ROBBIN BROSTERMAN Design Director - Books
ROBBIE BIEDERMAN Publication Design

BOB HARRAS VP - Editor-in-Chief

DIANE NELSON President DAN DIDIO and JIM LEE Co-Publishers
GEOFF JOHNS Chief Creative Officer
JOHN ROOD Executive VP - Sales, Marketing and Business Development
AMY GENKINS Senior VP - Business and Legal Affairs NAIRI GARDINER Senior VP - Finance
JEFF BOISON VP - Publishing Operations MARK CHIARELLO VP - Art Direction and Design
JOHN CUNNINGHAM VP - Marketing TERRI CUNNINGHAM VP - Talent Relations and Services
ALISON GILL Senior VP - Manufacturing and Operations DAVID HYDE VP - Publicity
HANK KANALZ Senior VP - Digital JAY KOGAN VP - Business and Legal Affairs, Publishing
JACK MAHAN VP - Business Affairs, Talent NICK NAPOLITANO VP - Manufacturing Administration
SUE POHJA VP - Book Sales COURTNEY SIMMONS Senior VP - Publicity
BOB WAYNE Senior VP - Sales

FRANKENSTEIN AGENT OF S.H.A.D.E. VOLUME ONE: WAR OF THE MONSTERS
Published by DC Comics.

DC Comics, 1700 Broadway, New York, NY 10019
A Warner Bros. Entertainment Company.
Printed by RR Donnelley, Salem, VA, USA. 5/18/12. First Printing.
ISBN: 978-1-4012-3471-3

SUSTAINABLE FORESTRY INITIATIVE
Certified Chain of Custody
At Least 25% Certified Forest Content
www.sfiprogram.org
SFI-01042
APPLIES TO TEXT STOCK ONLY

Lemire, Jeff.
Frankenstein, agent of S.H.A.D.E. Volume one, War of the monsters /
Jeff Lemire, Alberto Ponticelli.
p. cm. — (Frankenstein, agent of S.H.A.D.E. ; v. 1)
"Originally published in single magazine form in Frankenstein agent of S.H.A.D.E. 1-7."
ISBN 978-1-4012-3471-3
1. Frankenstein's monster (Fictitious character)—Comic books, strips, etc. 2. Graphic novels. I. Ponticelli, Alberto. II. Title. III. Title: Frankenstein, agent of SHADE. IV. Title: War of the monsters.
PN6733.L45F73 2012
741.5'973—dc23

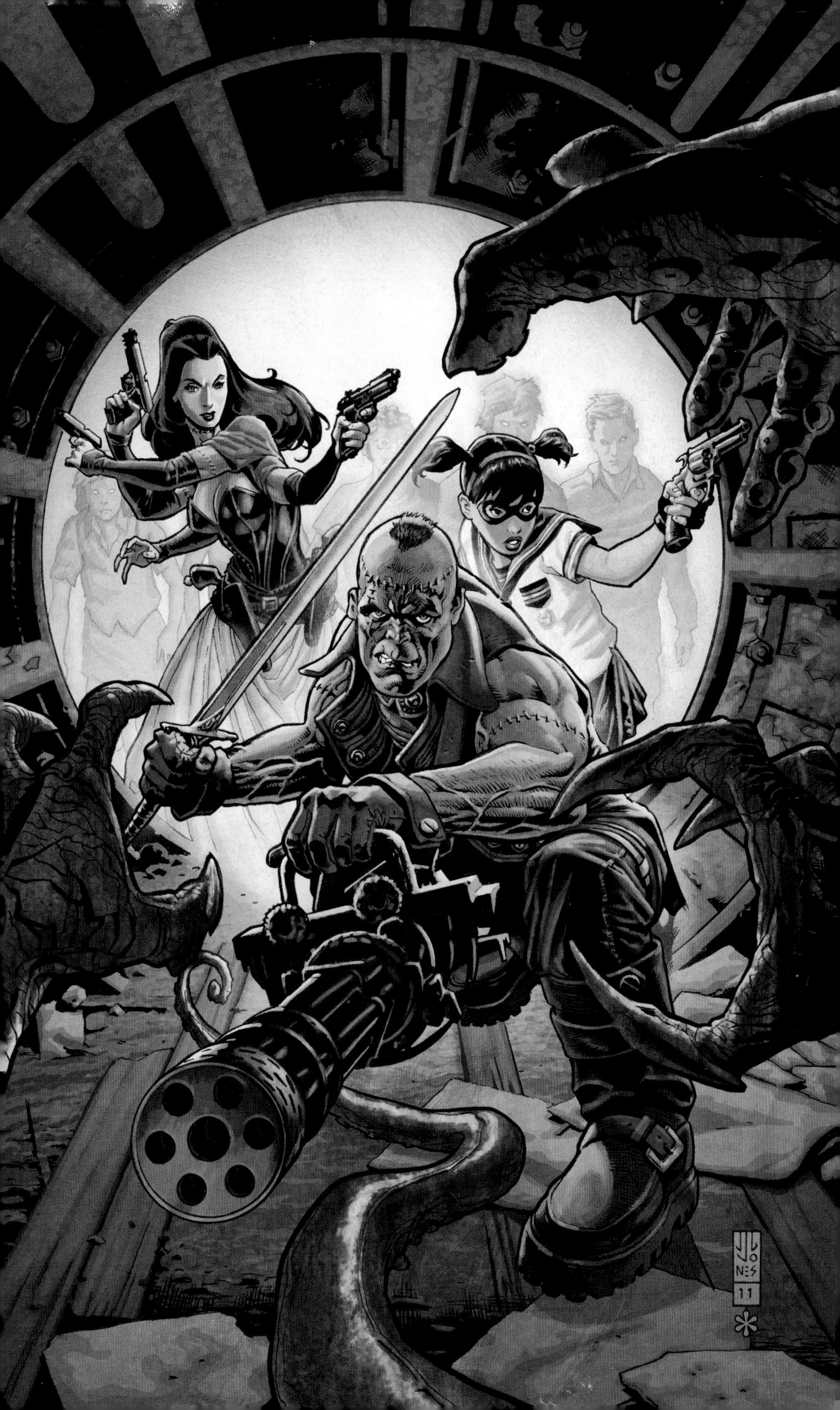

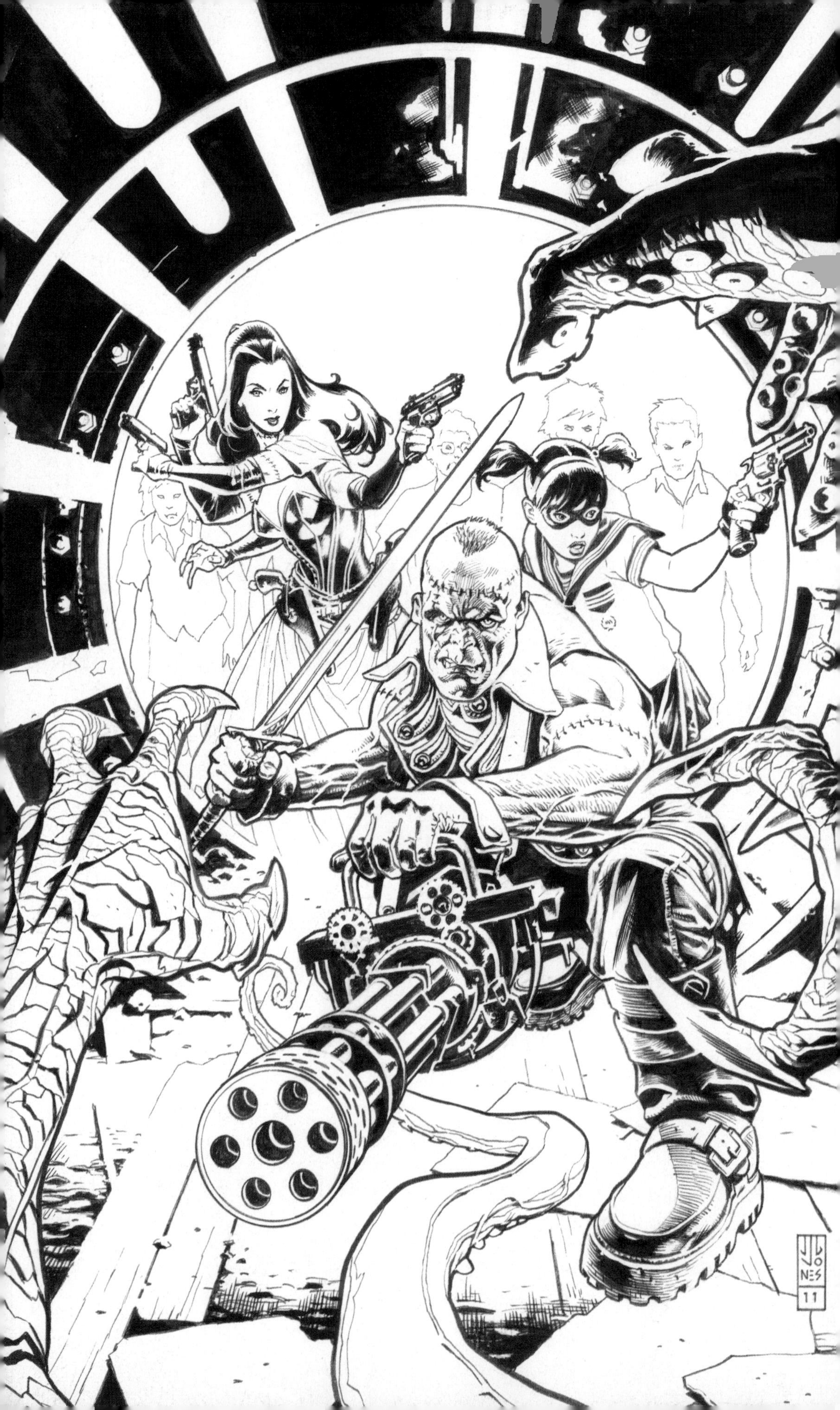

JG JONES
11

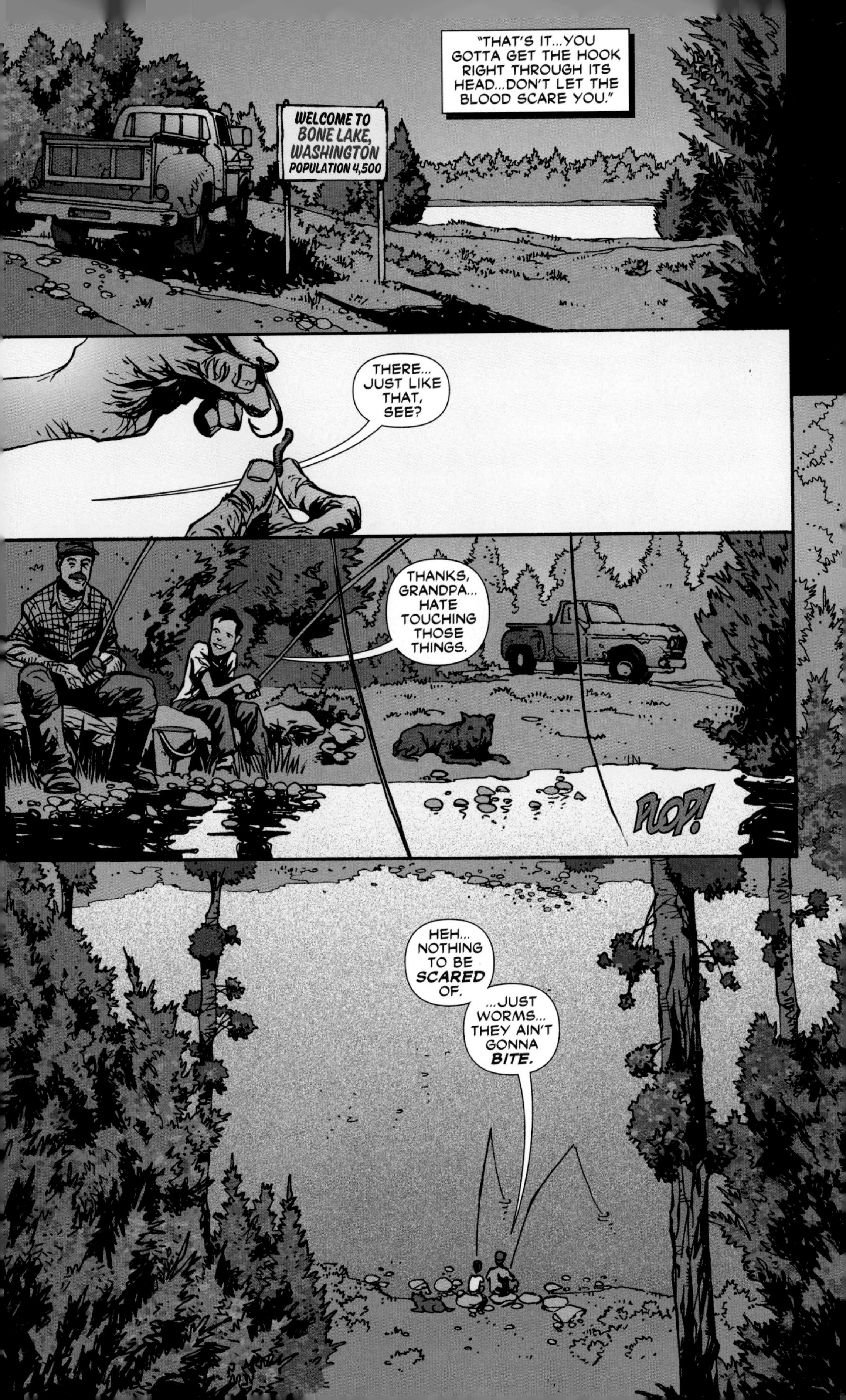
"THAT'S IT...YOU GOTTA GET THE HOOK RIGHT THROUGH ITS HEAD...DON'T LET THE BLOOD SCARE YOU."
WELCOME TO BONE LAKE, WASHINGTON POPULATION 4,500
THERE... JUST LIKE THAT, SEE?
THANKS, GRANDPA... HATE TOUCHING THOSE THINGS.
PLOP!
HEH... NOTHING TO BE SCARED OF.
...JUST WORMS... THEY AIN'T GONNA BITE.

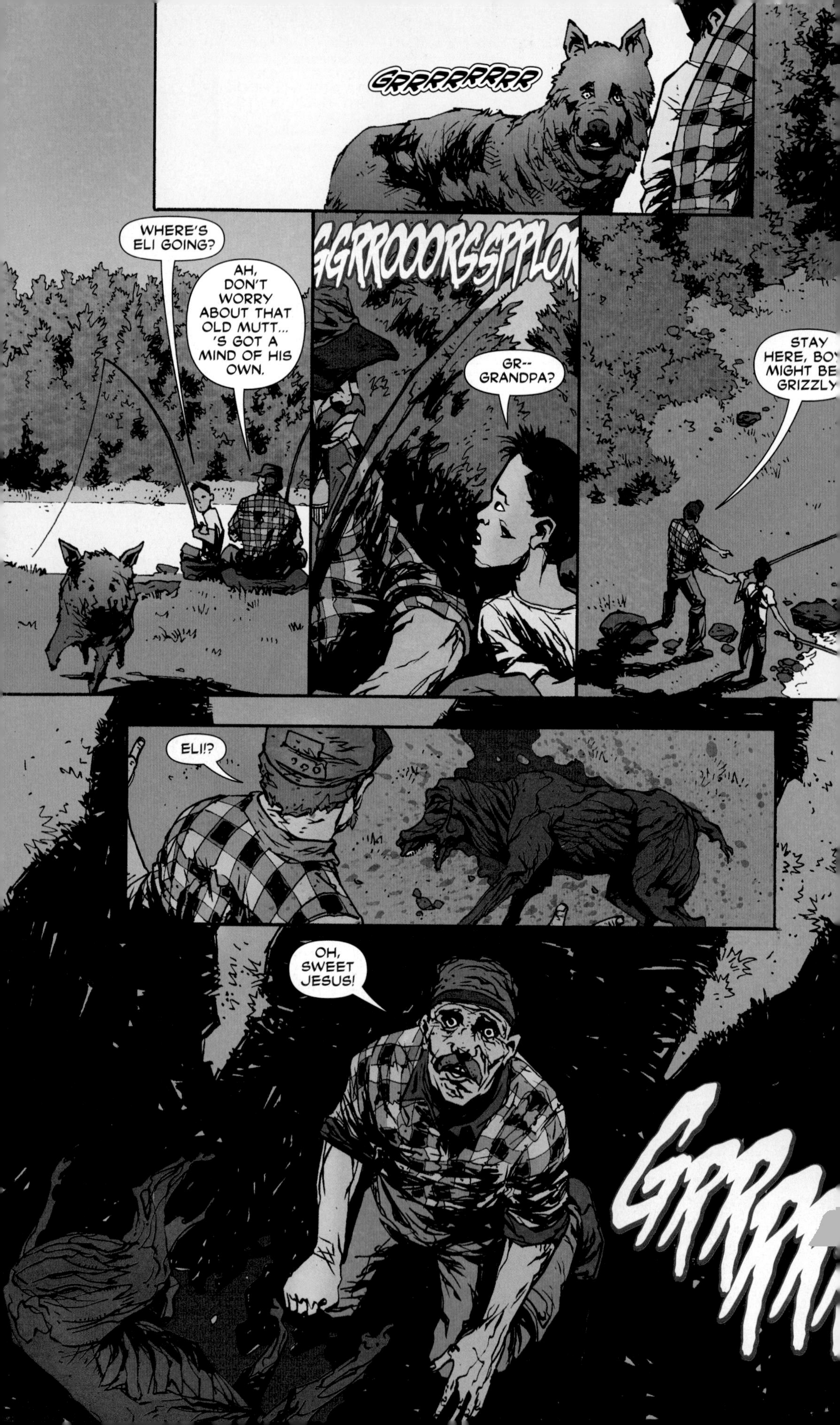
GRRRRRRRR
WHERE'S ELI GOING?
AH, DON'T WORRY ABOUT THAT OLD MUTT... 'S GOT A MIND OF HIS OWN.
GGRROOORSSPPLOK
GR-- GRANDPA?
STAY HERE, BO
MIGHT BE GRIZZLY
ELI!?
OH, SWEET JESUS!

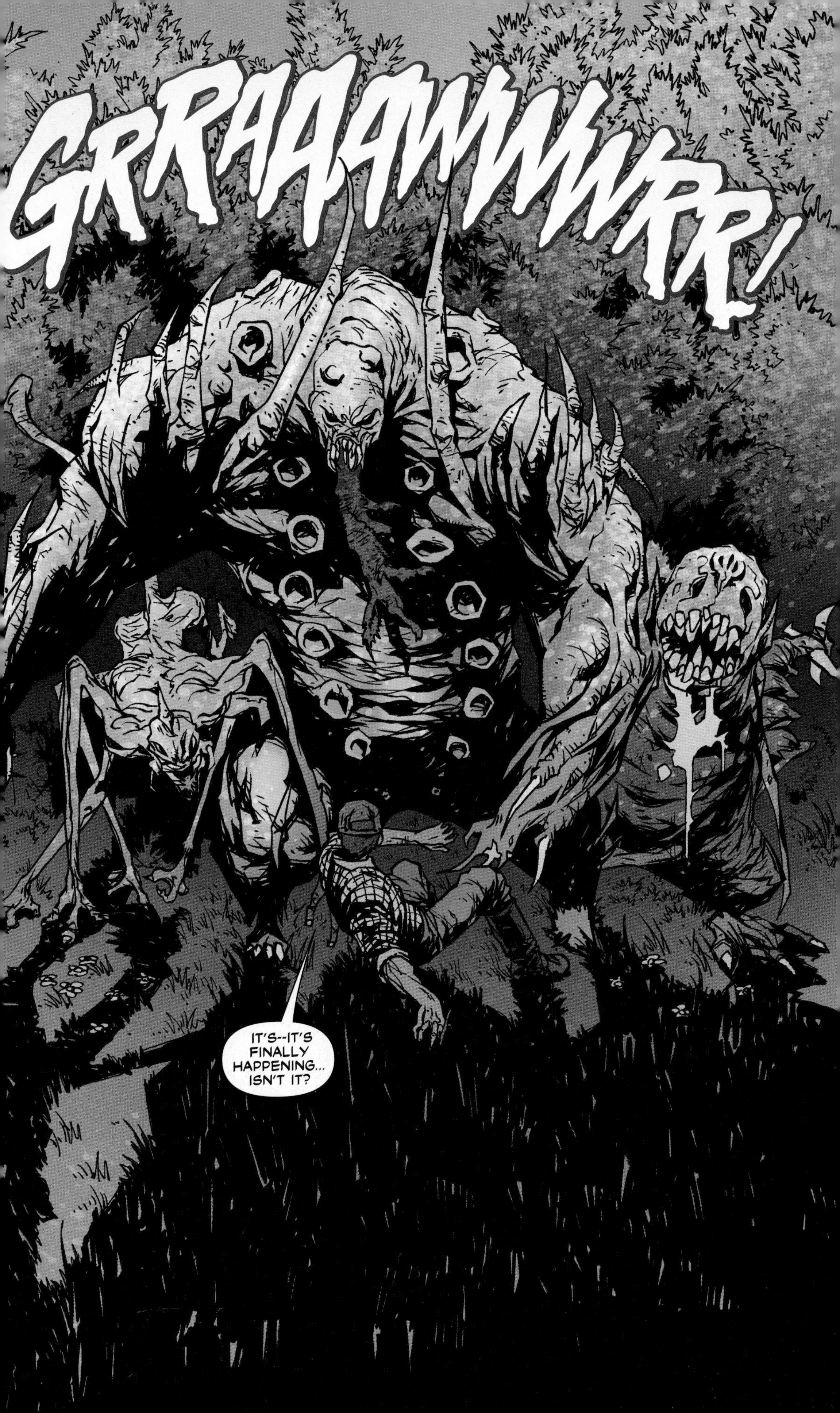
GRRAAAMMMWRR!
IT'S--IT'S FINALLY HAPPENING... ISN'T IT?

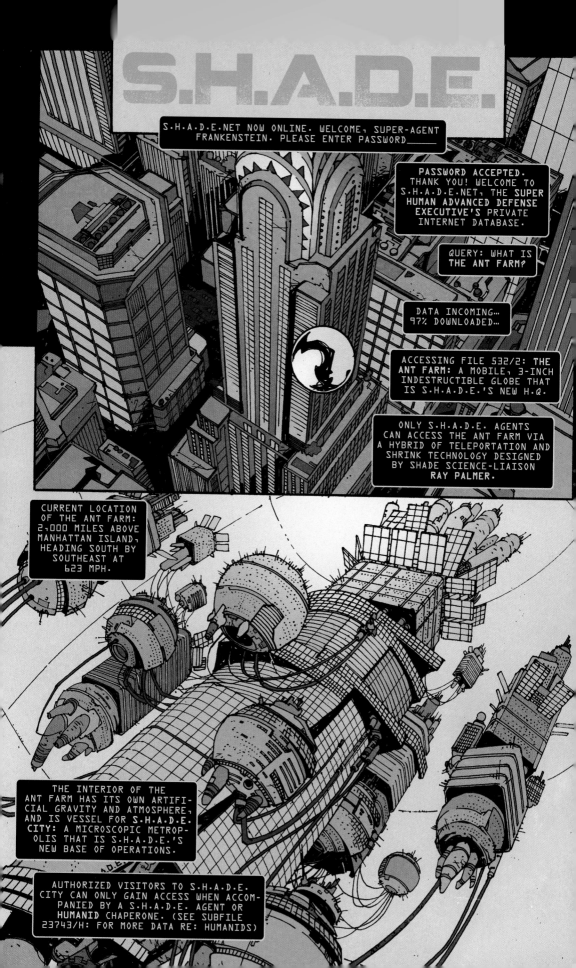

S.H.A.D.E.

S.H.A.D.E.NET NOW ONLINE. WELCOME, SUPER-AGENT FRANKENSTEIN. PLEASE ENTER PASSWORD_____

PASSWORD ACCEPTED. THANK YOU! WELCOME TO S.H.A.D.E.NET, THE SUPER HUMAN ADVANCED DEFENSE EXECUTIVE'S PRIVATE INTERNET DATABASE.

QUERY: WHAT IS THE ANT FARM?

DATA INCOMING... 97% DOWNLOADED...

ACCESSING FILE 532/2: THE ANT FARM: A MOBILE, 3-INCH INDESTRUCTIBLE GLOBE THAT IS S.H.A.D.E.'S NEW H.Q.

ONLY S.H.A.D.E. AGENTS CAN ACCESS THE ANT FARM VIA A HYBRID OF TELEPORTATION AND SHRINK TECHNOLOGY DESIGNED BY SHADE SCIENCE-LIAISON RAY PALMER.

CURRENT LOCATION OF THE ANT FARM: 2,000 MILES ABOVE MANHATTAN ISLAND, HEADING SOUTH BY SOUTHEAST AT 623 MPH.

THE INTERIOR OF THE ANT FARM HAS ITS OWN ARTIFICIAL GRAVITY AND ATMOSPHERE, AND IS VESSEL FOR S.H.A.D.E. CITY: A MICROSCOPIC METROPOLIS THAT IS S.H.A.D.E.'S NEW BASE OF OPERATIONS.

AUTHORIZED VISITORS TO S.H.A.D.E. CITY CAN ONLY GAIN ACCESS WHEN ACCOMPANIED BY A S.H.A.D.E. AGENT OR HUMANID CHAPERONE. (SEE SUBFILE 23743/H: FOR MORE DATA RE: HUMANIDS)

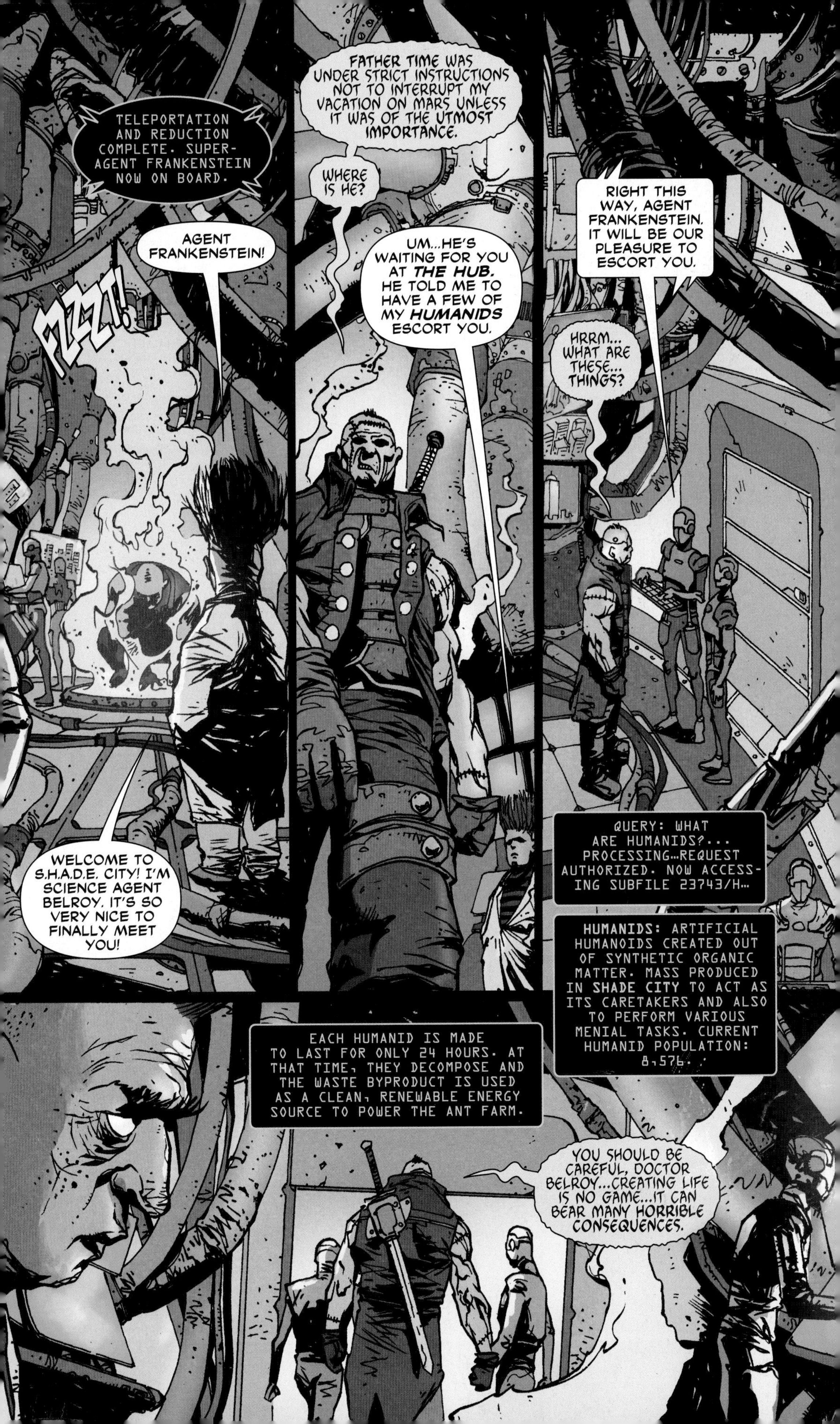
TELEPORTATION AND REDUCTION COMPLETE. SUPER-AGENT FRANKENSTEIN NOW ON BOARD.
AGENT FRANKENSTEIN!
FZZZT!
WELCOME TO S.H.A.D.E. CITY! I'M SCIENCE AGENT BELROY. IT'S SO VERY NICE TO FINALLY MEET YOU!
FATHER TIME WAS UNDER STRICT INSTRUCTIONS NOT TO INTERRUPT MY VACATION ON MARS UNLESS IT WAS OF THE UTMOST IMPORTANCE.
WHERE IS HE?
UM...HE'S WAITING FOR YOU AT THE HUB. HE TOLD ME TO HAVE A FEW OF MY HUMANIDS ESCORT YOU.
RIGHT THIS WAY, AGENT FRANKENSTEIN. IT WILL BE OUR PLEASURE TO ESCORT YOU.
HRRM... WHAT ARE THESE... THINGS?
QUERY: WHAT ARE HUMANIDS?... PROCESSING...REQUEST AUTHORIZED. NOW ACCESSING SUBFILE 23743/H...
HUMANIDS: ARTIFICIAL HUMANOIDS CREATED OUT OF SYNTHETIC ORGANIC MATTER. MASS PRODUCED IN SHADE CITY TO ACT AS ITS CARETAKERS AND ALSO TO PERFORM VARIOUS MENIAL TASKS. CURRENT HUMANID POPULATION: 8,576.
EACH HUMANID IS MADE TO LAST FOR ONLY 24 HOURS. AT THAT TIME, THEY DECOMPOSE AND THE WASTE BYPRODUCT IS USED AS A CLEAN, RENEWABLE ENERGY SOURCE TO POWER THE ANT FARM.
YOU SHOULD BE CAREFUL, DOCTOR BELROY...CREATING LIFE IS NO GAME...IT CAN BEAR MANY HORRIBLE CONSEQUENCES.

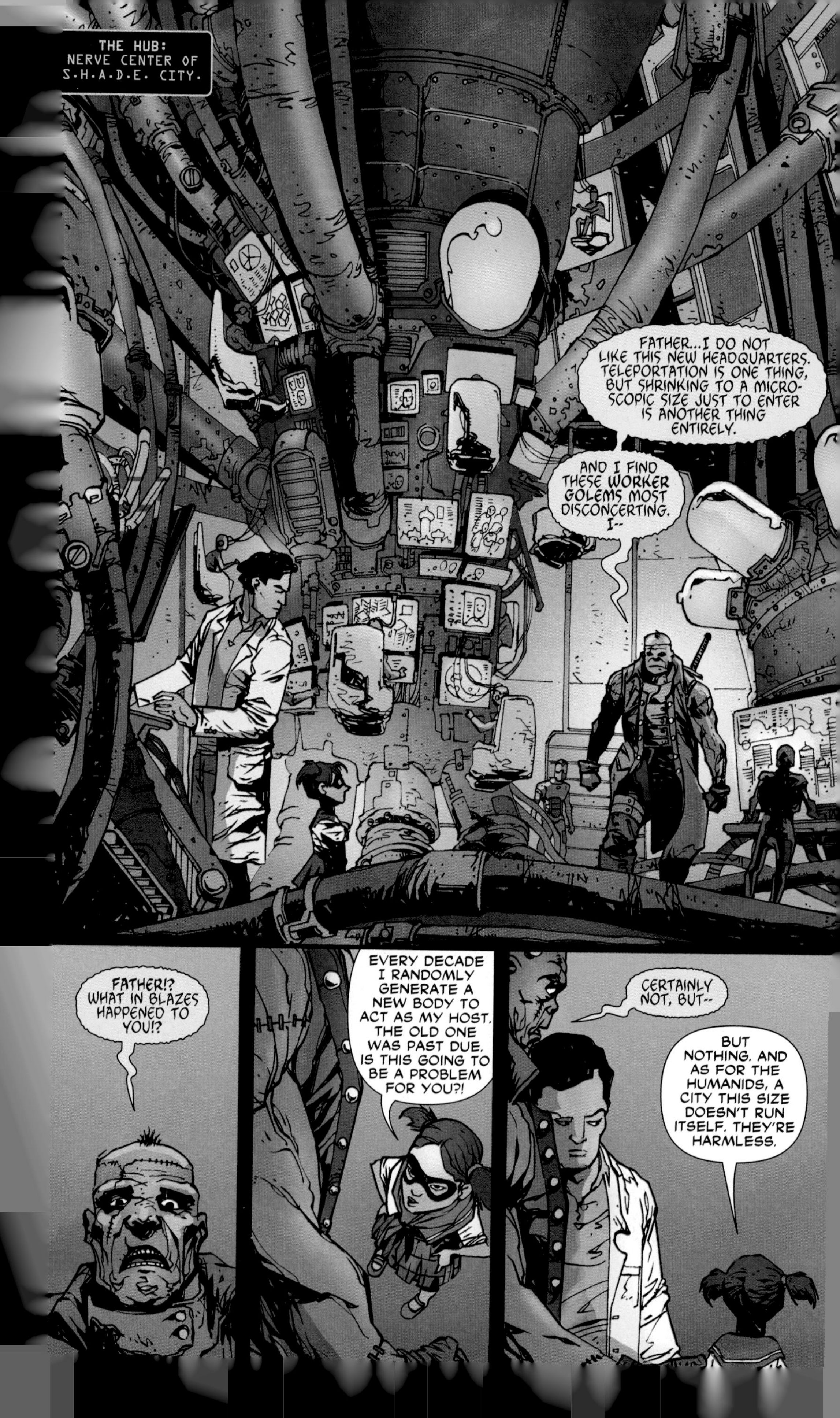
THE HUB: NERVE CENTER OF S.H.A.D.E. CITY.
FATHER...I DO NOT LIKE THIS NEW HEADQUARTERS. TELEPORTATION IS ONE THING, BUT SHRINKING TO A MICRO-SCOPIC SIZE JUST TO ENTER IS ANOTHER THING ENTIRELY.
AND I FIND THESE WORKER GOLEMS MOST DISCONCERTING. I--
FATHER!? WHAT IN BLAZES HAPPENED TO YOU!?
EVERY DECADE I RANDOMLY GENERATE A NEW BODY TO ACT AS MY HOST. THE OLD ONE WAS PAST DUE. IS THIS GOING TO BE A PROBLEM FOR YOU?!
CERTAINLY NOT, BUT--
BUT NOTHING. AND AS FOR THE HUMANIDS, A CITY THIS SIZE DOESN'T RUN ITSELF. THEY'RE HARMLESS.

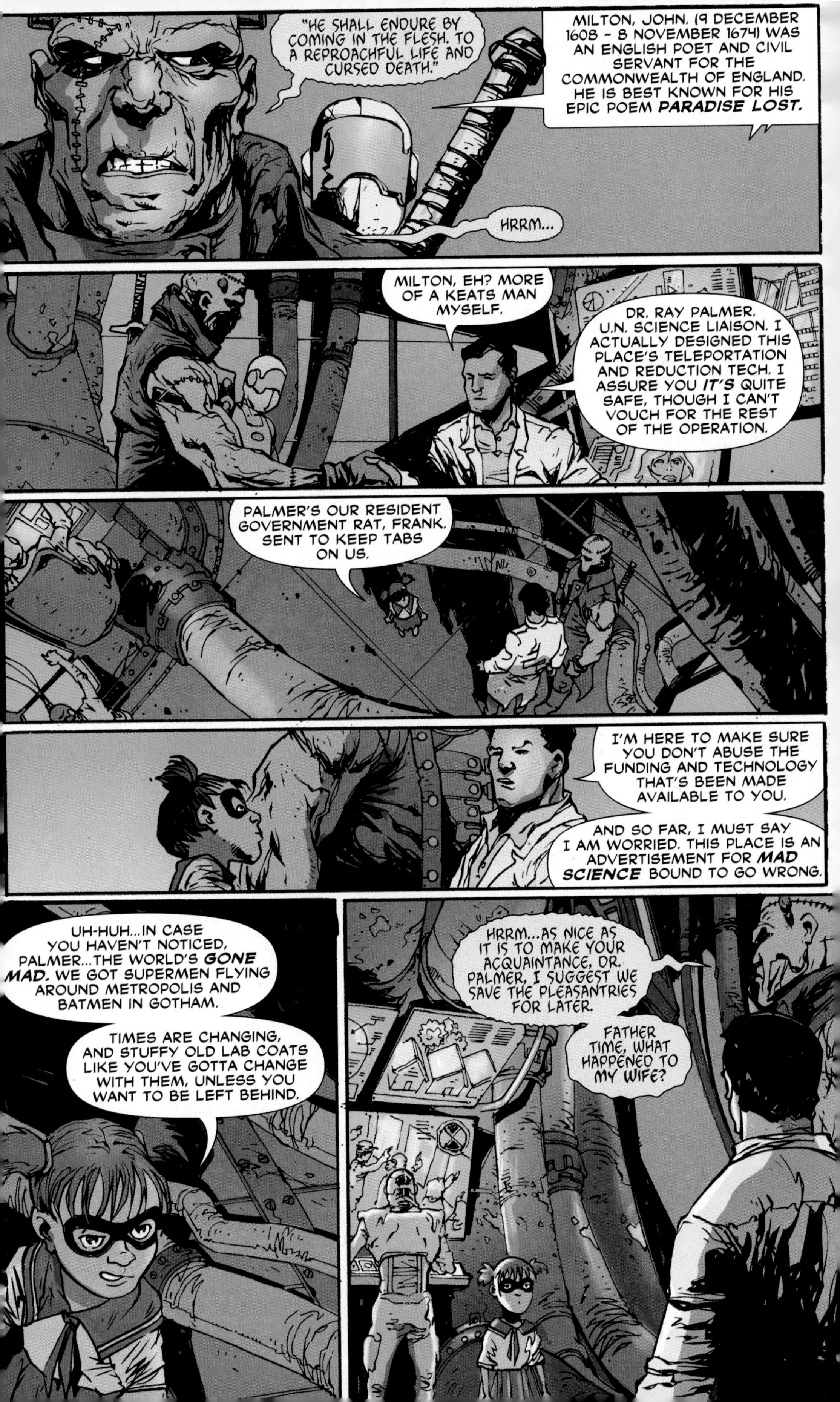
"HE SHALL ENDURE BY COMING IN THE FLESH. TO A REPROACHFUL LIFE AND CURSED DEATH."
MILTON, JOHN. (9 DECEMBER 1608 - 8 NOVEMBER 1674) WAS AN ENGLISH POET AND CIVIL SERVANT FOR THE COMMONWEALTH OF ENGLAND. HE IS BEST KNOWN FOR HIS EPIC POEM PARADISE LOST.
HRRM...
MILTON, EH? MORE OF A KEATS MAN MYSELF.
DR. RAY PALMER. U.N. SCIENCE LIAISON. I ACTUALLY DESIGNED THIS PLACE'S TELEPORTATION AND REDUCTION TECH. I ASSURE YOU IT'S QUITE SAFE, THOUGH I CAN'T VOUCH FOR THE REST OF THE OPERATION.
PALMER'S OUR RESIDENT GOVERNMENT RAT, FRANK. SENT TO KEEP TABS ON US.
I'M HERE TO MAKE SURE YOU DON'T ABUSE THE FUNDING AND TECHNOLOGY THAT'S BEEN MADE AVAILABLE TO YOU.
AND SO FAR, I MUST SAY I AM WORRIED. THIS PLACE IS AN ADVERTISEMENT FOR MAD SCIENCE BOUND TO GO WRONG.
UH-HUH...IN CASE YOU HAVEN'T NOTICED, PALMER...THE WORLD'S GONE MAD. WE GOT SUPERMEN FLYING AROUND METROPOLIS AND BATMEN IN GOTHAM.
TIMES ARE CHANGING, AND STUFFY OLD LAB COATS LIKE YOU'VE GOTTA CHANGE WITH THEM, UNLESS YOU WANT TO BE LEFT BEHIND.
HRRM...AS NICE AS IT IS TO MAKE YOUR ACQUAINTANCE, DR. PALMER, I SUGGEST WE SAVE THE PLEASANTRIES FOR LATER.
FATHER TIME, WHAT HAPPENED TO MY WIFE?

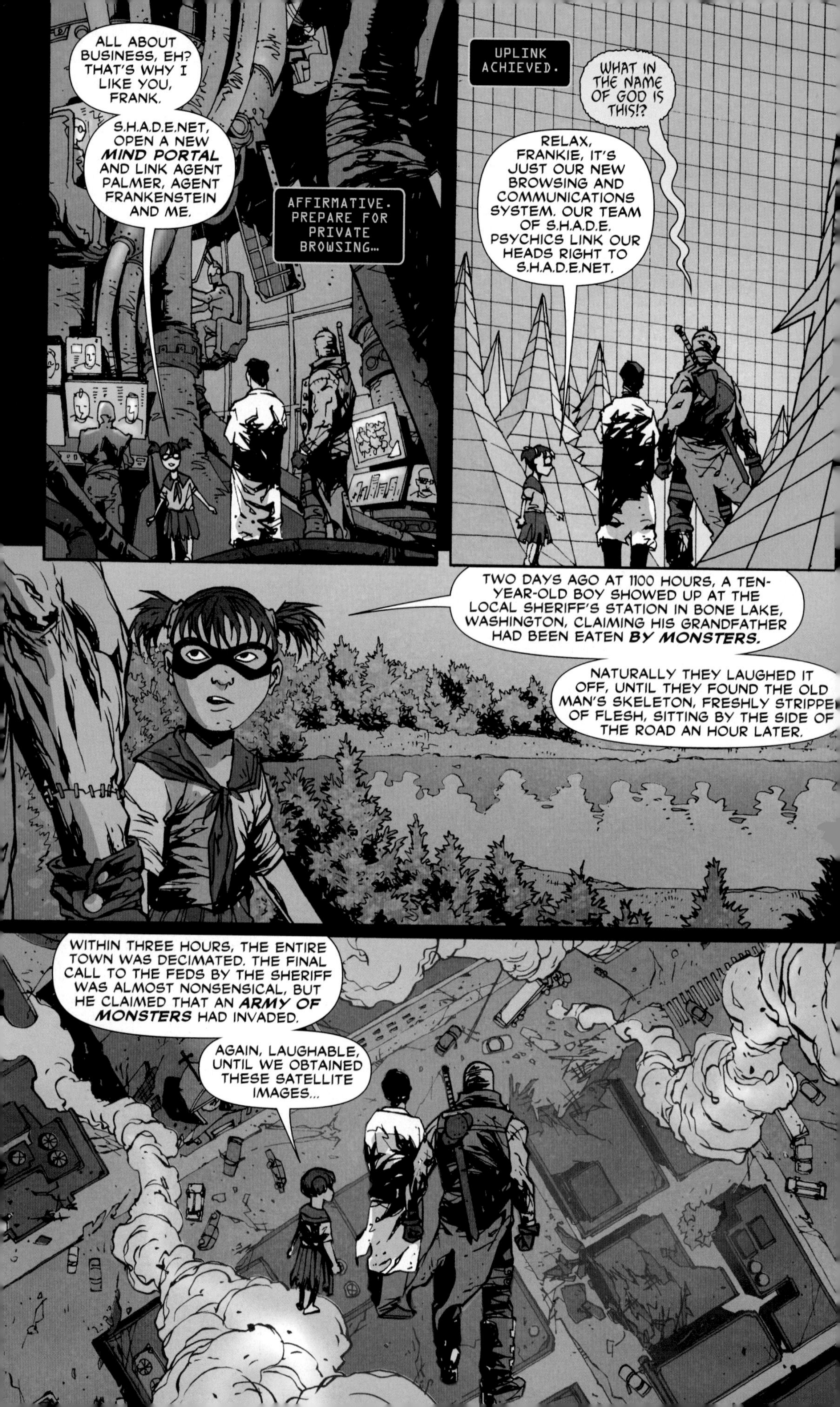

ALL ABOUT BUSINESS, EH? THAT'S WHY I LIKE YOU, FRANK.
S.H.A.D.E.NET, OPEN A NEW MIND PORTAL AND LINK AGENT PALMER, AGENT FRANKENSTEIN AND ME.
AFFIRMATIVE. PREPARE FOR PRIVATE BROWSING...
UPLINK ACHIEVED.
WHAT IN THE NAME OF GOD IS THIS!?
RELAX, FRANKIE, IT'S JUST OUR NEW BROWSING AND COMMUNICATIONS SYSTEM. OUR TEAM OF S.H.A.D.E. PSYCHICS LINK OUR HEADS RIGHT TO S.H.A.D.E.NET.
TWO DAYS AGO AT 1100 HOURS, A TEN-YEAR-OLD BOY SHOWED UP AT THE LOCAL SHERIFF'S STATION IN BONE LAKE, WASHINGTON, CLAIMING HIS GRANDFATHER HAD BEEN EATEN BY MONSTERS.
NATURALLY THEY LAUGHED IT OFF, UNTIL THEY FOUND THE OLD MAN'S SKELETON, FRESHLY STRIPPE OF FLESH, SITTING BY THE SIDE OF THE ROAD AN HOUR LATER.
WITHIN THREE HOURS, THE ENTIRE TOWN WAS DECIMATED. THE FINAL CALL TO THE FEDS BY THE SHERIFF WAS ALMOST NONSENSICAL, BUT HE CLAIMED THAT AN ARMY OF MONSTERS HAD INVADED.
AGAIN, LAUGHABLE, UNTIL WE OBTAINED THESE SATELLITE IMAGES...

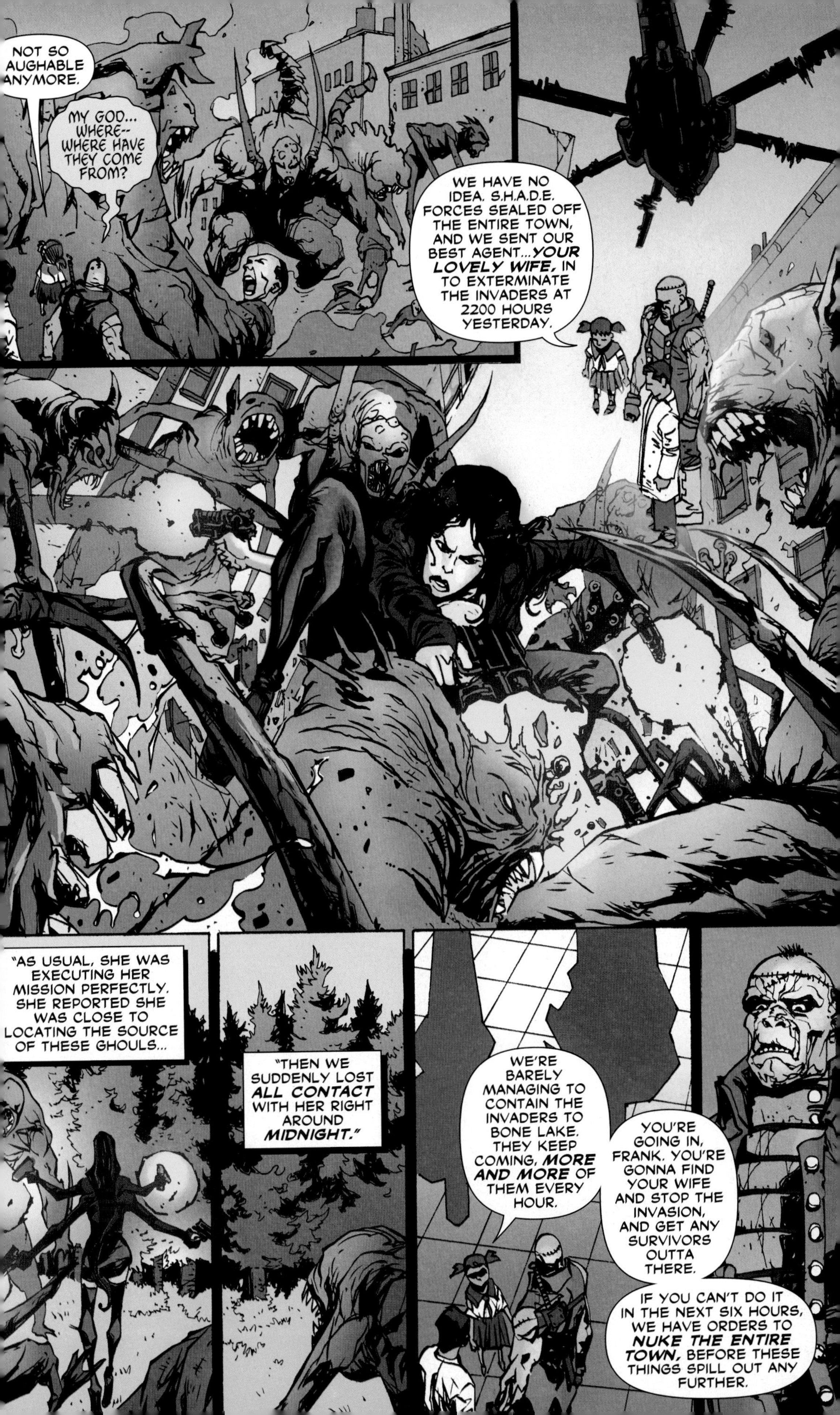

NOT SO AUGHABLE ANYMORE.
MY GOD... WHERE-- WHERE HAVE THEY COME FROM?
WE HAVE NO IDEA. S.H.A.D.E. FORCES SEALED OFF THE ENTIRE TOWN, AND WE SENT OUR BEST AGENT...YOUR LOVELY WIFE, IN TO EXTERMINATE THE INVADERS AT 2200 HOURS YESTERDAY.
"AS USUAL, SHE WAS EXECUTING HER MISSION PERFECTLY. SHE REPORTED SHE WAS CLOSE TO LOCATING THE SOURCE OF THESE GHOULS...
"THEN WE SUDDENLY LOST ALL CONTACT WITH HER RIGHT AROUND MIDNIGHT."
WE'RE BARELY MANAGING TO CONTAIN THE INVADERS TO BONE LAKE. THEY KEEP COMING, MORE AND MORE OF THEM EVERY HOUR.
YOU'RE GOING IN, FRANK. YOU'RE GONNA FIND YOUR WIFE AND STOP THE INVASION, AND GET ANY SURVIVORS OUTTA THERE.
IF YOU CAN'T DO IT IN THE NEXT SIX HOURS, WE HAVE ORDERS TO NUKE THE ENTIRE TOWN, BEFORE THESE THINGS SPILL OUT ANY FURTHER.

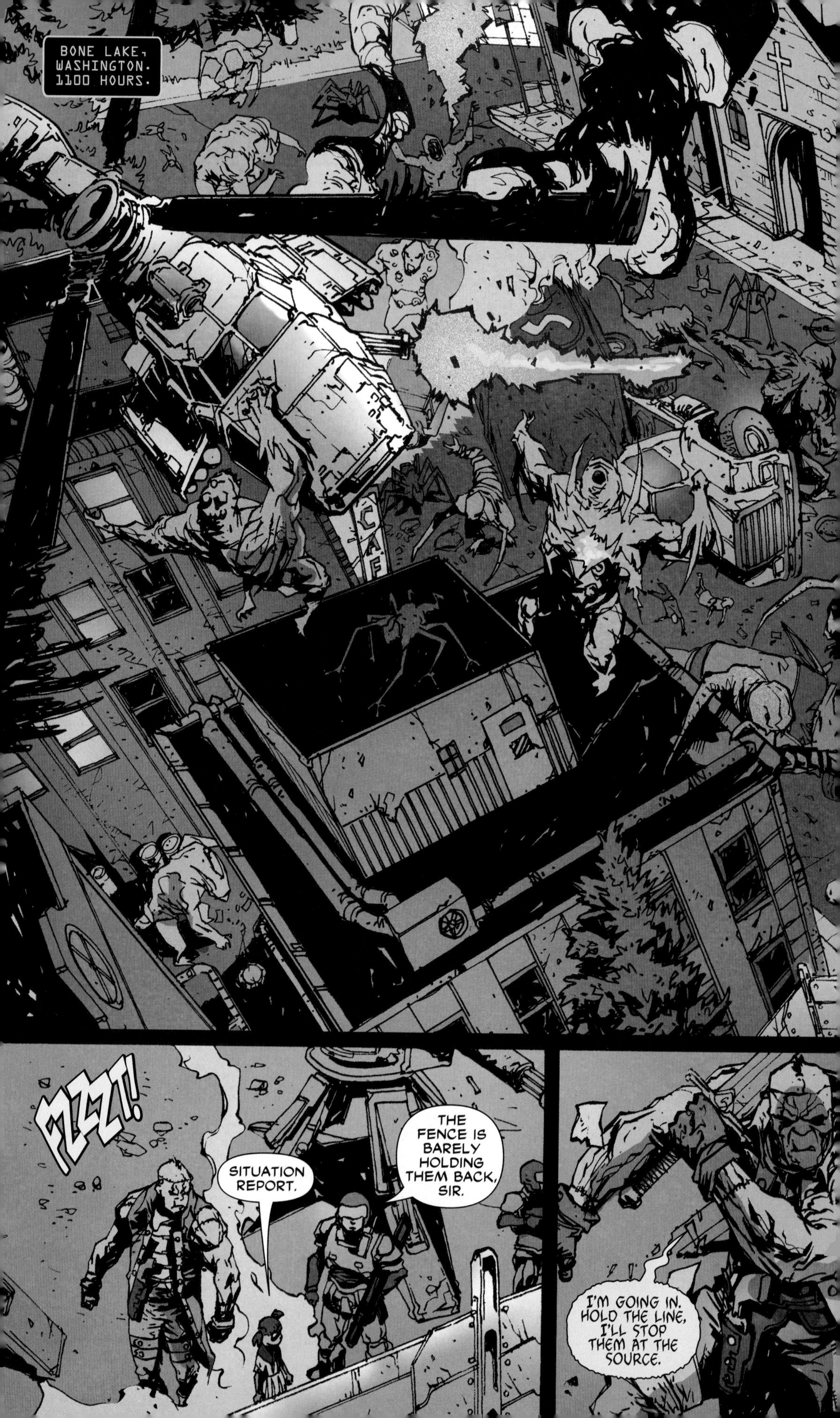
BONE LAKE, WASHINGTON. 1100 HOURS.
CAF
FZZZT!
SITUATION REPORT.
THE FENCE IS BARELY HOLDING THEM BACK, SIR.
I'M GOING IN. HOLD THE LINE, I'LL STOP THEM AT THE SOURCE.

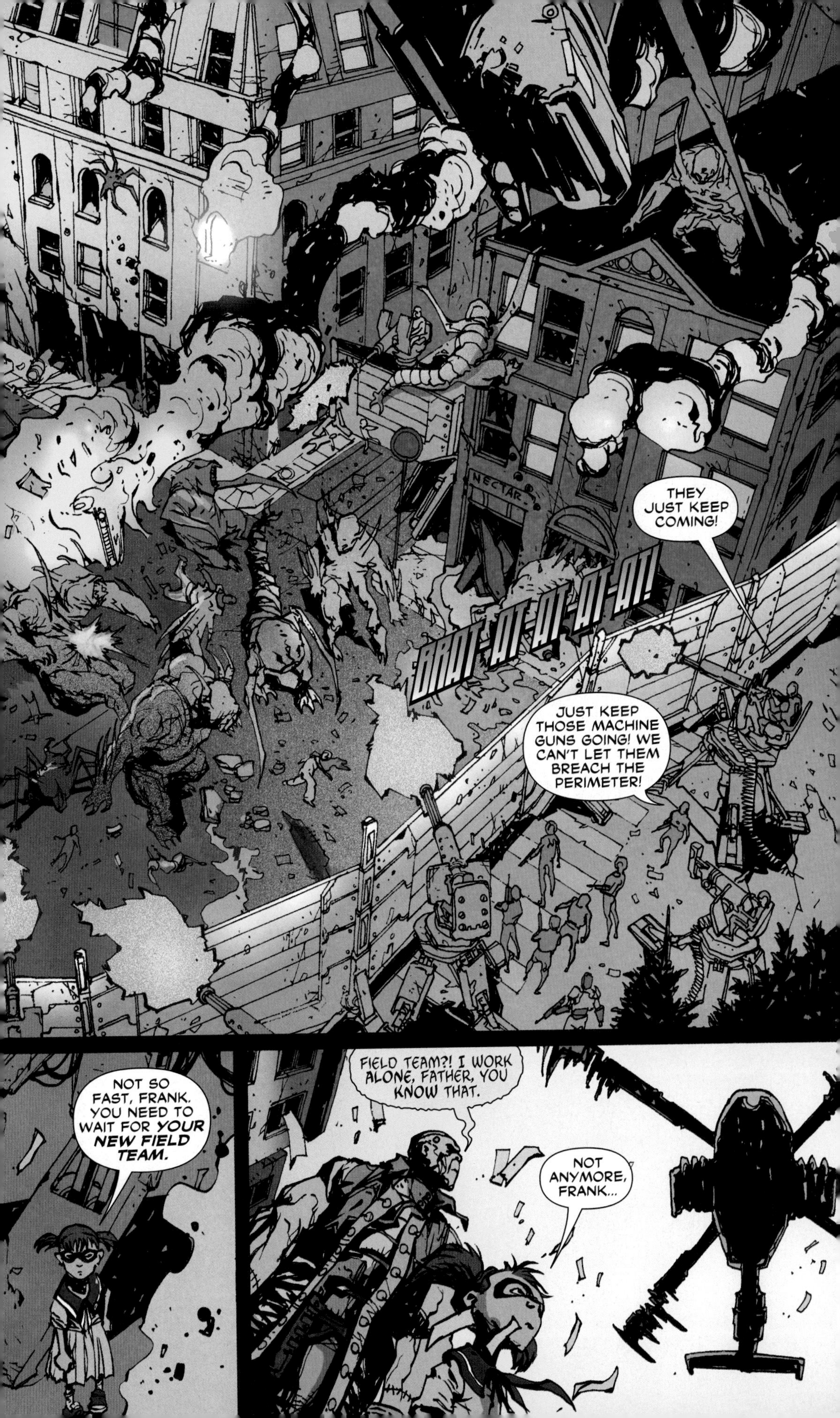

THEY JUST KEEP COMING!
BRAT-AT-AT-AT-AT!
JUST KEEP THOSE MACHINE GUNS GOING! WE CAN'T LET THEM BREACH THE PERIMETER!
NOT SO FAST, FRANK. YOU NEED TO WAIT FOR YOUR NEW FIELD TEAM.
FIELD TEAM?! I WORK ALONE, FATHER, YOU KNOW THAT.
NOT ANYMORE, FRANK...
NECTAR

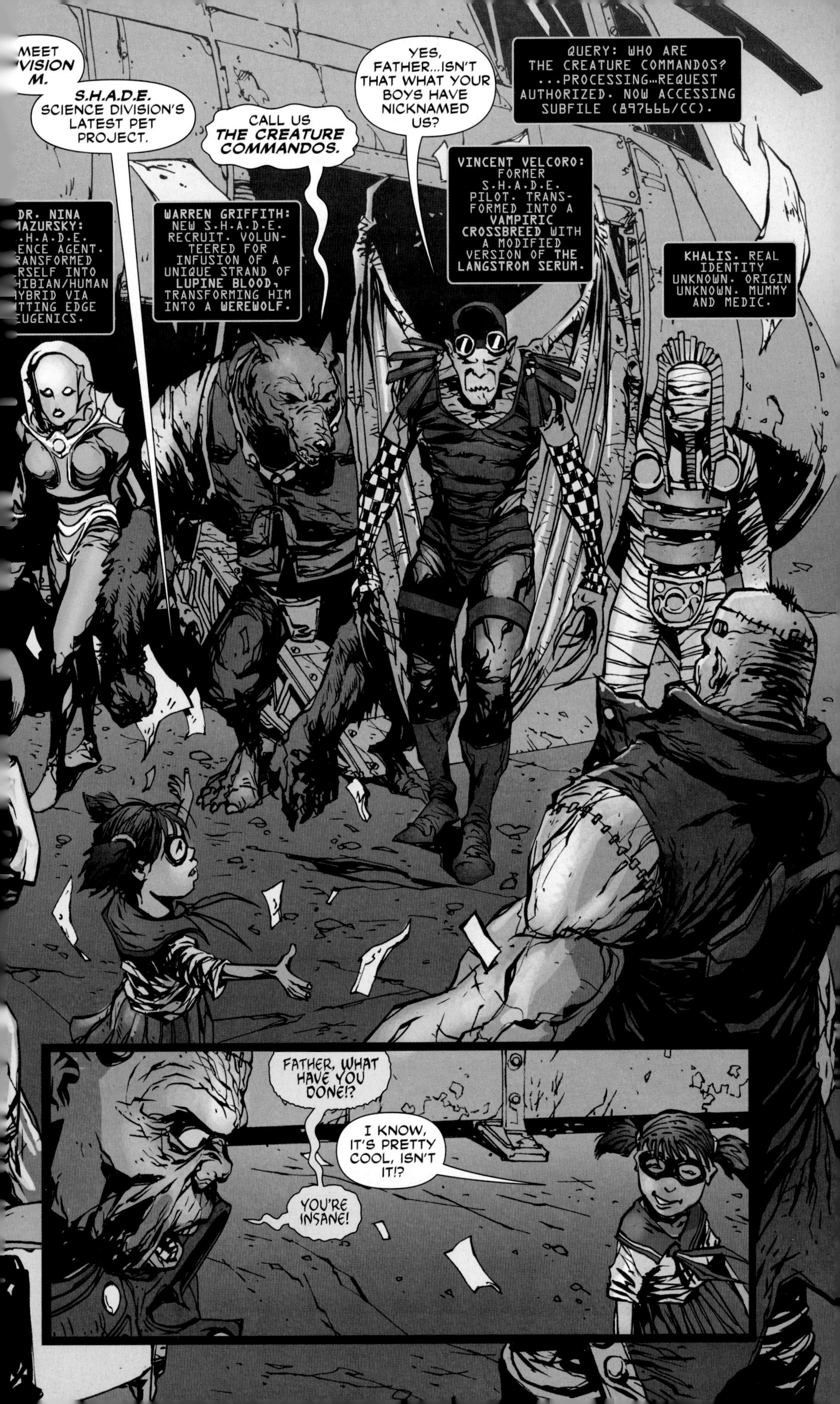

MEET VISION M.
S.H.A.D.E. SCIENCE DIVISION'S LATEST PET PROJECT.
CALL US THE CREATURE COMMANDOS.
YES, FATHER...ISN'T THAT WHAT YOUR BOYS HAVE NICKNAMED US?
QUERY: WHO ARE THE CREATURE COMMANDOS? ...PROCESSING...REQUEST AUTHORIZED. NOW ACCESSING SUBFILE (897666/CC).
DR. NINA MAZURSKY: .H.A.D.E. ENCE AGENT. RANSFORMED RSELF INTO HIBIAN/HUMAN HYBRID VIA TTING EDGE EUGENICS.
WARREN GRIFFITH: NEW S.H.A.D.E. RECRUIT. VOLUNTEERED FOR INFUSION OF A UNIQUE STRAND OF LUPINE BLOOD, TRANSFORMING HIM INTO A WEREWOLF.
VINCENT VELCORO: FORMER S.H.A.D.E. PILOT. TRANSFORMED INTO A VAMPIRIC CROSSBREED WITH A MODIFIED VERSION OF THE LANGSTROM SERUM.
KHALIS. REAL IDENTITY UNKNOWN. ORIGIN UNKNOWN. MUMMY AND MEDIC.
FATHER, WHAT HAVE YOU DONE!?
YOU'RE INSANE!
I KNOW, IT'S PRETTY COOL, ISN'T IT!?

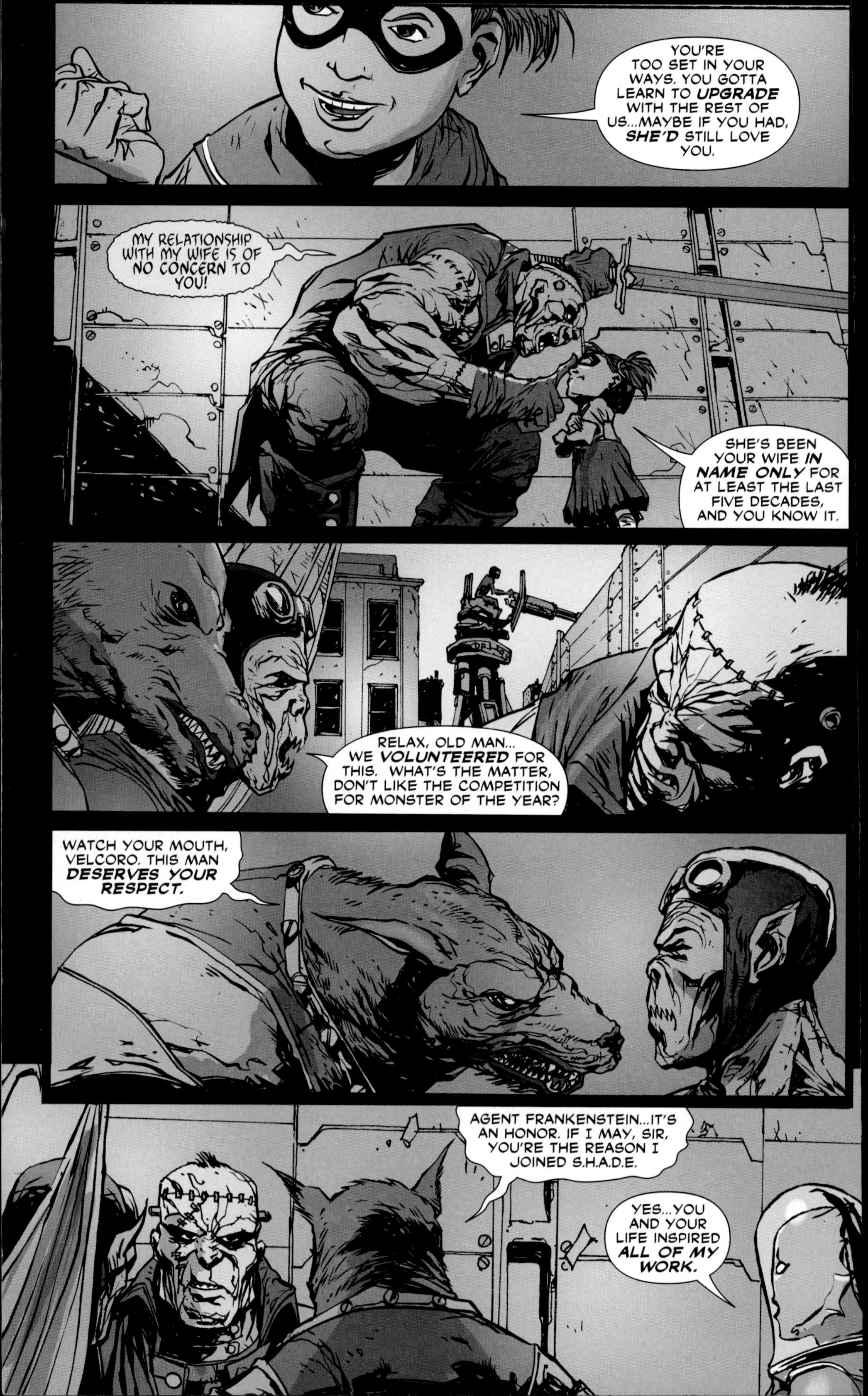
YOU'RE TOO SET IN YOUR WAYS. YOU GOTTA LEARN TO UPGRADE WITH THE REST OF US...MAYBE IF YOU HAD, SHE'D STILL LOVE YOU.
MY RELATIONSHIP WITH MY WIFE IS OF NO CONCERN TO YOU!
SHE'S BEEN YOUR WIFE IN NAME ONLY FOR AT LEAST THE LAST FIVE DECADES, AND YOU KNOW IT.
RELAX, OLD MAN... WE VOLUNTEERED FOR THIS. WHAT'S THE MATTER, DON'T LIKE THE COMPETITION FOR MONSTER OF THE YEAR?
WATCH YOUR MOUTH, VELCORO. THIS MAN DESERVES YOUR RESPECT.
AGENT FRANKENSTEIN...IT'S AN HONOR. IF I MAY, SIR, YOU'RE THE REASON I JOINED S.H.A.D.E.
YES...YOU AND YOUR LIFE INSPIRED ALL OF MY WORK.

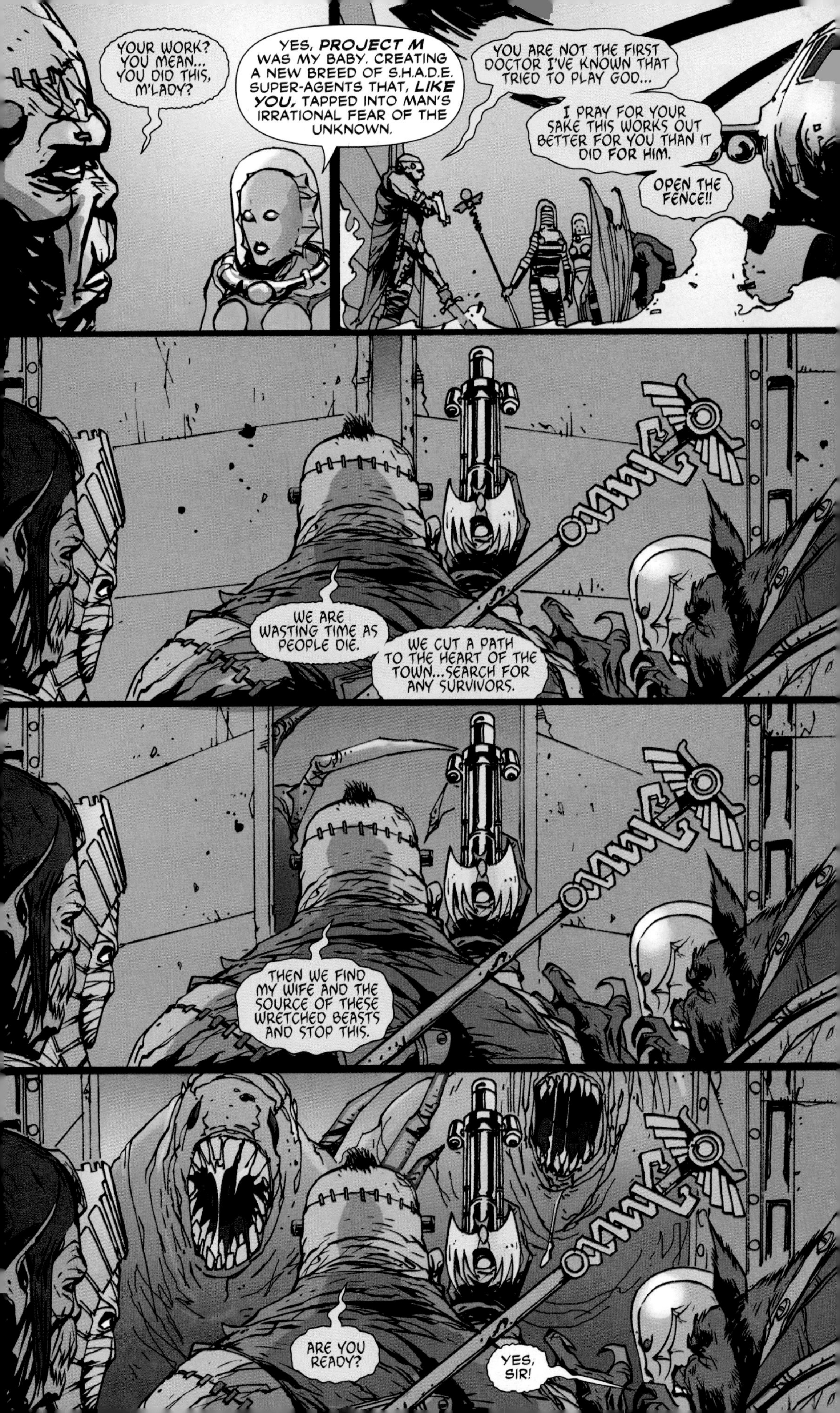
YOUR WORK? YOU MEAN... YOU DID THIS, M'LADY?
YES, PROJECT M WAS MY BABY. CREATING A NEW BREED OF S.H.A.D.E. SUPER-AGENTS THAT, LIKE YOU, TAPPED INTO MAN'S IRRATIONAL FEAR OF THE UNKNOWN.
YOU ARE NOT THE FIRST DOCTOR I'VE KNOWN THAT TRIED TO PLAY GOD...
I PRAY FOR YOUR SAKE THIS WORKS OUT BETTER FOR YOU THAN IT DID FOR HIM.
OPEN THE FENCE!!
WE ARE WASTING TIME AS PEOPLE DIE.
WE CUT A PATH TO THE HEART OF THE TOWN...SEARCH FOR ANY SURVIVORS.
THEN WE FIND MY WIFE AND THE SOURCE OF THESE WRETCHED BEASTS AND STOP THIS.
ARE YOU READY?
YES, SIR!

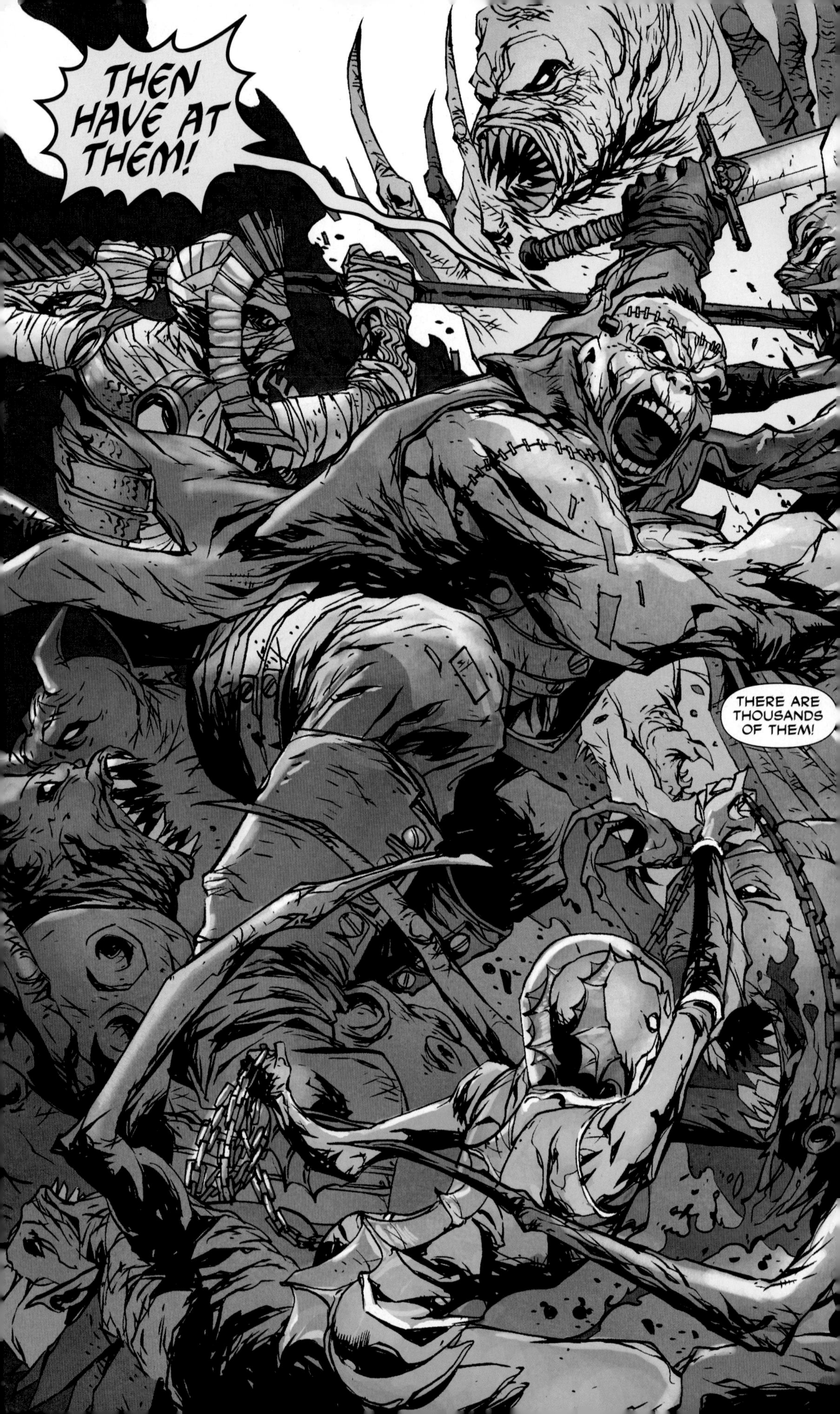
THEN HAVE AT THEM!
THERE ARE THOUSANDS OF THEM!

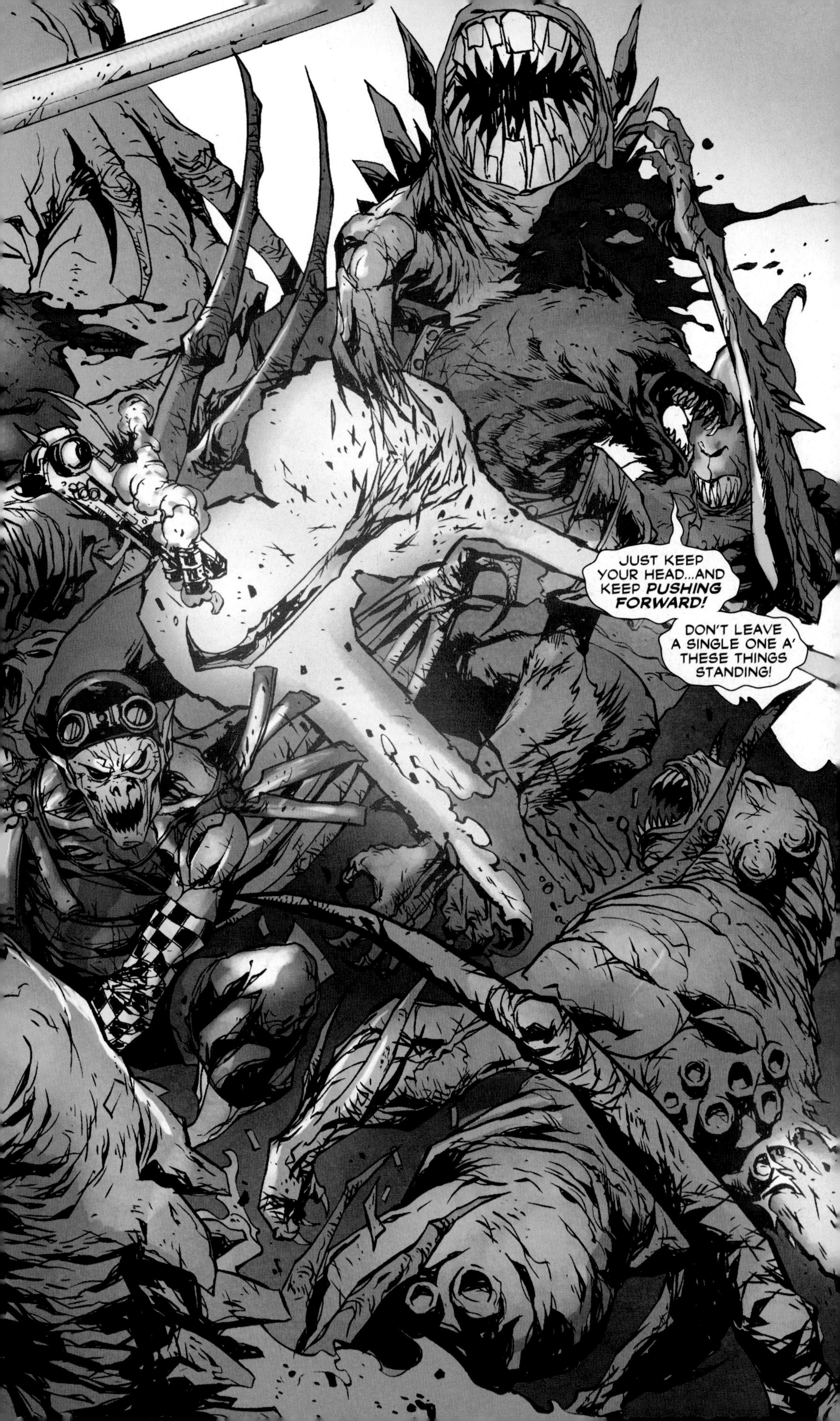
JUST KEEP YOUR HEAD...AND KEEP PUSHING FORWARD!
DON'T LEAVE A SINGLE ONE A' THESE THINGS STANDING!

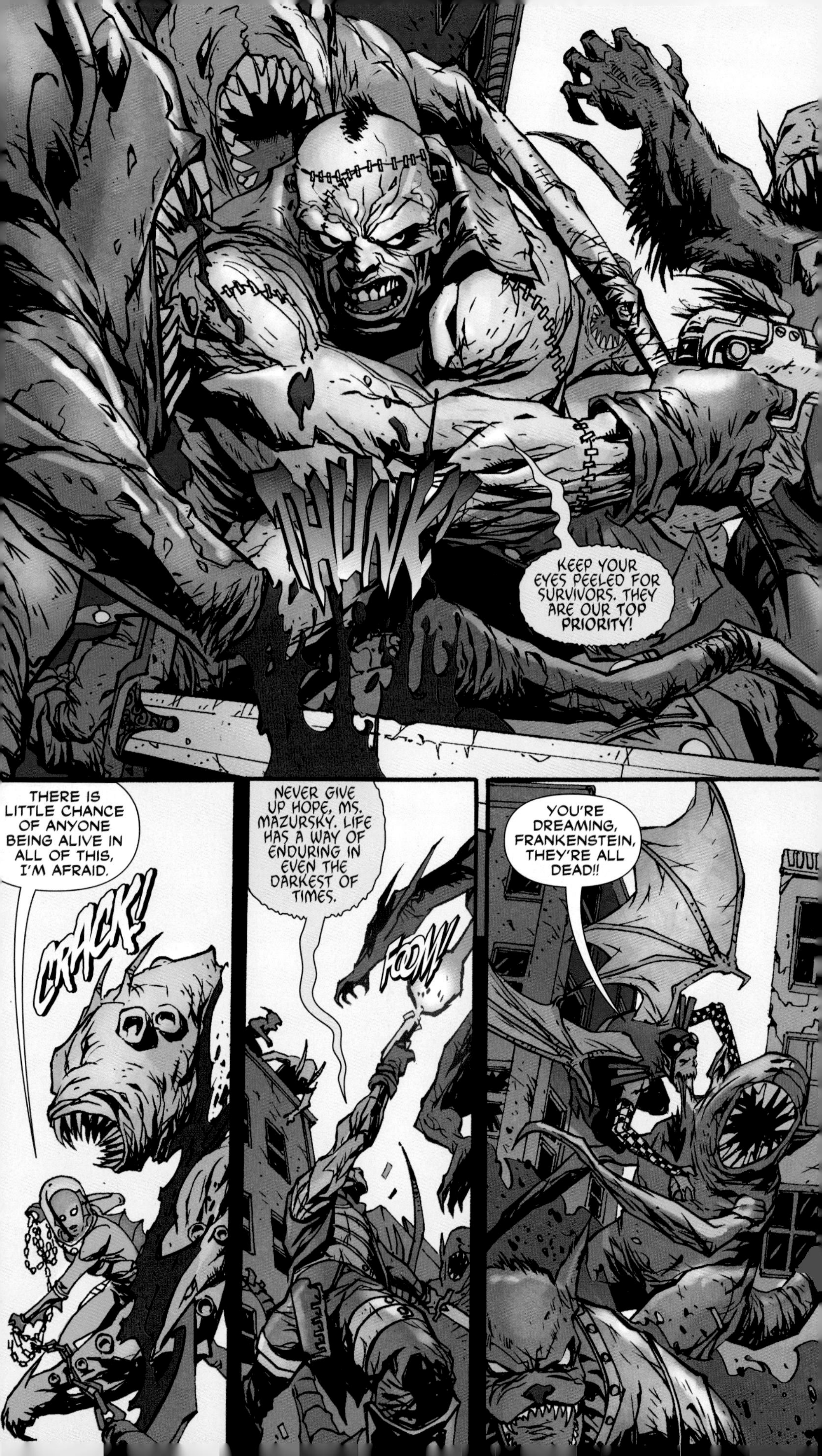
THUNK
KEEP YOUR EYES PEELED FOR SURVIVORS. THEY ARE OUR TOP PRIORITY!
THERE IS LITTLE CHANCE OF ANYONE BEING ALIVE IN ALL OF THIS, I'M AFRAID.
CRACK!
NEVER GIVE UP HOPE, MS. MAZURSKY. LIFE HAS A WAY OF ENDURING IN EVEN THE DARKEST OF TIMES.
FOOM!
YOU'RE DREAMING, FRANKENSTEIN, THEY'RE ALL DEAD!!

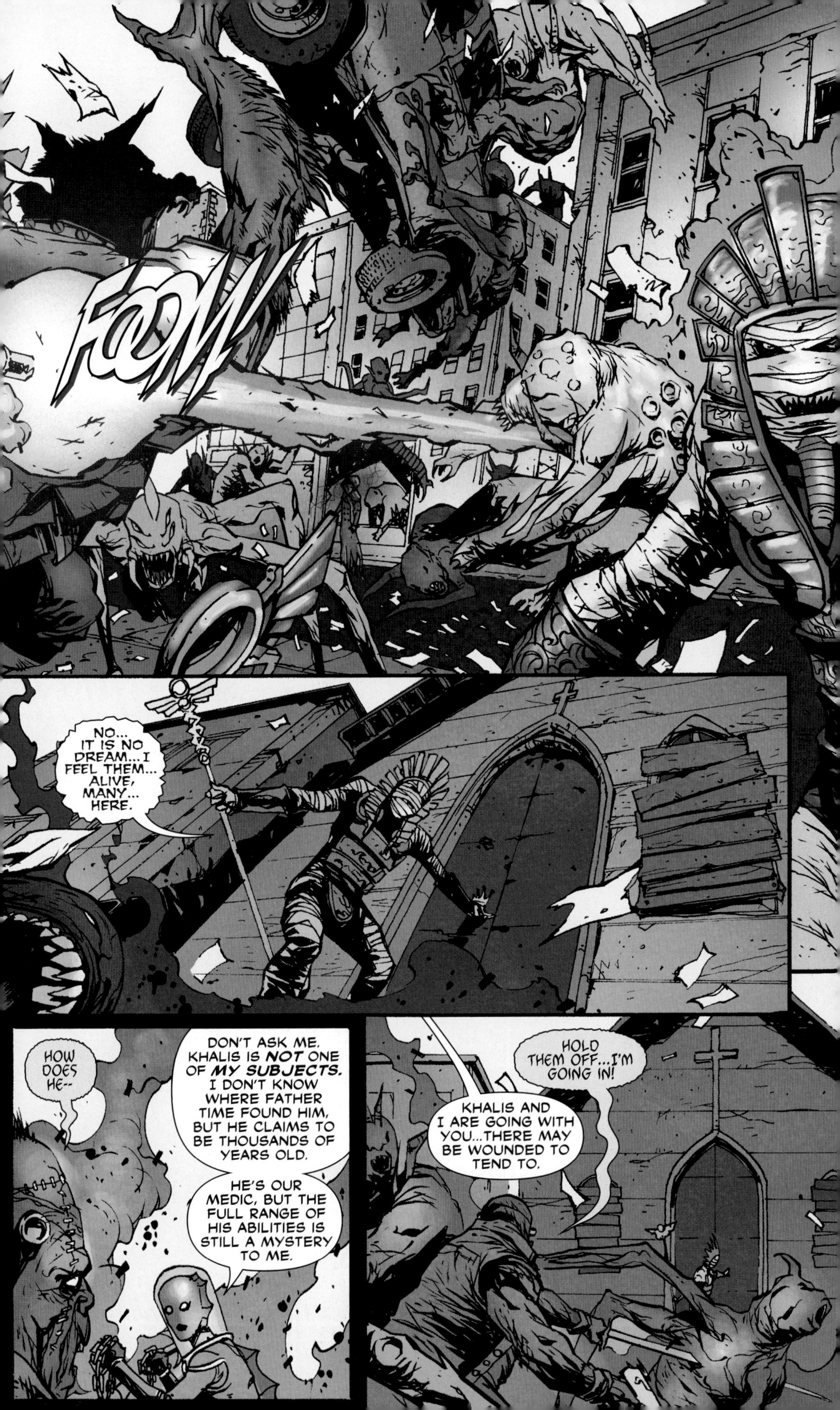
FOOM
NO... IT IS NO DREAM... I FEEL THEM... ALIVE, MANY... HERE.
HOW DOES HE--
DON'T ASK ME. KHALIS IS **NOT** ONE OF **MY SUBJECTS.** I DON'T KNOW WHERE FATHER TIME FOUND HIM, BUT HE CLAIMS TO BE THOUSANDS OF YEARS OLD.
HE'S OUR MEDIC, BUT THE FULL RANGE OF HIS ABILITIES IS STILL A MYSTERY TO ME.
HOLD THEM OFF...I'M GOING IN!
KHALIS AND I ARE GOING WITH YOU...THERE MAY BE WOUNDED TO TEND TO.

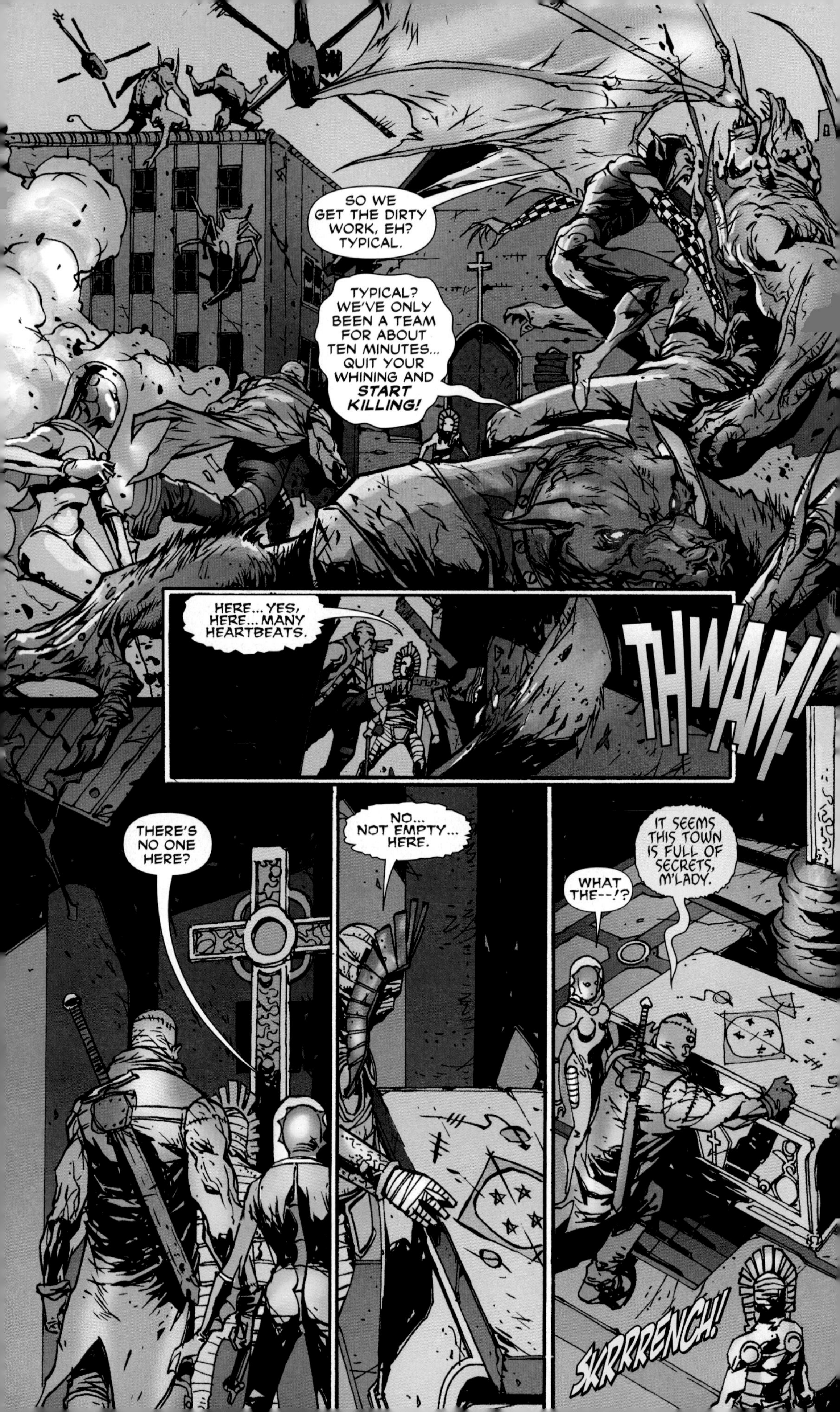
SO WE GET THE DIRTY WORK, EH? TYPICAL.
TYPICAL? WE'VE ONLY BEEN A TEAM FOR ABOUT TEN MINUTES... QUIT YOUR WHINING AND START KILLING!
HERE... YES, HERE... MANY HEARTBEATS.
THWAM!
THERE'S NO ONE HERE?
NO... NOT EMPTY... HERE.
WHAT THE--!?
IT SEEMS THIS TOWN IS FULL OF SECRETS, M'LADY.
SKRRRENCH!

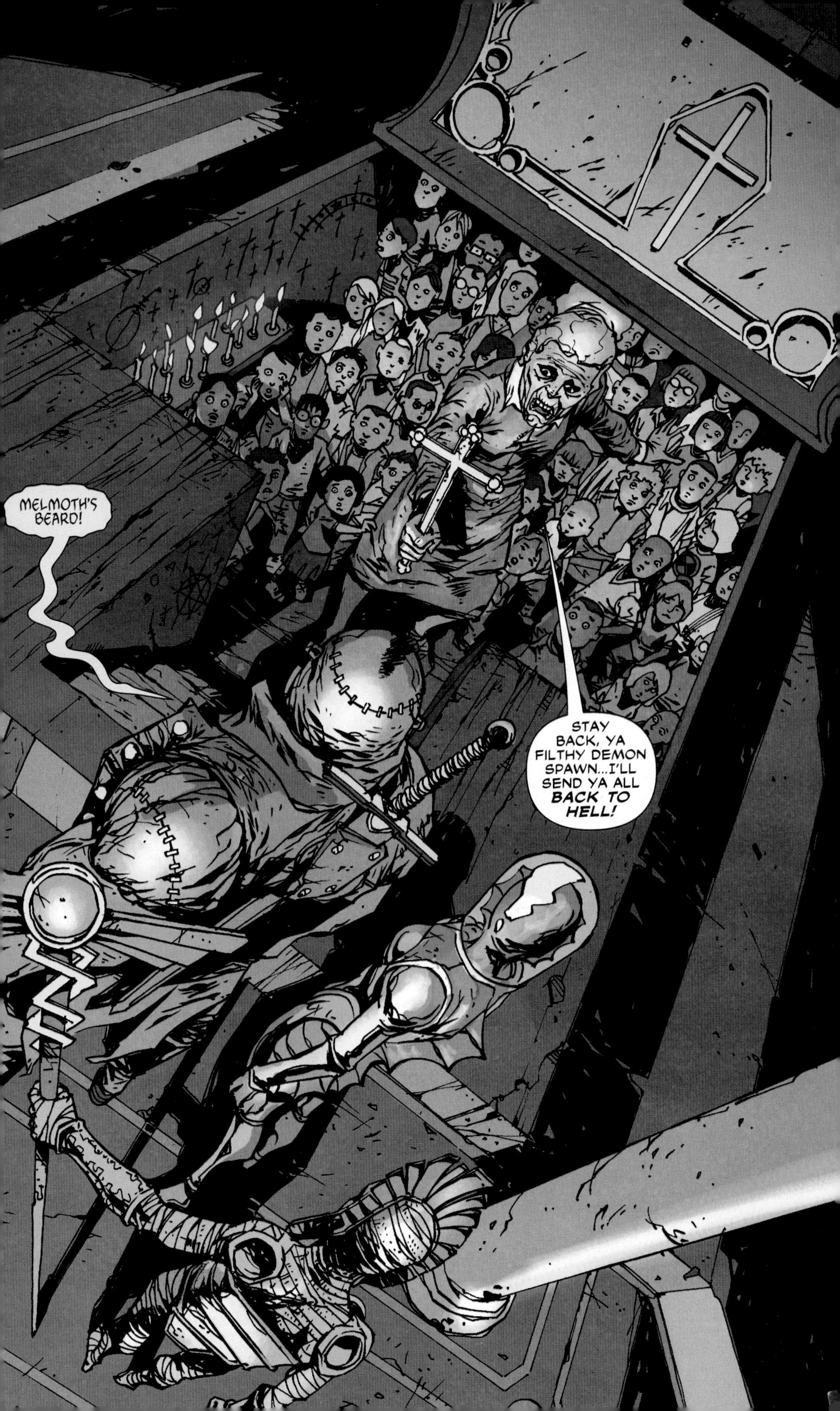
MELMOTH'S BEARD!
STAY BACK, YA FILTHY DEMON SPAWN...I'LL SEND YA ALL BACK TO HELL!

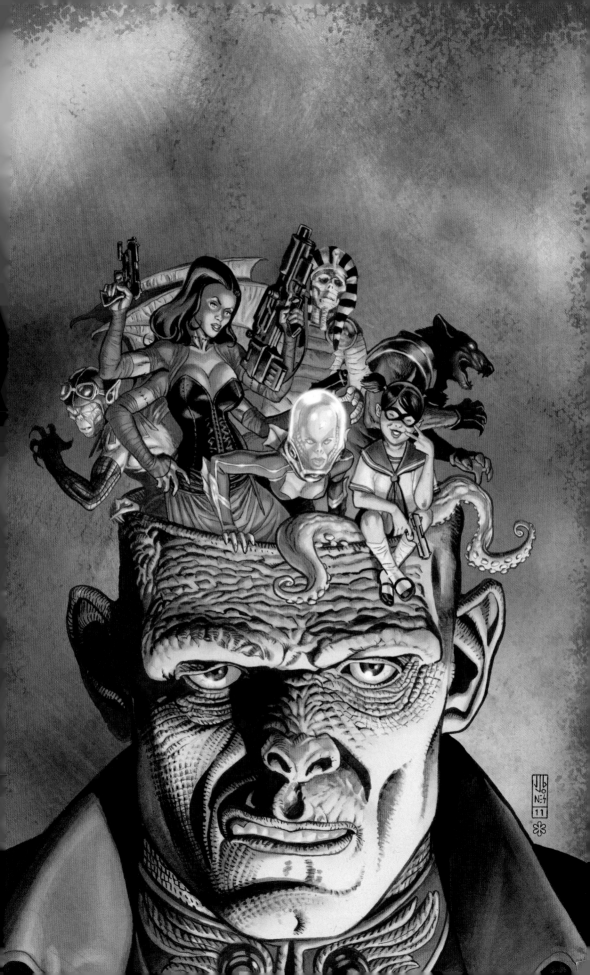

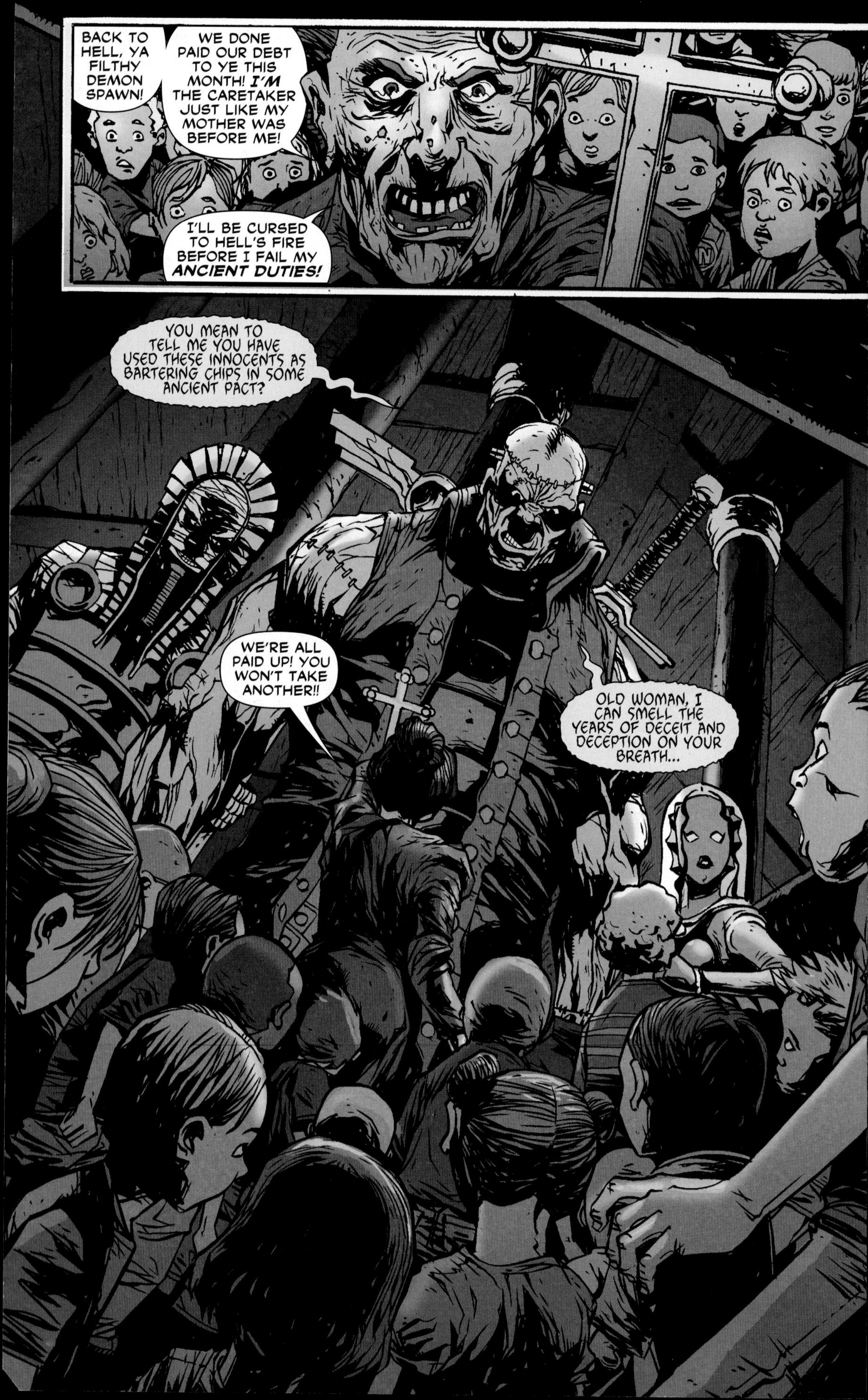
BACK TO HELL, YA FILTHY DEMON SPAWN!
WE DONE PAID OUR DEBT TO YE THIS MONTH! *I'M* THE CARETAKER JUST LIKE MY MOTHER WAS BEFORE ME!
I'LL BE CURSED TO HELL'S FIRE BEFORE I FAIL MY ***ANCIENT DUTIES!***
YOU MEAN TO TELL ME YOU HAVE USED THESE INNOCENTS AS BARTERING CHIPS IN SOME ANCIENT PACT?
WE'RE ALL PAID UP! YOU WON'T TAKE ANOTHER!!
OLD WOMAN, I CAN SMELL THE YEARS OF DECEIT AND DECEPTION ON YOUR BREATH...

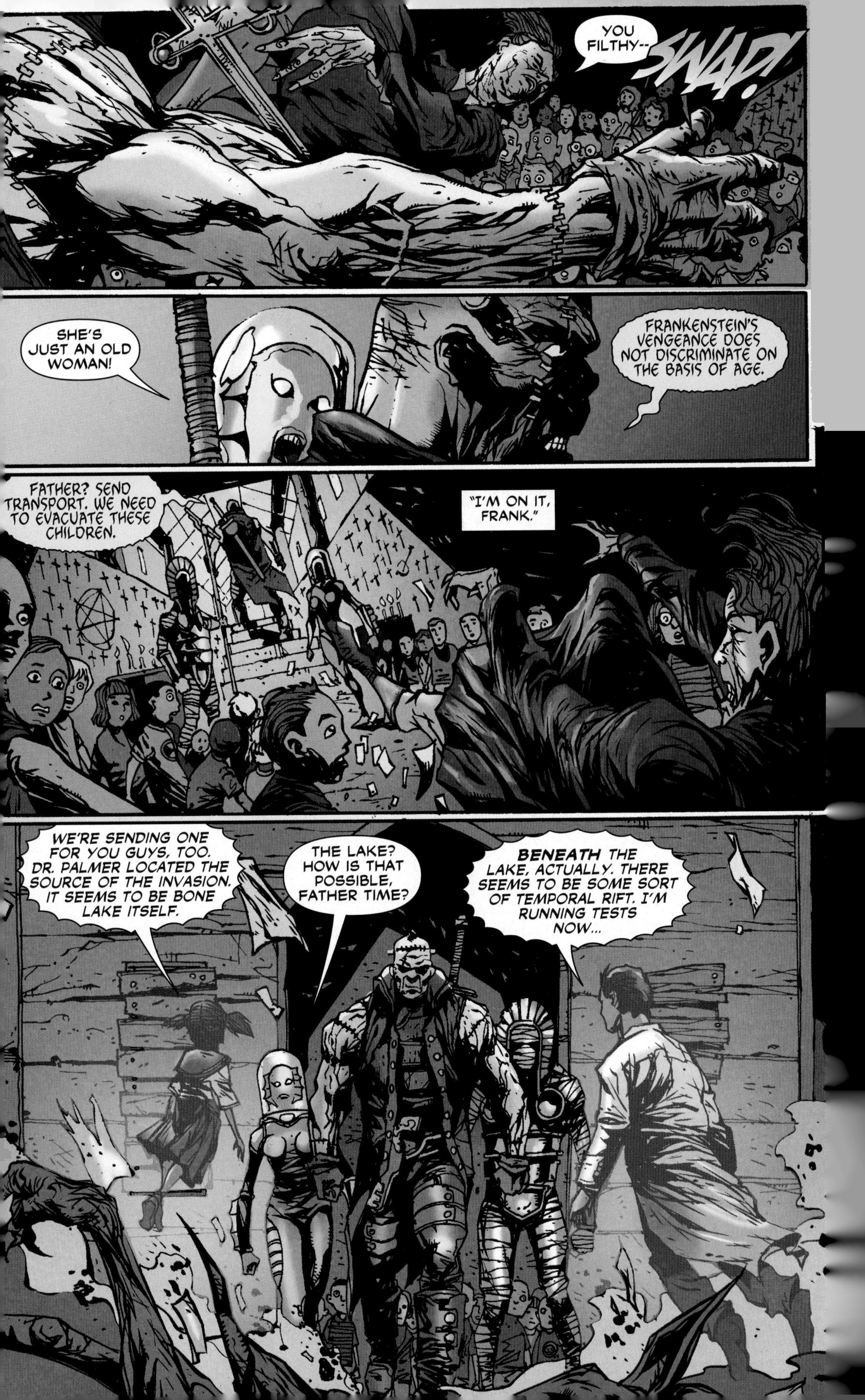
YOU FILTHY--
SNAP!
SHE'S JUST AN OLD WOMAN!
FRANKENSTEIN'S VENGEANCE DOES NOT DISCRIMINATE ON THE BASIS OF AGE.
FATHER? SEND TRANSPORT. WE NEED TO EVACUATE THESE CHILDREN.
"I'M ON IT, FRANK."
WE'RE SENDING ONE FOR YOU GUYS, TOO. DR. PALMER LOCATED THE SOURCE OF THE INVASION. IT SEEMS TO BE BONE LAKE ITSELF.
THE LAKE? HOW IS THAT POSSIBLE, FATHER TIME?
BENEATH THE LAKE, ACTUALLY. THERE SEEMS TO BE SOME SORT OF TEMPORAL RIFT. I'M RUNNING TESTS NOW...

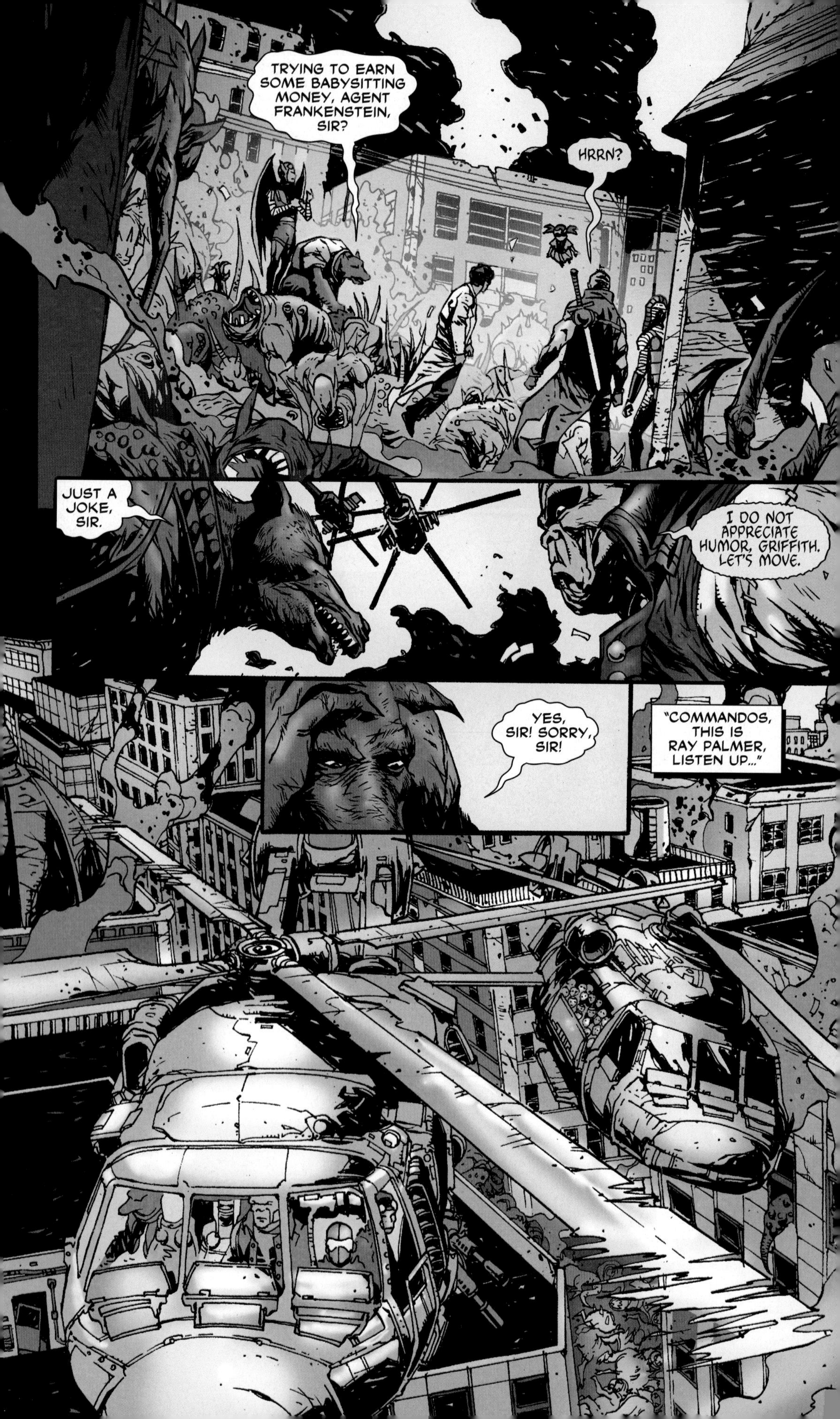
TRYING TO EARN SOME BABYSITTING MONEY, AGENT FRANKENSTEIN, SIR?
HRRN?
JUST A JOKE, SIR.
I DO NOT APPRECIATE HUMOR, GRIFFITH. LET'S MOVE.
YES, SIR! SORRY, SIR!
"COMMANDOS, THIS IS RAY PALMER, LISTEN UP..."

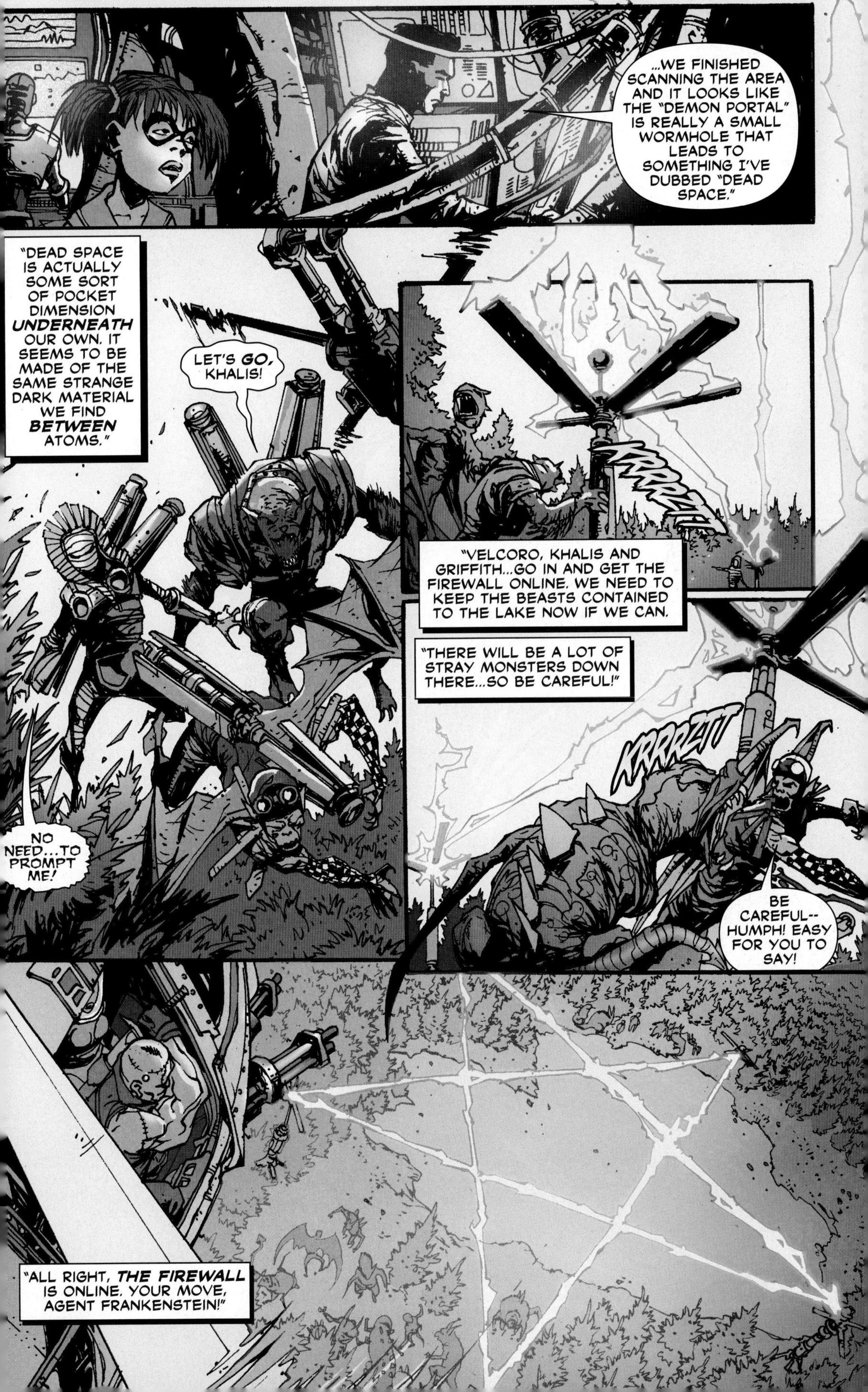
...WE FINISHED SCANNING THE AREA AND IT LOOKS LIKE THE "DEMON PORTAL" IS REALLY A SMALL WORMHOLE THAT LEADS TO SOMETHING I'VE DUBBED "DEAD SPACE."
"DEAD SPACE IS ACTUALLY SOME SORT OF POCKET DIMENSION UNDERNEATH OUR OWN. IT SEEMS TO BE MADE OF THE SAME STRANGE DARK MATERIAL WE FIND BETWEEN ATOMS."
LET'S GO, KHALIS!
NO NEED...TO PROMPT ME!
KRRRZTT
"VELCORO, KHALIS AND GRIFFITH...GO IN AND GET THE FIREWALL ONLINE. WE NEED TO KEEP THE BEASTS CONTAINED TO THE LAKE NOW IF WE CAN.
"THERE WILL BE A LOT OF STRAY MONSTERS DOWN THERE...SO BE CAREFUL!"
KRRRZTT
BE CAREFUL-- HUMPH! EASY FOR YOU TO SAY!
"ALL RIGHT, THE FIREWALL IS ONLINE. YOUR MOVE, AGENT FRANKENSTEIN!"

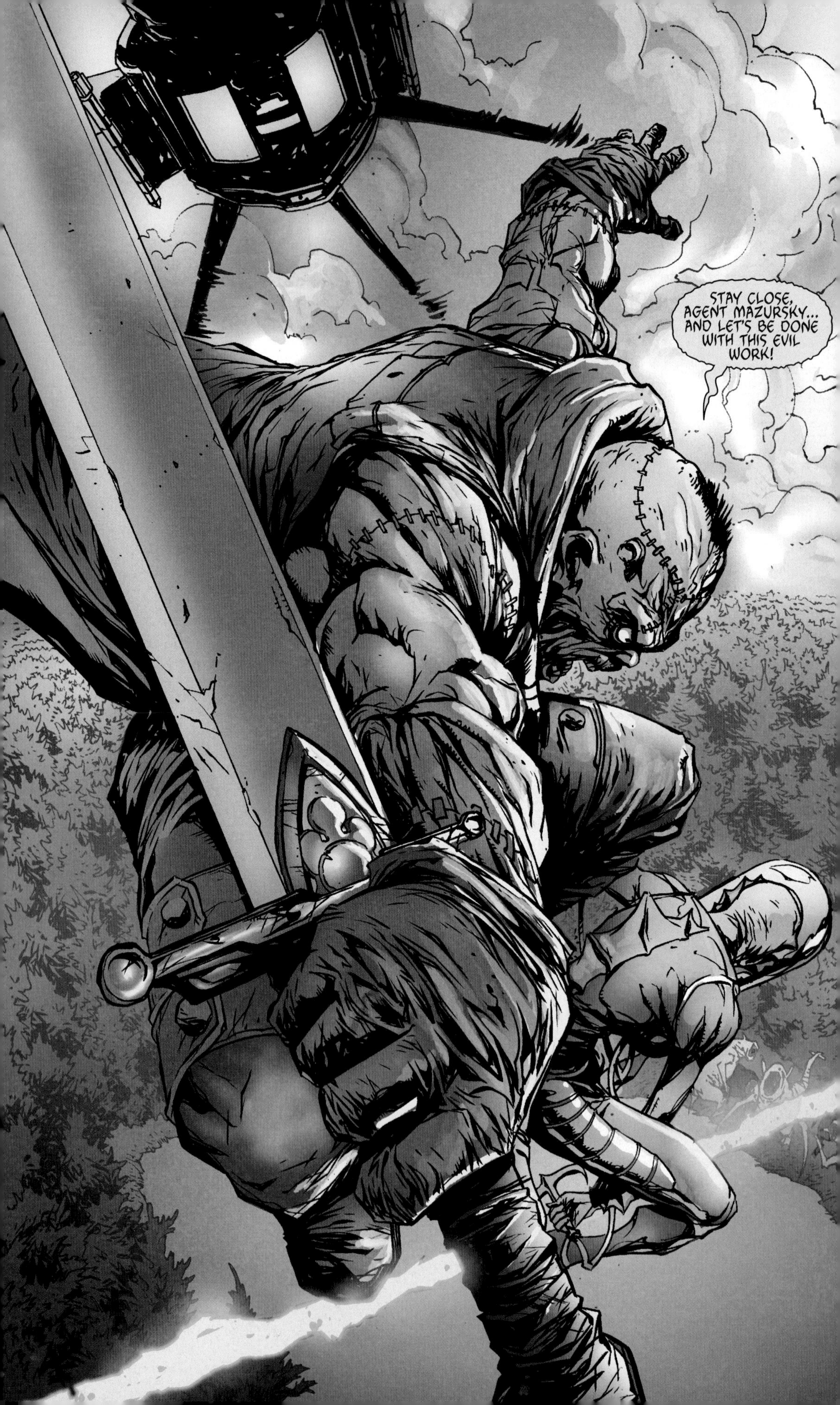
STAY CLOSE, AGENT MAZURSKY... AND LET'S BE DONE WITH THIS EVIL WORK!

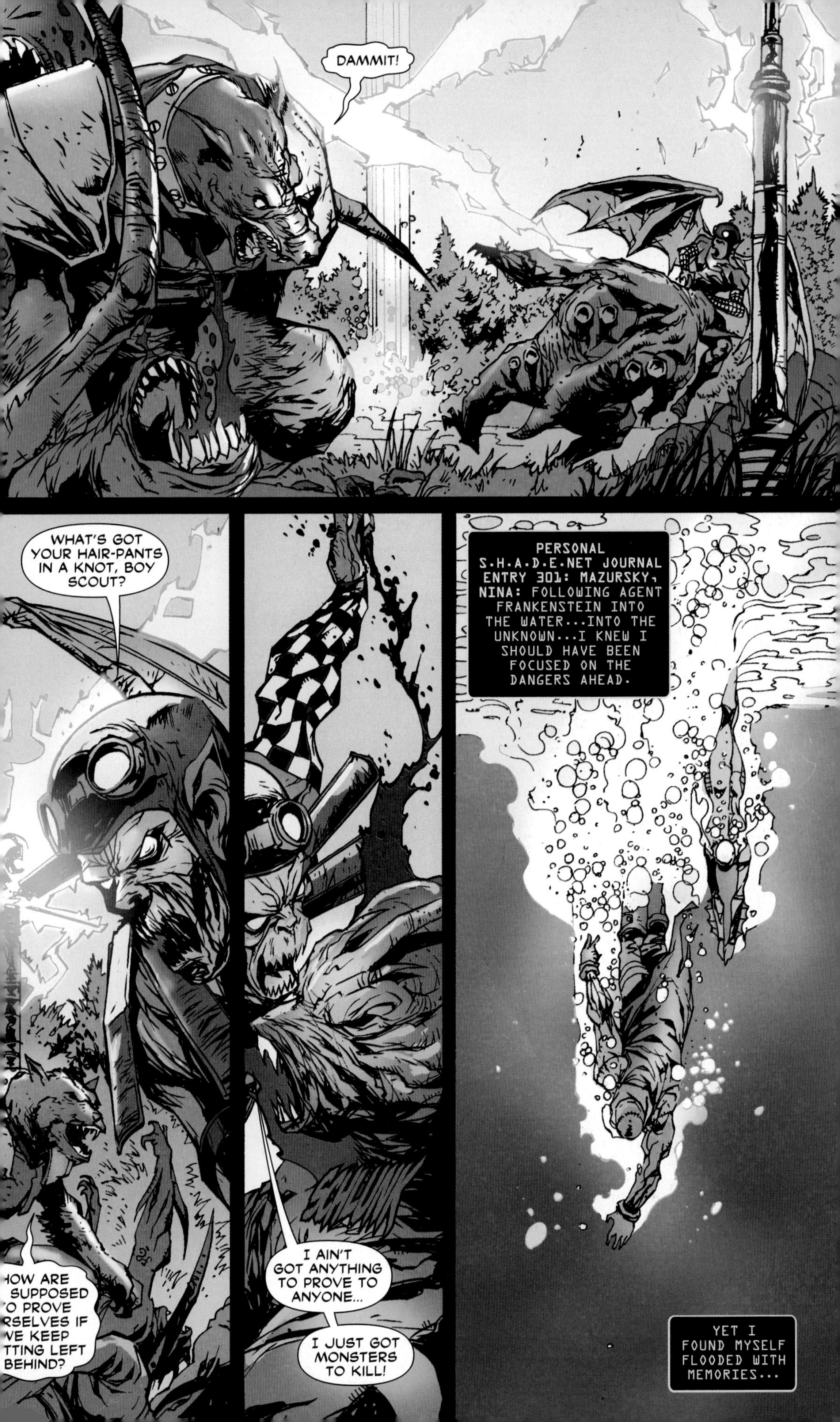
DAMMIT!
WHAT'S GOT YOUR HAIR-PANTS IN A KNOT, BOY SCOUT?
HOW ARE SUPPOSED O PROVE RSELVES IF VE KEEP TTING LEFT BEHIND?
I AIN'T GOT ANYTHING TO PROVE TO ANYONE...
I JUST GOT MONSTERS TO KILL!
PERSONAL S.H.A.D.E.NET JOURNAL ENTRY 301: MAZURSKY, NINA: FOLLOWING AGENT FRANKENSTEIN INTO THE WATER...INTO THE UNKNOWN...I KNEW I SHOULD HAVE BEEN FOCUSED ON THE DANGERS AHEAD.
YET I FOUND MYSELF FLOODED WITH MEMORIES...

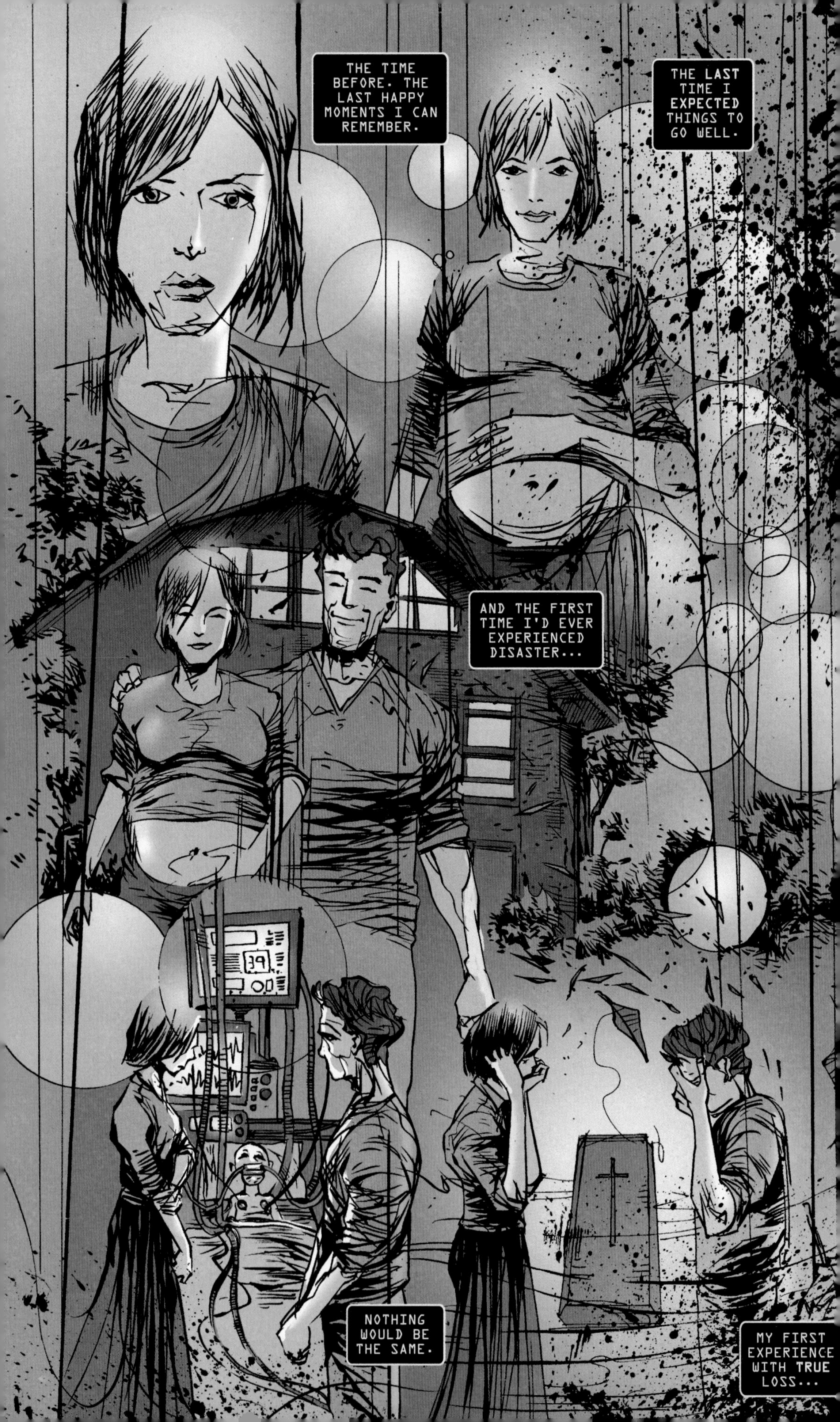
THE TIME BEFORE. THE LAST HAPPY MOMENTS I CAN REMEMBER.
THE LAST TIME I EXPECTED THINGS TO GO WELL.
AND THE FIRST TIME I'D EVER EXPERIENCED DISASTER...
NOTHING WOULD BE THE SAME.
MY FIRST EXPERIENCE WITH TRUE LOSS...

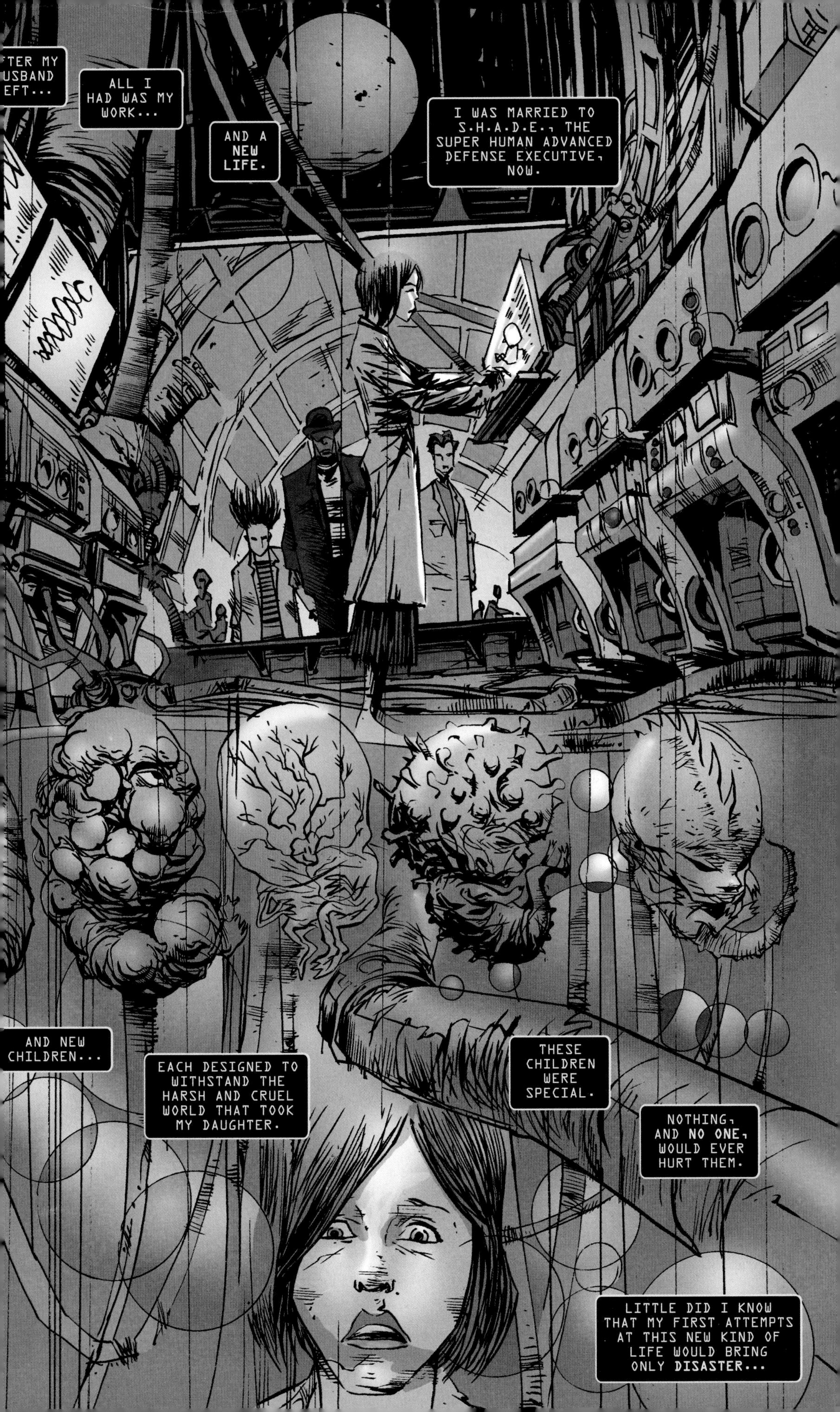

FTER MY USBAND EFT...
ALL I HAD WAS MY WORK...
AND A NEW LIFE.
I WAS MARRIED TO S.H.A.D.E., THE SUPER HUMAN ADVANCED DEFENSE EXECUTIVE, NOW.
AND NEW CHILDREN...
EACH DESIGNED TO WITHSTAND THE HARSH AND CRUEL WORLD THAT TOOK MY DAUGHTER.
THESE CHILDREN WERE SPECIAL.
NOTHING, AND NO ONE, WOULD EVER HURT THEM.
LITTLE DID I KNOW THAT MY FIRST ATTEMPTS AT THIS NEW KIND OF LIFE WOULD BRING ONLY DISASTER...

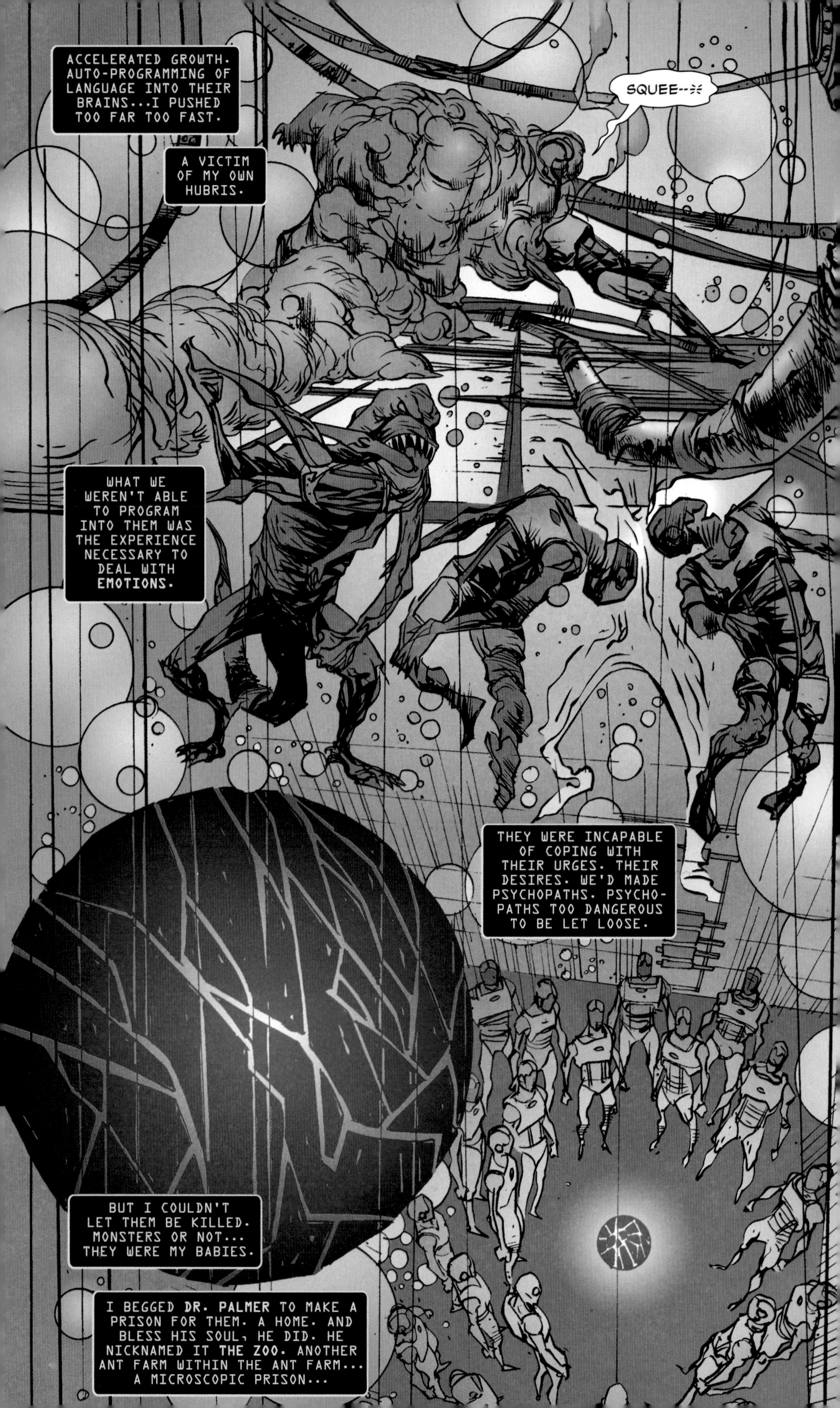
ACCELERATED GROWTH. AUTO-PROGRAMMING OF LANGUAGE INTO THEIR BRAINS...I PUSHED TOO FAR TOO FAST.
A VICTIM OF MY OWN HUBRIS.
SQUEE--
WHAT WE WEREN'T ABLE TO PROGRAM INTO THEM WAS THE EXPERIENCE NECESSARY TO DEAL WITH EMOTIONS.
THEY WERE INCAPABLE OF COPING WITH THEIR URGES. THEIR DESIRES. WE'D MADE PSYCHOPATHS. PSYCHO-PATHS TOO DANGEROUS TO BE LET LOOSE.
BUT I COULDN'T LET THEM BE KILLED. MONSTERS OR NOT... THEY WERE MY BABIES.
I BEGGED DR. PALMER TO MAKE A PRISON FOR THEM. A HOME. AND BLESS HIS SOUL, HE DID. HE NICKNAMED IT THE ZOO. ANOTHER ANT FARM WITHIN THE ANT FARM... A MICROSCOPIC PRISON...

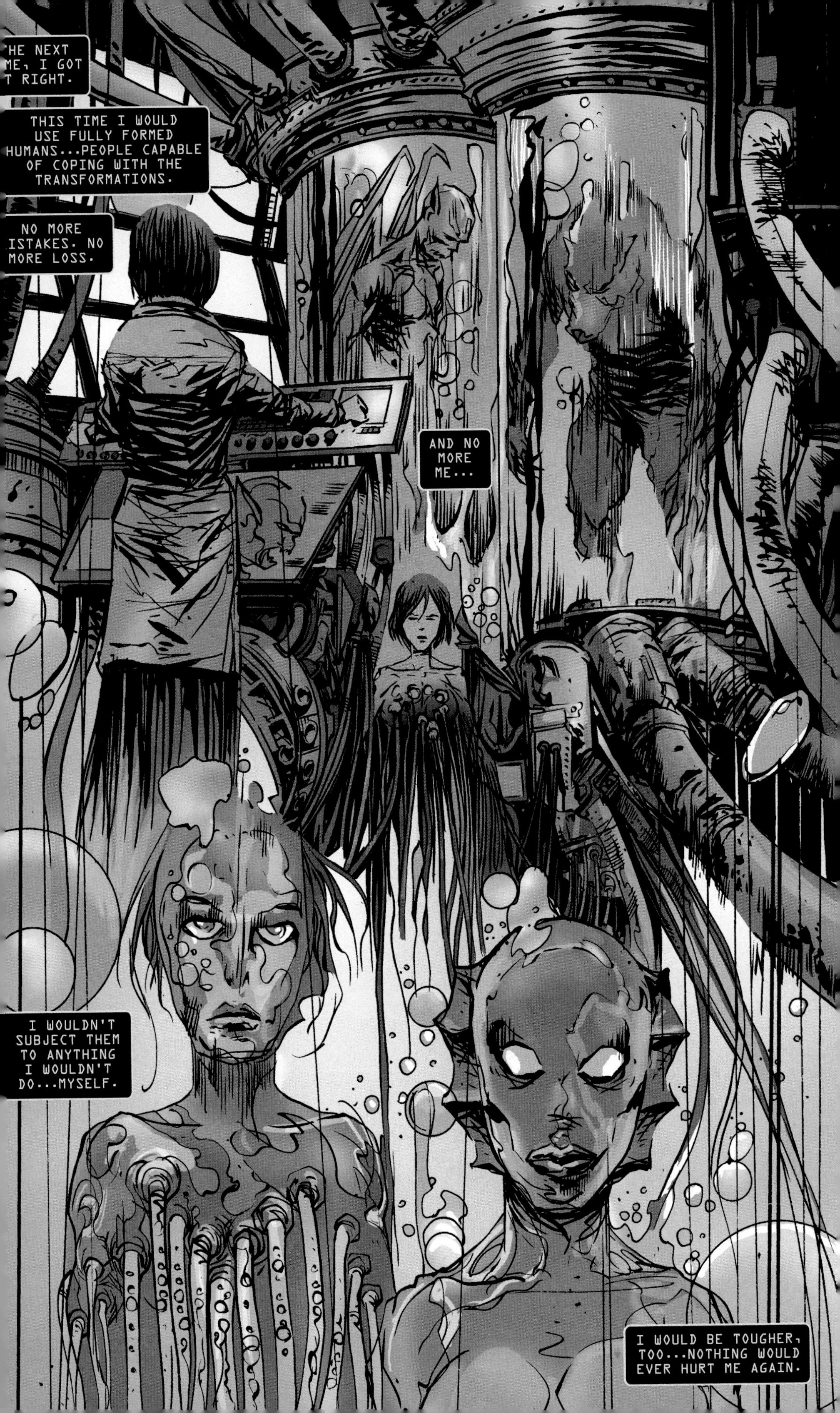
HE NEXT ME, I GOT T RIGHT.
THIS TIME I WOULD USE FULLY FORMED HUMANS...PEOPLE CAPABLE OF COPING WITH THE TRANSFORMATIONS.
NO MORE ISTAKES. NO MORE LOSS.
AND NO MORE ME...
I WOULDN'T SUBJECT THEM TO ANYTHING I WOULDN'T DO...MYSELF.
I WOULD BE TOUGHER, TOO...NOTHING WOULD EVER HURT ME AGAIN.

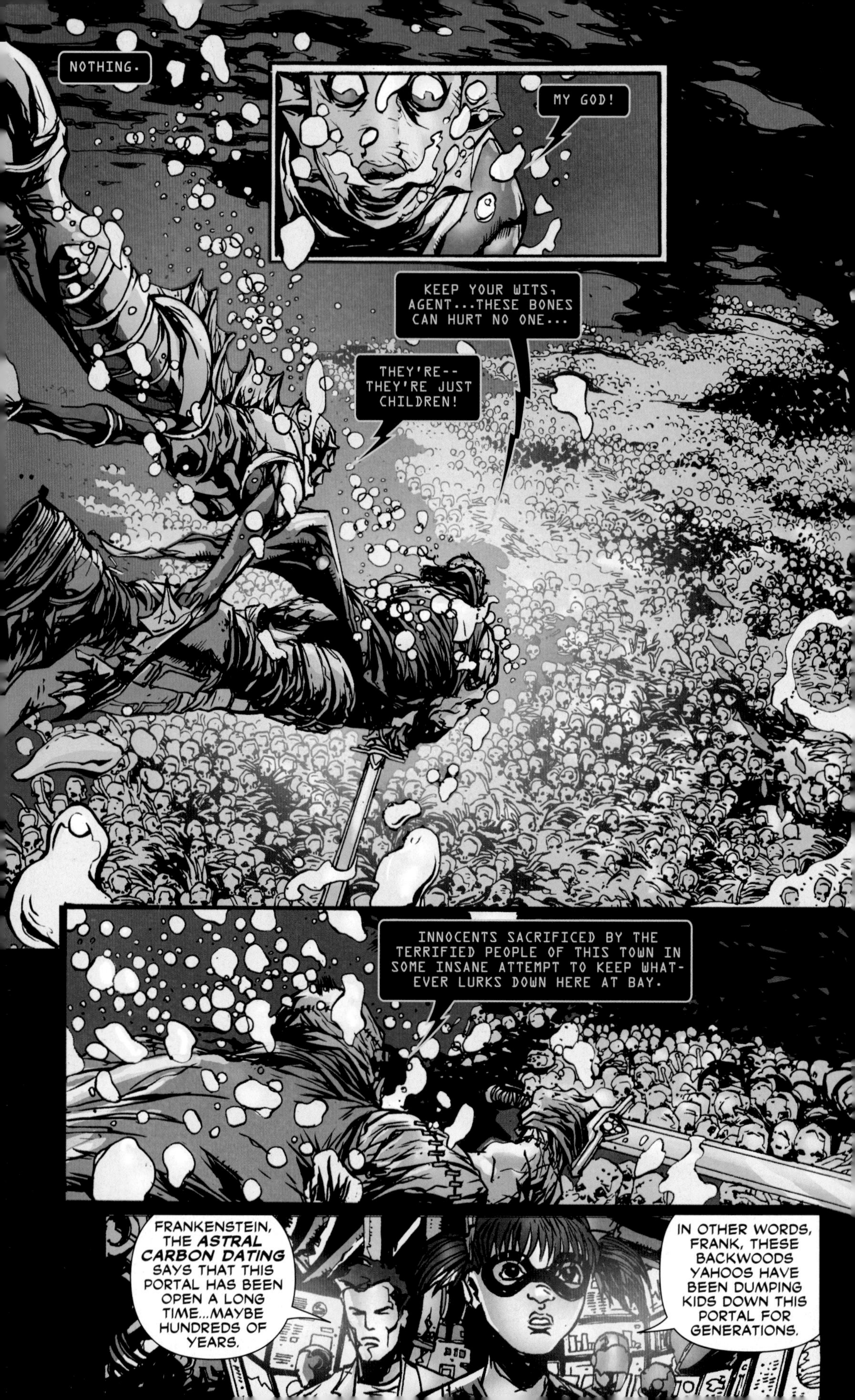
NOTHING.
MY GOD!
THEY'RE-- THEY'RE JUST CHILDREN!
KEEP YOUR WITS, AGENT...THESE BONES CAN HURT NO ONE...
INNOCENTS SACRIFICED BY THE TERRIFIED PEOPLE OF THIS TOWN IN SOME INSANE ATTEMPT TO KEEP WHATEVER LURKS DOWN HERE AT BAY.
FRANKENSTEIN, THE ASTRAL CARBON DATING SAYS THAT THIS PORTAL HAS BEEN OPEN A LONG TIME...MAYBE HUNDREDS OF YEARS.
IN OTHER WORDS, FRANK, THESE BACKWOODS YAHOOS HAVE BEEN DUMPING KIDS DOWN THIS PORTAL FOR GENERATIONS.

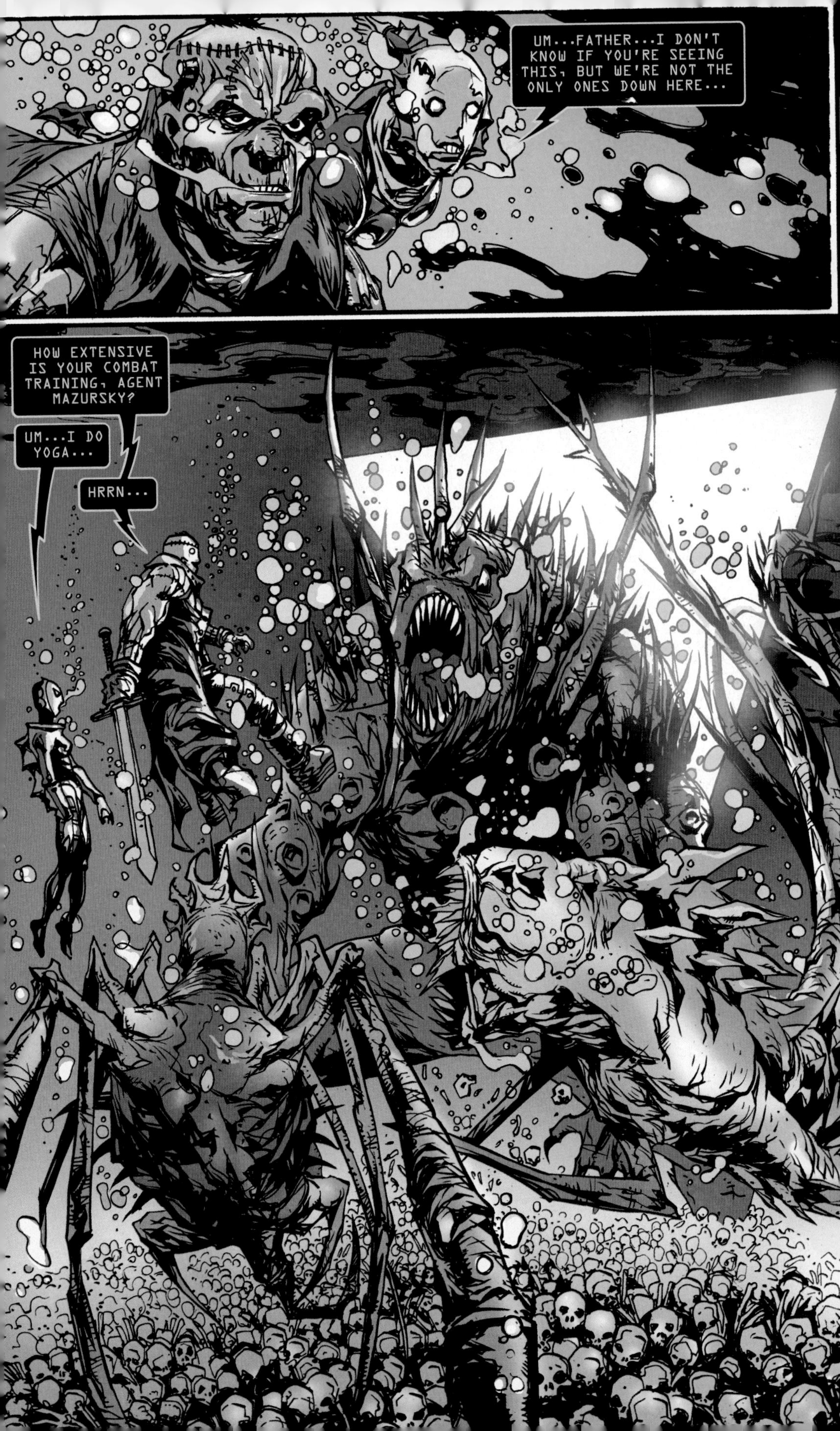
UM...FATHER...I DON'T KNOW IF YOU'RE SEEING THIS, BUT WE'RE NOT THE ONLY ONES DOWN HERE...
HOW EXTENSIVE IS YOUR COMBAT TRAINING, AGENT MAZURSKY?
UM...I DO YOGA...
HRRN...

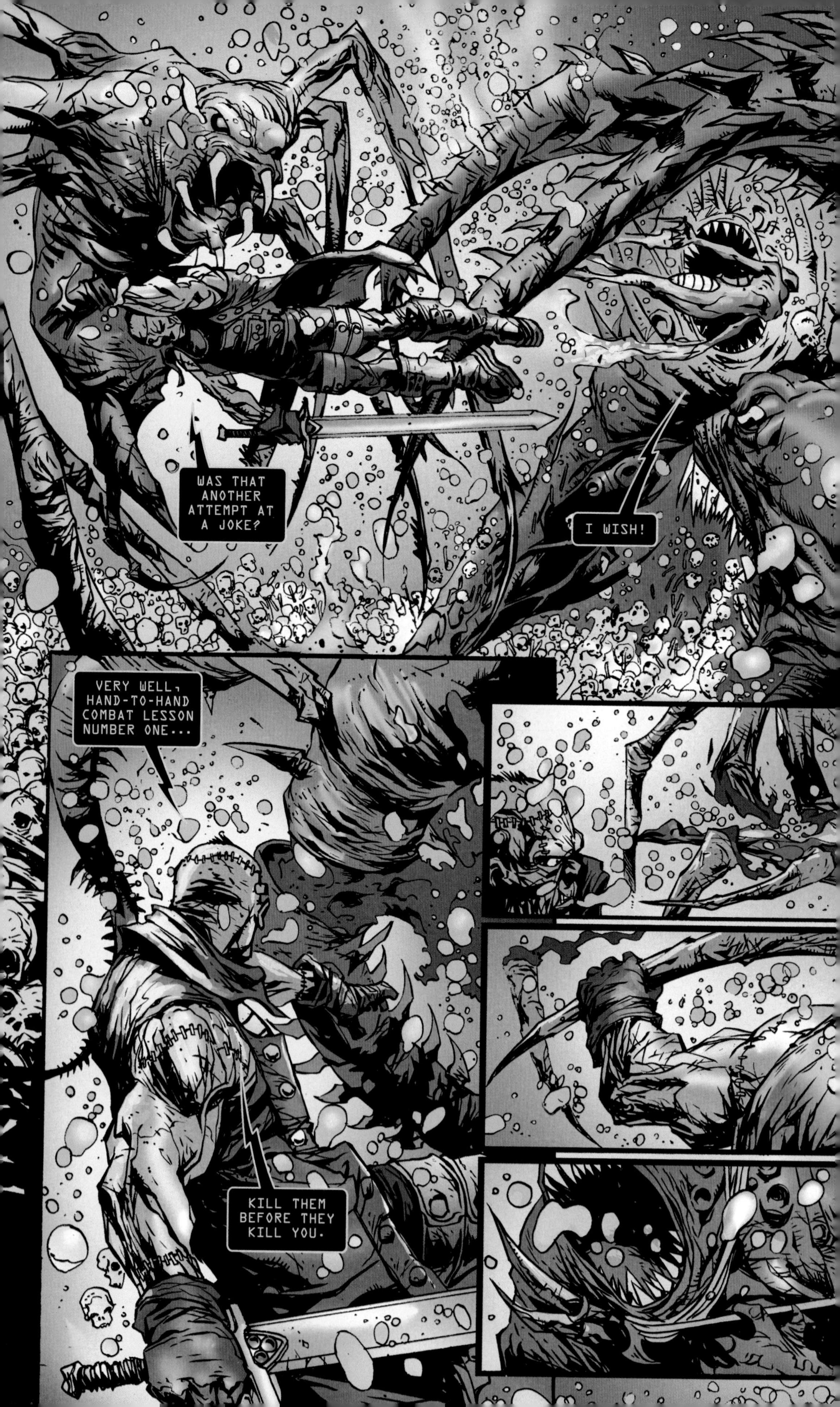

WAS THAT ANOTHER ATTEMPT AT A JOKE?
I WISH!
VERY WELL, HAND-TO-HAND COMBAT LESSON NUMBER ONE...
KILL THEM BEFORE THEY KILL YOU.

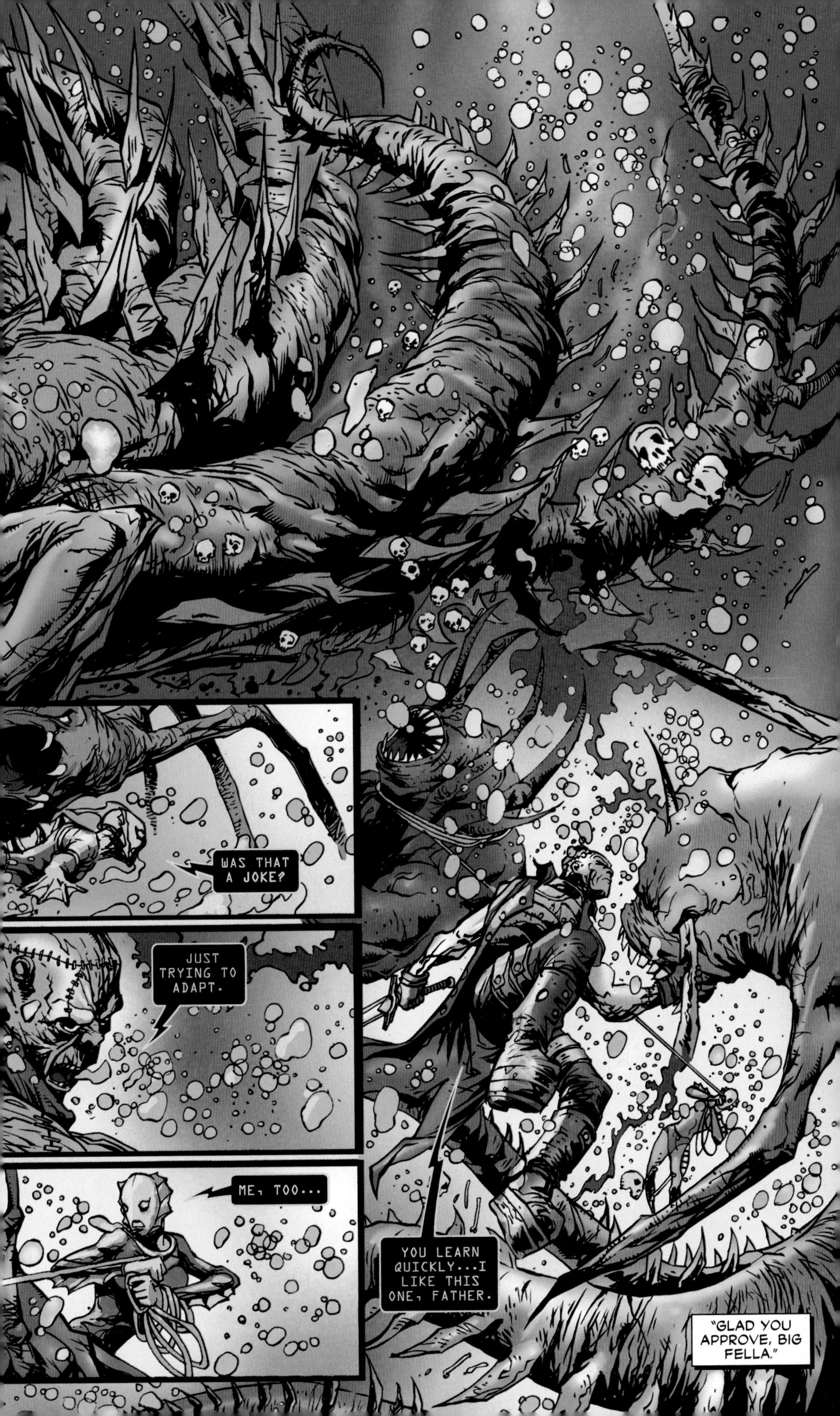
WAS THAT A JOKE?
JUST TRYING TO ADAPT.
ME, TOO...
YOU LEARN QUICKLY...I LIKE THIS ONE, FATHER.
"GLAD YOU APPROVE, BIG FELLA."

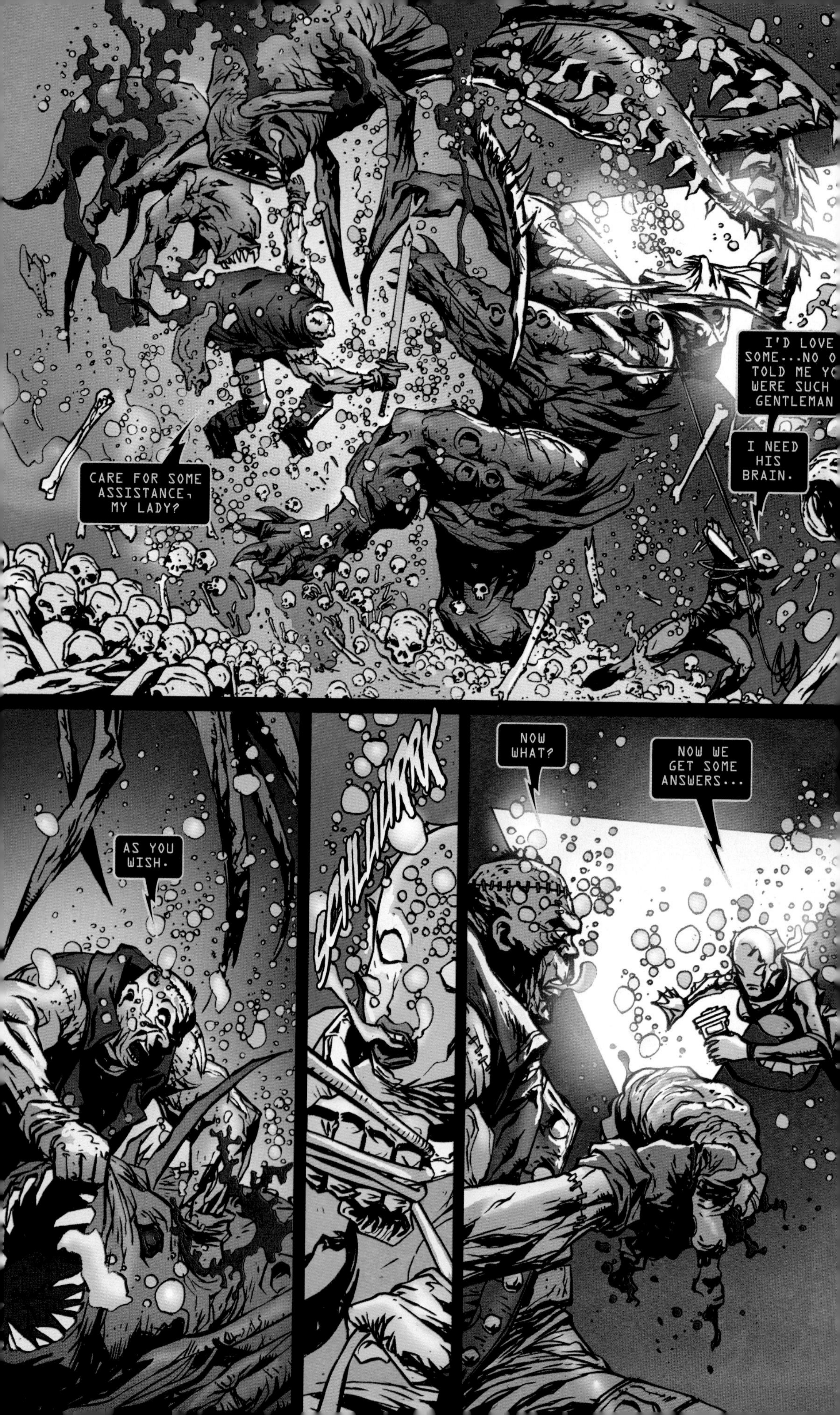
CARE FOR SOME ASSISTANCE, MY LADY?
I'D LOVE SOME...NO O TOLD ME YO WERE SUCH GENTLEMAN
I NEED HIS BRAIN.
AS YOU WISH.
NOW WHAT?
NOW WE GET SOME ANSWERS...

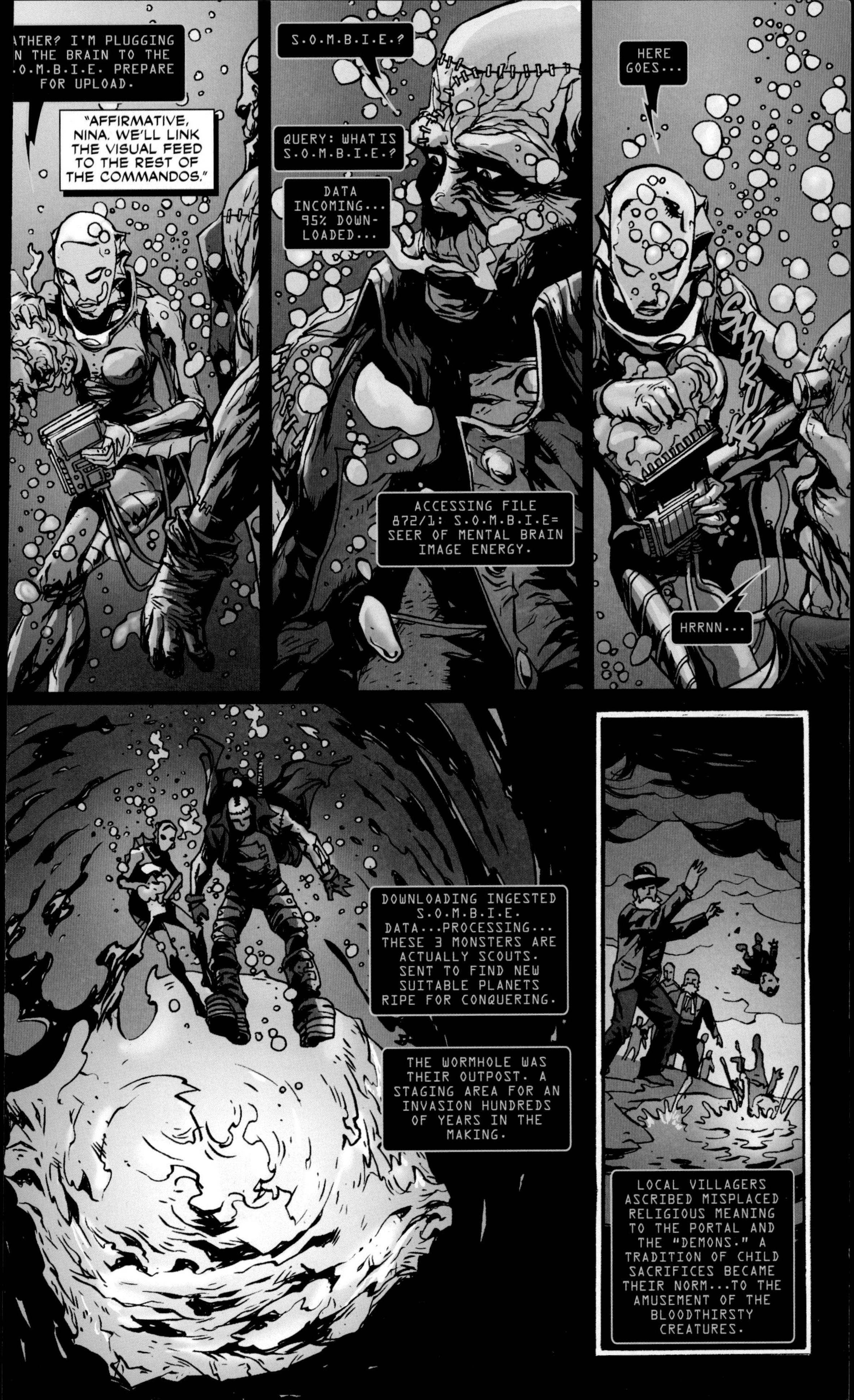
ATHER? I'M PLUGGING N THE BRAIN TO THE .O.M.B.I.E. PREPARE FOR UPLOAD.
"AFFIRMATIVE, NINA. WE'LL LINK THE VISUAL FEED TO THE REST OF THE COMMANDOS."
S.O.M.B.I.E.?
QUERY: WHAT IS S.O.M.B.I.E.?
DATA INCOMING... 95% DOWN-LOADED...
ACCESSING FILE 872/1: S.O.M.B.I.E= SEER OF MENTAL BRAIN IMAGE ENERGY.
HERE GOES...
HRRNN...
DOWNLOADING INGESTED S.O.M.B.I.E. DATA...PROCESSING... THESE 3 MONSTERS ARE ACTUALLY SCOUTS. SENT TO FIND NEW SUITABLE PLANETS RIPE FOR CONQUERING.
THE WORMHOLE WAS THEIR OUTPOST. A STAGING AREA FOR AN INVASION HUNDREDS OF YEARS IN THE MAKING.
LOCAL VILLAGERS ASCRIBED MISPLACED RELIGIOUS MEANING TO THE PORTAL AND THE "DEMONS." A TRADITION OF CHILD SACRIFICES BECAME THEIR NORM...TO THE AMUSEMENT OF THE BLOODTHIRSTY CREATURES.

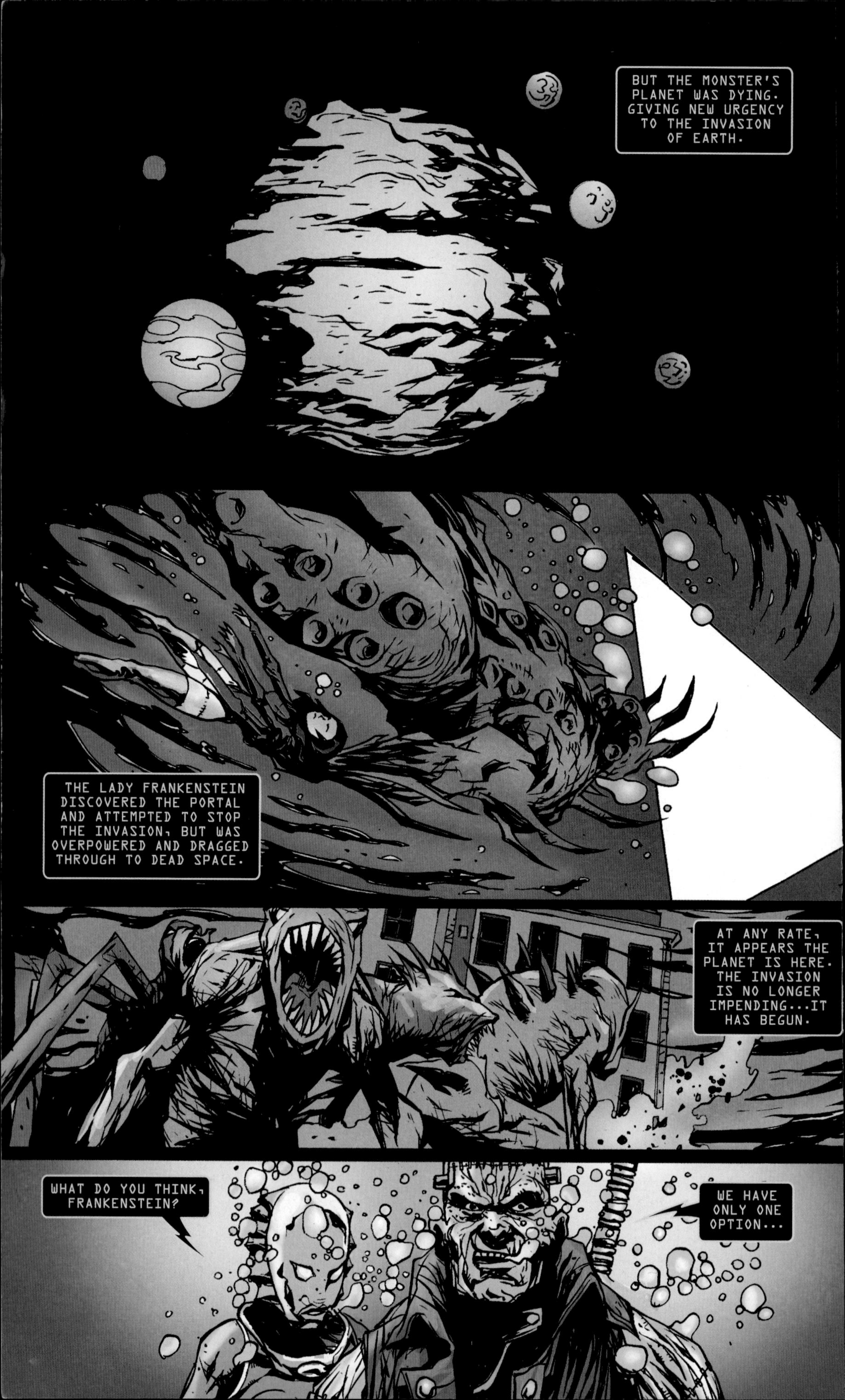
BUT THE MONSTER'S PLANET WAS DYING. GIVING NEW URGENCY TO THE INVASION OF EARTH.
THE LADY FRANKENSTEIN DISCOVERED THE PORTAL AND ATTEMPTED TO STOP THE INVASION, BUT WAS OVERPOWERED AND DRAGGED THROUGH TO DEAD SPACE.
AT ANY RATE, IT APPEARS THE PLANET IS HERE. THE INVASION IS NO LONGER IMPENDING...IT HAS BEGUN.
WHAT DO YOU THINK, FRANKENSTEIN?
WE HAVE ONLY ONE OPTION...

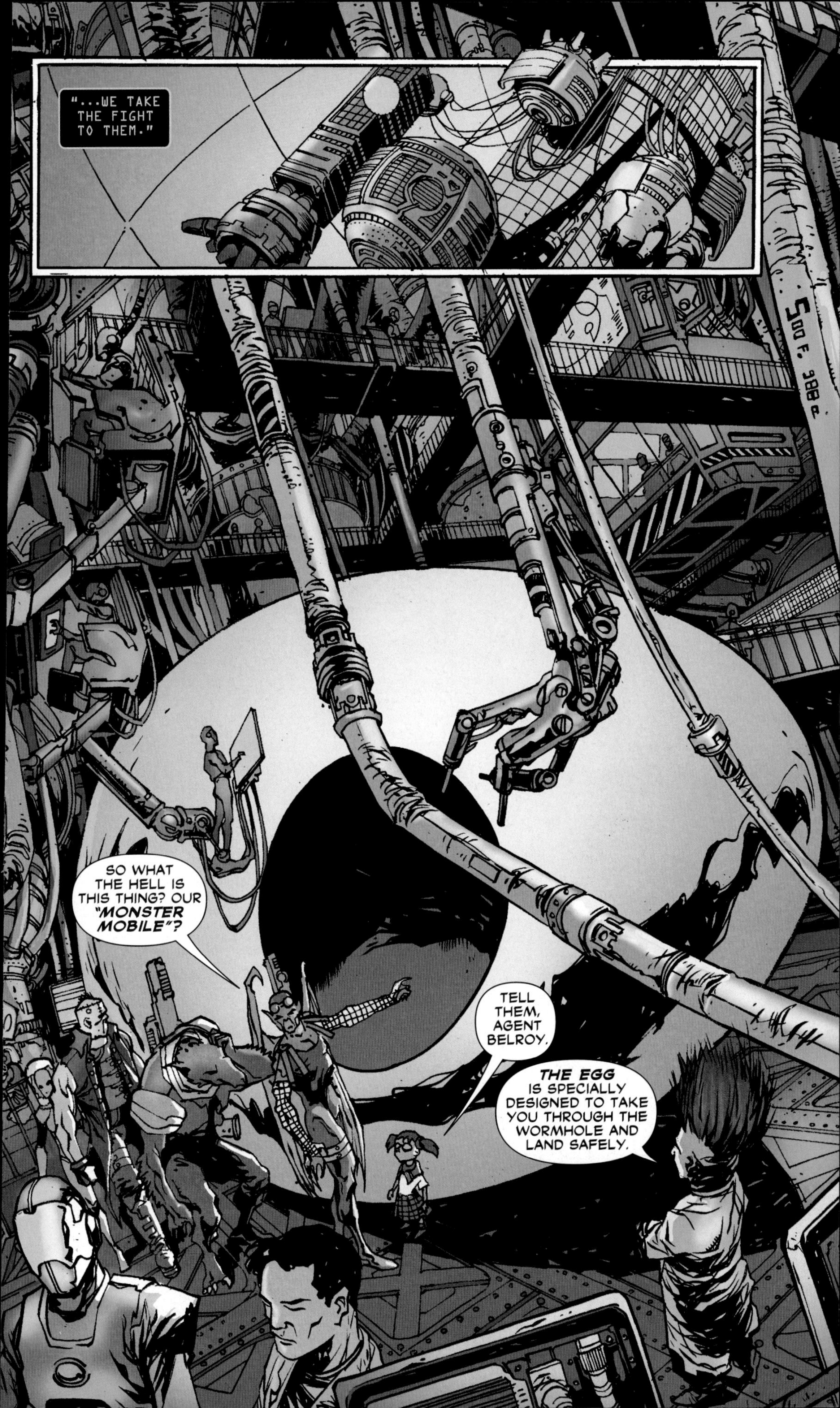
"...WE TAKE THE FIGHT TO THEM."
SO WHAT THE HELL IS THIS THING? OUR *"MONSTER MOBILE"*?
TELL THEM, AGENT BELROY.
THE EGG IS SPECIALLY DESIGNED TO TAKE YOU THROUGH THE WORMHOLE AND LAND SAFELY.

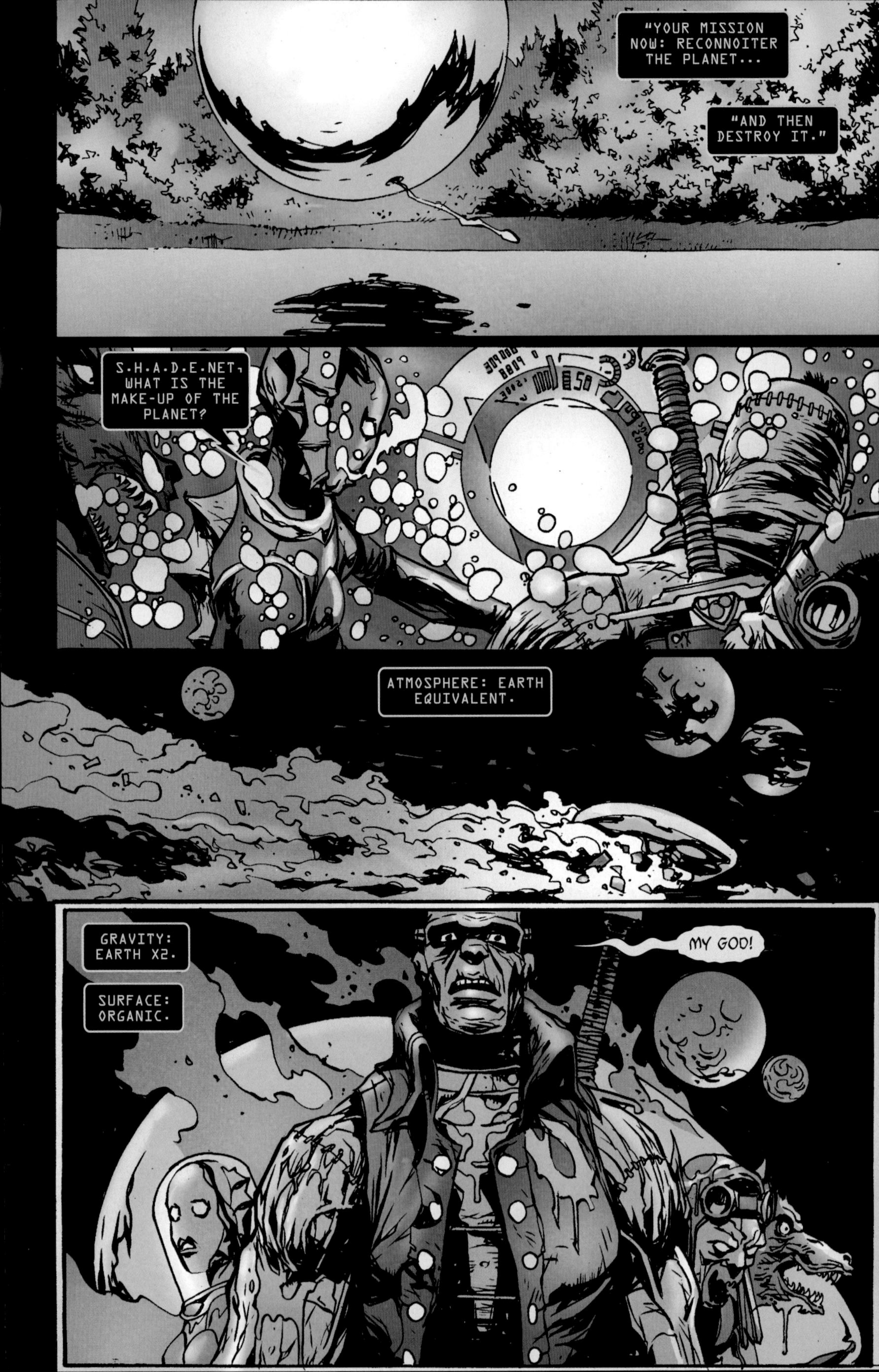
"YOUR MISSION NOW: RECONNOITER THE PLANET...
"AND THEN DESTROY IT."
S.H.A.D.E.NET, WHAT IS THE MAKE-UP OF THE PLANET?
ATMOSPHERE: EARTH EQUIVALENT.
GRAVITY: EARTH X2.
SURFACE: ORGANIC.
MY GOD!

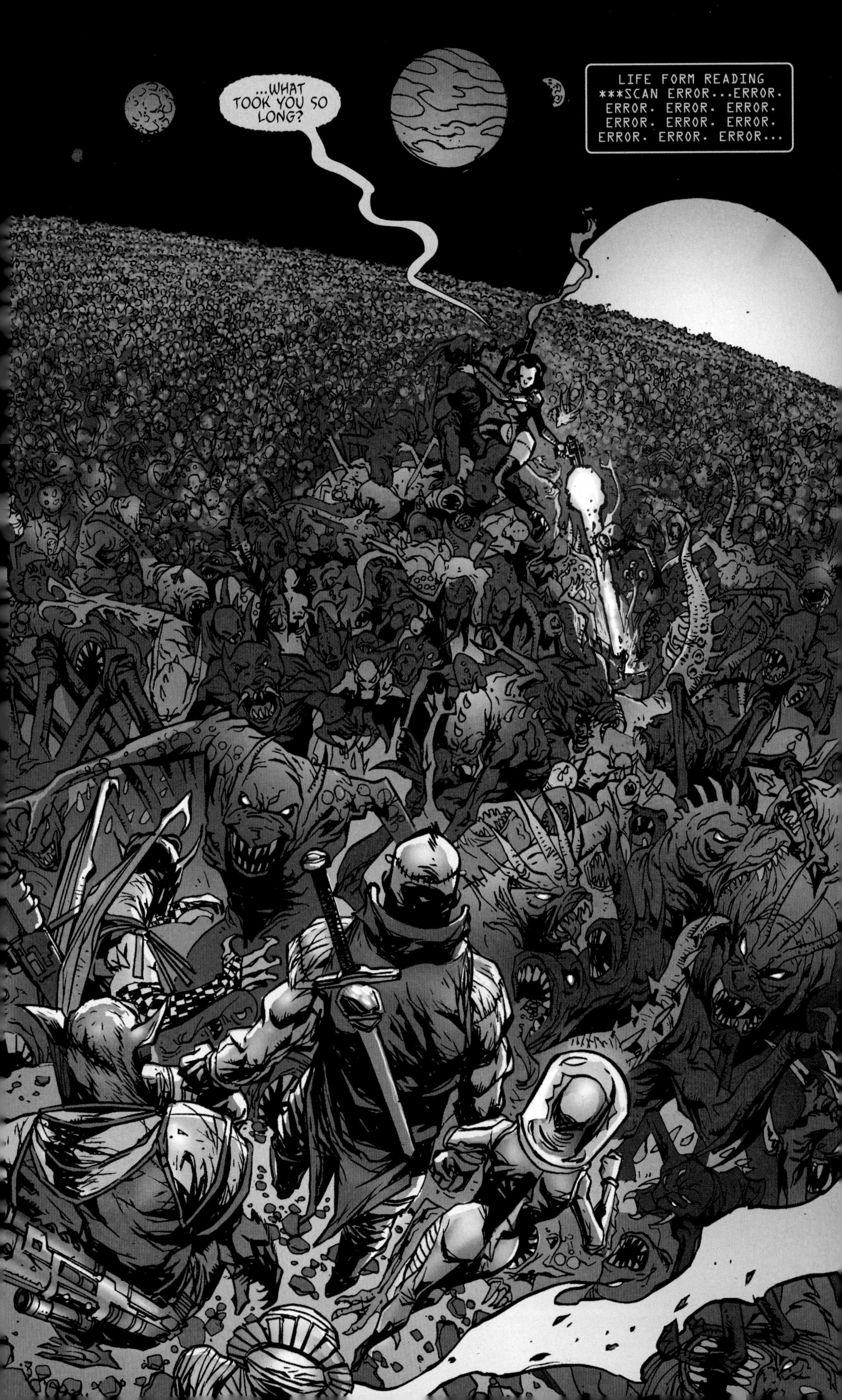
LIFE FORM READING
***SCAN ERROR...ERROR. ERROR. ERROR. ERROR. ERROR. ERROR. ERROR. ERROR. ERROR. ERROR...
...WHAT TOOK YOU SO LONG?

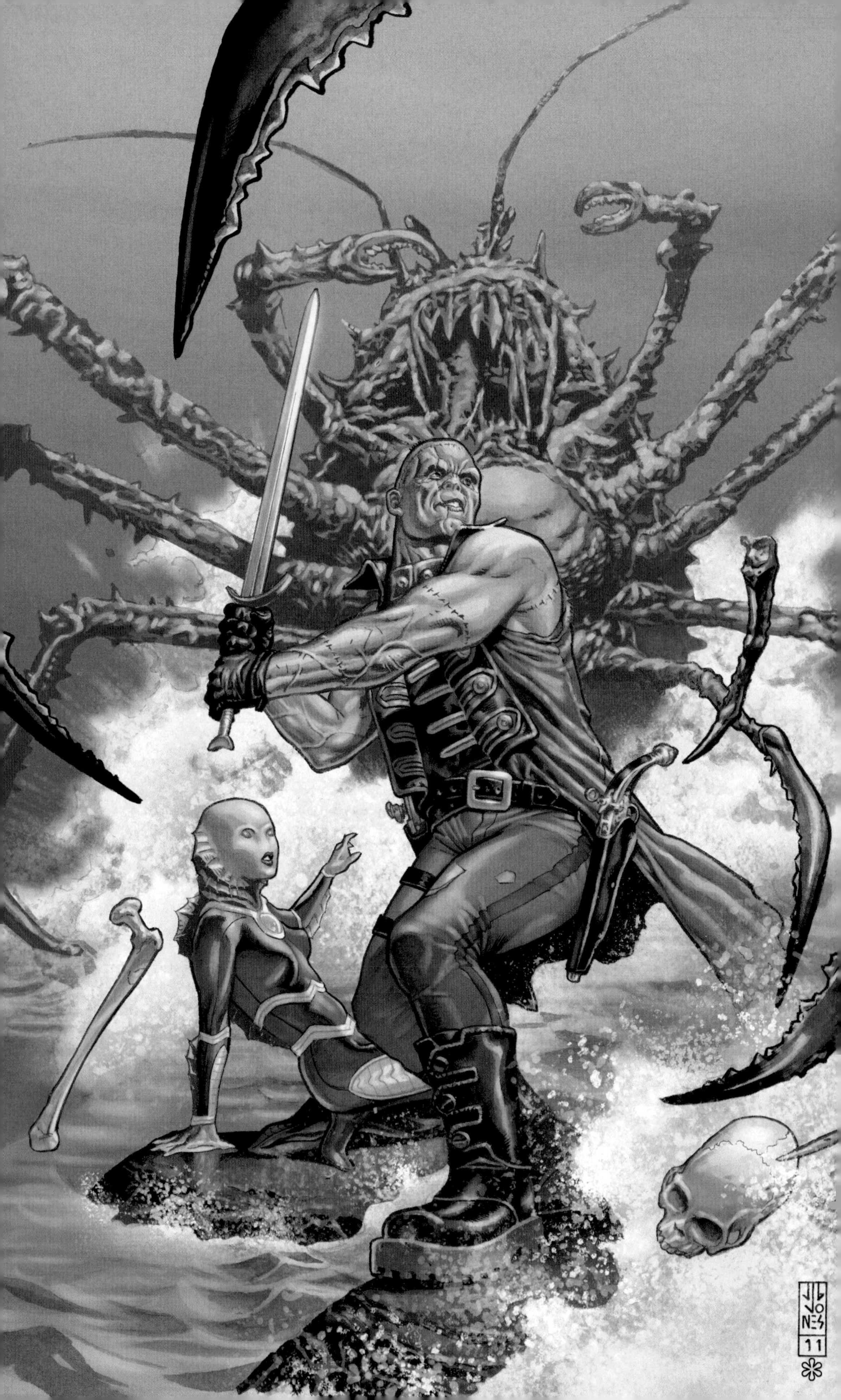

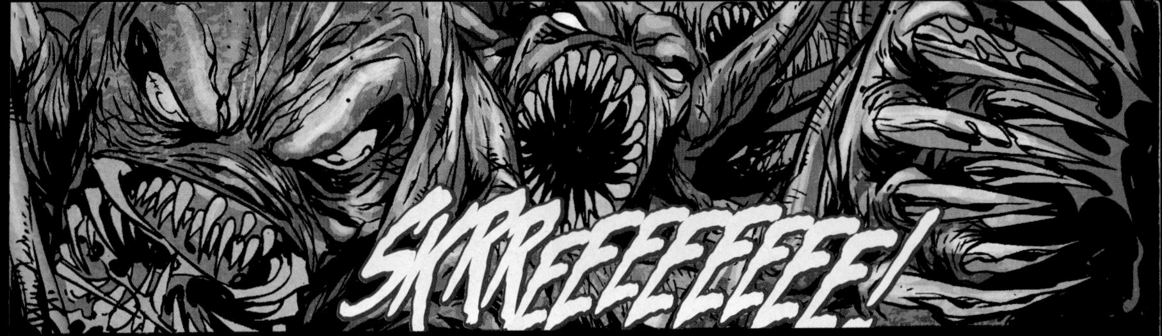
SKRREEEEEEEE!

TRANS-DIMENSIONAL BROADCAST IN
PROGRESS...BUFFERING...78%...

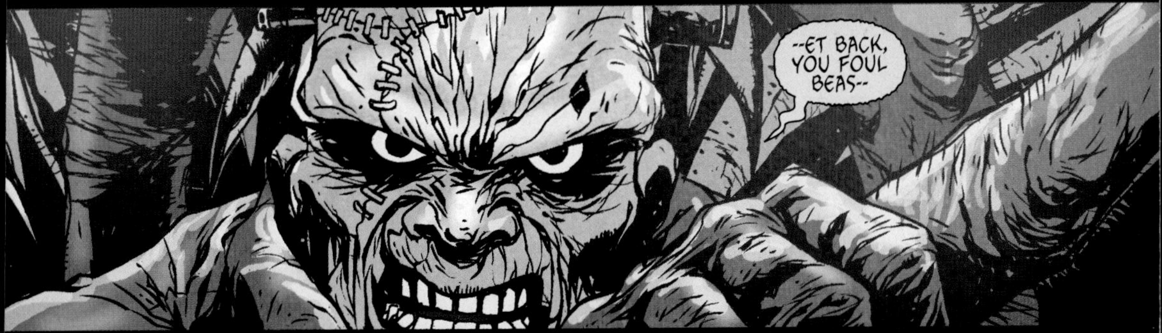
--ET BACK, YOU FOUL BEAS--

TRANS-DIMENSIONAL BROADCAST IN
PROGRESS...BUFFERING...89%...

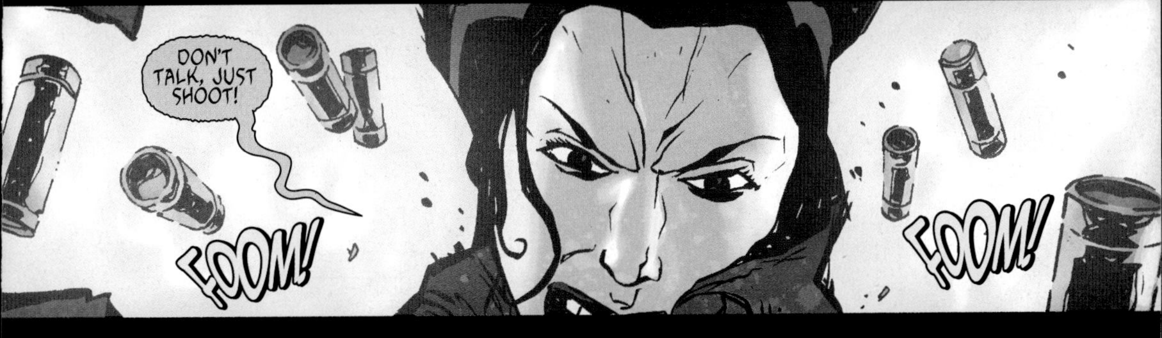
DON'T TALK, JUST SHOOT!
FOOM!
FOOM!

TRANS-DIMENSIONAL BROADCAST IN
PROGRESS...BUFFERING...99%...

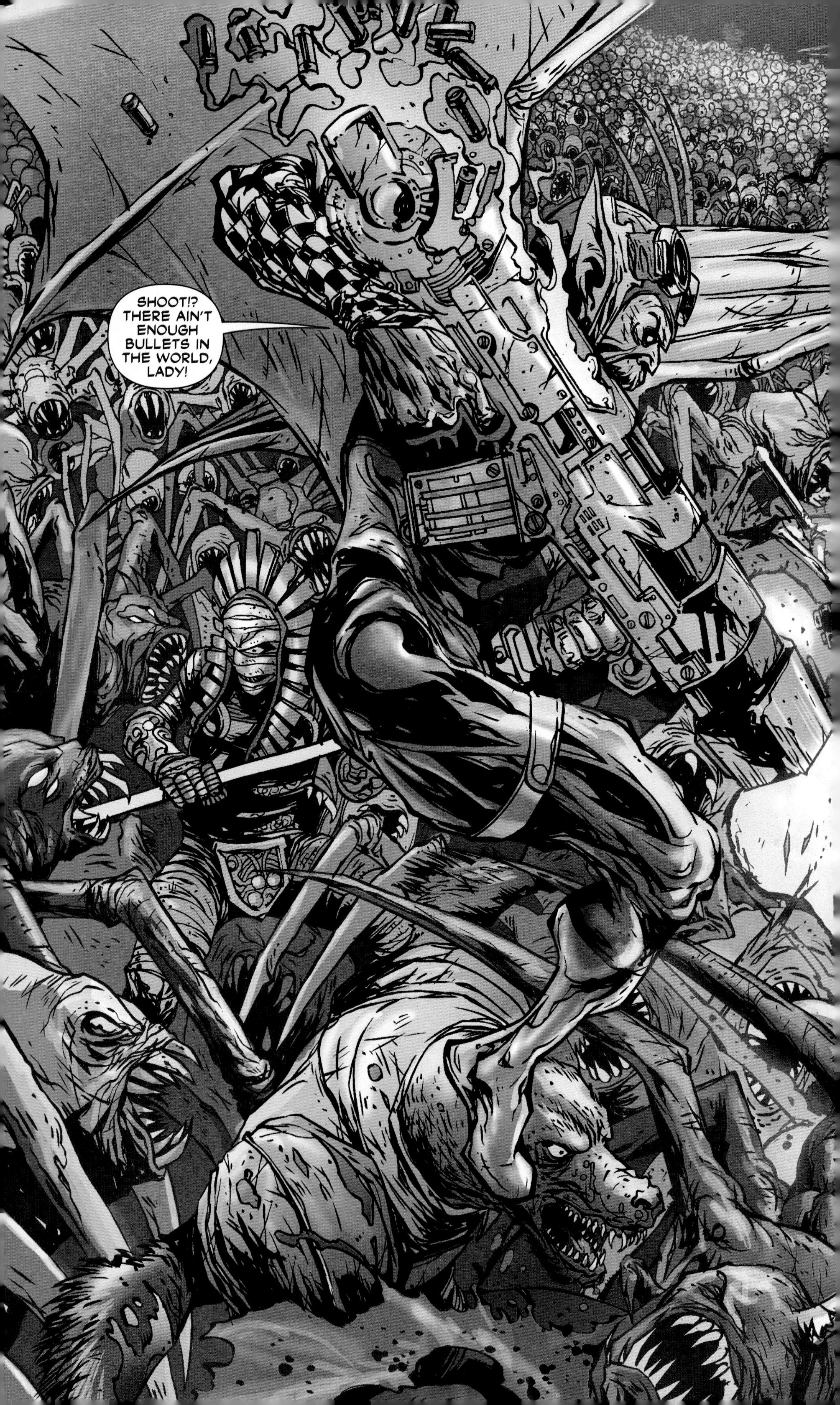
SHOOT!? THERE AIN'T ENOUGH BULLETS IN THE WORLD, LADY!

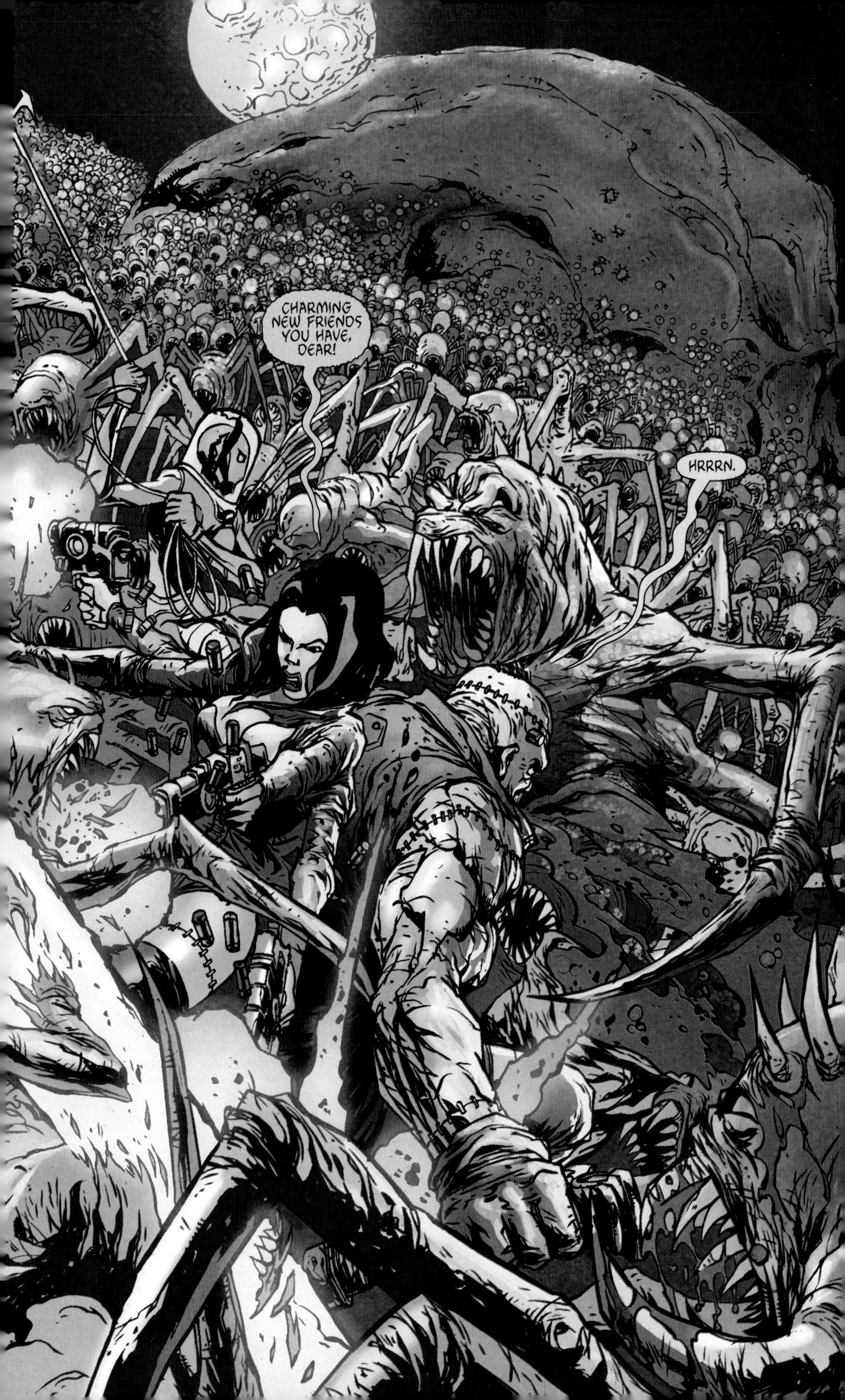
CHARMING NEW FRIENDS YOU HAVE, DEAR!
HRRRN.

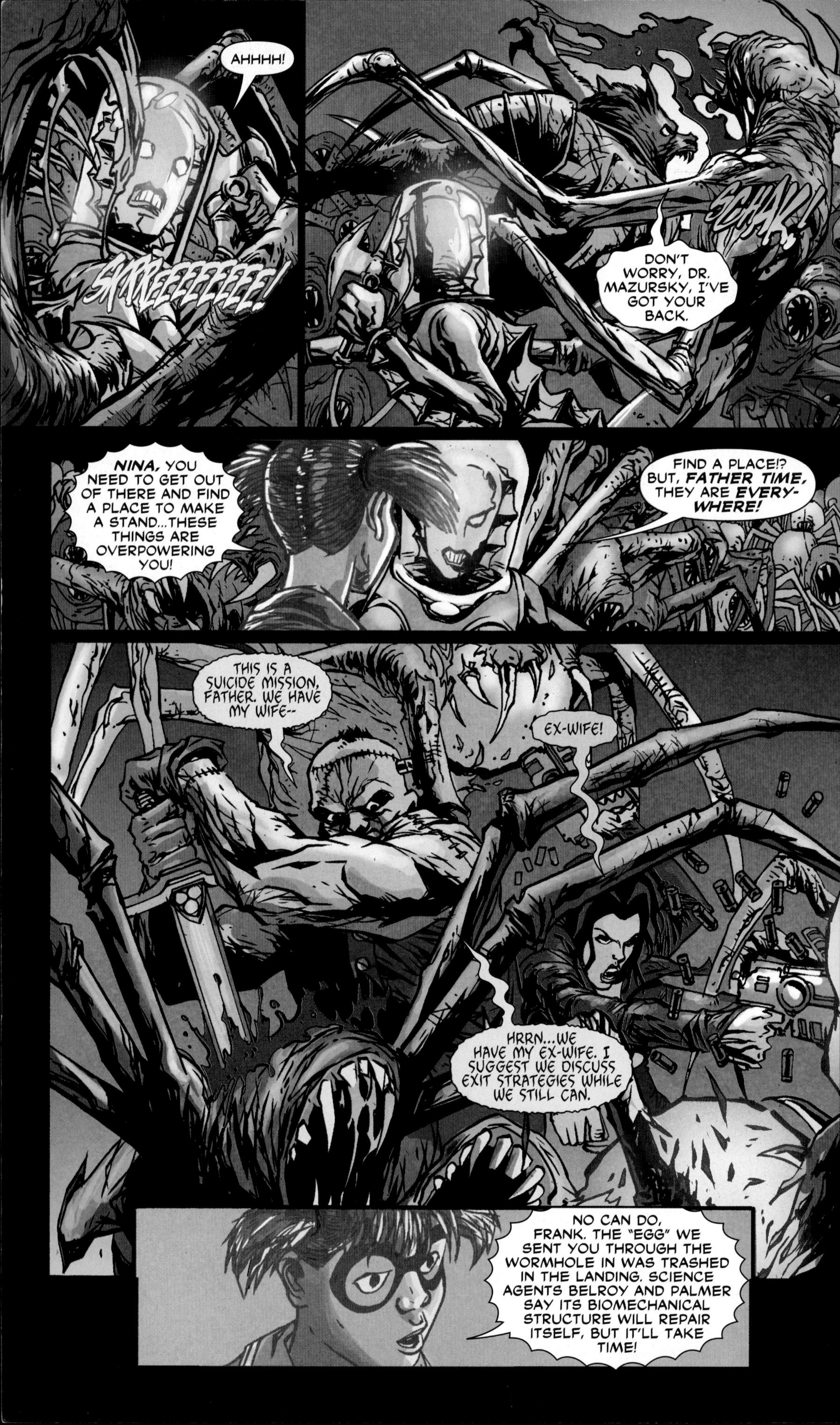
AHHHH!
SKRREEEEEEEEEE!
SCHAK!
DON'T WORRY, DR. MAZURSKY, I'VE GOT YOUR BACK.
NINA, YOU NEED TO GET OUT OF THERE AND FIND A PLACE TO MAKE A STAND...THESE THINGS ARE OVERPOWERING YOU!
FIND A PLACE!? BUT, FATHER TIME, THEY ARE EVERY-WHERE!
THIS IS A SUICIDE MISSION, FATHER. WE HAVE MY WIFE--
EX-WIFE!
HRRN...WE HAVE MY EX-WIFE. I SUGGEST WE DISCUSS EXIT STRATEGIES WHILE WE STILL CAN.
NO CAN DO, FRANK. THE "EGG" WE SENT YOU THROUGH THE WORMHOLE IN WAS TRASHED IN THE LANDING. SCIENCE AGENTS BELROY AND PALMER SAY ITS BIOMECHANICAL STRUCTURE WILL REPAIR ITSELF, BUT IT'LL TAKE TIME!

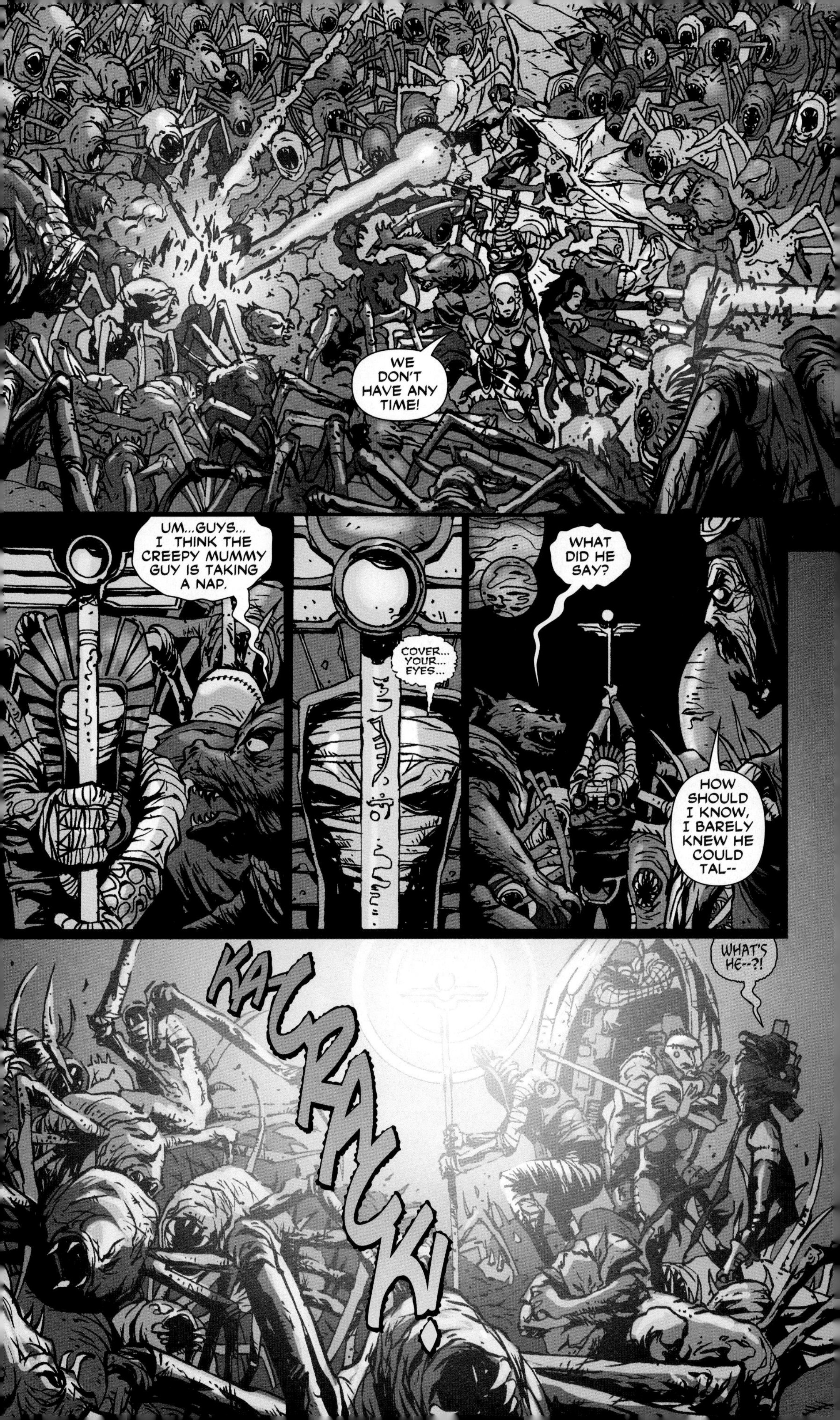
WE DON'T HAVE ANY TIME!
UM...GUYS... I THINK THE CREEPY MUMMY GUY IS TAKING A NAP.
COVER... YOUR... EYES...
WHAT DID HE SAY?
HOW SHOULD I KNOW, I BARELY KNEW HE COULD TAL--
KA-CRANK!
WHAT'S HE--?!

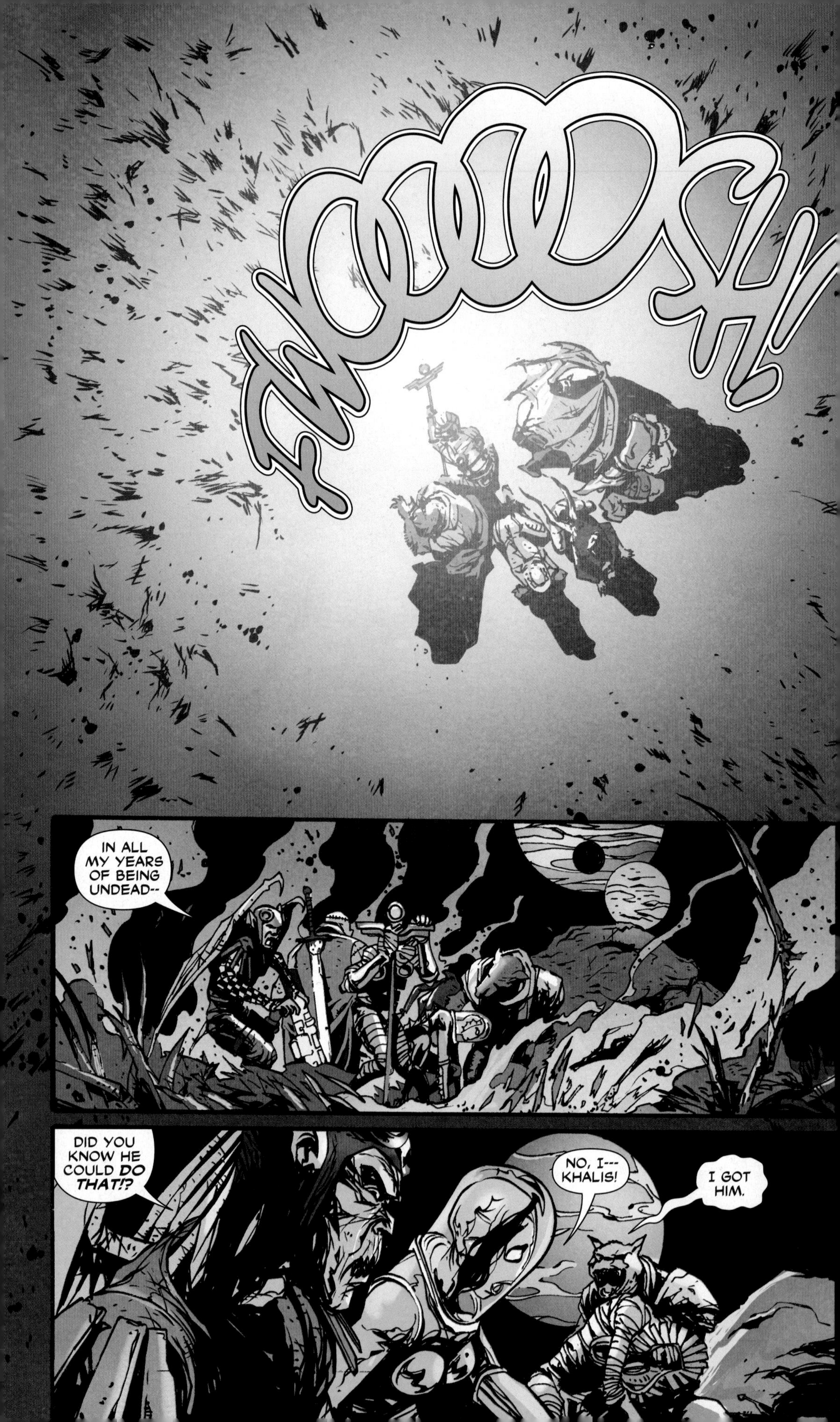
FWOOOOSH!
IN ALL MY YEARS OF BEING UNDEAD--
DID YOU KNOW HE COULD **DO THAT!?**
NO, I--- KHALIS!
I GOT HIM.

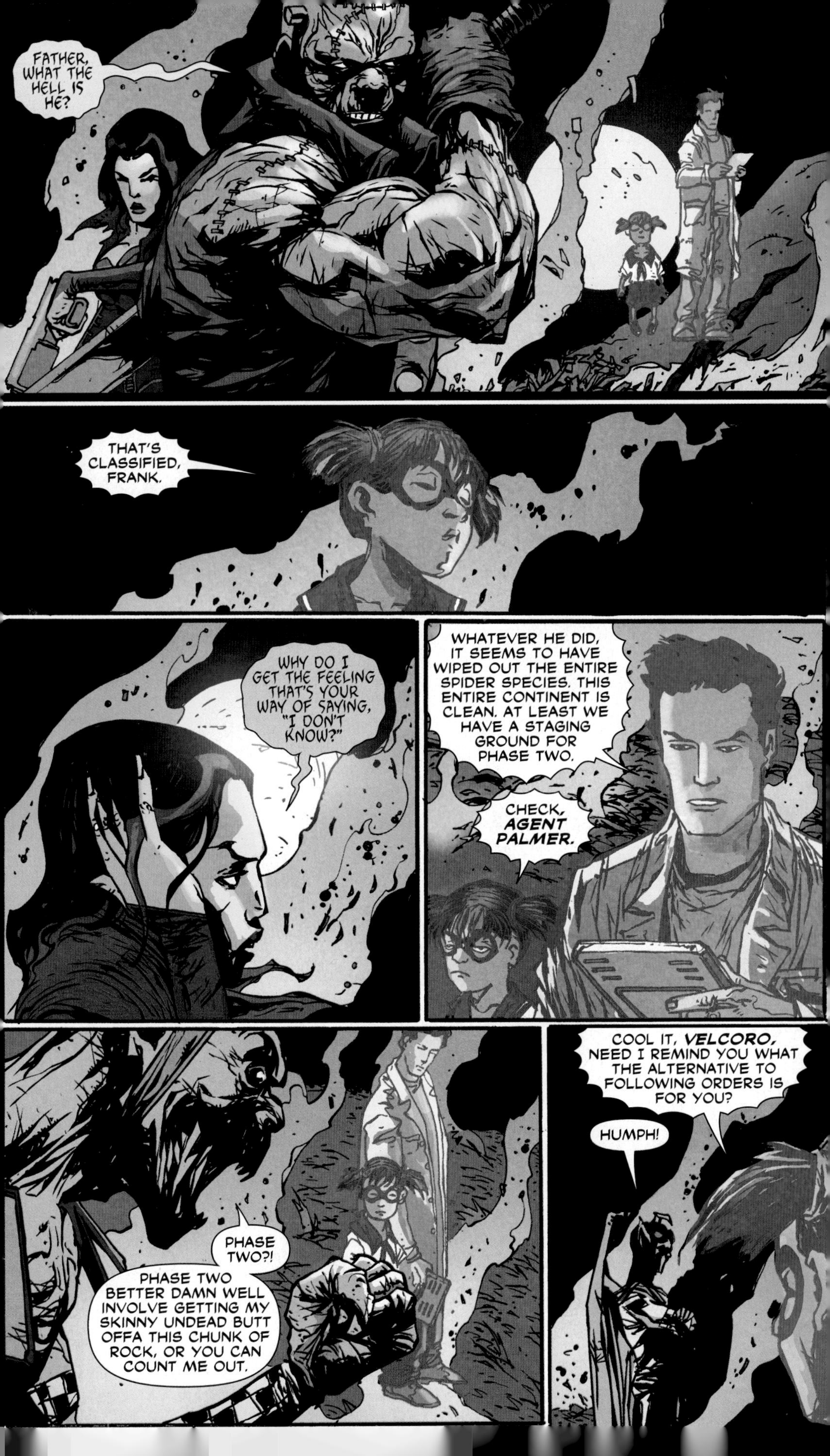
FATHER, WHAT THE HELL IS HE?
THAT'S CLASSIFIED, FRANK.
WHY DO I GET THE FEELING THAT'S YOUR WAY OF SAYING, "I DON'T KNOW?"
WHATEVER HE DID, IT SEEMS TO HAVE WIPED OUT THE ENTIRE SPIDER SPECIES. THIS ENTIRE CONTINENT IS CLEAN. AT LEAST WE HAVE A STAGING GROUND FOR PHASE TWO.
CHECK, ***AGENT PALMER.***
PHASE TWO?!
PHASE TWO BETTER DAMN WELL INVOLVE GETTING MY SKINNY UNDEAD BUTT OFFA THIS CHUNK OF ROCK, OR YOU CAN COUNT ME OUT.
COOL IT, ***VELCORO,*** NEED I REMIND YOU WHAT THE ALTERNATIVE TO FOLLOWING ORDERS IS FOR YOU?
HUMPH!

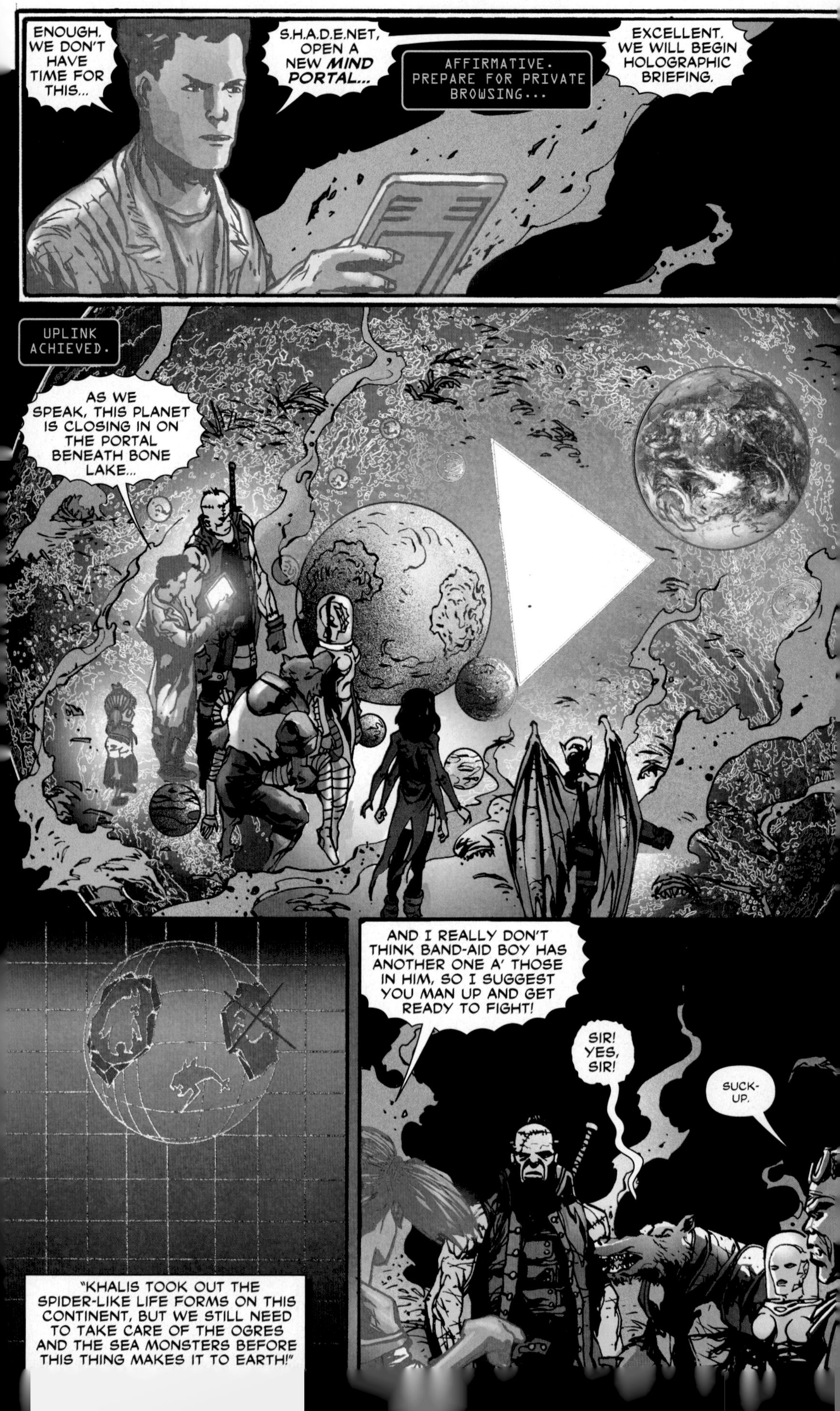

ENOUGH. WE DON'T HAVE TIME FOR THIS...
S.H.A.D.E.NET, OPEN A NEW *MIND PORTAL...*
AFFIRMATIVE. PREPARE FOR PRIVATE BROWSING...
EXCELLENT. WE WILL BEGIN HOLOGRAPHIC BRIEFING.
UPLINK ACHIEVED.
AS WE SPEAK, THIS PLANET IS CLOSING IN ON THE PORTAL BENEATH BONE LAKE...
"KHALIS TOOK OUT THE SPIDER-LIKE LIFE FORMS ON THIS CONTINENT, BUT WE STILL NEED TO TAKE CARE OF THE OGRES AND THE SEA MONSTERS BEFORE THIS THING MAKES IT TO EARTH!"
AND I REALLY DON'T THINK BAND-AID BOY HAS ANOTHER ONE A' THOSE IN HIM, SO I SUGGEST YOU MAN UP AND GET READY TO FIGHT!
SIR! YES, SIR!
SUCK-UP.

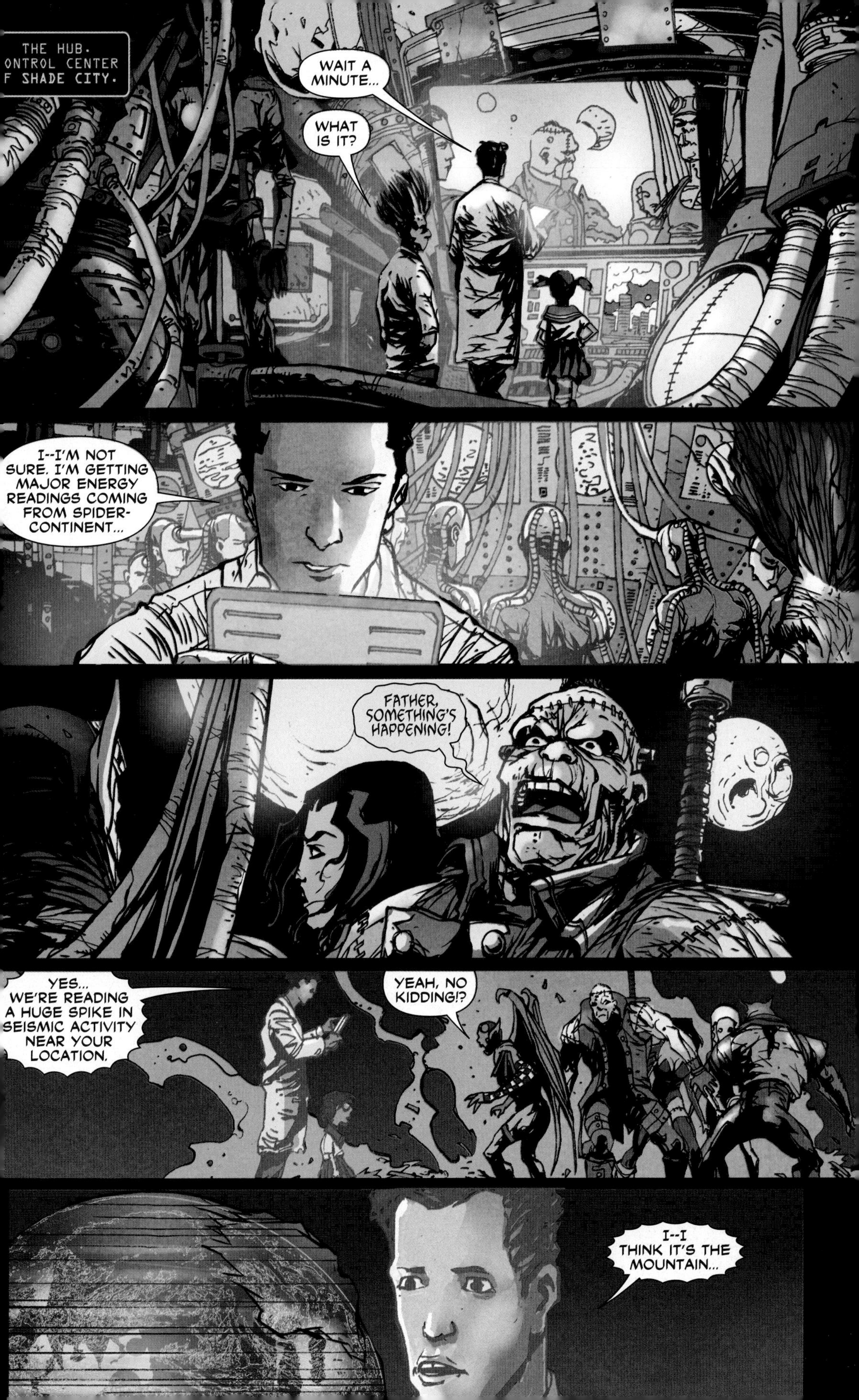
THE HUB.
ONTROL CENTER
F SHADE CITY.
WAIT A MINUTE...
WHAT IS IT?
I--I'M NOT SURE. I'M GETTING MAJOR ENERGY READINGS COMING FROM SPIDER-CONTINENT...
FATHER, SOMETHING'S HAPPENING!
YES... WE'RE READING A HUGE SPIKE IN SEISMIC ACTIVITY NEAR YOUR LOCATION.
YEAH, NO KIDDING!?
I--I THINK IT'S THE MOUNTAIN...

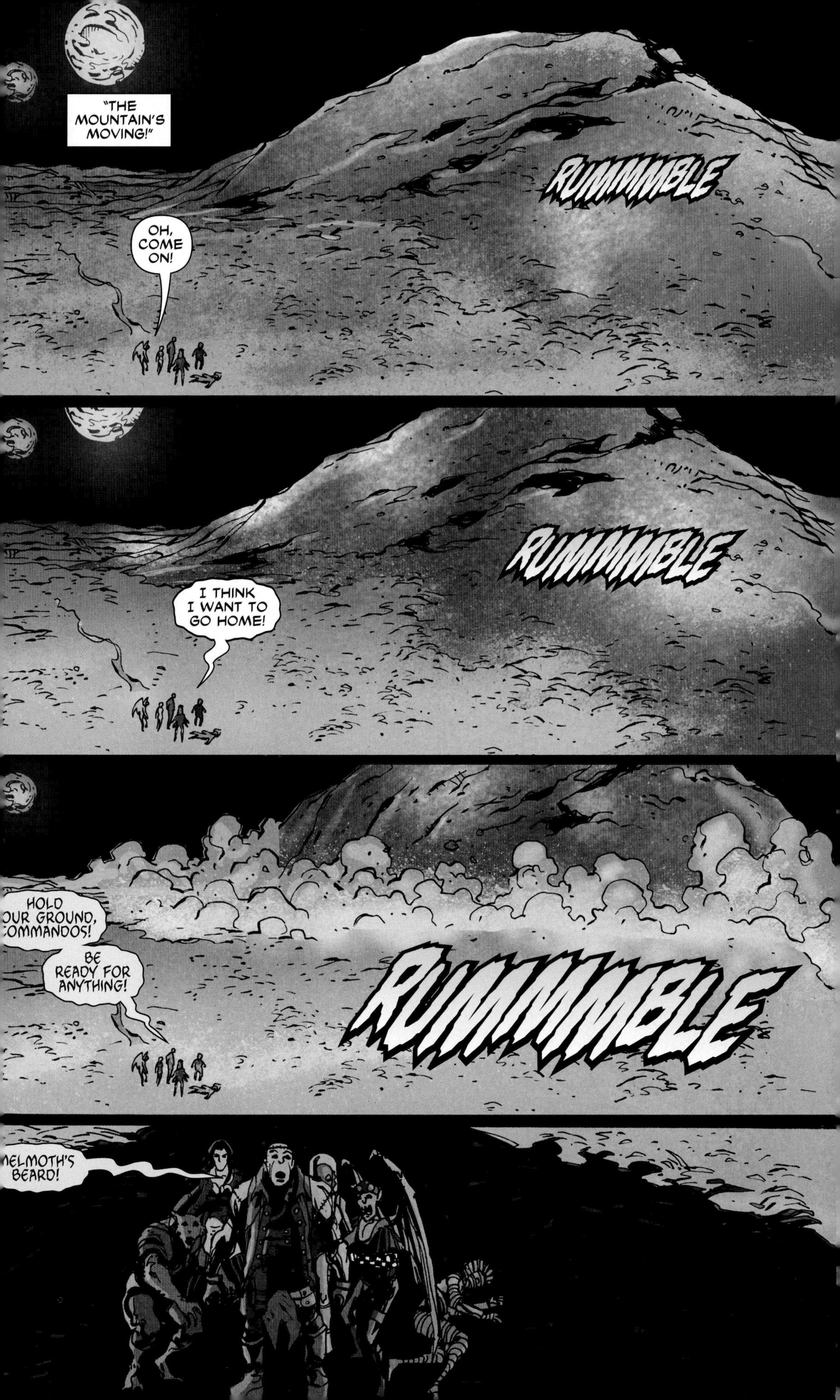
"THE MOUNTAIN'S MOVING!"
RUMMMBLE
OH, COME ON!
RUMMMBLE
I THINK I WANT TO GO HOME!
HOLD OUR GROUND, COMMANDOS!
BE READY FOR ANYTHING!
RUMMMBLE
MELMOTH'S BEARD!

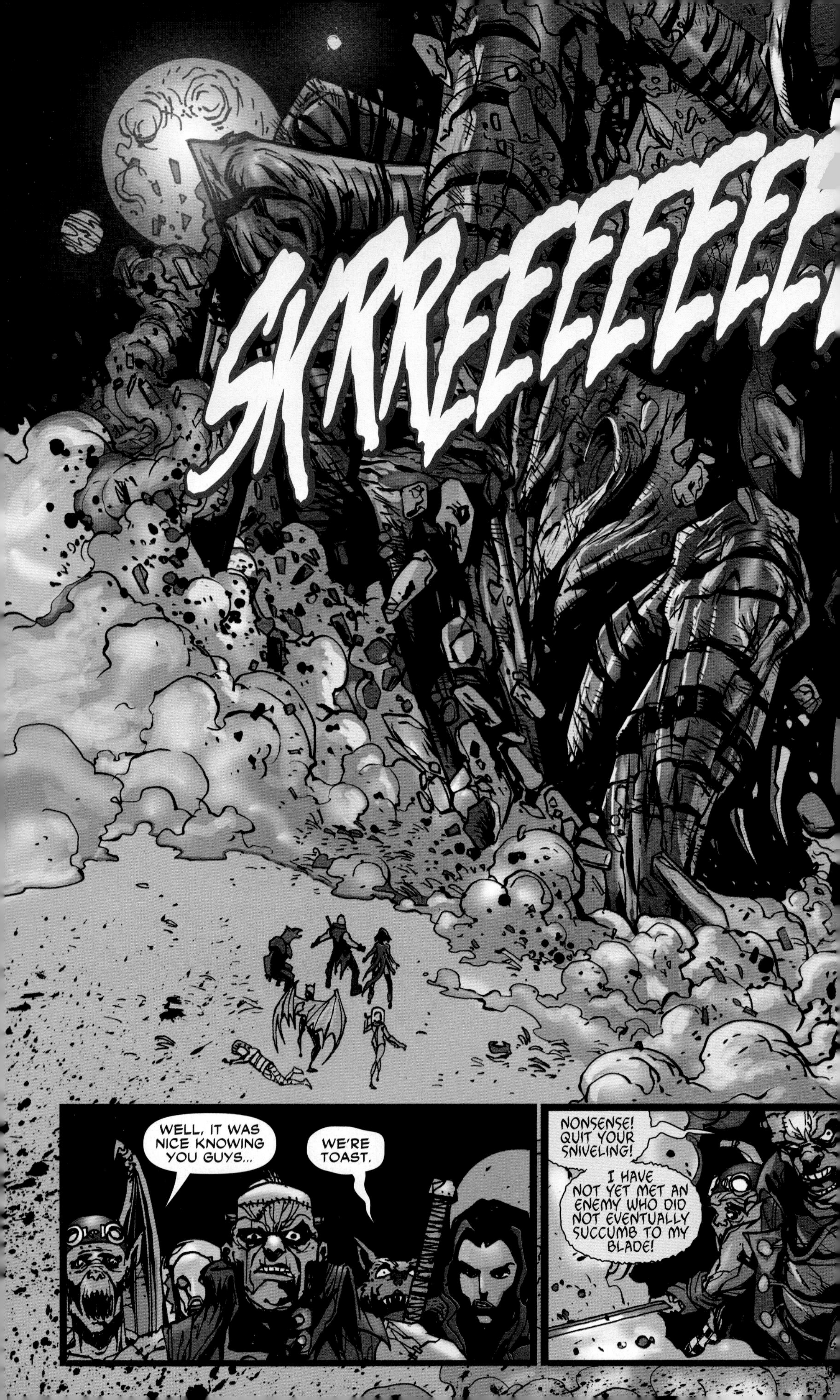

SKRREEEEEEEE
WELL, IT WAS NICE KNOWING YOU GUYS...
WE'RE TOAST.
NONSENSE! QUIT YOUR SNIVELING!
I HAVE NOT YET MET AN ENEMY WHO DID NOT EVENTUALLY SUCCUMB TO MY BLADE!

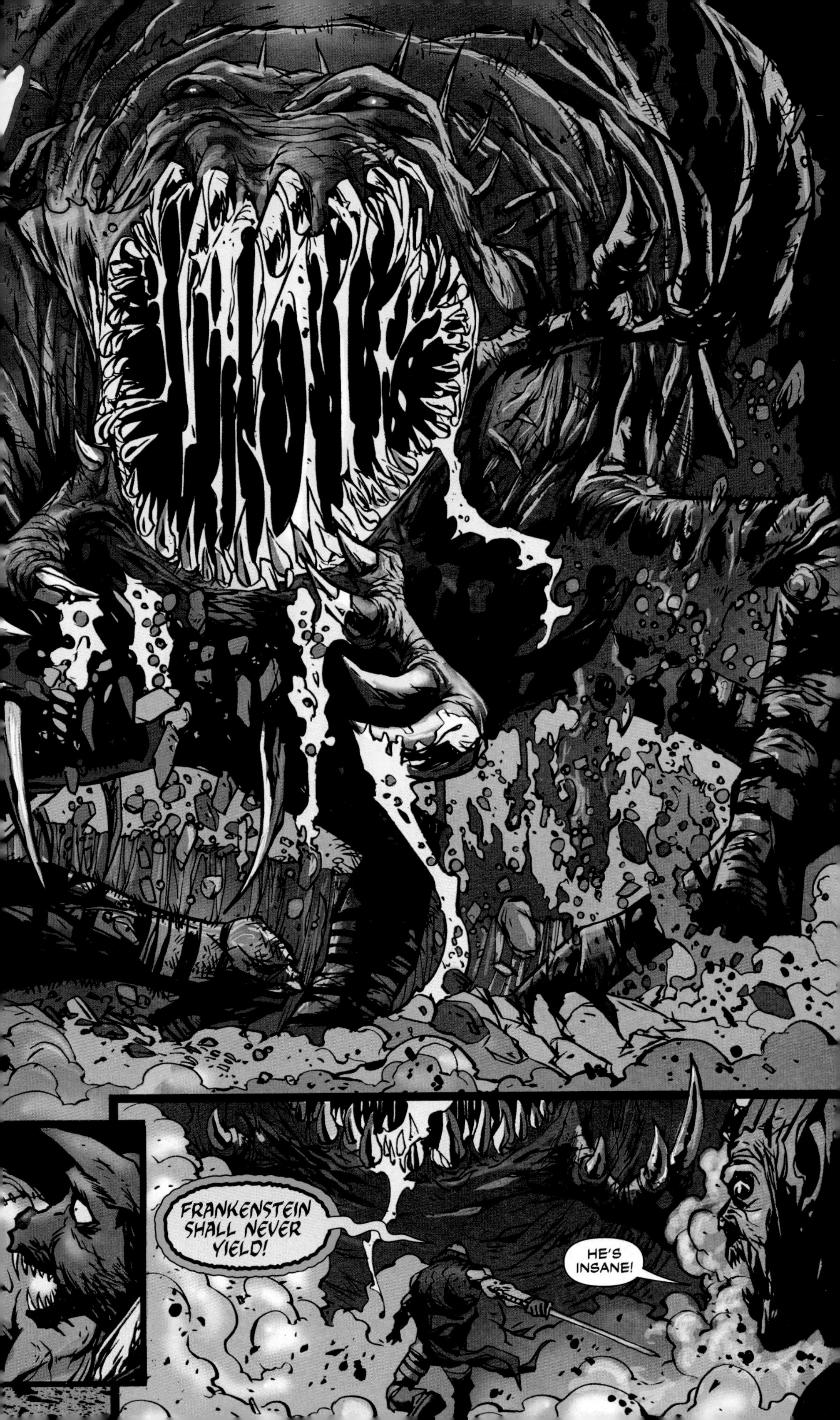
FRANKENSTEIN SHALL NEVER YIELD!
HE'S INSANE!

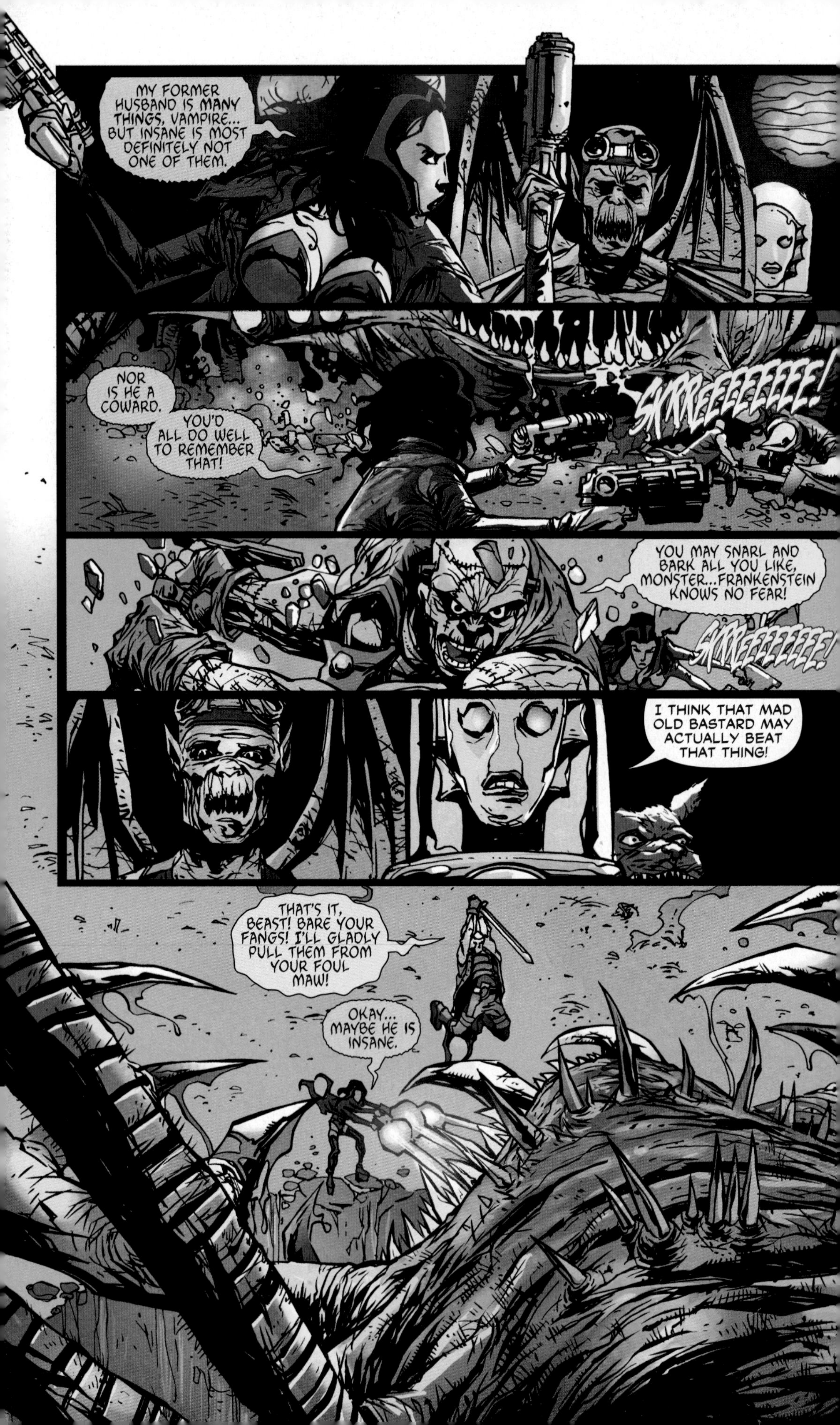
MY FORMER HUSBAND IS MANY THINGS, VAMPIRE... BUT INSANE IS MOST DEFINITELY NOT ONE OF THEM.
NOR IS HE A COWARD.
YOU'D ALL DO WELL TO REMEMBER THAT!
SKRREEEEEEEEE!
YOU MAY SNARL AND BARK ALL YOU LIKE, MONSTER...FRANKENSTEIN KNOWS NO FEAR!
SKRREEEEEEEE!
I THINK THAT MAD OLD BASTARD MAY ACTUALLY BEAT THAT THING!
THAT'S IT, BEAST! BARE YOUR FANGS! I'LL GLADLY PULL THEM FROM YOUR FOUL MAW!
OKAY... MAYBE HE IS INSANE.

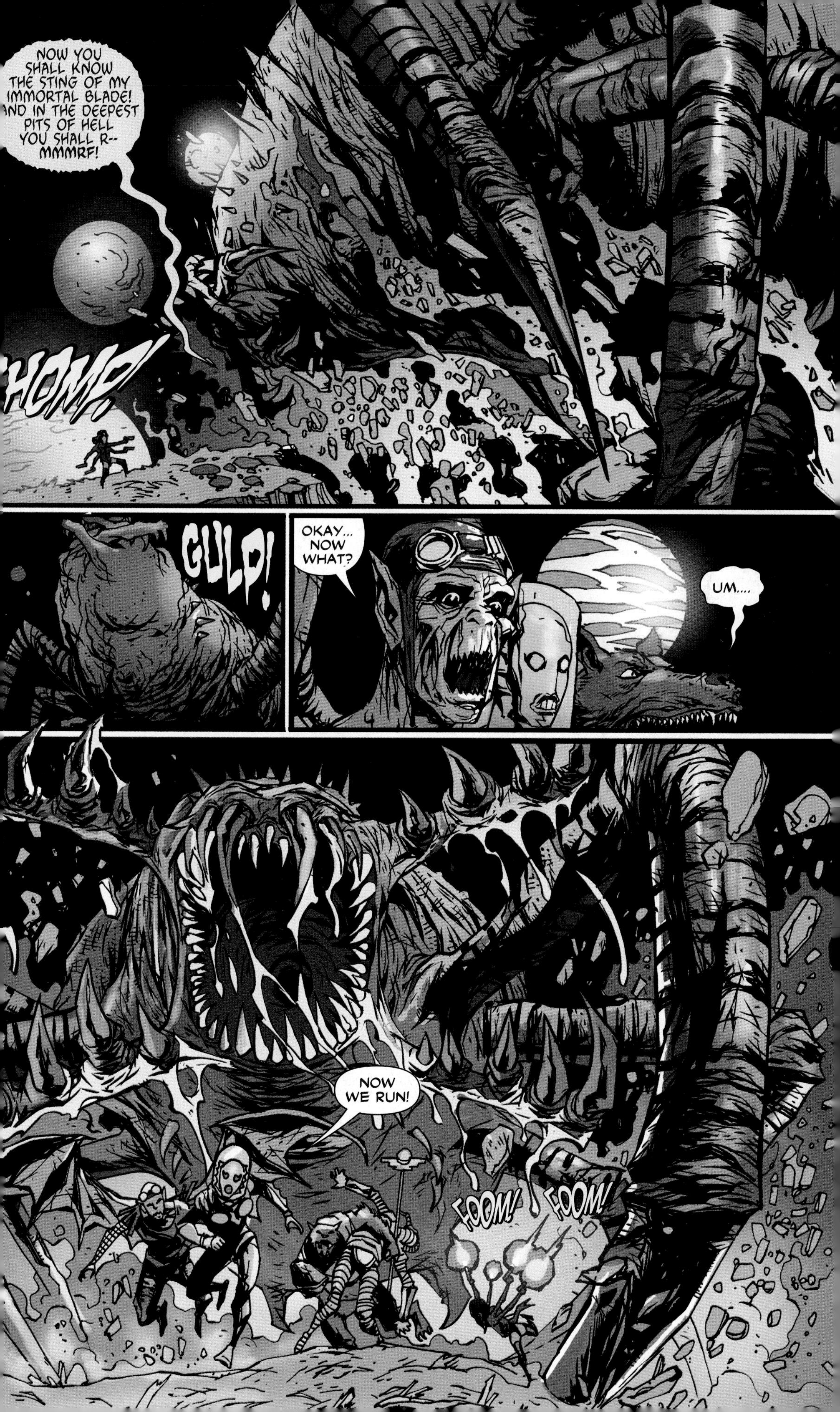

NOW YOU SHALL KNOW THE STING OF MY IMMORTAL BLADE! AND IN THE DEEPEST PITS OF HELL YOU SHALL R-- MMMRF!
CHOMP!
GULP!
OKAY... NOW WHAT?
UM....
NOW WE RUN!
FOOM! FOOM!

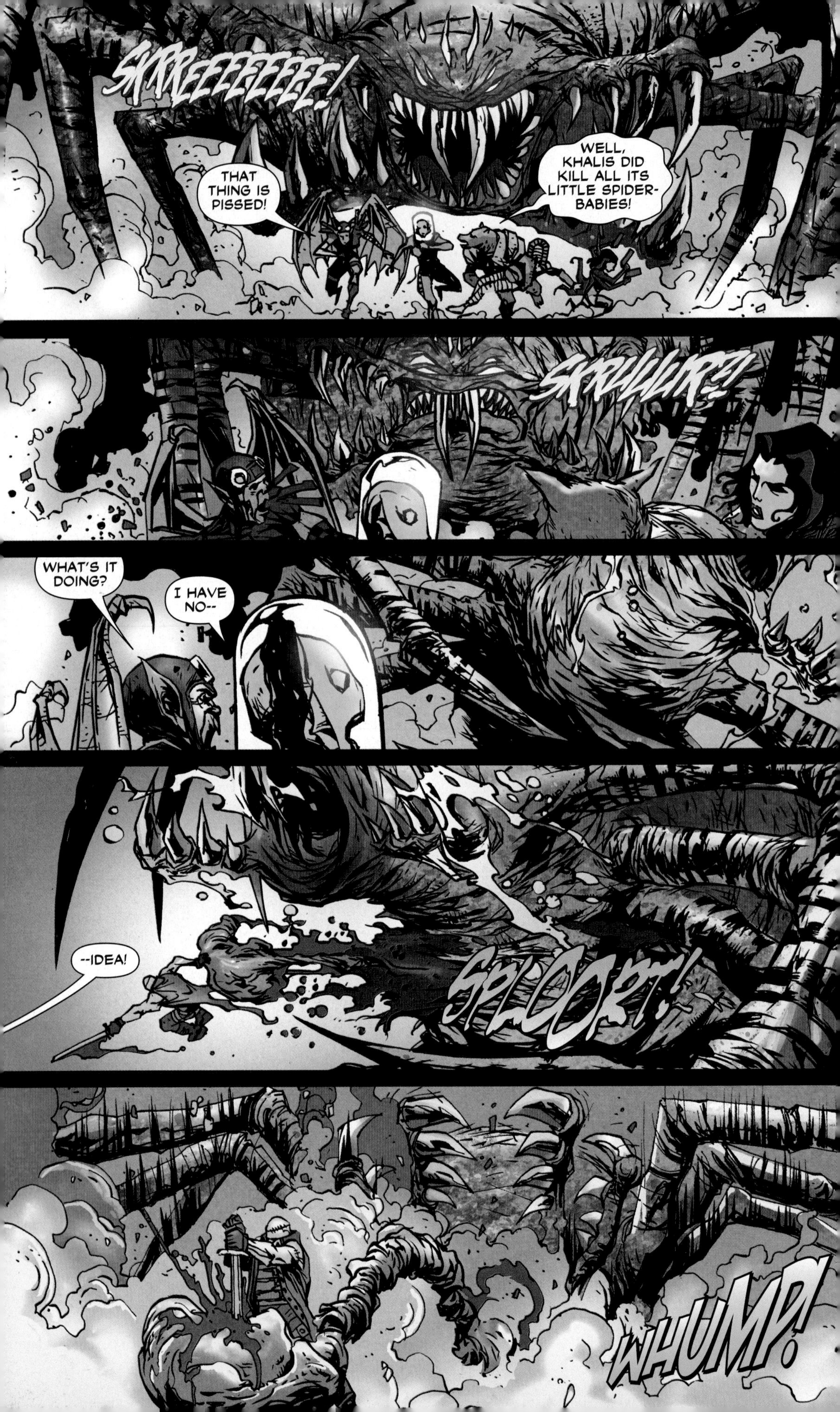
SKRREEEEEEEEEE!
THAT THING IS PISSED!
WELL, KHALIS DID KILL ALL ITS LITTLE SPIDER-BABIES!
WHAT'S IT DOING?
I HAVE NO--
--IDEA!
SPLOORT!
WHUMP!

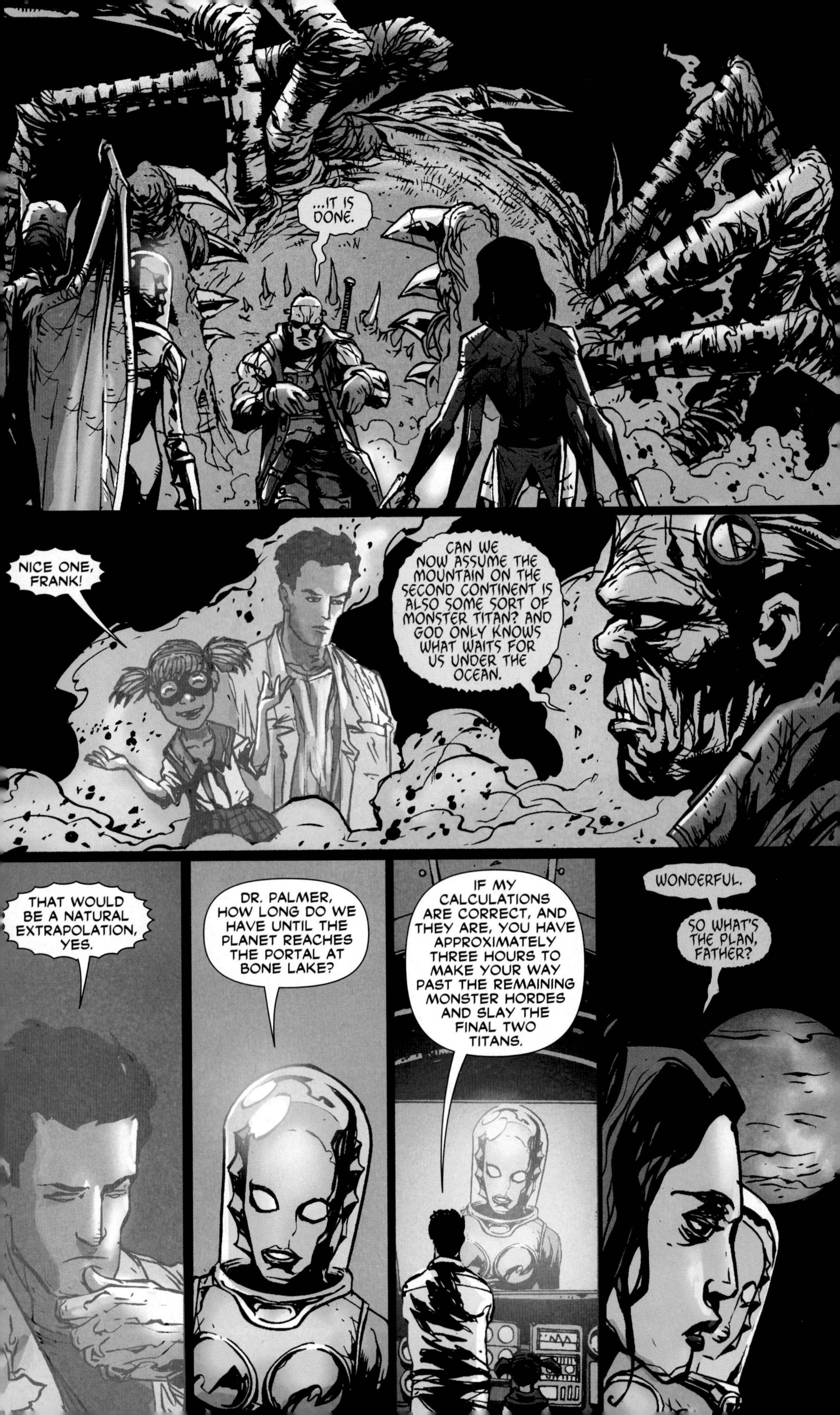
...IT IS DONE.
NICE ONE, FRANK!
CAN WE NOW ASSUME THE MOUNTAIN ON THE SECOND CONTINENT IS ALSO SOME SORT OF MONSTER TITAN? AND GOD ONLY KNOWS WHAT WAITS FOR US UNDER THE OCEAN.
THAT WOULD BE A NATURAL EXTRAPOLATION, YES.
DR. PALMER, HOW LONG DO WE HAVE UNTIL THE PLANET REACHES THE PORTAL AT BONE LAKE?
IF MY CALCULATIONS ARE CORRECT, AND THEY ARE, YOU HAVE APPROXIMATELY THREE HOURS TO MAKE YOUR WAY PAST THE REMAINING MONSTER HORDES AND SLAY THE FINAL TWO TITANS.
WONDERFUL.
SO WHAT'S THE PLAN, FATHER?

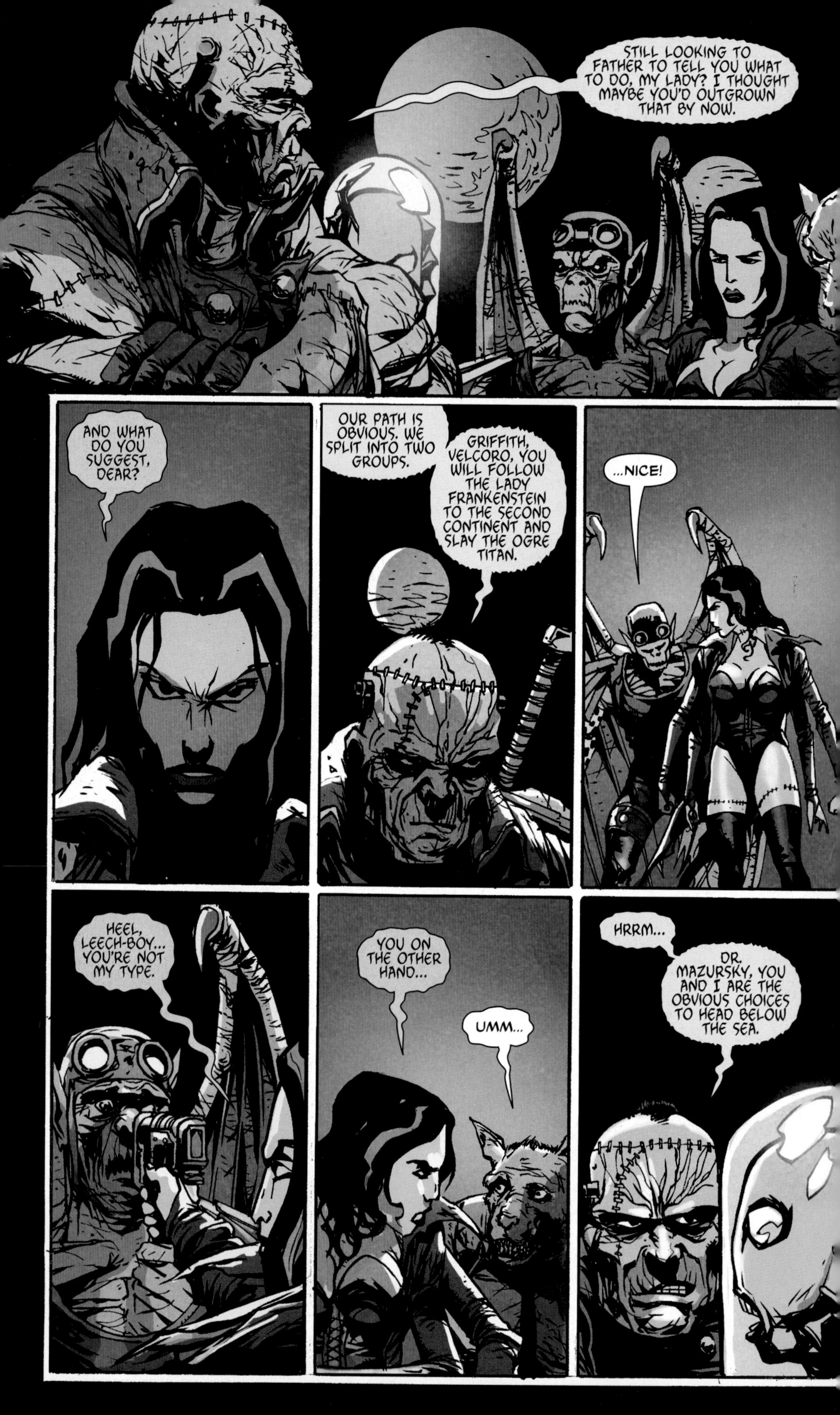
STILL LOOKING TO FATHER TO TELL YOU WHAT TO DO, MY LADY? I THOUGHT MAYBE YOU'D OUTGROWN THAT BY NOW.
AND WHAT DO YOU SUGGEST, DEAR?
OUR PATH IS OBVIOUS. WE SPLIT INTO TWO GROUPS.
GRIFFITH, VELCORO, YOU WILL FOLLOW THE LADY FRANKENSTEIN TO THE SECOND CONTINENT AND SLAY THE OGRE TITAN.
...NICE!
HEEL, LEECH-BOY... YOU'RE NOT MY TYPE.
YOU ON THE OTHER HAND...
UMM...
HRRM...
DR. MAZURSKY, YOU AND I ARE THE OBVIOUS CHOICES TO HEAD BELOW THE SEA.

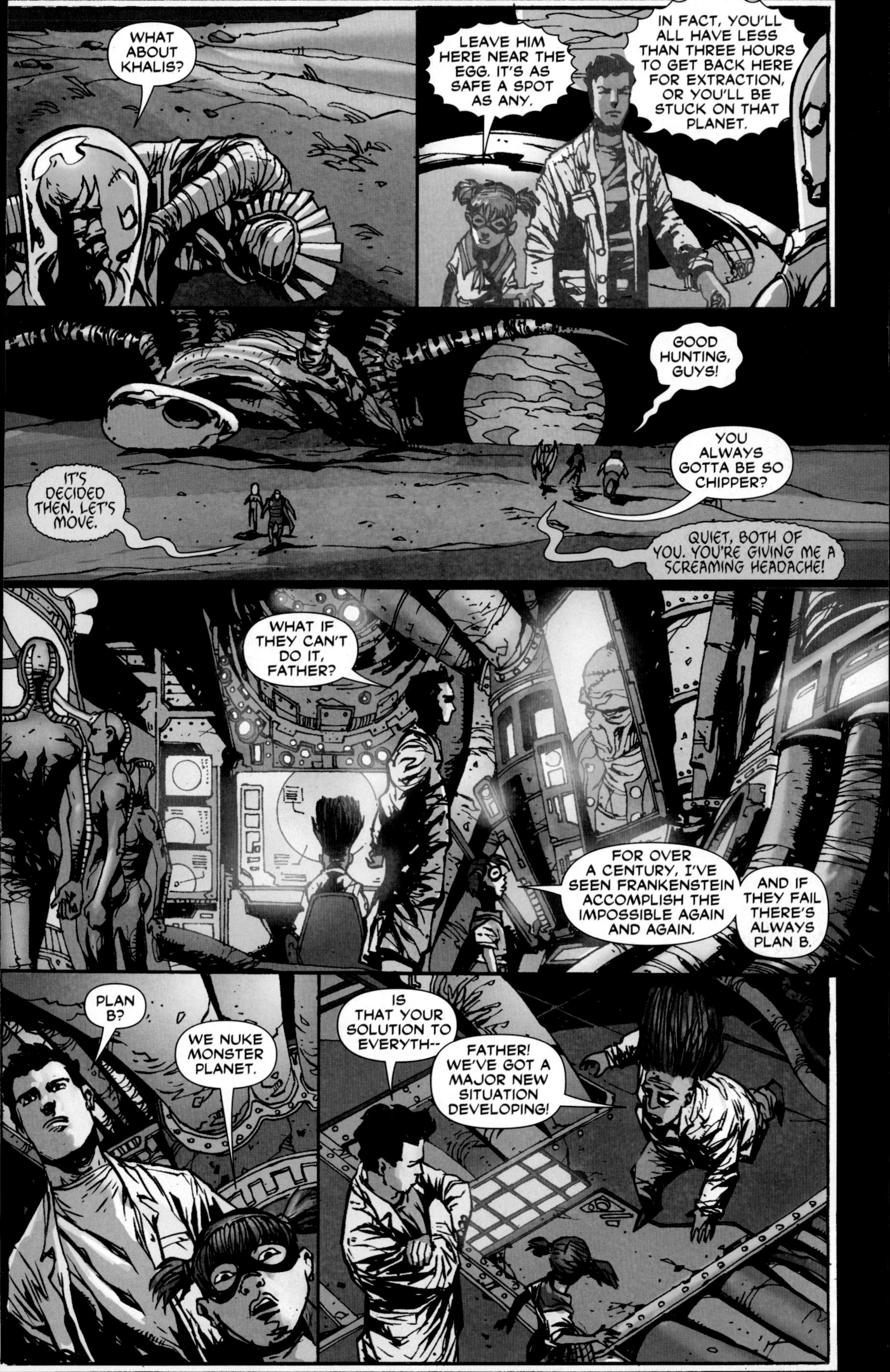
WHAT ABOUT KHALIS?
LEAVE HIM HERE NEAR THE EGG. IT'S AS SAFE A SPOT AS ANY.
IN FACT, YOU'LL ALL HAVE LESS THAN THREE HOURS TO GET BACK HERE FOR EXTRACTION, OR YOU'LL BE STUCK ON THAT PLANET.
GOOD HUNTING, GUYS!
YOU ALWAYS GOTTA BE SO CHIPPER?
IT'S DECIDED THEN. LET'S MOVE.
QUIET, BOTH OF YOU. YOU'RE GIVING ME A SCREAMING HEADACHE!
WHAT IF THEY CAN'T DO IT, FATHER?
FOR OVER A CENTURY, I'VE SEEN FRANKENSTEIN ACCOMPLISH THE IMPOSSIBLE AGAIN AND AGAIN.
AND IF THEY FAIL THERE'S ALWAYS PLAN B.
PLAN B?
WE NUKE MONSTER PLANET.
IS THAT YOUR SOLUTION TO EVERYTH--
FATHER! WE'VE GOT A MAJOR NEW SITUATION DEVELOPING!

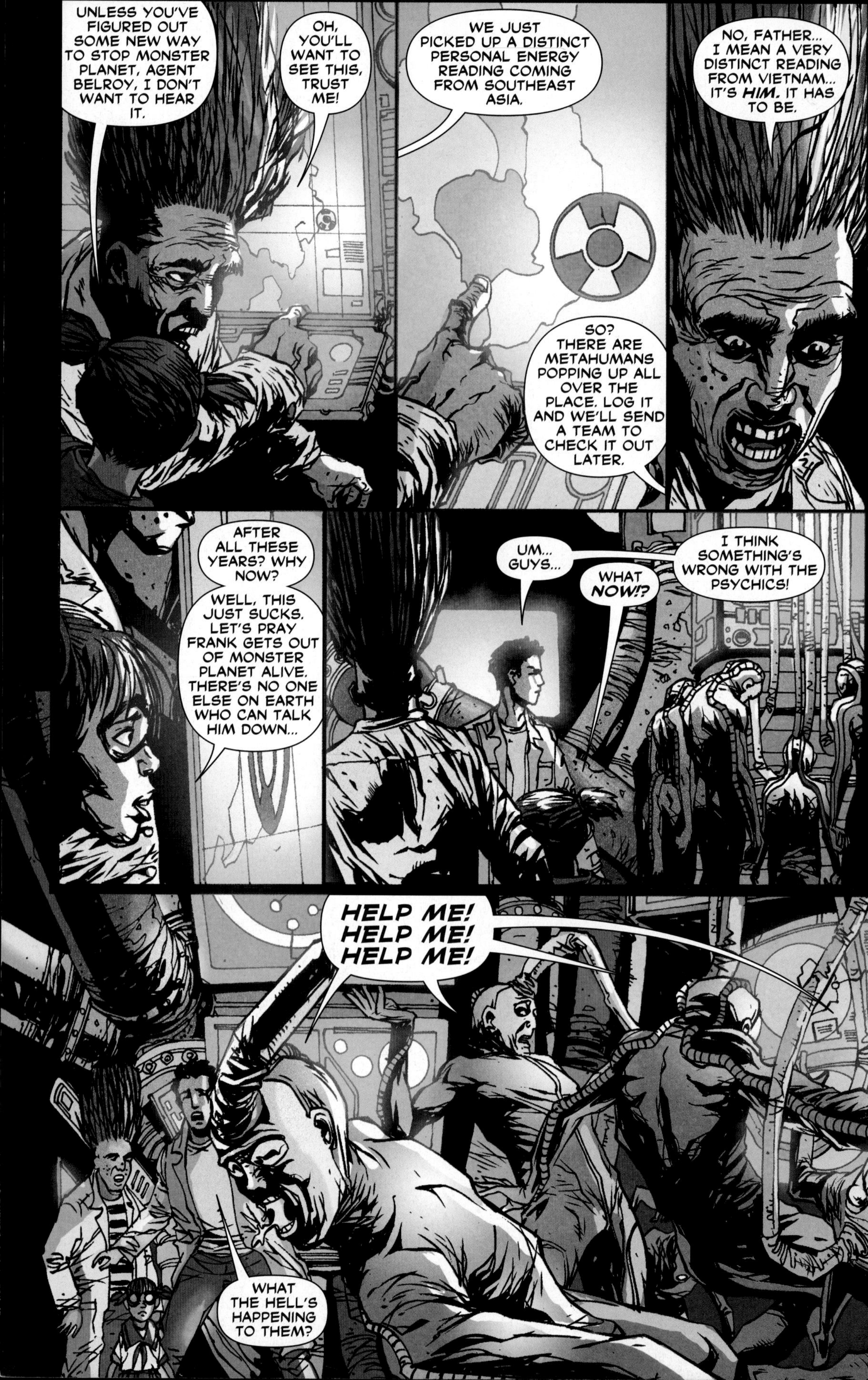
UNLESS YOU'VE FIGURED OUT SOME NEW WAY TO STOP MONSTER PLANET, AGENT BELROY, I DON'T WANT TO HEAR IT.
OH, YOU'LL WANT TO SEE THIS, TRUST ME!
WE JUST PICKED UP A DISTINCT PERSONAL ENERGY READING COMING FROM SOUTHEAST ASIA.
SO? THERE ARE METAHUMANS POPPING UP ALL OVER THE PLACE. LOG IT AND WE'LL SEND A TEAM TO CHECK IT OUT LATER.
NO, FATHER... I MEAN A VERY DISTINCT READING FROM VIETNAM... IT'S HIM. IT HAS TO BE.
AFTER ALL THESE YEARS? WHY NOW?
WELL, THIS JUST SUCKS. LET'S PRAY FRANK GETS OUT OF MONSTER PLANET ALIVE. THERE'S NO ONE ELSE ON EARTH WHO CAN TALK HIM DOWN...
UM... GUYS...
WHAT NOW!?
I THINK SOMETHING'S WRONG WITH THE PSYCHICS!
HELP ME! HELP ME! HELP ME!
WHAT THE HELL'S HAPPENING TO THEM?

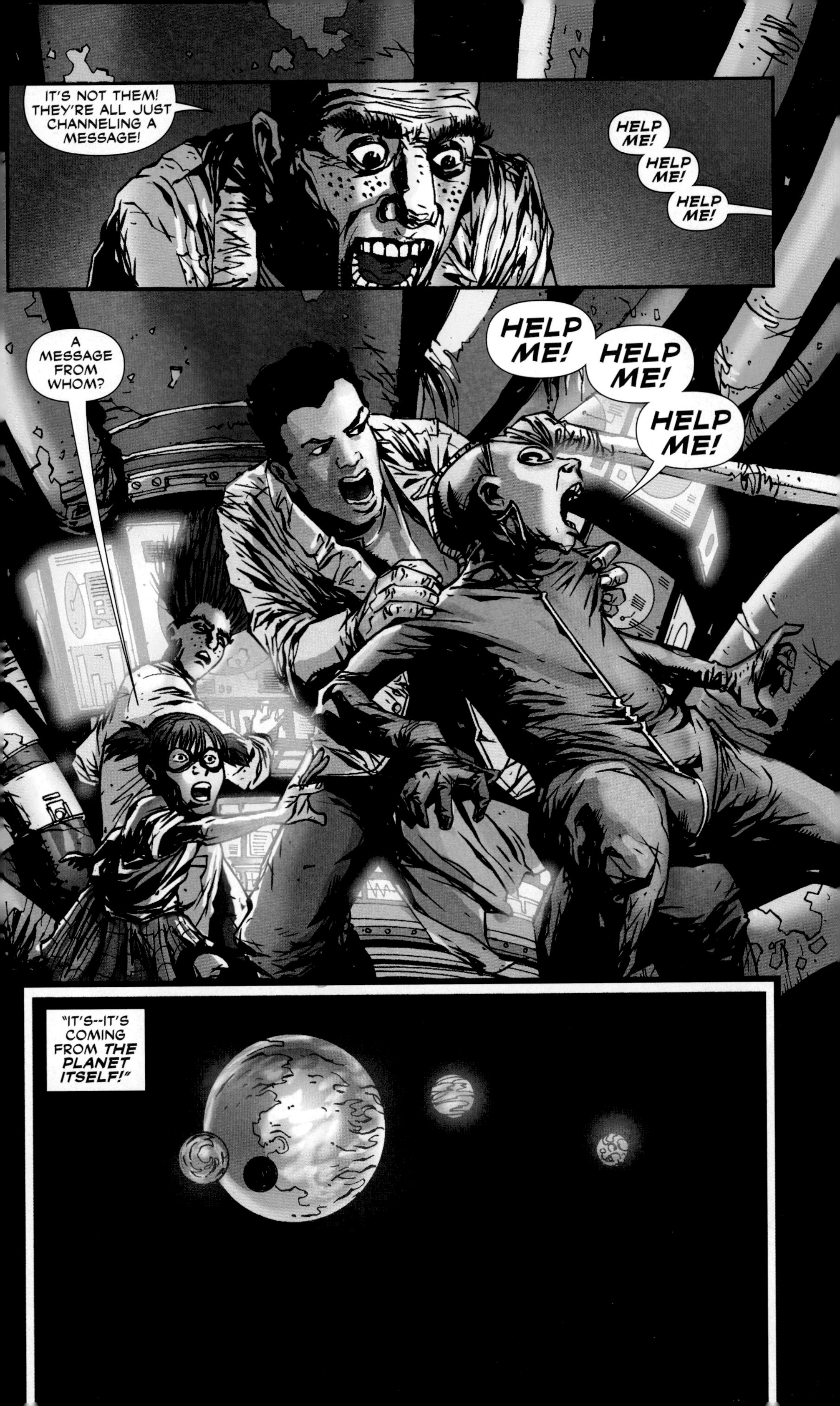
IT'S NOT THEM! THEY'RE ALL JUST CHANNELING A MESSAGE!
HELP ME!
HELP ME!
HELP ME!
A MESSAGE FROM WHOM?
HELP ME!
HELP ME!
HELP ME!
"IT'S--IT'S COMING FROM THE PLANET ITSELF!"

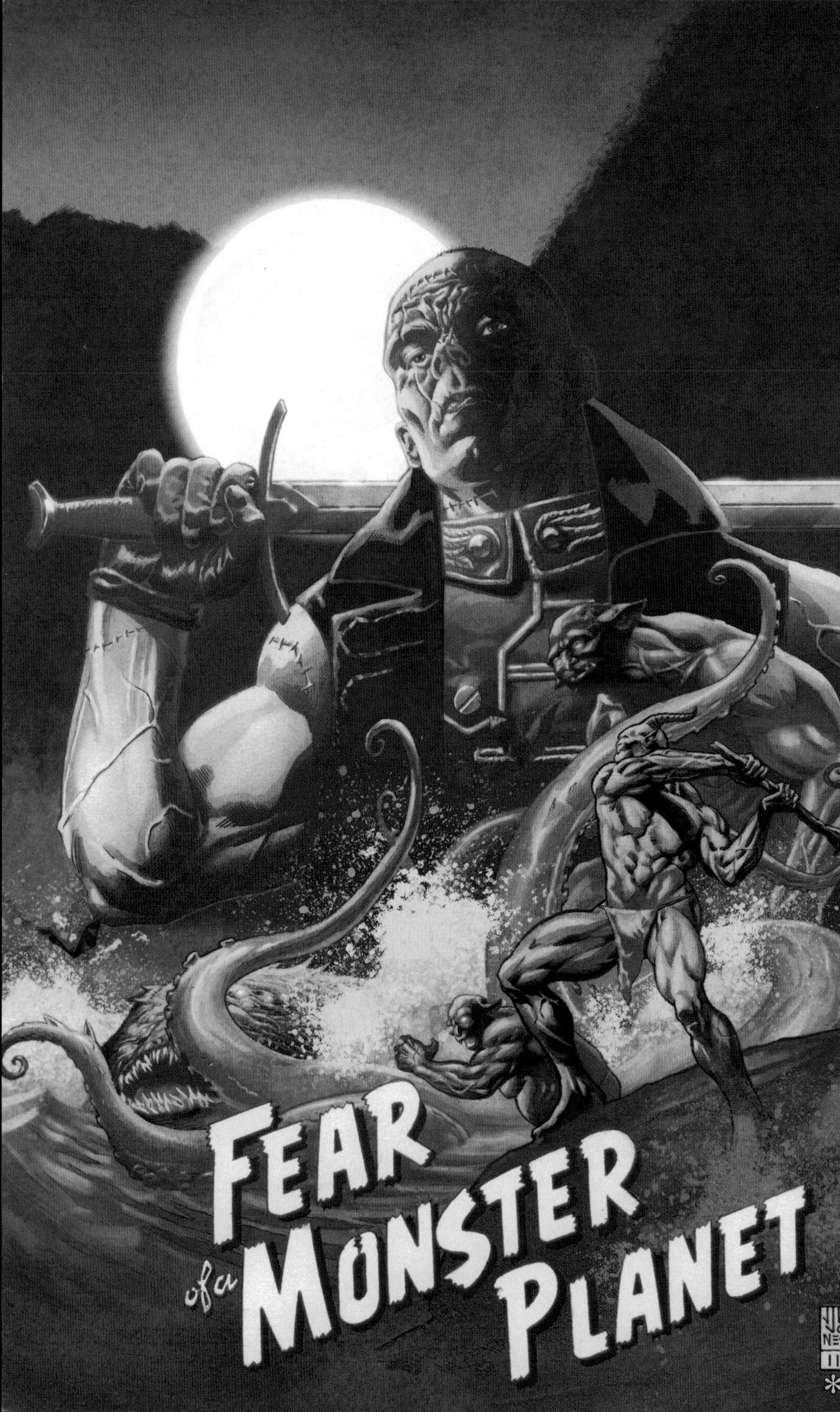

FEAR
of a
MONSTER
PLANET

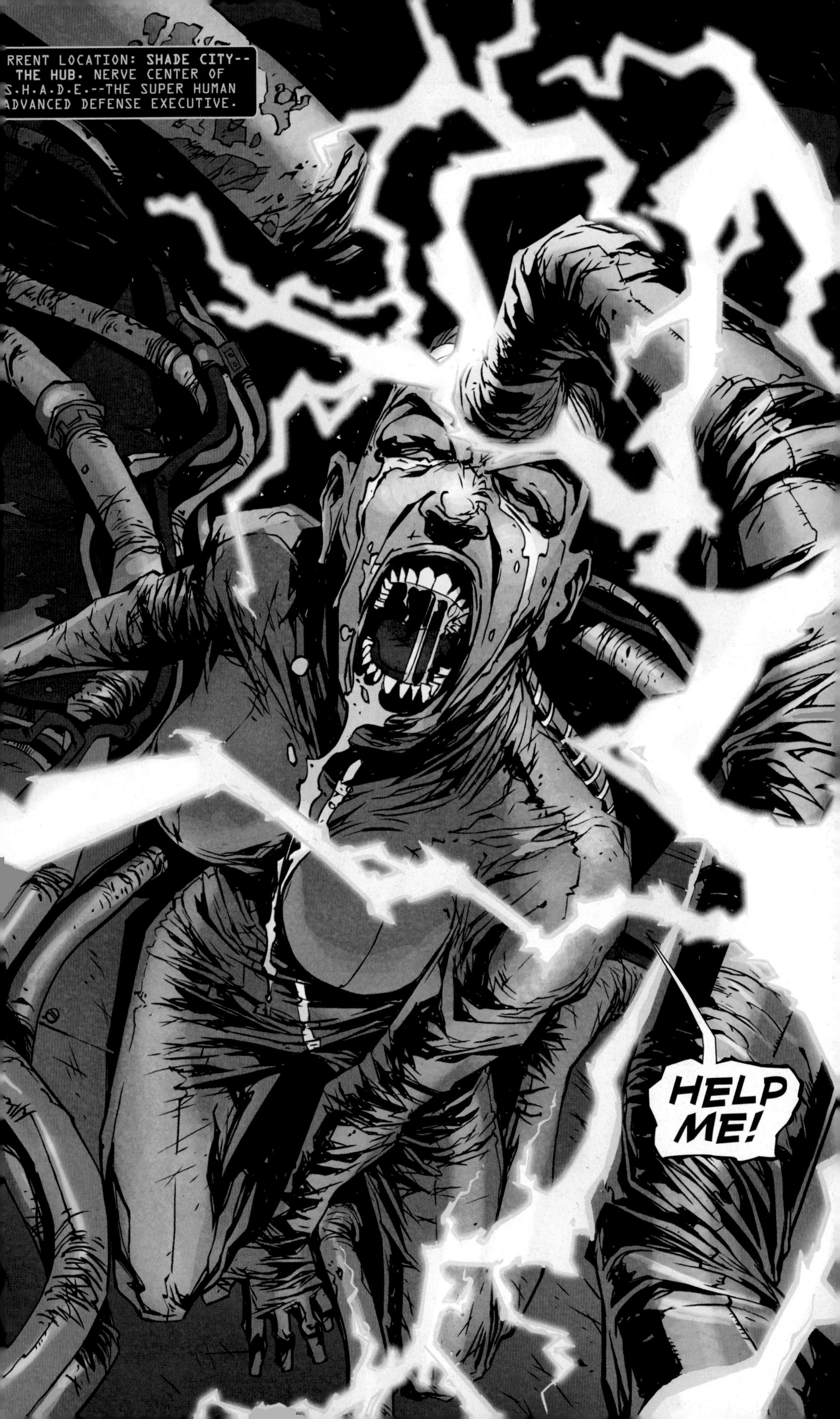
RRENT LOCATION: SHADE CITY--
THE HUB. NERVE CENTER OF
S.H.A.D.E.--THE SUPER HUMAN
ADVANCED DEFENSE EXECUTIVE.
HELP ME!

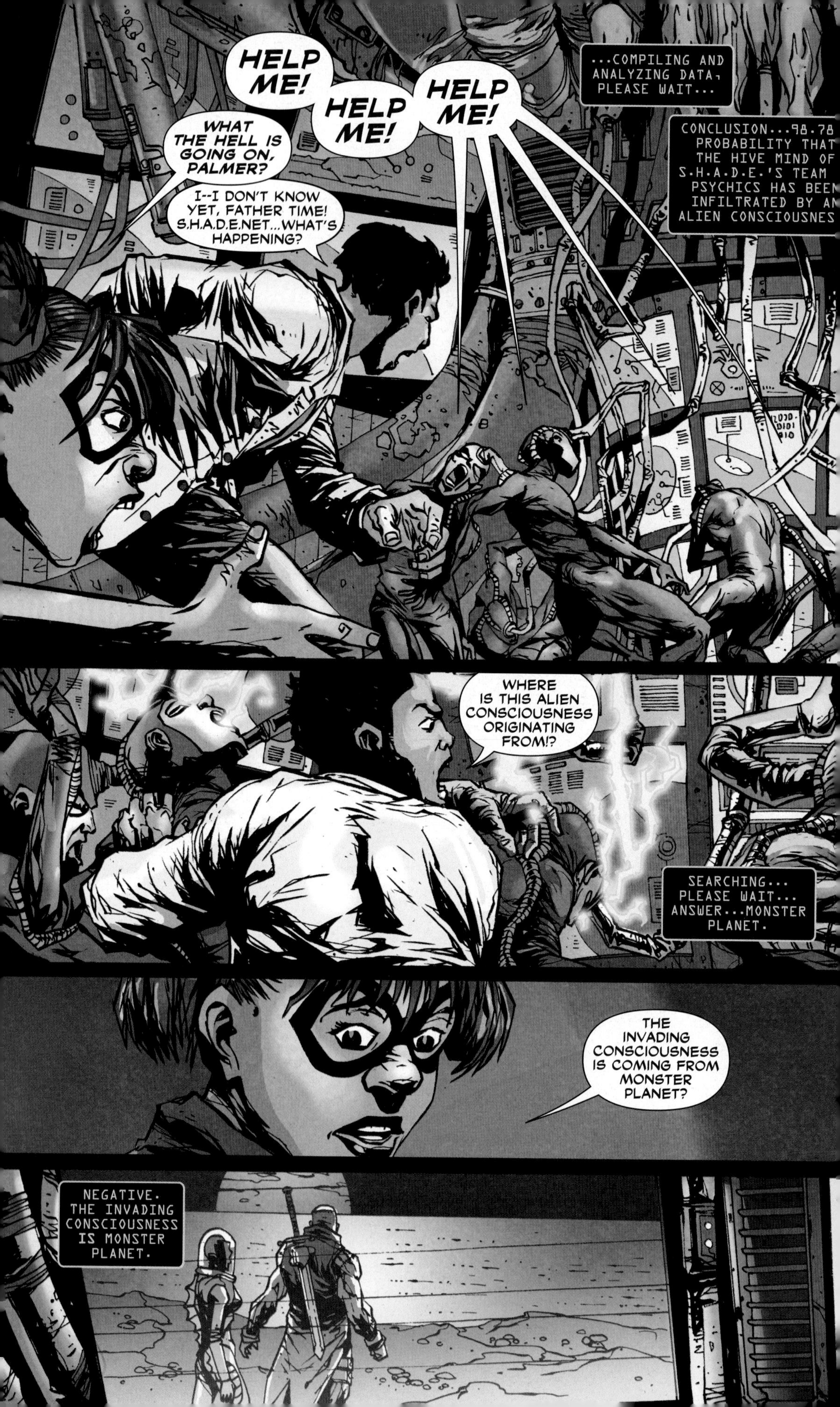
HELP ME!
HELP ME!
HELP ME!
...COMPILING AND ANALYZING DATA, PLEASE WAIT...
WHAT THE HELL IS GOING ON, PALMER?
I--I DON'T KNOW YET, FATHER TIME! S.H.A.D.E.NET...WHAT'S HAPPENING?
CONCLUSION...98.78 PROBABILITY THAT THE HIVE MIND OF S.H.A.D.E.'S TEAM PSYCHICS HAS BEEN INFILTRATED BY AN ALIEN CONSCIOUSNES
WHERE IS THIS ALIEN CONSCIOUSNESS ORIGINATING FROM!?
SEARCHING... PLEASE WAIT... ANSWER...MONSTER PLANET.
THE INVADING CONSCIOUSNESS IS COMING FROM MONSTER PLANET?
NEGATIVE. THE INVADING CONSCIOUSNESS IS MONSTER PLANET.

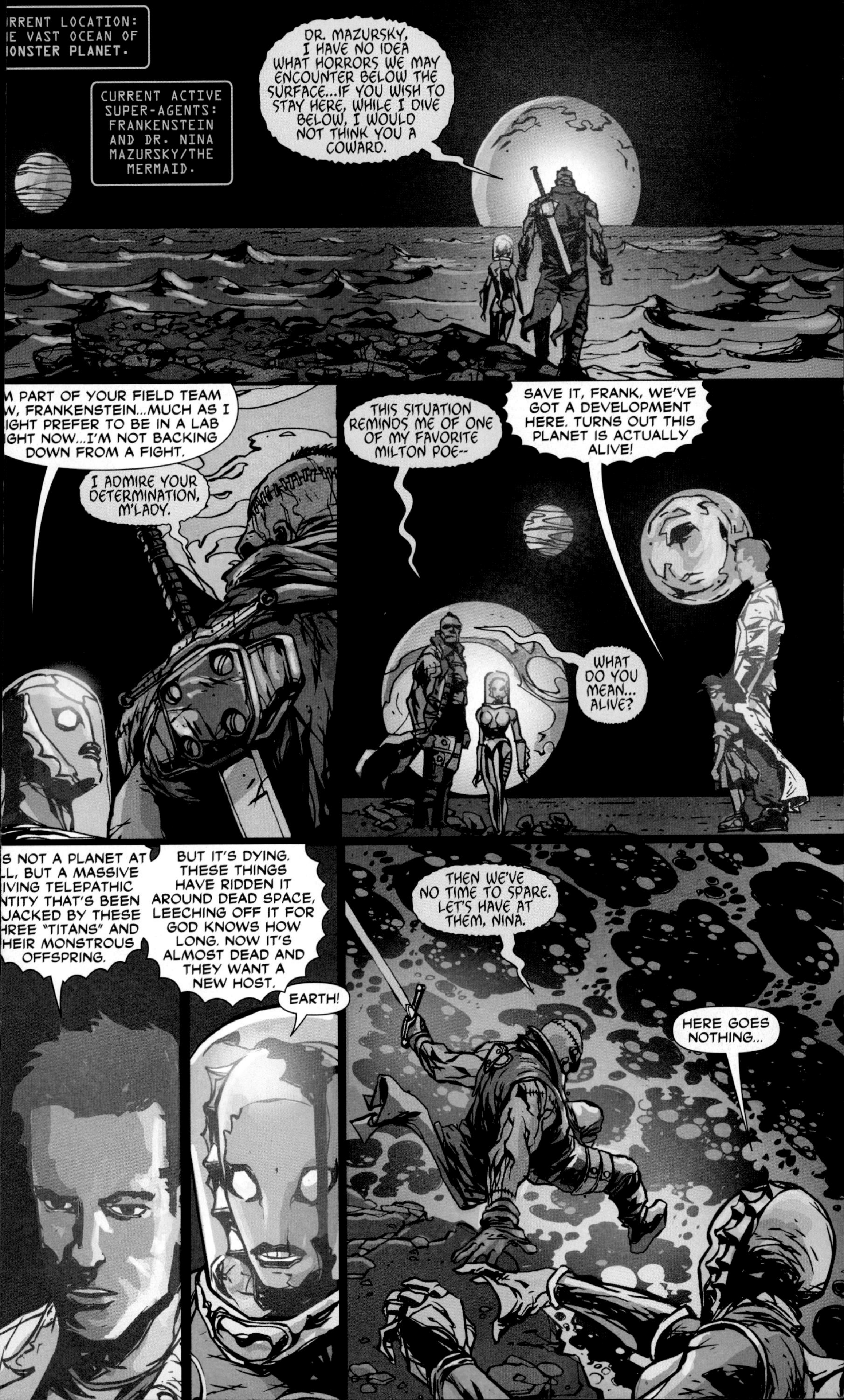

RRENT LOCATION:
E VAST OCEAN OF
ONSTER PLANET.
CURRENT ACTIVE SUPER-AGENTS: FRANKENSTEIN AND DR. NINA MAZURSKY/THE MERMAID.
DR. MAZURSKY, I HAVE NO IDEA WHAT HORRORS WE MAY ENCOUNTER BELOW THE SURFACE...IF YOU WISH TO STAY HERE, WHILE I DIVE BELOW, I WOULD NOT THINK YOU A COWARD.
M PART OF YOUR FIELD TEAM W, FRANKENSTEIN...MUCH AS I IGHT PREFER TO BE IN A LAB IGHT NOW...I'M NOT BACKING DOWN FROM A FIGHT.
I ADMIRE YOUR DETERMINATION, M'LADY.
THIS SITUATION REMINDS ME OF ONE OF MY FAVORITE MILTON POE--
SAVE IT, FRANK, WE'VE GOT A DEVELOPMENT HERE. TURNS OUT THIS PLANET IS ACTUALLY ALIVE!
WHAT DO YOU MEAN... ALIVE?
S NOT A PLANET AT LL, BUT A MASSIVE IVING TELEPATHIC NTITY THAT'S BEEN JACKED BY THESE HREE "TITANS" AND HEIR MONSTROUS OFFSPRING.
BUT IT'S DYING. THESE THINGS HAVE RIDDEN IT AROUND DEAD SPACE, LEECHING OFF IT FOR GOD KNOWS HOW LONG. NOW IT'S ALMOST DEAD AND THEY WANT A NEW HOST.
EARTH!
THEN WE'VE NO TIME TO SPARE. LET'S HAVE AT THEM, NINA.
HERE GOES NOTHING...

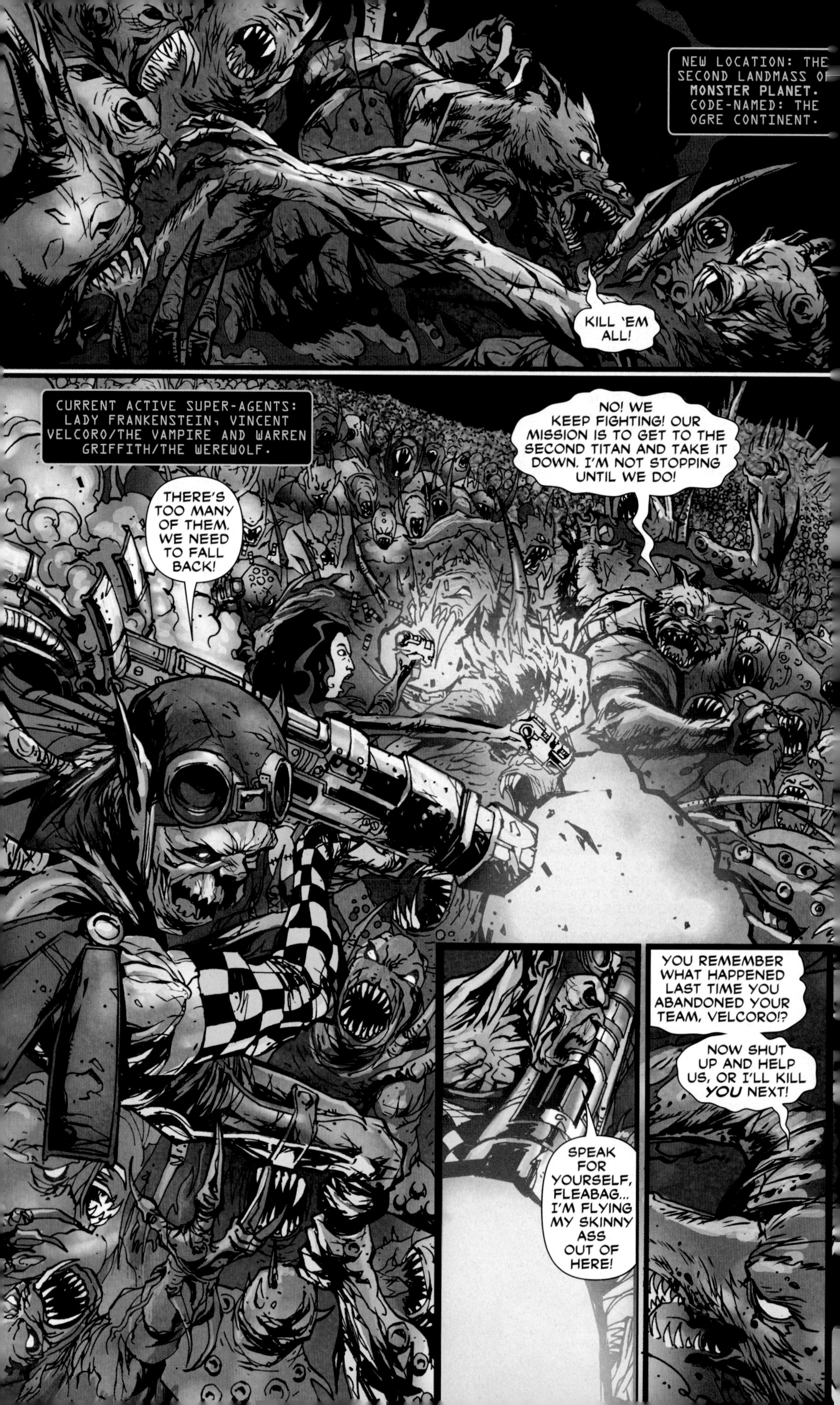
NEW LOCATION: THE SECOND LANDMASS OF MONSTER PLANET. CODE-NAMED: THE OGRE CONTINENT.
KILL 'EM ALL!
CURRENT ACTIVE SUPER-AGENTS: LADY FRANKENSTEIN, VINCENT VELCORO/THE VAMPIRE AND WARREN GRIFFITH/THE WEREWOLF.
THERE'S TOO MANY OF THEM. WE NEED TO FALL BACK!
NO! WE KEEP FIGHTING! OUR MISSION IS TO GET TO THE SECOND TITAN AND TAKE IT DOWN. I'M NOT STOPPING UNTIL WE DO!
SPEAK FOR YOURSELF, FLEABAG... I'M FLYING MY SKINNY ASS OUT OF HERE!
YOU REMEMBER WHAT HAPPENED LAST TIME YOU ABANDONED YOUR TEAM, VELCORO!?
NOW SHUT UP AND HELP US, OR I'LL KILL YOU NEXT!

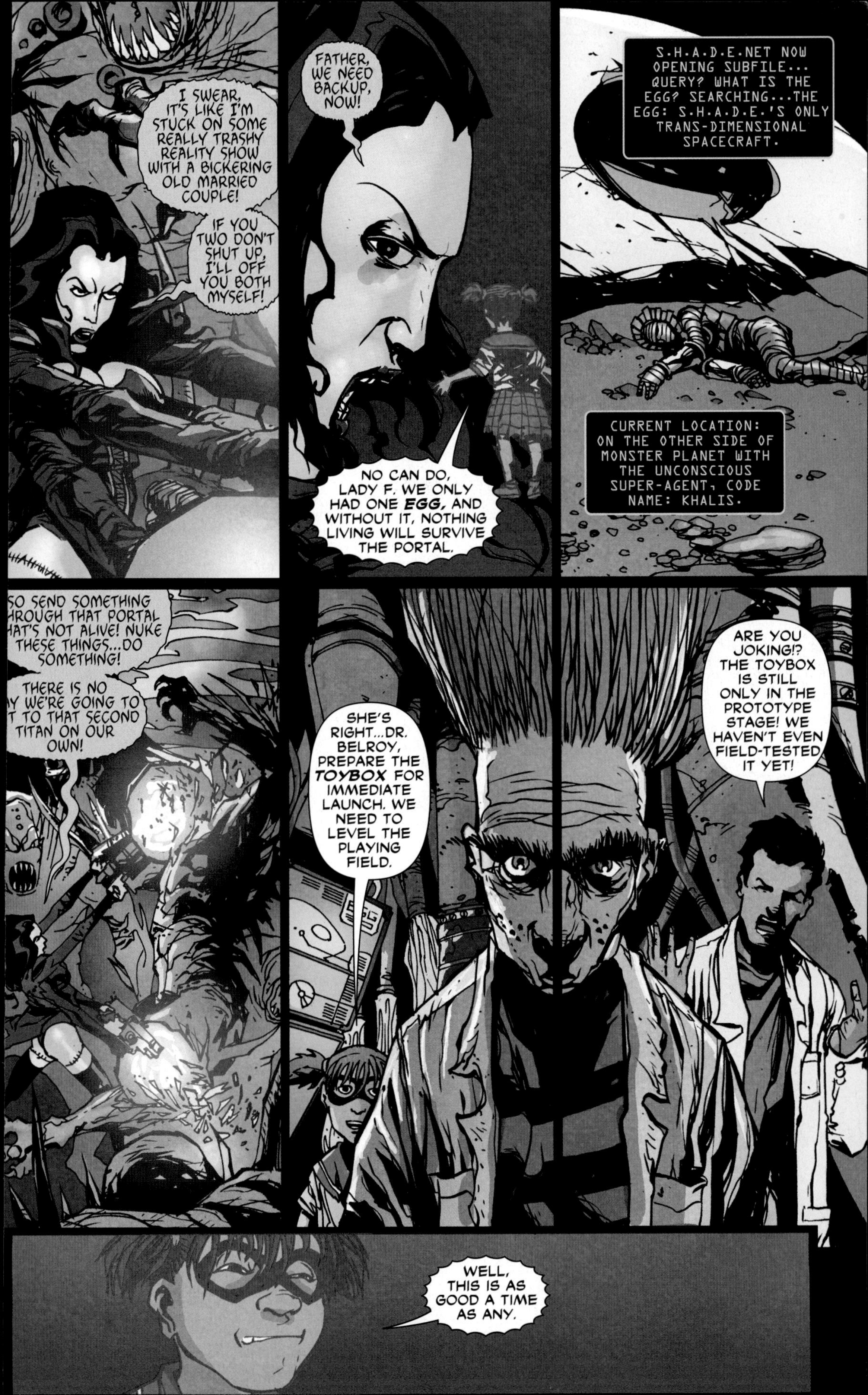

I SWEAR, IT'S LIKE I'M STUCK ON SOME REALLY TRASHY REALITY SHOW WITH A BICKERING OLD MARRIED COUPLE!
IF YOU TWO DON'T SHUT UP, I'LL OFF YOU BOTH MYSELF!
FATHER, WE NEED BACKUP, NOW!
NO CAN DO, LADY F. WE ONLY HAD ONE EGG, AND WITHOUT IT, NOTHING LIVING WILL SURVIVE THE PORTAL.
S.H.A.D.E.NET NOW OPENING SUBFILE... QUERY? WHAT IS THE EGG? SEARCHING...THE EGG: S.H.A.D.E.'S ONLY TRANS-DIMENSIONAL SPACECRAFT.
CURRENT LOCATION: ON THE OTHER SIDE OF MONSTER PLANET WITH THE UNCONSCIOUS SUPER-AGENT, CODE NAME: KHALIS.
SO SEND SOMETHING HROUGH THAT PORTAL HAT'S NOT ALIVE! NUKE THESE THINGS...DO SOMETHING!
THERE IS NO AY WE'RE GOING TO T TO THAT SECOND TITAN ON OUR OWN!
SHE'S RIGHT...DR. BELROY, PREPARE THE TOYBOX FOR IMMEDIATE LAUNCH. WE NEED TO LEVEL THE PLAYING FIELD.
ARE YOU JOKING!? THE TOYBOX IS STILL ONLY IN THE PROTOTYPE STAGE! WE HAVEN'T EVEN FIELD-TESTED IT YET!
WELL, THIS IS AS GOOD A TIME AS ANY.

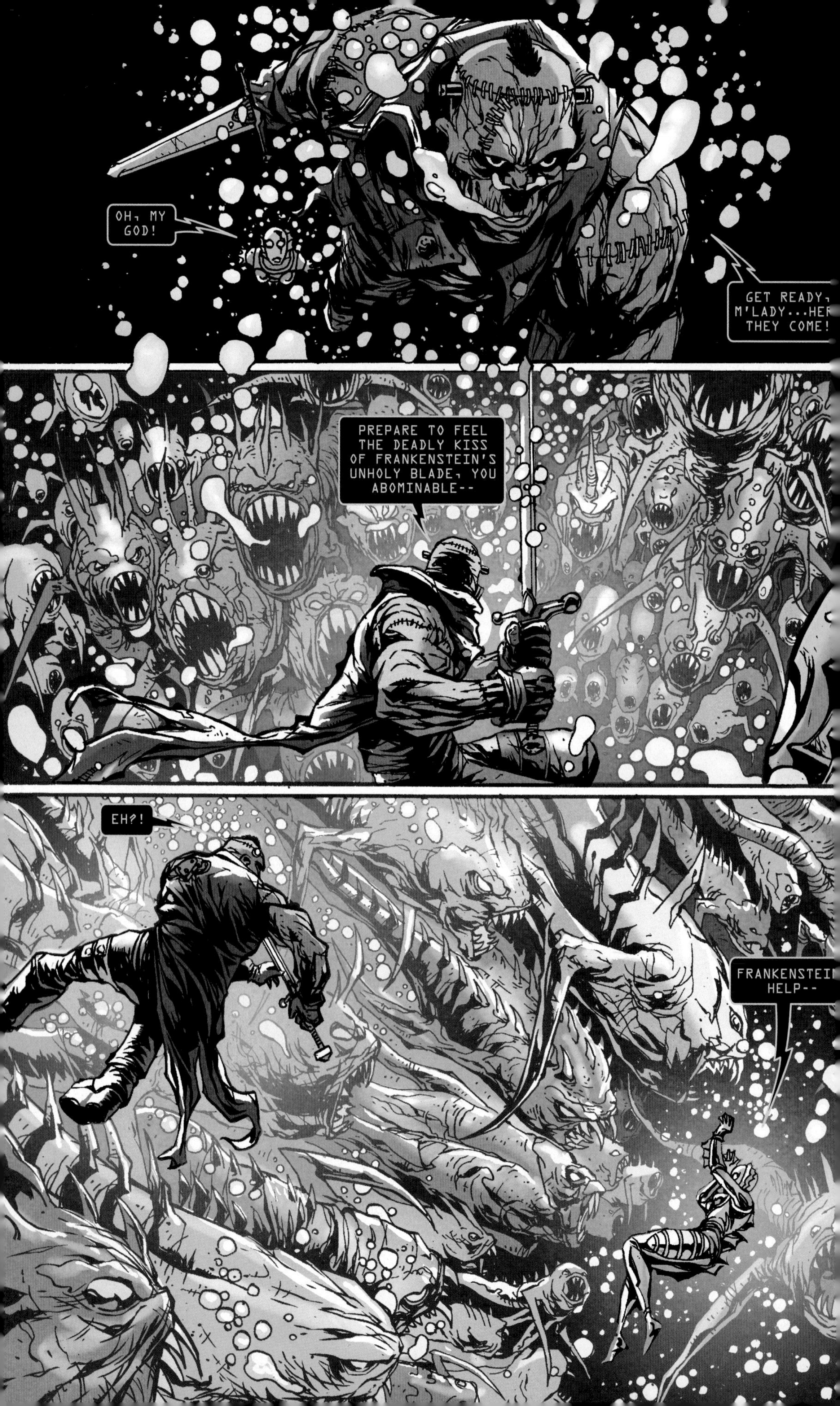
OH, MY GOD!
GET READY, M'LADY...HER THEY COME!
PREPARE TO FEEL THE DEADLY KISS OF FRANKENSTEIN'S UNHOLY BLADE, YOU ABOMINABLE--
EH?!
FRANKENSTEI HELP--

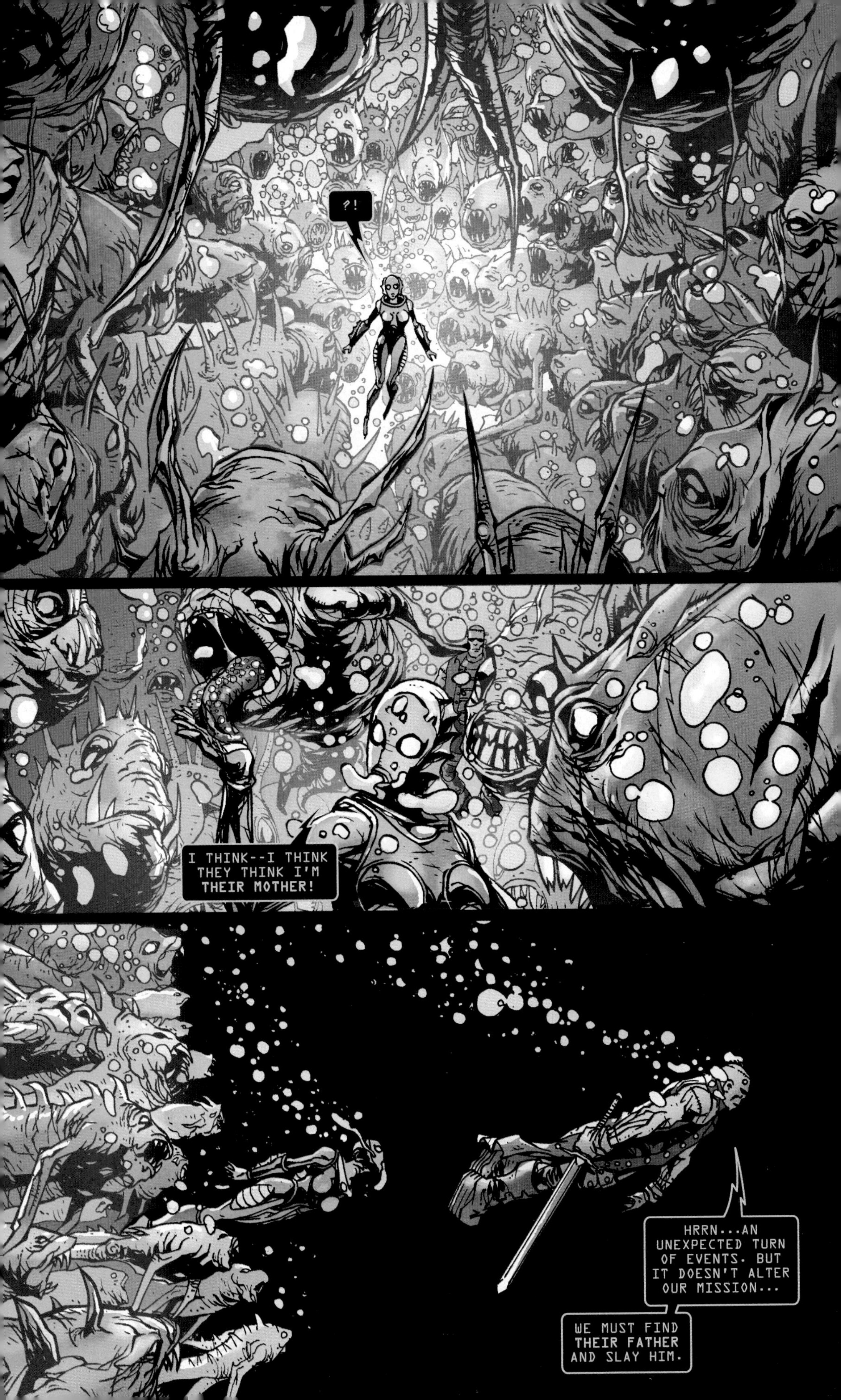
?!
I THINK--I THINK THEY THINK I'M THEIR MOTHER!
HRRN...AN UNEXPECTED TURN OF EVENTS. BUT IT DOESN'T ALTER OUR MISSION...
WE MUST FIND THEIR FATHER AND SLAY HIM.

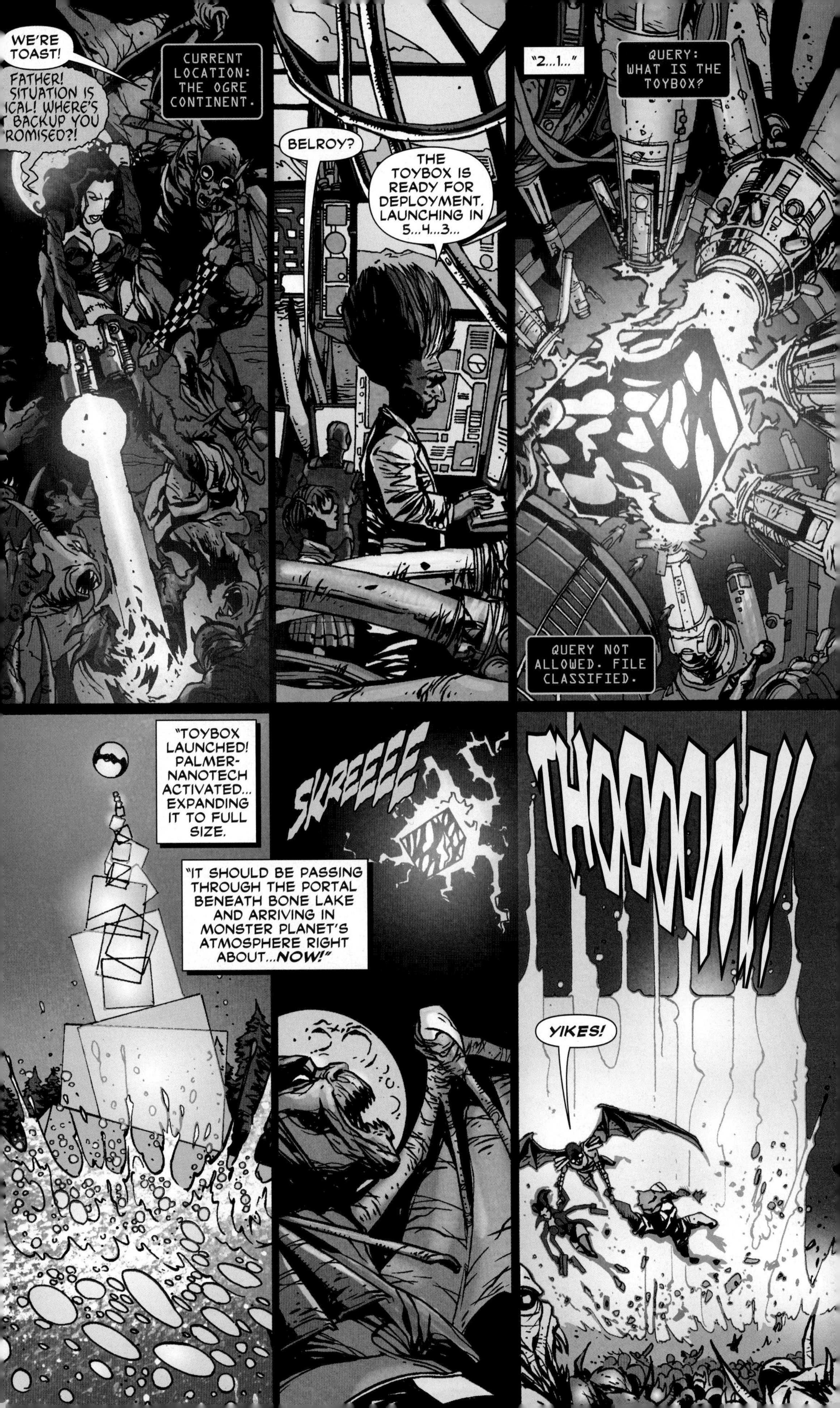
WE'RE TOAST!
FATHER! SITUATION IS ICAL! WHERE'S BACKUP YOU ROMISED?!
CURRENT LOCATION: THE OGRE CONTINENT.
BELROY?
THE TOYBOX IS READY FOR DEPLOYMENT. LAUNCHING IN 5...4...3...
"2...1..."
QUERY: WHAT IS THE TOYBOX?
QUERY NOT ALLOWED. FILE CLASSIFIED.
"TOYBOX LAUNCHED! PALMER-NANOTECH ACTIVATED... EXPANDING IT TO FULL SIZE.
"IT SHOULD BE PASSING THROUGH THE PORTAL BENEATH BONE LAKE AND ARRIVING IN MONSTER PLANET'S ATMOSPHERE RIGHT ABOUT...NOW!"
SKREEEE
THOOOOM!!
YIKES!

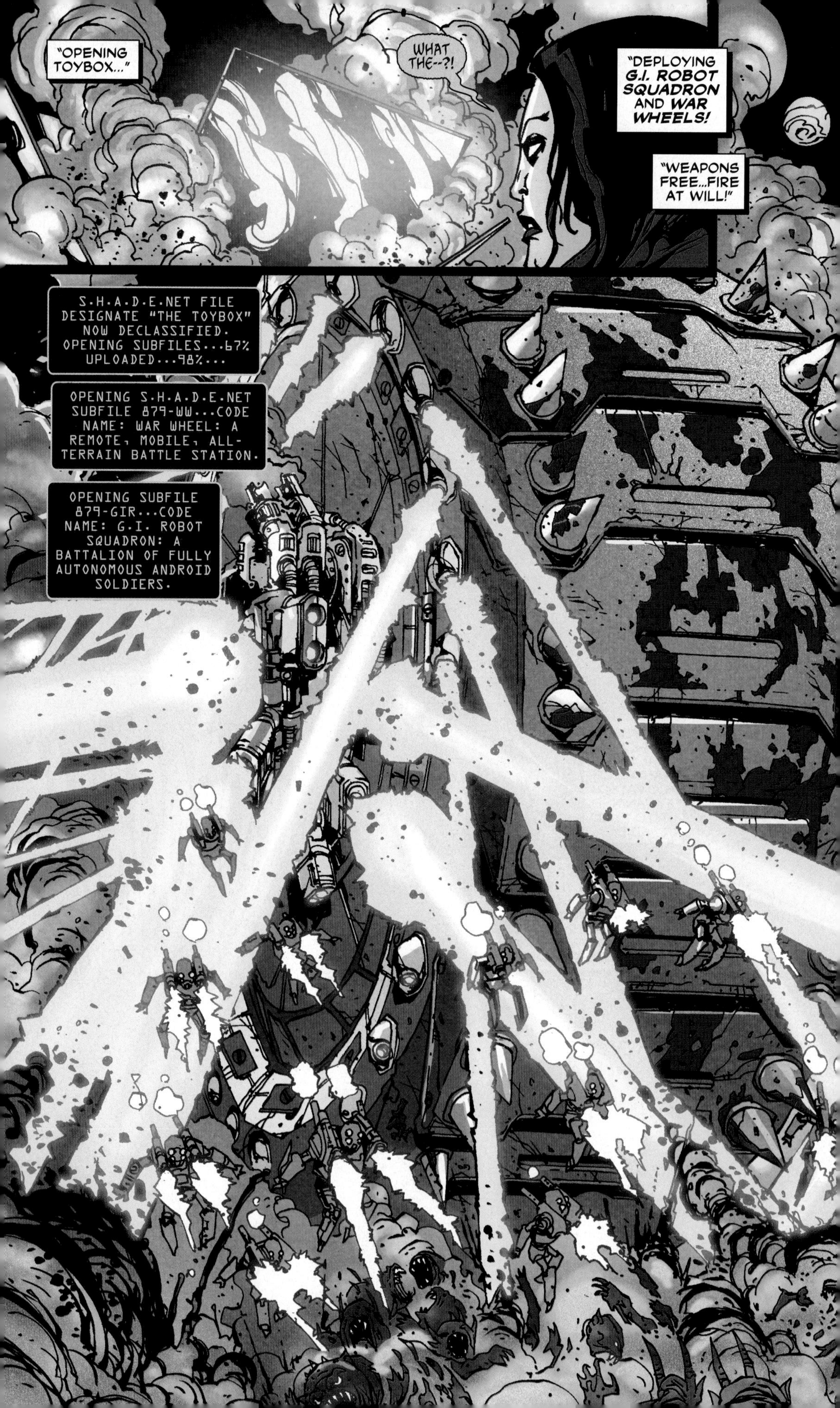
"OPENING TOYBOX..."
WHAT THE--?!
"DEPLOYING G.I. ROBOT SQUADRON AND WAR WHEELS!
"WEAPONS FREE...FIRE AT WILL!"
S.H.A.D.E.NET FILE DESIGNATE "THE TOYBOX" NOW DECLASSIFIED. OPENING SUBFILES...67% UPLOADED...98%...
OPENING S.H.A.D.E.NET SUBFILE 879-WW...CODE NAME: WAR WHEEL: A REMOTE, MOBILE, ALL-TERRAIN BATTLE STATION.
OPENING SUBFILE 879-GIR...CODE NAME: G.I. ROBOT SQUADRON: A BATTALION OF FULLY AUTONOMOUS ANDROID SOLDIERS.

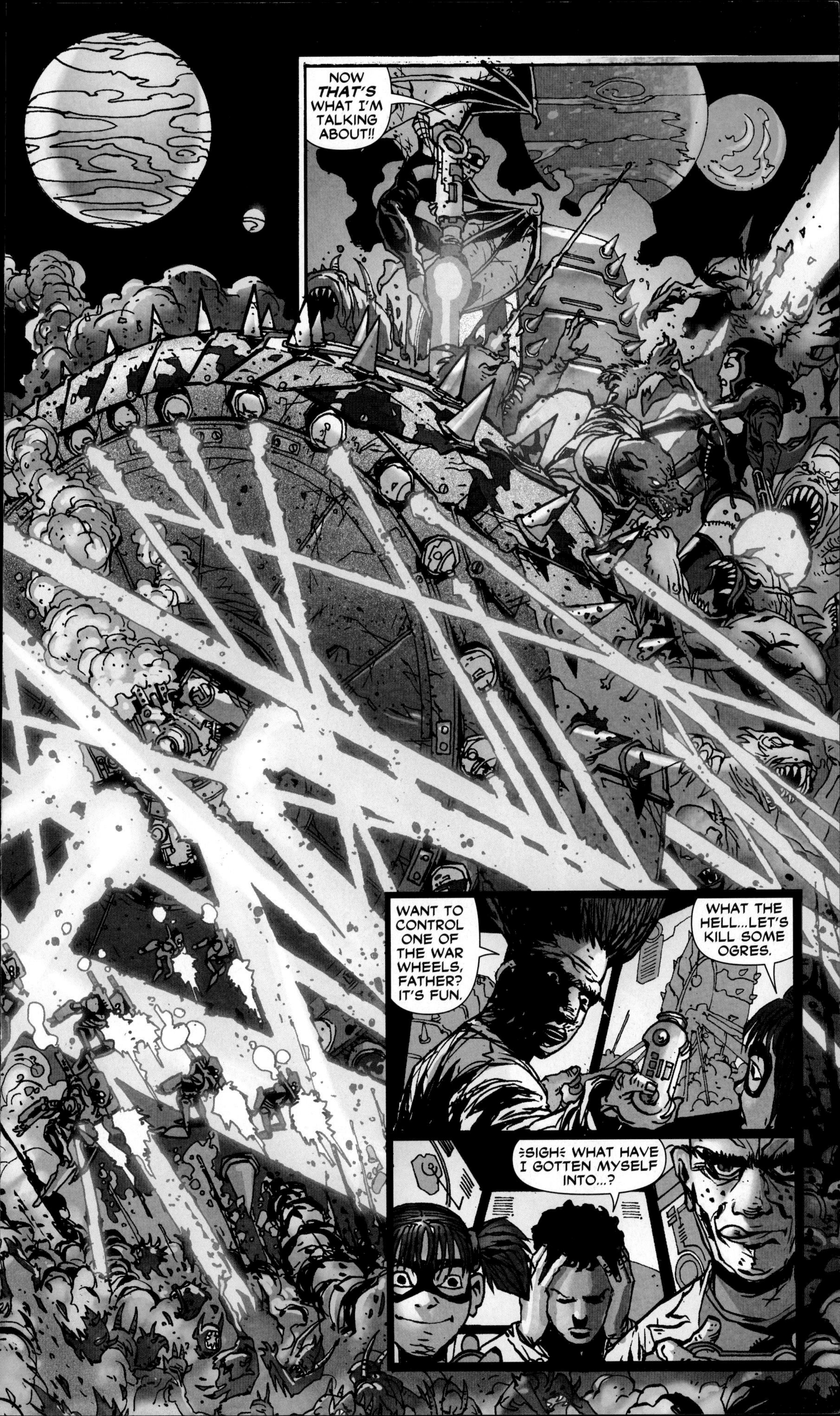
NOW *THAT'S* WHAT I'M TALKING ABOUT!!
WANT TO CONTROL ONE OF THE WAR WHEELS, FATHER? IT'S FUN.
WHAT THE HELL...LET'S KILL SOME OGRES.
≥SIGH≤ WHAT HAVE I GOTTEN MYSELF INTO...?

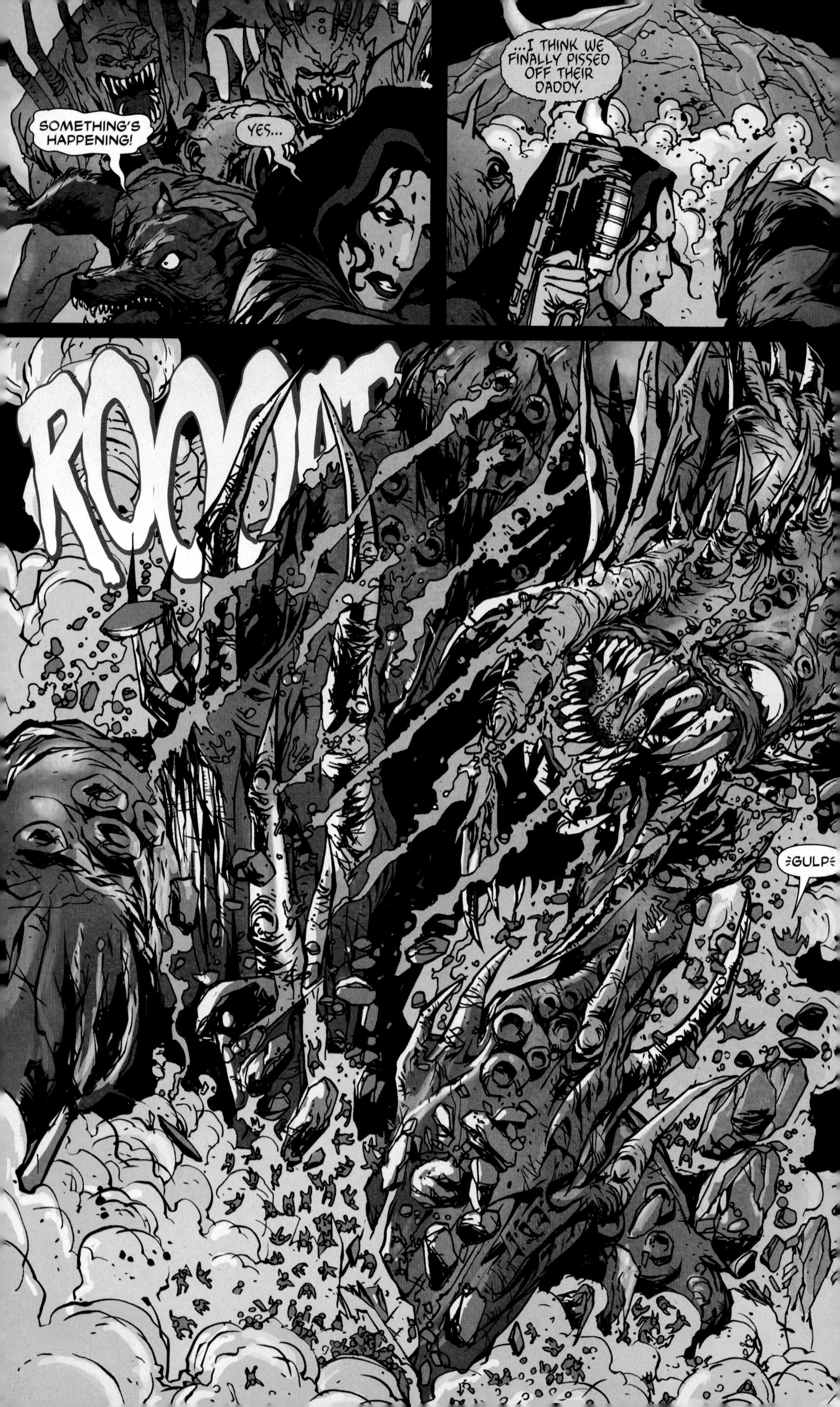
SOMETHING'S HAPPENING!
YES...
...I THINK WE FINALLY PISSED OFF THEIR DADDY.
ROOOM
GULP

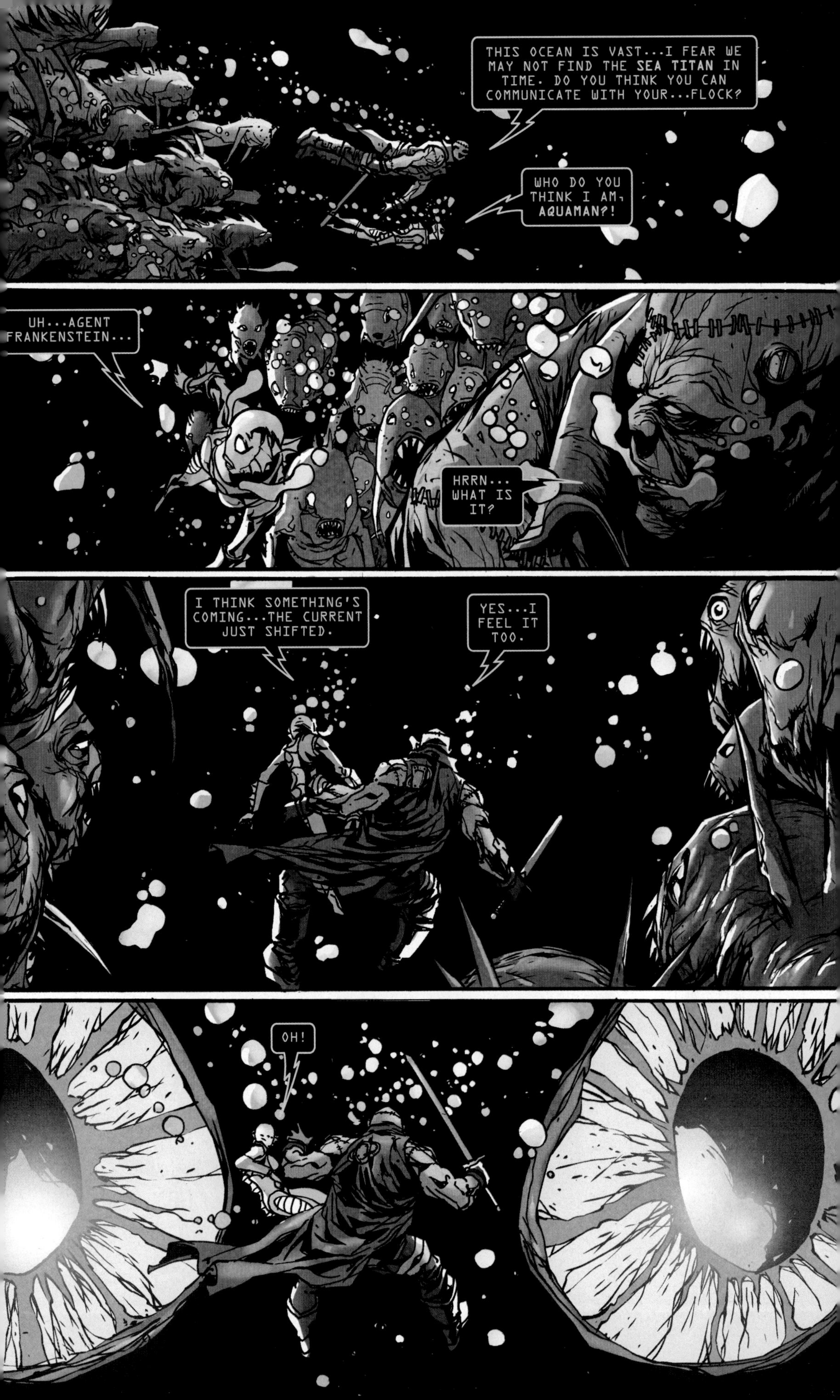

THIS OCEAN IS VAST...I FEAR WE MAY NOT FIND THE SEA TITAN IN TIME. DO YOU THINK YOU CAN COMMUNICATE WITH YOUR...FLOCK?
WHO DO YOU THINK I AM, AQUAMAN?!
UH...AGENT FRANKENSTEIN...
HRRN... WHAT IS IT?
I THINK SOMETHING'S COMING...THE CURRENT JUST SHIFTED.
YES...I FEEL IT TOO.
OH!

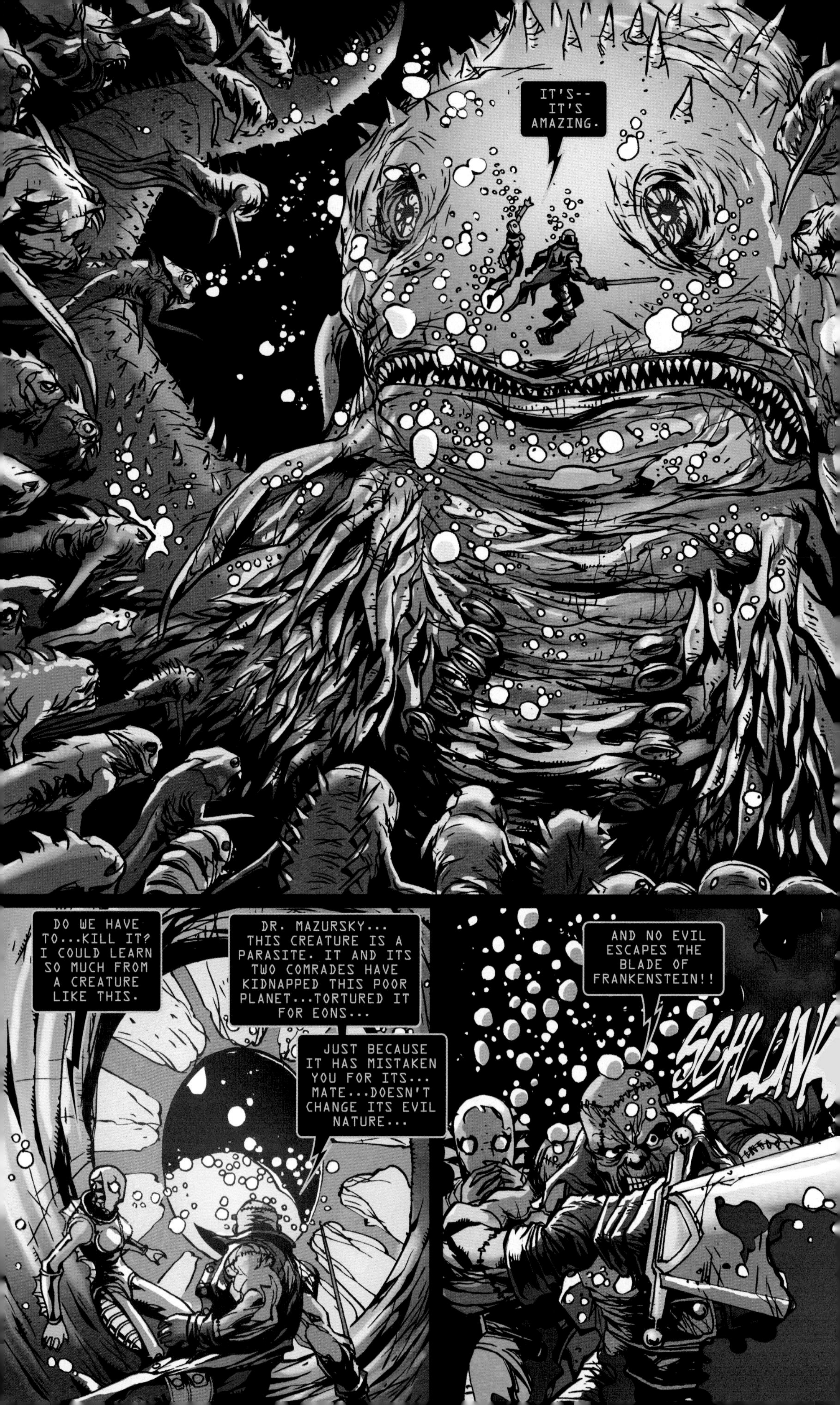
IT'S-- IT'S AMAZING.
DO WE HAVE TO...KILL IT? I COULD LEARN SO MUCH FROM A CREATURE LIKE THIS.
DR. MAZURSKY... THIS CREATURE IS A PARASITE. IT AND ITS TWO COMRADES HAVE KIDNAPPED THIS POOR PLANET...TORTURED IT FOR EONS...
JUST BECAUSE IT HAS MISTAKEN YOU FOR ITS... MATE...DOESN'T CHANGE ITS EVIL NATURE...
AND NO EVIL ESCAPES THE BLADE OF FRANKENSTEIN!!
SCHLUNK

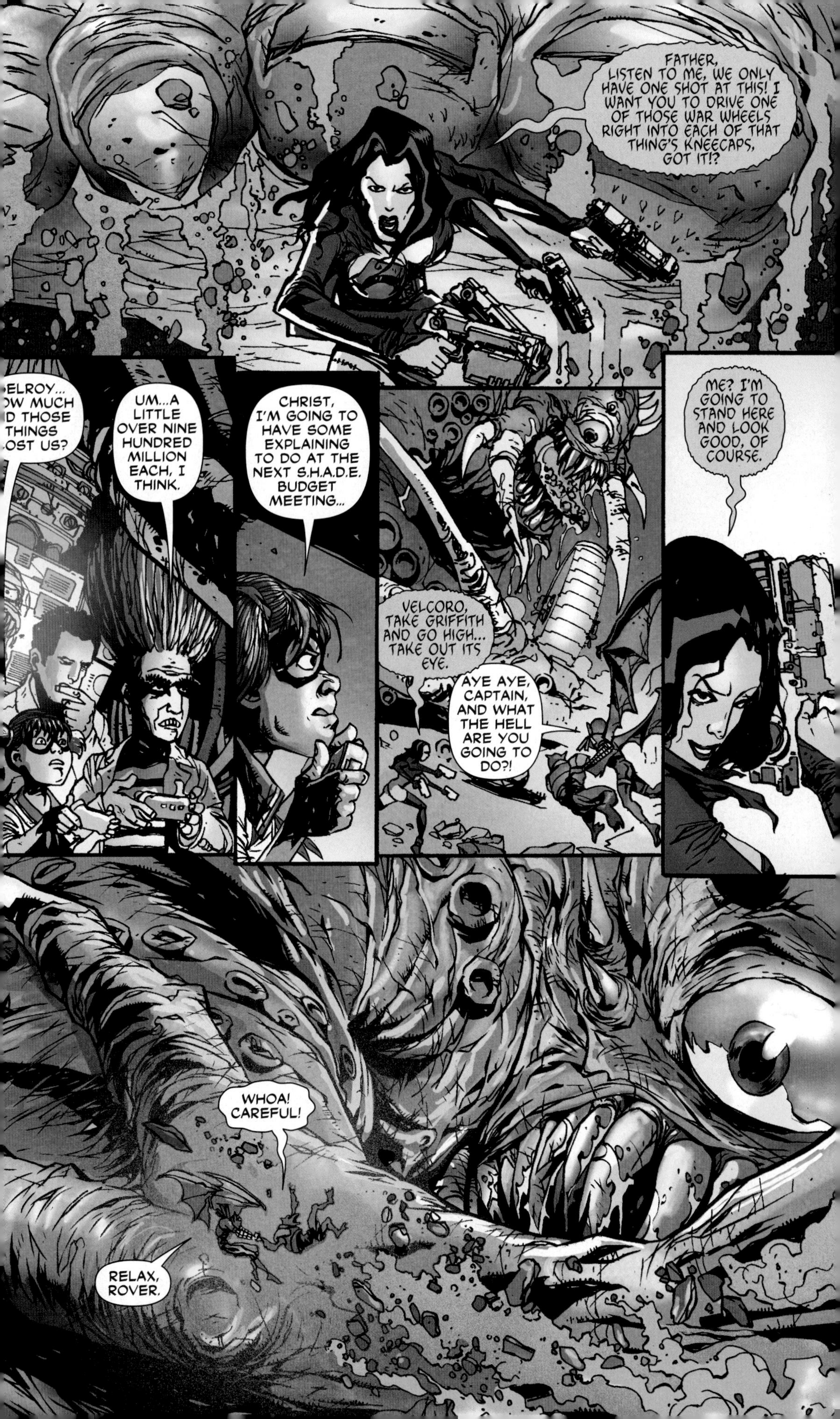
FATHER, LISTEN TO ME, WE ONLY HAVE ONE SHOT AT THIS! I WANT YOU TO DRIVE ONE OF THOSE WAR WHEELS RIGHT INTO EACH OF THAT THING'S KNEECAPS, GOT IT!?
ELROY... OW MUCH D THOSE THINGS OST US?
UM...A LITTLE OVER NINE HUNDRED MILLION EACH, I THINK.
CHRIST, I'M GOING TO HAVE SOME EXPLAINING TO DO AT THE NEXT S.H.A.D.E. BUDGET MEETING...
VELCORO, TAKE GRIFFITH AND GO HIGH... TAKE OUT ITS EYE.
AYE AYE, CAPTAIN, AND WHAT THE HELL ARE YOU GOING TO DO?!
ME? I'M GOING TO STAND HERE AND LOOK GOOD, OF COURSE.
WHOA! CAREFUL!
RELAX, ROVER.

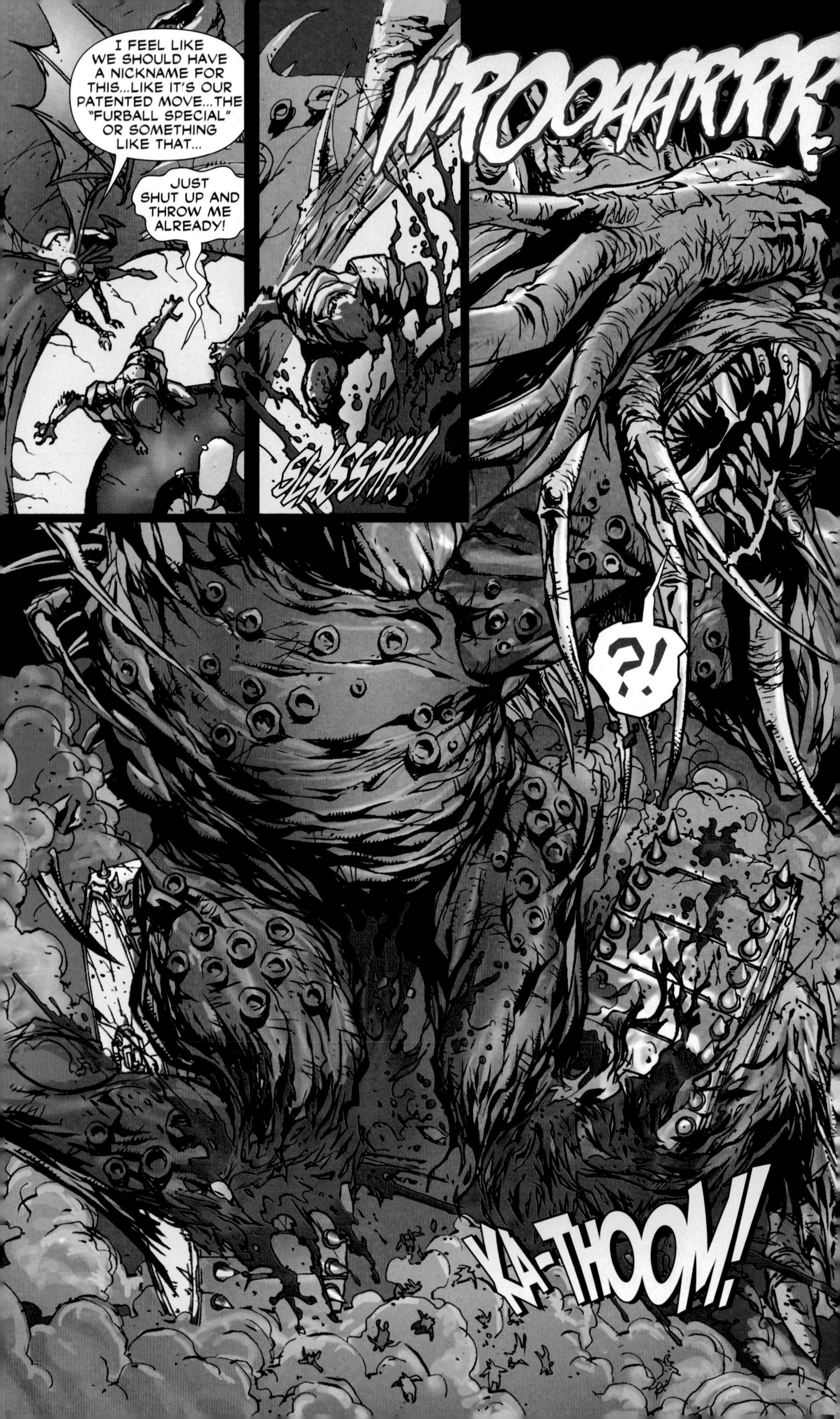
I FEEL LIKE WE SHOULD HAVE A NICKNAME FOR THIS...LIKE IT'S OUR PATENTED MOVE...THE "FURBALL SPECIAL" OR SOMETHING LIKE THAT...
JUST SHUT UP AND THROW ME ALREADY!
SLASSHH!
WROOAARRRR
?!
KA-THOOM!!

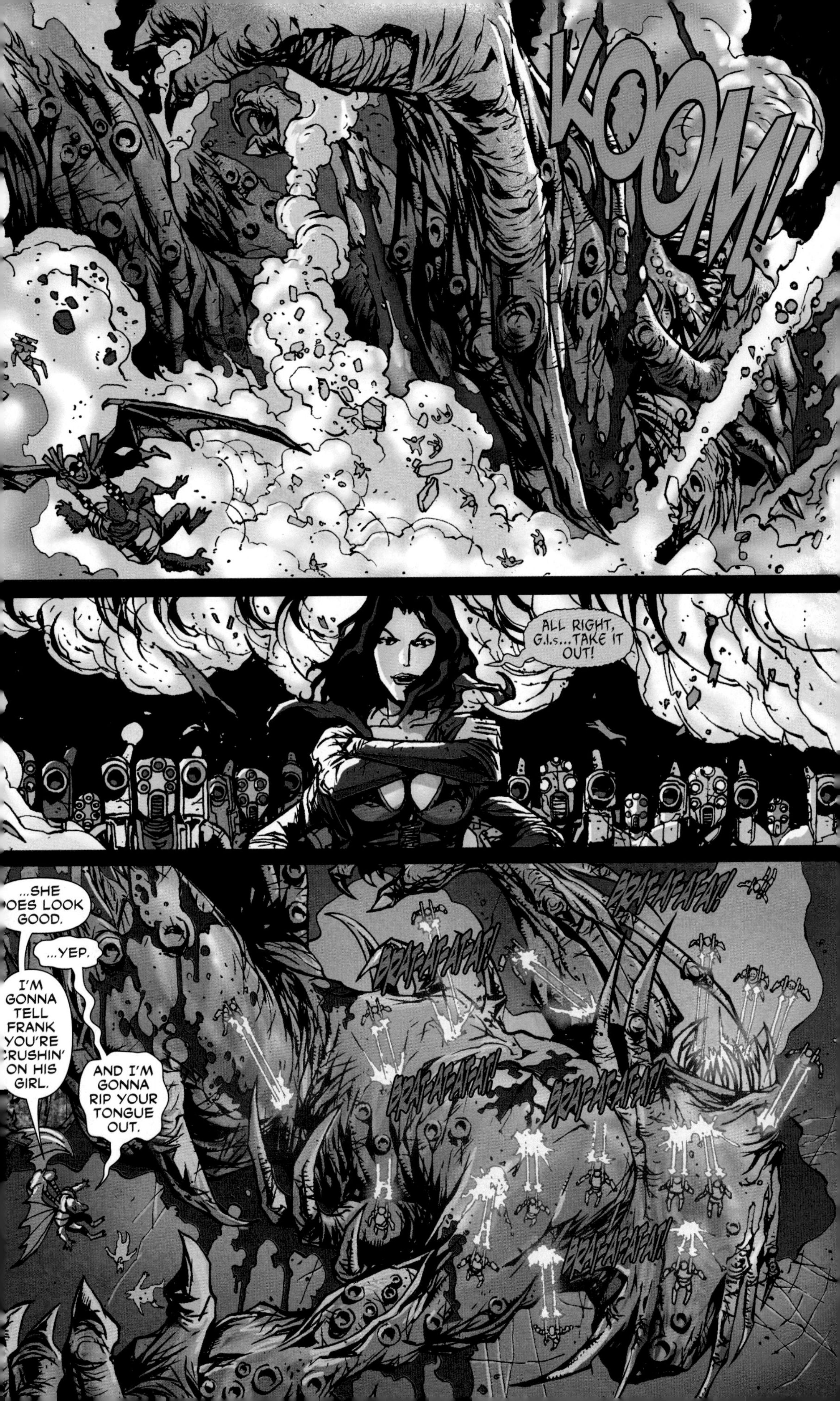
KOOM!
ALL RIGHT, G.I.s...TAKE IT OUT!
...SHE DOES LOOK GOOD.
...YEP.
I'M GONNA TELL FRANK YOU'RE CRUSHIN' ON HIS GIRL.
AND I'M GONNA RIP YOUR TONGUE OUT.

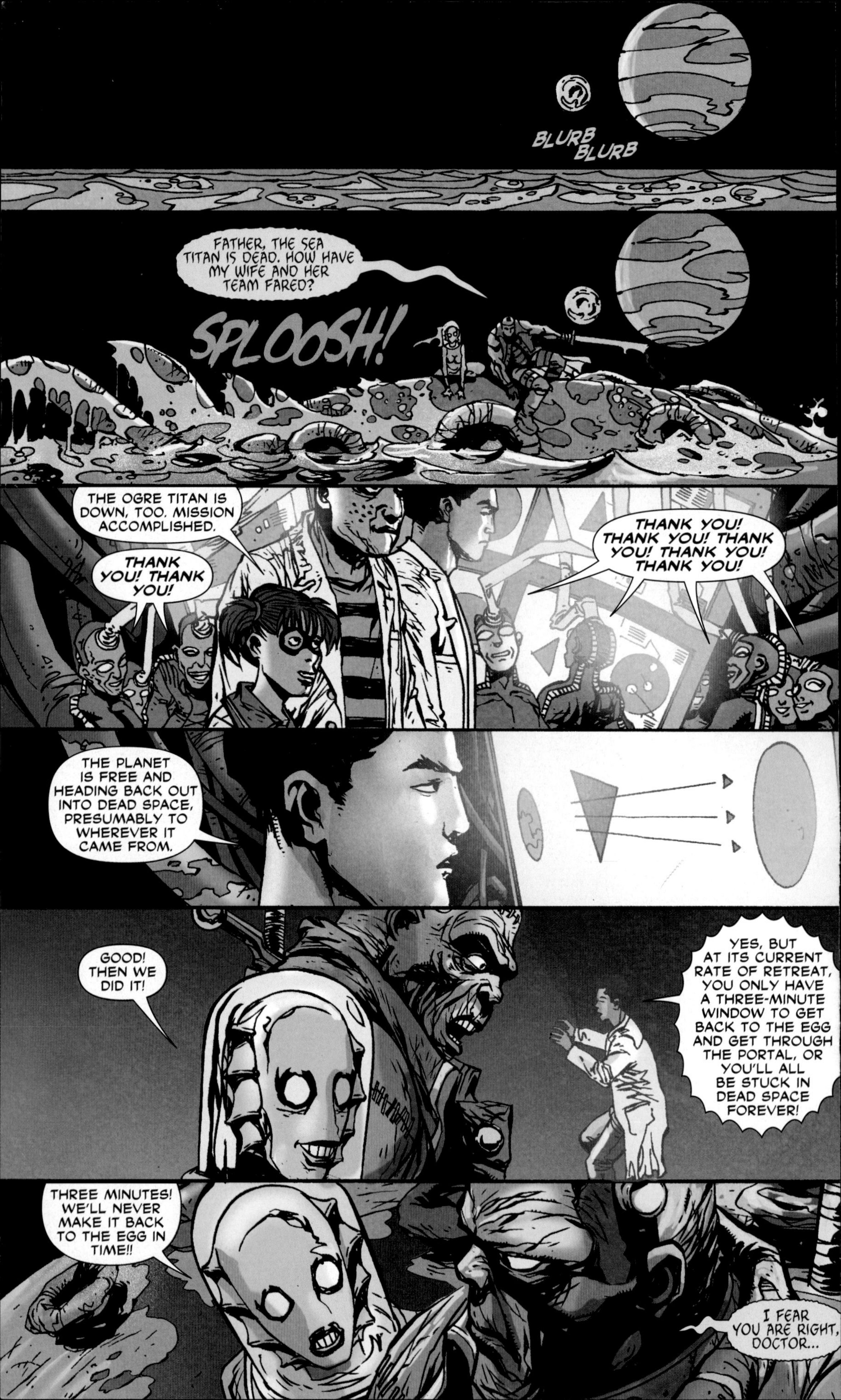

BLURB BLURB
FATHER, THE SEA TITAN IS DEAD. HOW HAVE MY WIFE AND HER TEAM FARED?
SPLOOSH!
THE OGRE TITAN IS DOWN, TOO. MISSION ACCOMPLISHED.
THANK YOU! THANK YOU!
THANK YOU! THANK YOU! THANK YOU! THANK YOU! THANK YOU!
THE PLANET IS FREE AND HEADING BACK OUT INTO DEAD SPACE, PRESUMABLY TO WHEREVER IT CAME FROM.
GOOD! THEN WE DID IT!
YES, BUT AT ITS CURRENT RATE OF RETREAT, YOU ONLY HAVE A THREE-MINUTE WINDOW TO GET BACK TO THE EGG AND GET THROUGH THE PORTAL, OR YOU'LL ALL BE STUCK IN DEAD SPACE FOREVER!
THREE MINUTES! WE'LL NEVER MAKE IT BACK TO THE EGG IN TIME!!
I FEAR YOU ARE RIGHT, DOCTOR...

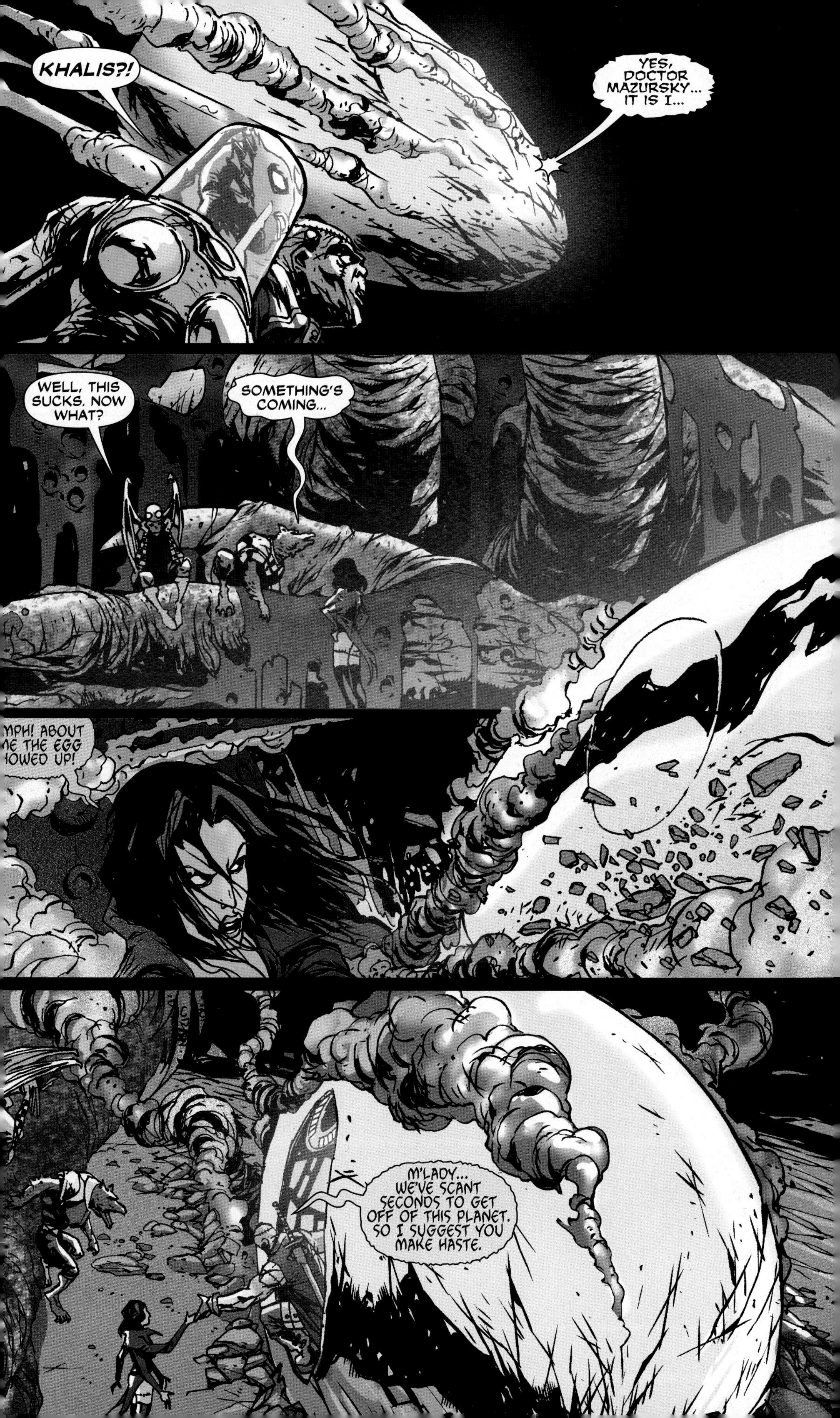
KHALIS?!
YES, DOCTOR MAZURSKY... IT IS I...
WELL, THIS SUCKS. NOW WHAT?
SOMETHING'S COMING...
MPH! ABOUT ME THE EGG HOWED UP!
M'LADY... WE'VE SCANT SECONDS TO GET OFF OF THIS PLANET. SO I SUGGEST YOU MAKE HASTE.

WHAT ABOUT THE G.I. ROBOTS?

WE'LL LEAVE THEM HERE... REPROGRAM THEM TO WATCH OVER THE PLANET...PREVENT ANY MORE UNWANTED GUESTS FROM TAKING ROOT.

NOW GET YOUR GREEN BUTT IN THE EGG!

MOVE! WE ONLY HAVE FOUR SECONDS LEFT UNTIL THE LAUNCH WINDOW CLOSES!

THREE SECONDS!

 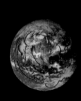

TWO!

ONE!

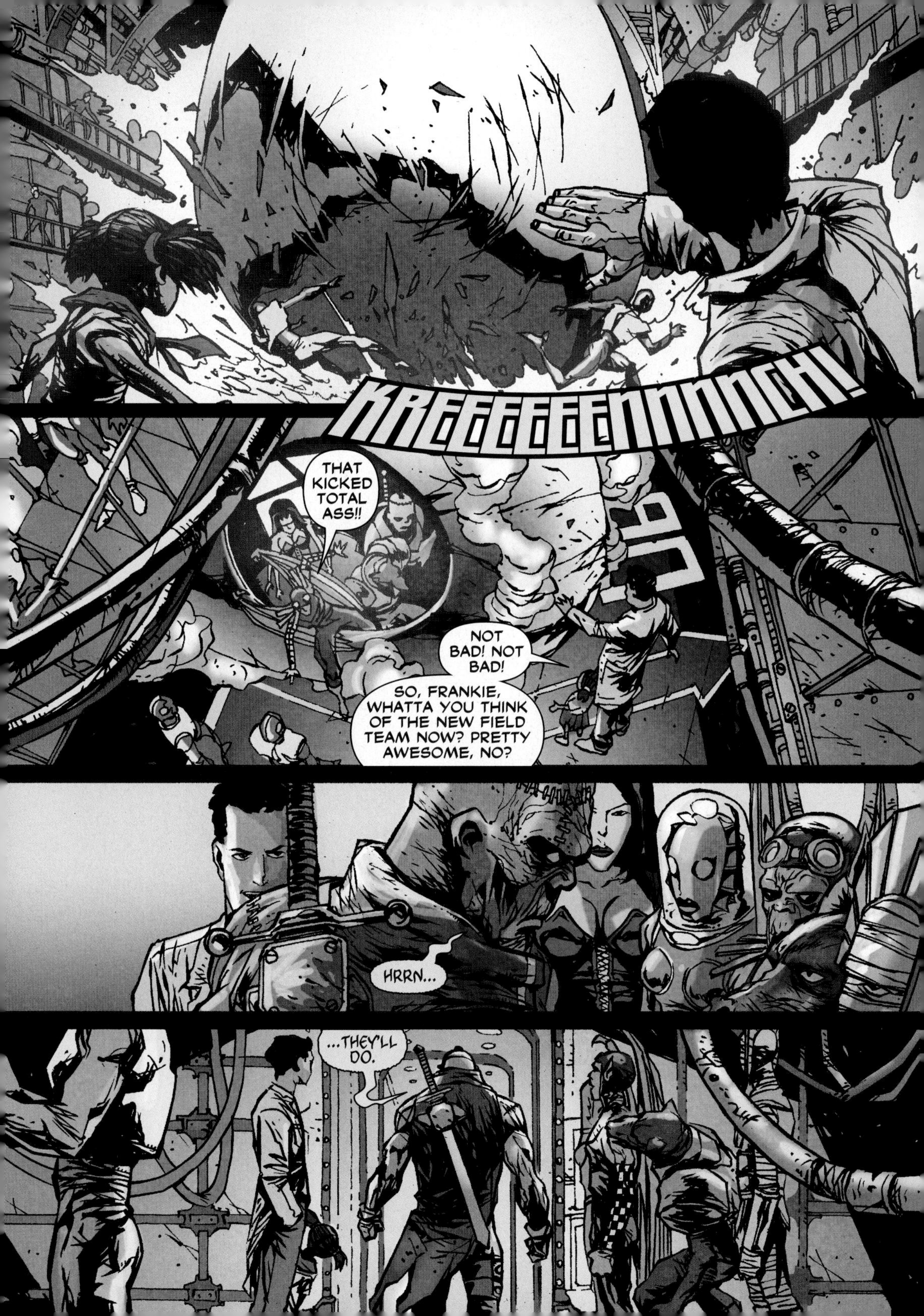
KREEEEEENNNNCH!
THAT KICKED TOTAL ASS!!
NOT BAD! NOT BAD!
SO, FRANKIE, WHATTA YOU THINK OF THE NEW FIELD TEAM NOW? PRETTY AWESOME, NO?
HRRN...
...THEY'LL DO.

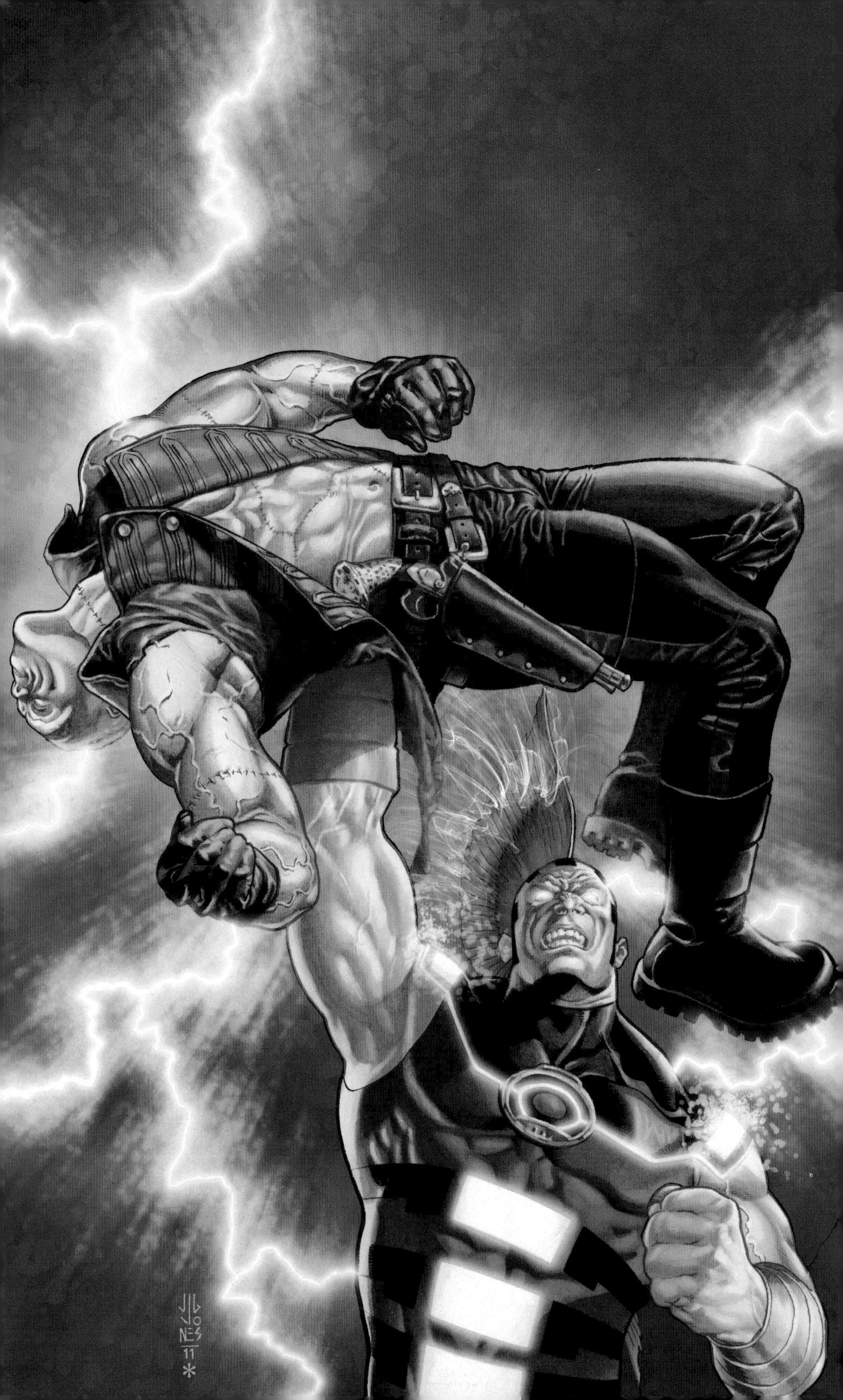

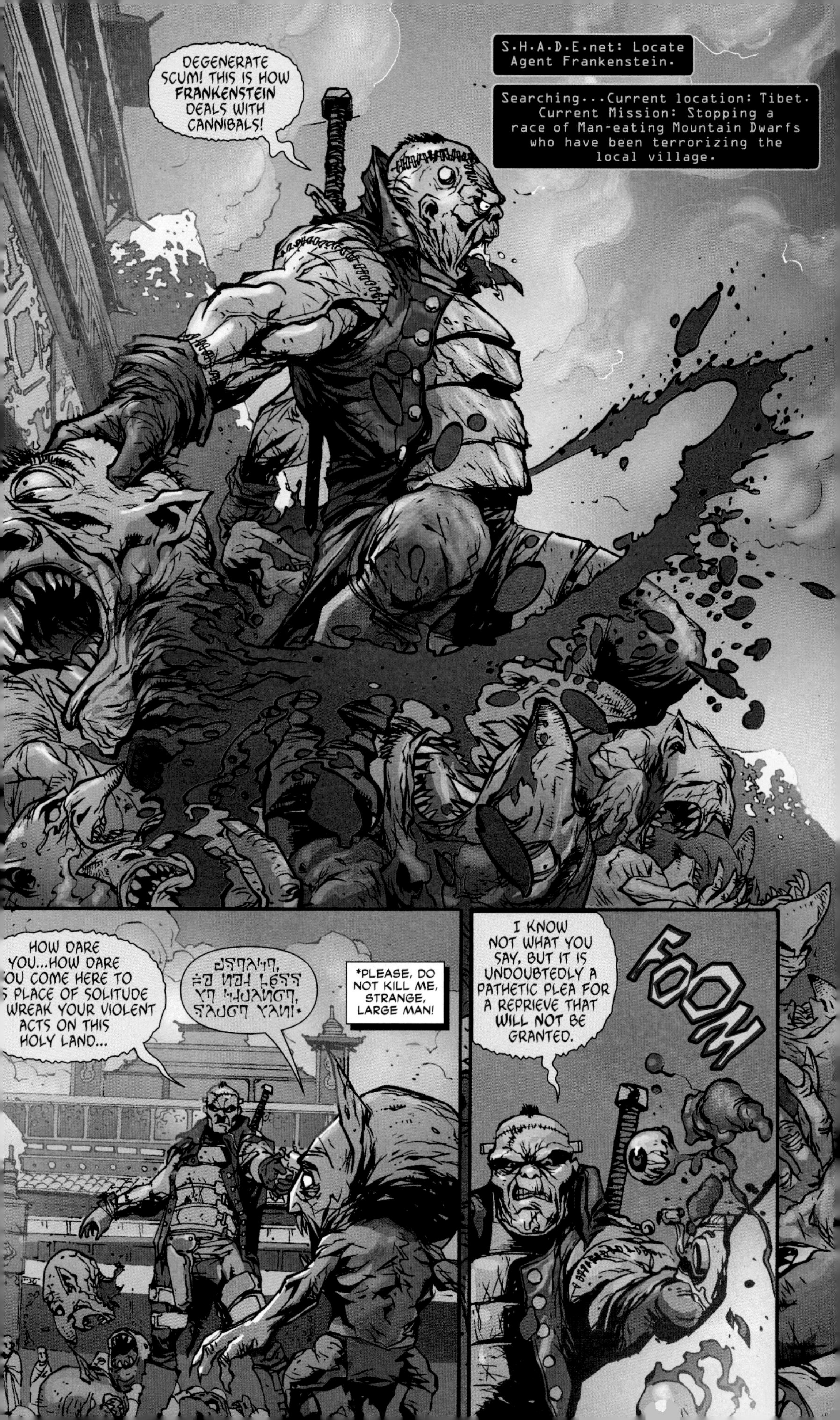
S.H.A.D.E.net: Locate Agent Frankenstein.
Searching...Current location: Tibet. Current Mission: Stopping a race of Man-eating Mountain Dwarfs who have been terrorizing the local village.
DEGENERATE SCUM! THIS IS HOW FRANKENSTEIN DEALS WITH CANNIBALS!
HOW DARE YOU...HOW DARE OU COME HERE TO S PLACE OF SOLITUDE WREAK YOUR VIOLENT ACTS ON THIS HOLY LAND...
*PLEASE, DO NOT KILL ME, STRANGE, LARGE MAN!
I KNOW NOT WHAT YOU SAY, BUT IT IS UNDOUBTEDLY A PATHETIC PLEA FOR A REPRIEVE THAT WILL NOT BE GRANTED.
FOOM

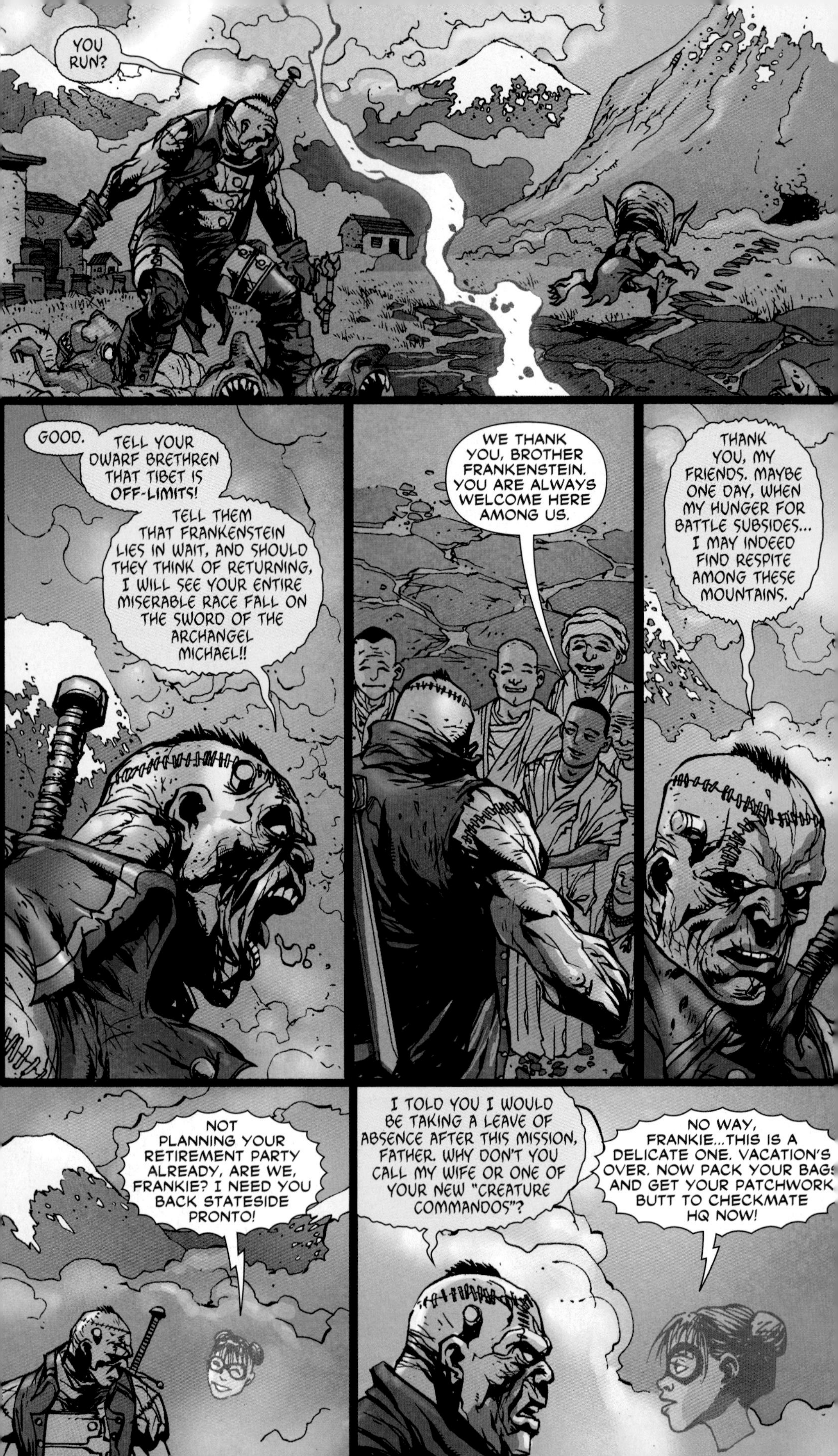
YOU RUN?
GOOD.
TELL YOUR DWARF BRETHREN THAT TIBET IS OFF-LIMITS!
TELL THEM THAT FRANKENSTEIN LIES IN WAIT, AND SHOULD THEY THINK OF RETURNING, I WILL SEE YOUR ENTIRE MISERABLE RACE FALL ON THE SWORD OF THE ARCHANGEL MICHAEL!!
WE THANK YOU, BROTHER FRANKENSTEIN. YOU ARE ALWAYS WELCOME HERE AMONG US.
THANK YOU, MY FRIENDS. MAYBE ONE DAY, WHEN MY HUNGER FOR BATTLE SUBSIDES... I MAY INDEED FIND RESPITE AMONG THESE MOUNTAINS.
NOT PLANNING YOUR RETIREMENT PARTY ALREADY, ARE WE, FRANKIE? I NEED YOU BACK STATESIDE PRONTO!
I TOLD YOU I WOULD BE TAKING A LEAVE OF ABSENCE AFTER THIS MISSION, FATHER. WHY DON'T YOU CALL MY WIFE OR ONE OF YOUR NEW "CREATURE COMMANDOS"?
NO WAY, FRANKIE...THIS IS A DELICATE ONE. VACATION'S OVER. NOW PACK YOUR BAGS AND GET YOUR PATCHWORK BUTT TO CHECKMATE HQ NOW!

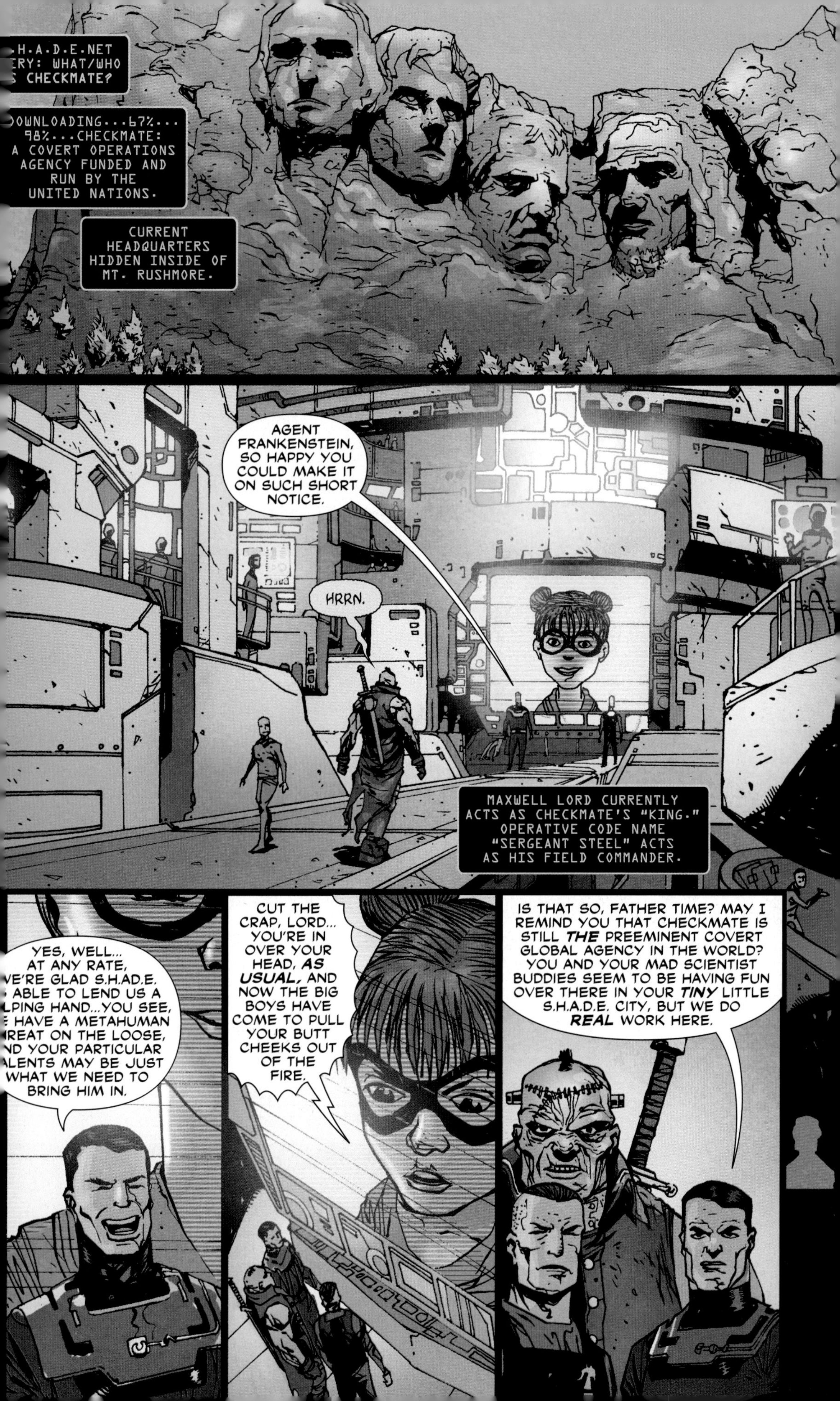

S.H.A.D.E.NET
ERY: WHAT/WHO
S CHECKMATE?
DOWNLOADING...67%...
98%...CHECKMATE:
A COVERT OPERATIONS AGENCY FUNDED AND RUN BY THE UNITED NATIONS.
CURRENT HEADQUARTERS HIDDEN INSIDE OF MT. RUSHMORE.
AGENT FRANKENSTEIN, SO HAPPY YOU COULD MAKE IT ON SUCH SHORT NOTICE.
HRRN.
MAXWELL LORD CURRENTLY ACTS AS CHECKMATE'S "KING." OPERATIVE CODE NAME "SERGEANT STEEL" ACTS AS HIS FIELD COMMANDER.
YES, WELL... AT ANY RATE, WE'RE GLAD S.H.A.D.E. IS ABLE TO LEND US A HELPING HAND...YOU SEE, WE HAVE A METAHUMAN THREAT ON THE LOOSE, AND YOUR PARTICULAR TALENTS MAY BE JUST WHAT WE NEED TO BRING HIM IN.
CUT THE CRAP, LORD... YOU'RE IN OVER YOUR HEAD, AS USUAL, AND NOW THE BIG BOYS HAVE COME TO PULL YOUR BUTT CHEEKS OUT OF THE FIRE.
IS THAT SO, FATHER TIME? MAY I REMIND YOU THAT CHECKMATE IS STILL THE PREEMINENT COVERT GLOBAL AGENCY IN THE WORLD? YOU AND YOUR MAD SCIENTIST BUDDIES SEEM TO BE HAVING FUN OVER THERE IN YOUR TINY LITTLE S.H.A.D.E. CITY, BUT WE DO REAL WORK HERE.

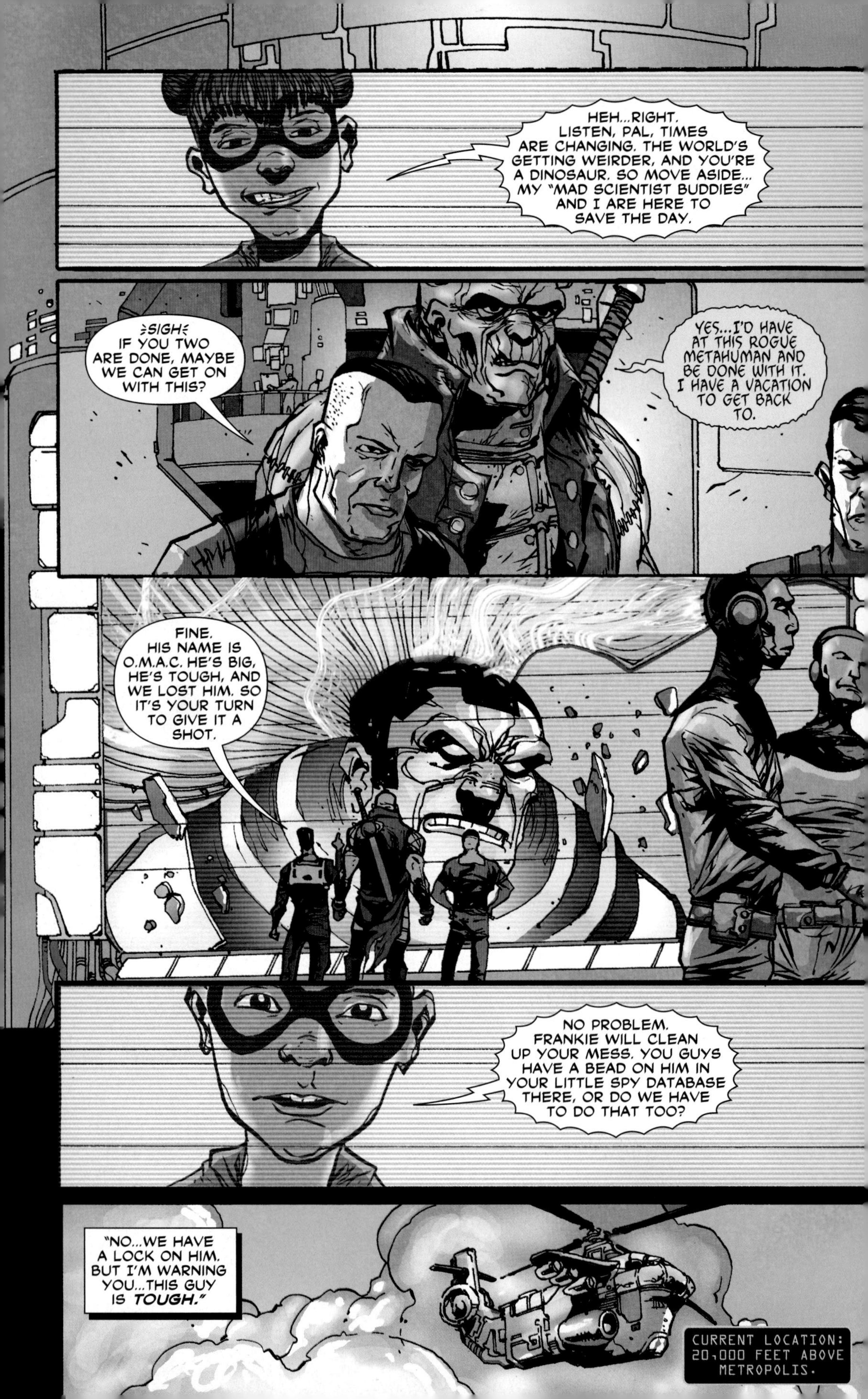
HEH...RIGHT. LISTEN, PAL, TIMES ARE CHANGING. THE WORLD'S GETTING WEIRDER, AND YOU'RE A DINOSAUR. SO MOVE ASIDE... MY "MAD SCIENTIST BUDDIES" AND I ARE HERE TO SAVE THE DAY.
SIGH
IF YOU TWO ARE DONE, MAYBE WE CAN GET ON WITH THIS?
YES...I'D HAVE AT THIS ROGUE METAHUMAN AND BE DONE WITH IT. I HAVE A VACATION TO GET BACK TO.
FINE. HIS NAME IS O.M.A.C. HE'S BIG, HE'S TOUGH, AND WE LOST HIM. SO IT'S YOUR TURN TO GIVE IT A SHOT.
NO PROBLEM. FRANKIE WILL CLEAN UP YOUR MESS. YOU GUYS HAVE A BEAD ON HIM IN YOUR LITTLE SPY DATABASE THERE, OR DO WE HAVE TO DO THAT TOO?
"NO...WE HAVE A LOCK ON HIM. BUT I'M WARNING YOU...THIS GUY IS TOUGH."
CURRENT LOCATION: 20,000 FEET ABOVE METROPOLIS.

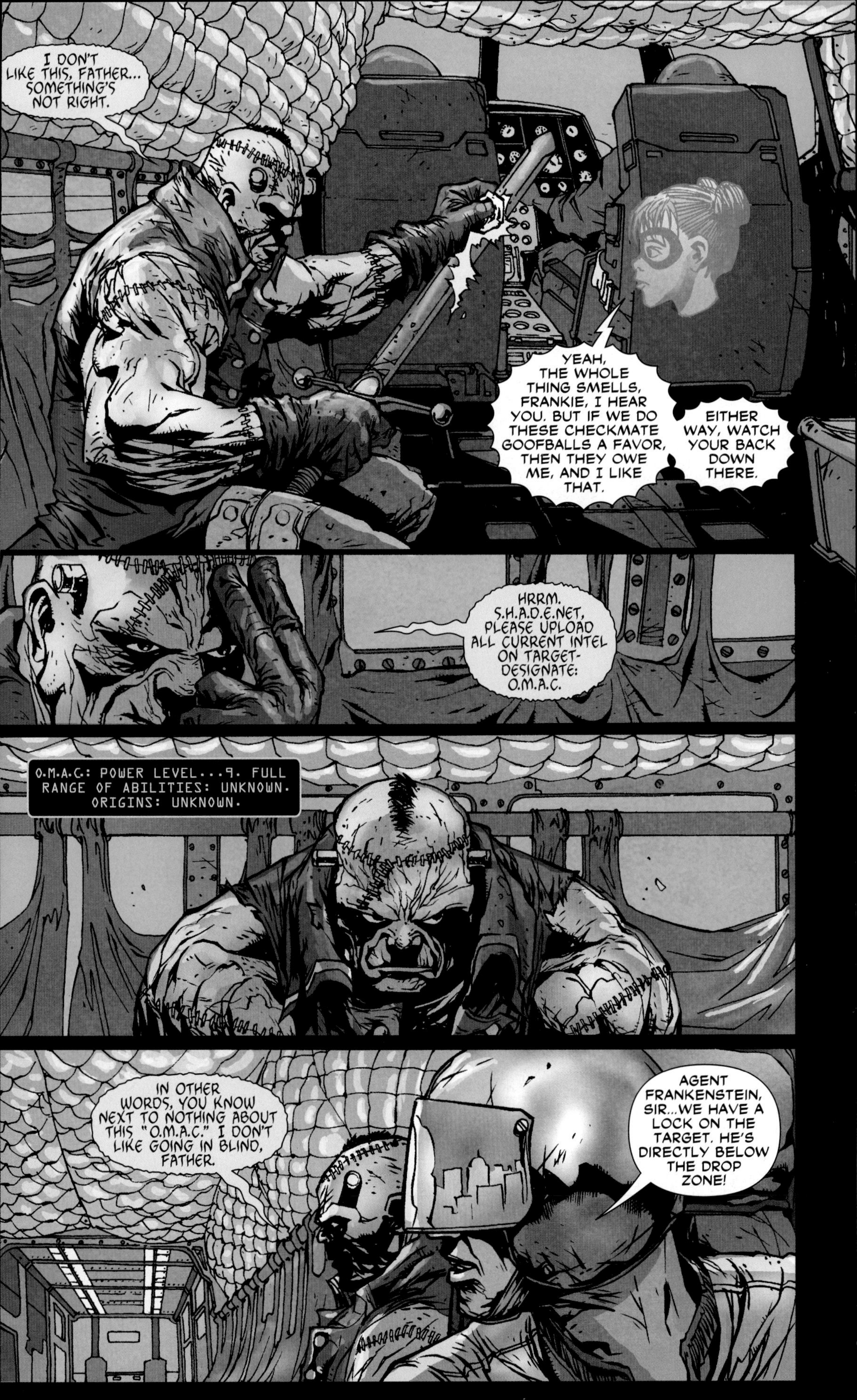
I DON'T LIKE THIS, FATHER... SOMETHING'S NOT RIGHT.
YEAH, THE WHOLE THING SMELLS, FRANKIE, I HEAR YOU. BUT IF WE DO THESE CHECKMATE GOOFBALLS A FAVOR, THEN THEY OWE ME, AND I LIKE THAT.
EITHER WAY, WATCH YOUR BACK DOWN THERE.
HRRM. S.H.A.D.E.NET, PLEASE UPLOAD ALL CURRENT INTEL ON TARGET-DESIGNATE: O.M.A.C.
O.M.A.C: POWER LEVEL...9. FULL RANGE OF ABILITIES: UNKNOWN. ORIGINS: UNKNOWN.
IN OTHER WORDS, YOU KNOW NEXT TO NOTHING ABOUT THIS "O.M.A.C." I DON'T LIKE GOING IN BLIND, FATHER.
AGENT FRANKENSTEIN, SIR...WE HAVE A LOCK ON THE TARGET. HE'S DIRECTLY BELOW THE DROP ZONE!

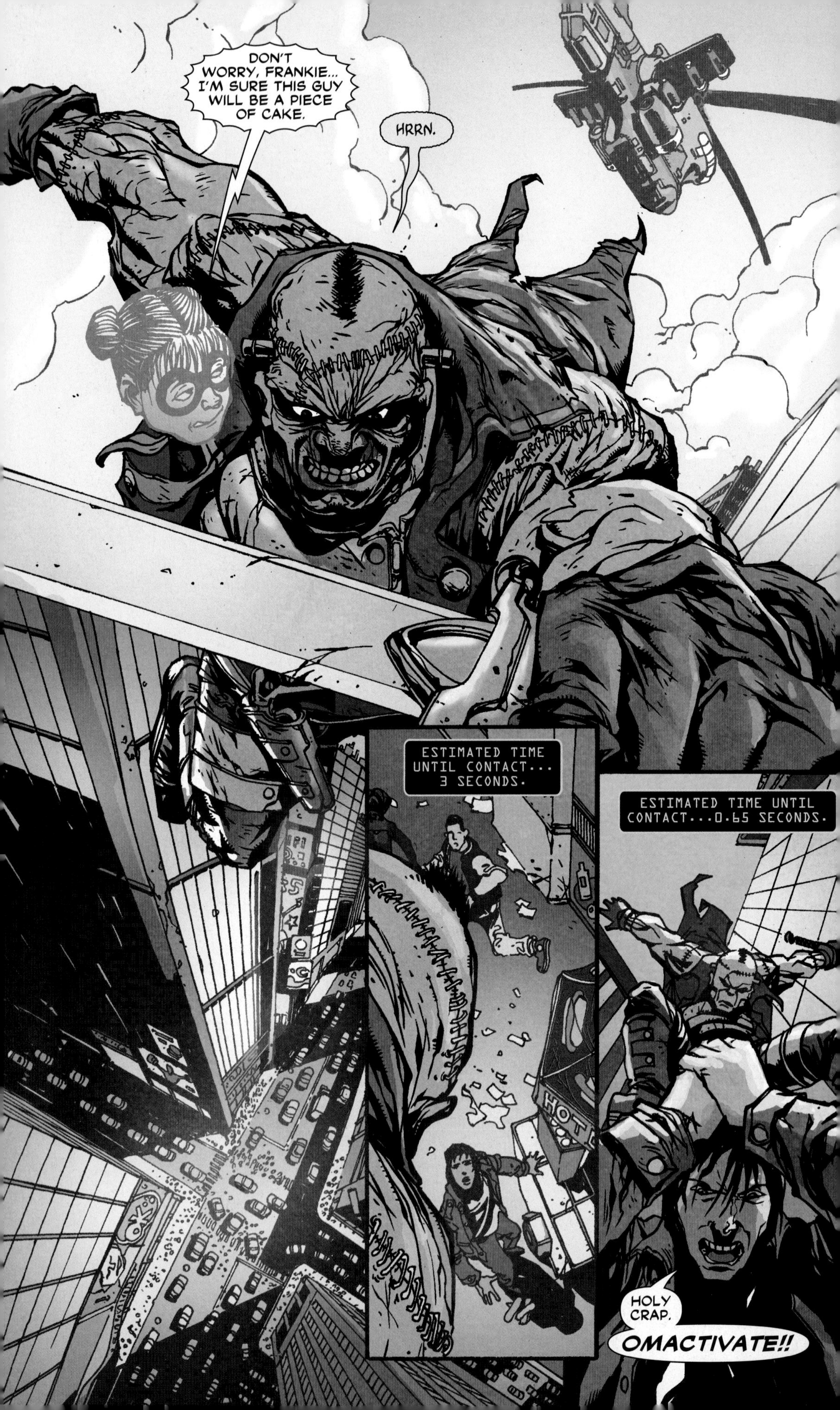
DON'T WORRY, FRANKIE... I'M SURE THIS GUY WILL BE A PIECE OF CAKE.
HRRN.
ESTIMATED TIME UNTIL CONTACT... 3 SECONDS.
ESTIMATED TIME UNTIL CONTACT...0.65 SECONDS.
HOLY CRAP.
OMACTIVATE!!

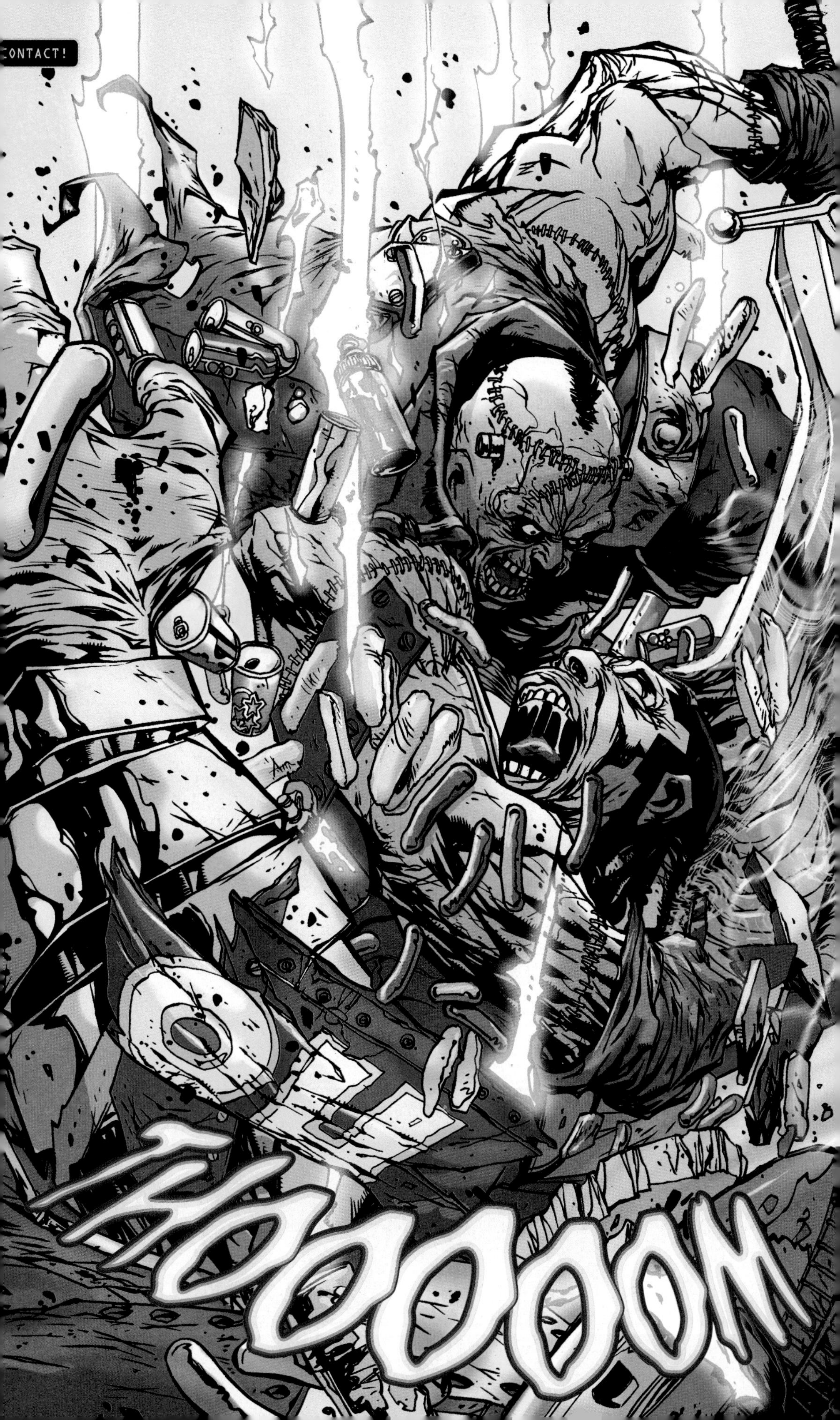

ONTACT!
THOOOOOM

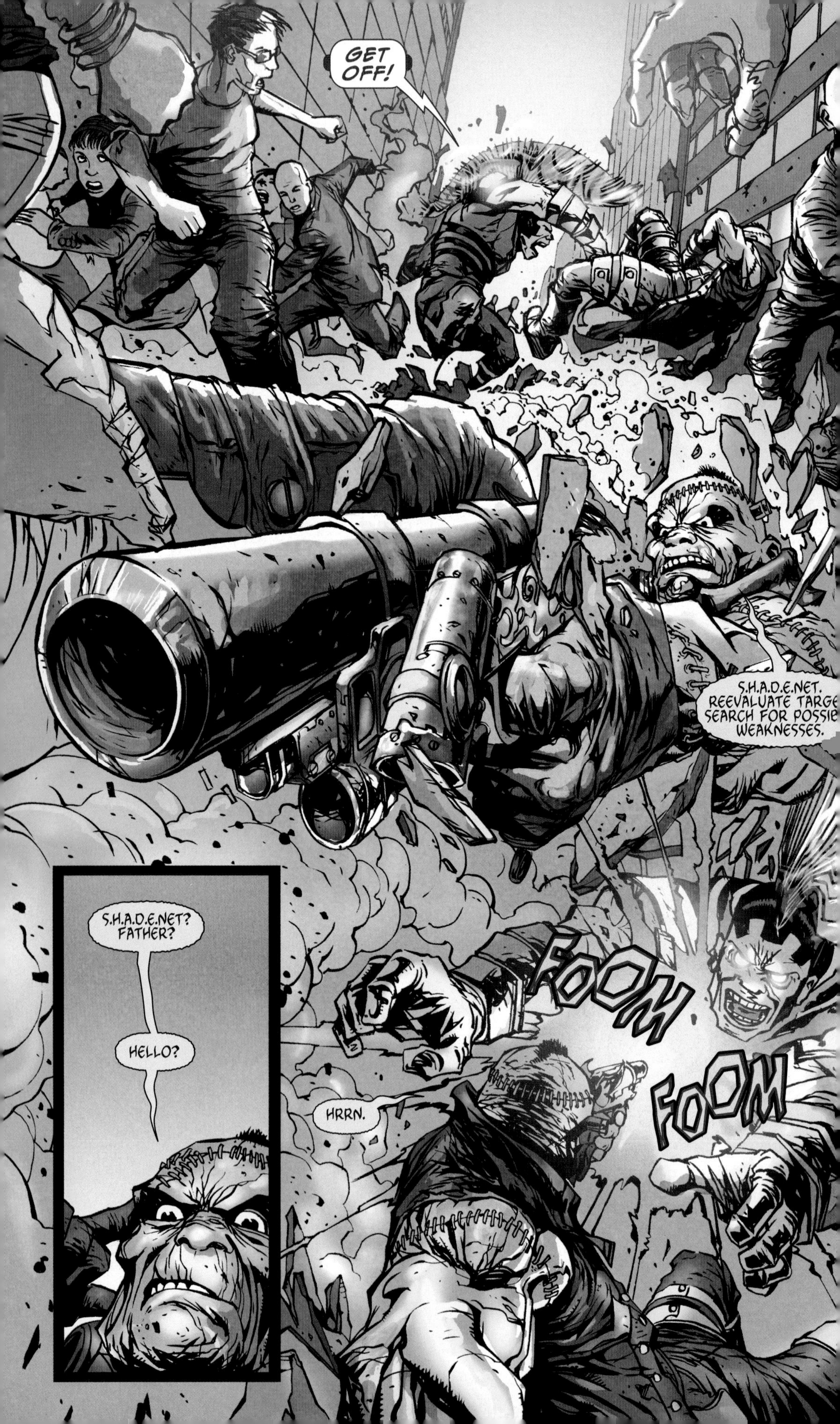
GET OFF!
S.H.A.D.E.NET. REEVALUATE TARGE SEARCH FOR POSSIB WEAKNESSES.
S.H.A.D.E.NET? FATHER?
HELLO?
HRRN.
FOOM
FOOM

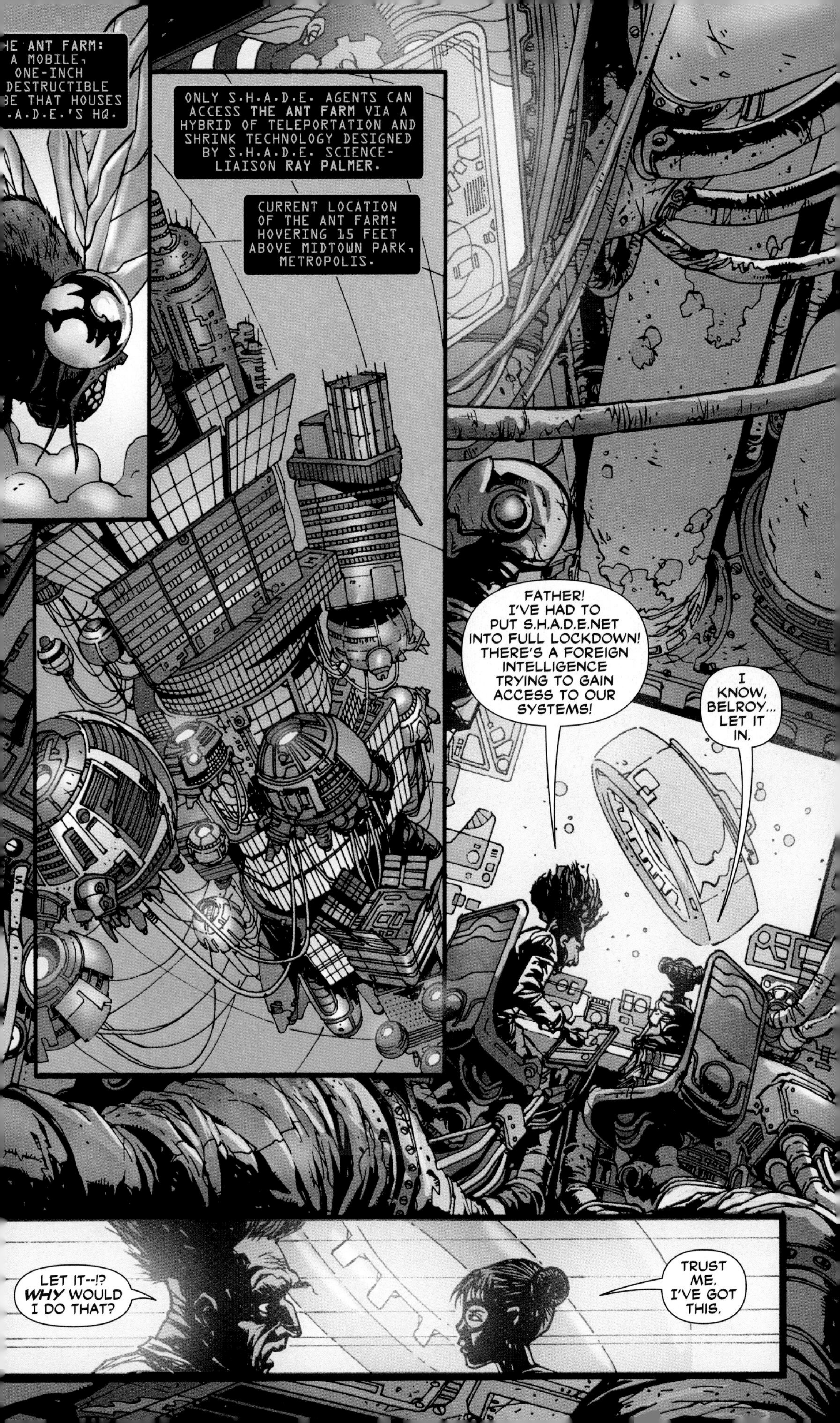

HE ANT FARM: A MOBILE, ONE-INCH DESTRUCTIBLE BE THAT HOUSES .A.D.E.'S HQ.
ONLY S.H.A.D.E. AGENTS CAN ACCESS THE ANT FARM VIA A HYBRID OF TELEPORTATION AND SHRINK TECHNOLOGY DESIGNED BY S.H.A.D.E. SCIENCE-LIAISON RAY PALMER.
CURRENT LOCATION OF THE ANT FARM: HOVERING 15 FEET ABOVE MIDTOWN PARK, METROPOLIS.
FATHER! I'VE HAD TO PUT S.H.A.D.E.NET INTO FULL LOCKDOWN! THERE'S A FOREIGN INTELLIGENCE TRYING TO GAIN ACCESS TO OUR SYSTEMS!
I KNOW, BELROY... LET IT IN.
LET IT--!? WHY WOULD I DO THAT?
TRUST ME. I'VE GOT THIS.

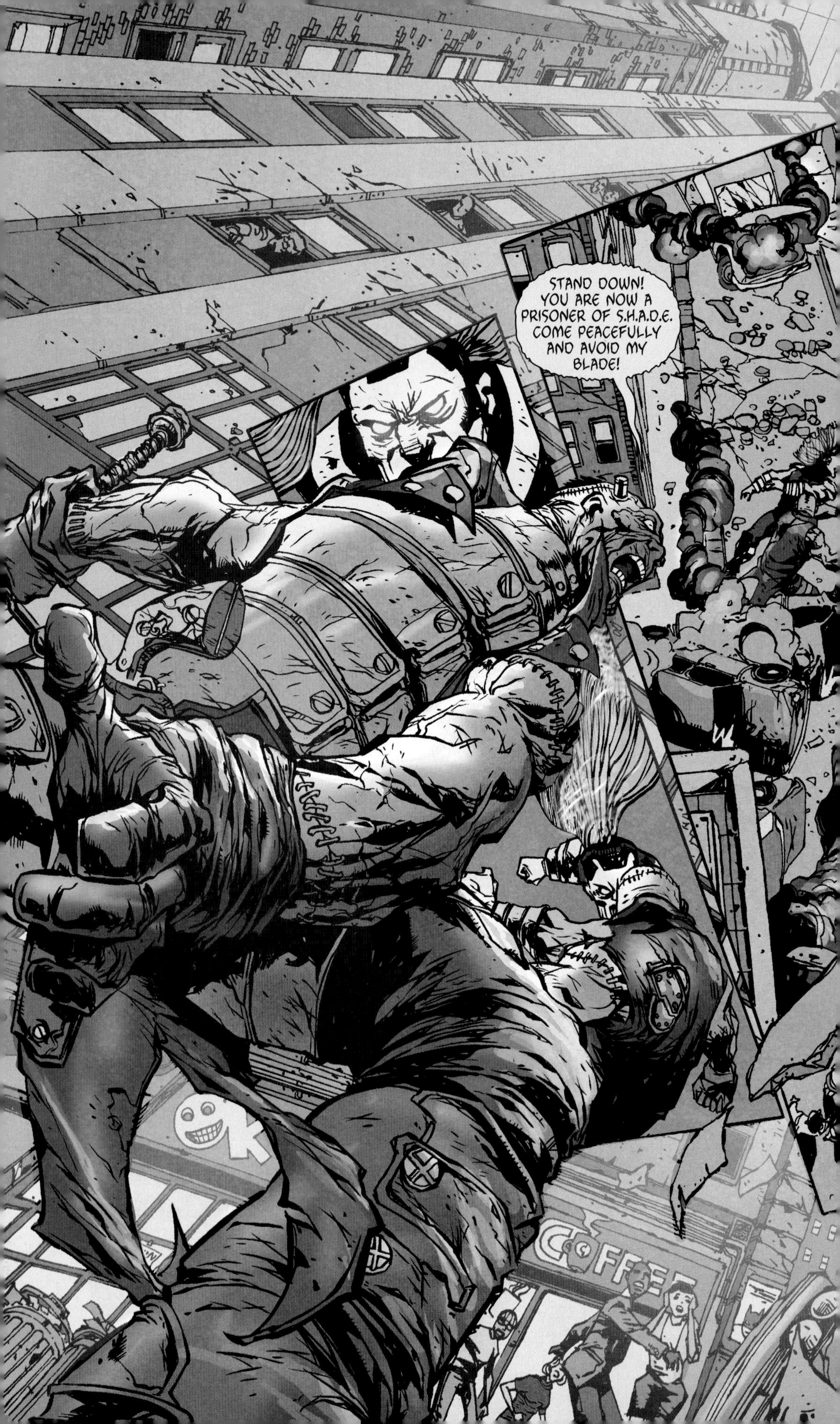
STAND DOWN! YOU ARE NOW A PRISONER OF S.H.A.D.E. COME PEACEFULLY AND AVOID MY BLADE!
COFFEE

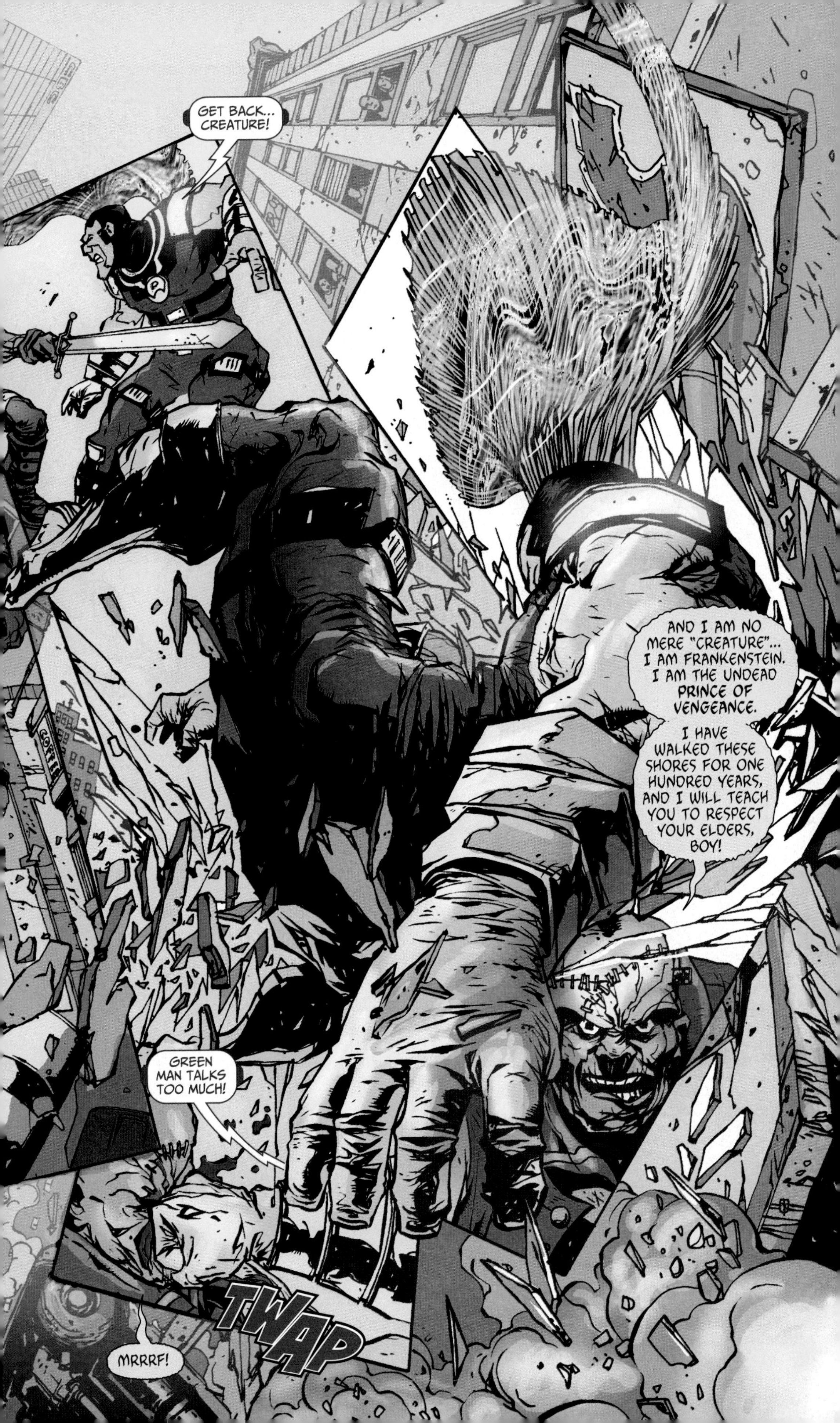
GET BACK... CREATURE!
AND I AM NO MERE "CREATURE"... I AM FRANKENSTEIN. I AM THE UNDEAD PRINCE OF VENGEANCE.
I HAVE WALKED THESE SHORES FOR ONE HUNDRED YEARS, AND I WILL TEACH YOU TO RESPECT YOUR ELDERS, BOY!
GREEN MAN TALKS TOO MUCH!
TWAP
MRRRF!

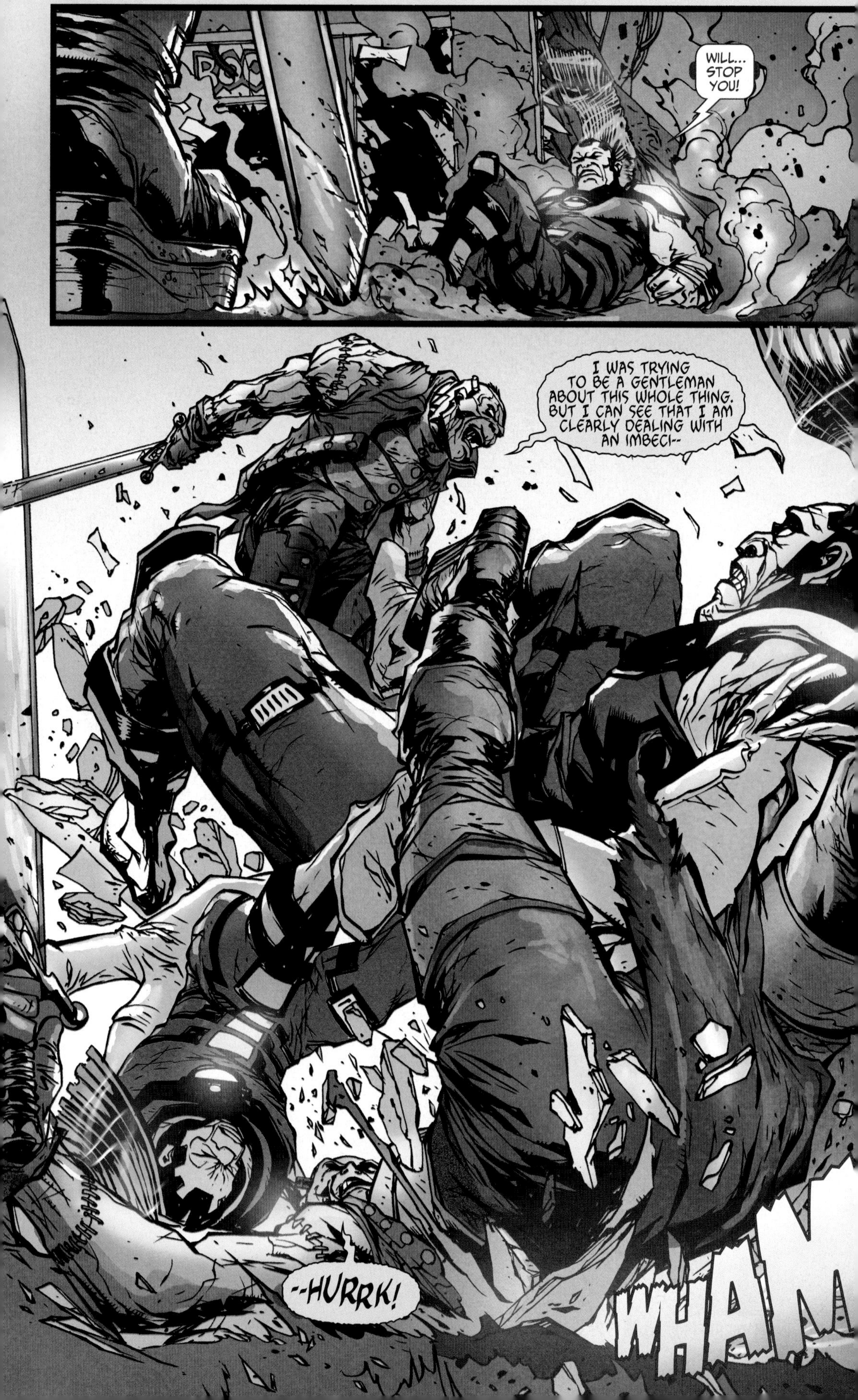
WILL... STOP YOU!
I WAS TRYING TO BE A GENTLEMAN ABOUT THIS WHOLE THING. BUT I CAN SEE THAT I AM CLEARLY DEALING WITH AN IMBECI--
--HURRK!
WHAM

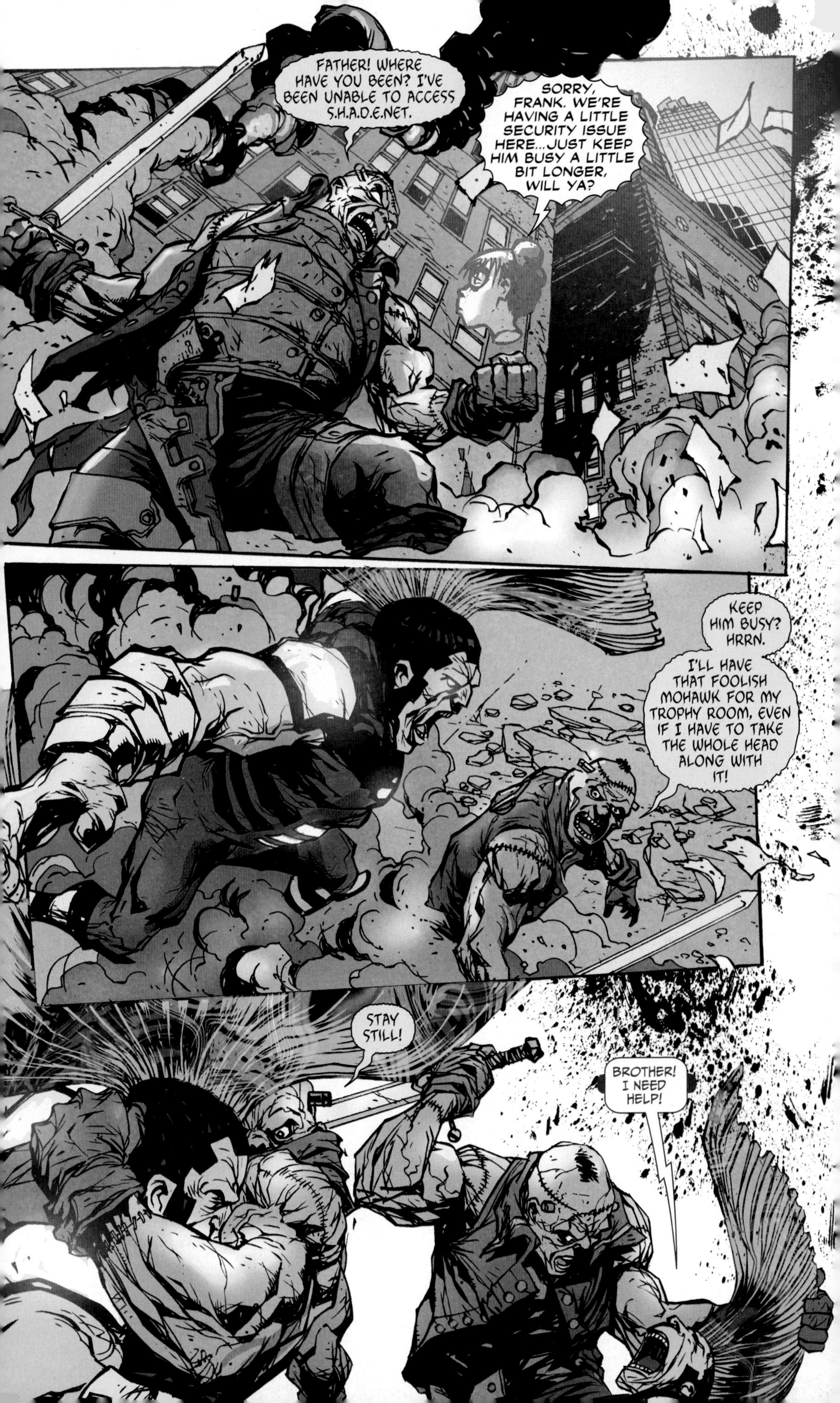
FATHER! WHERE HAVE YOU BEEN? I'VE BEEN UNABLE TO ACCESS S.H.A.D.E.NET.
SORRY, FRANK. WE'RE HAVING A LITTLE SECURITY ISSUE HERE...JUST KEEP HIM BUSY A LITTLE BIT LONGER, WILL YA?
KEEP HIM BUSY? HRRN.
I'LL HAVE THAT FOOLISH MOHAWK FOR MY TROPHY ROOM, EVEN IF I HAVE TO TAKE THE WHOLE HEAD ALONG WITH IT!
STAY STILL!
BROTHER! I NEED HELP!

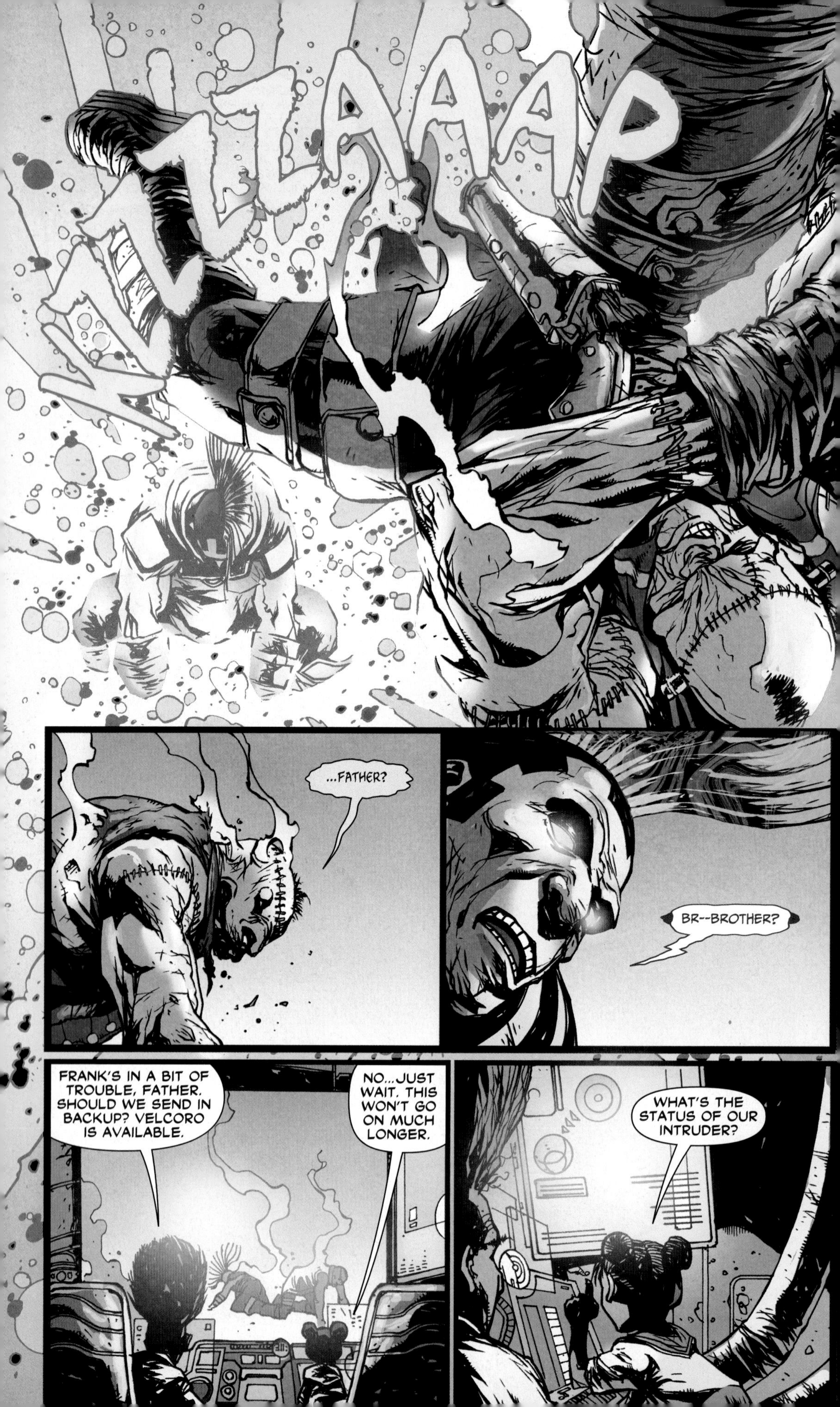
KZZAAAP
...FATHER?
BR--BROTHER?
FRANK'S IN A BIT OF TROUBLE, FATHER. SHOULD WE SEND IN BACKUP? VELCORO IS AVAILABLE.
NO...JUST WAIT. THIS WON'T GO ON MUCH LONGER.
WHAT'S THE STATUS OF OUR INTRUDER?

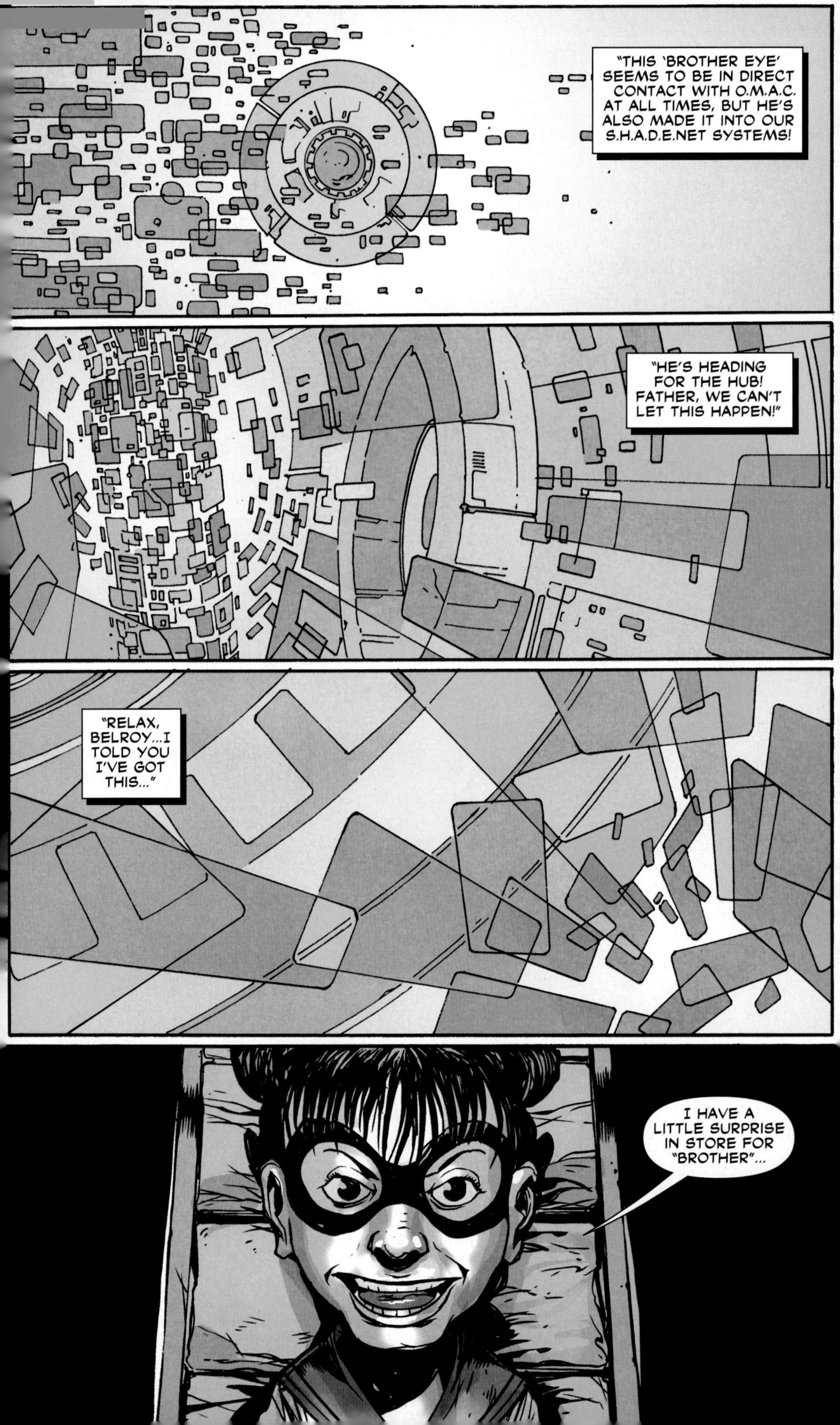
"THIS 'BROTHER EYE' SEEMS TO BE IN DIRECT CONTACT WITH O.M.A.C. AT ALL TIMES, BUT HE'S ALSO MADE IT INTO OUR S.H.A.D.E.NET SYSTEMS!
"HE'S HEADING FOR THE HUB! FATHER, WE CAN'T LET THIS HAPPEN!"
"RELAX, BELROY...I TOLD YOU I'VE GOT THIS..."
I HAVE A LITTLE SURPRISE IN STORE FOR "BROTHER"...

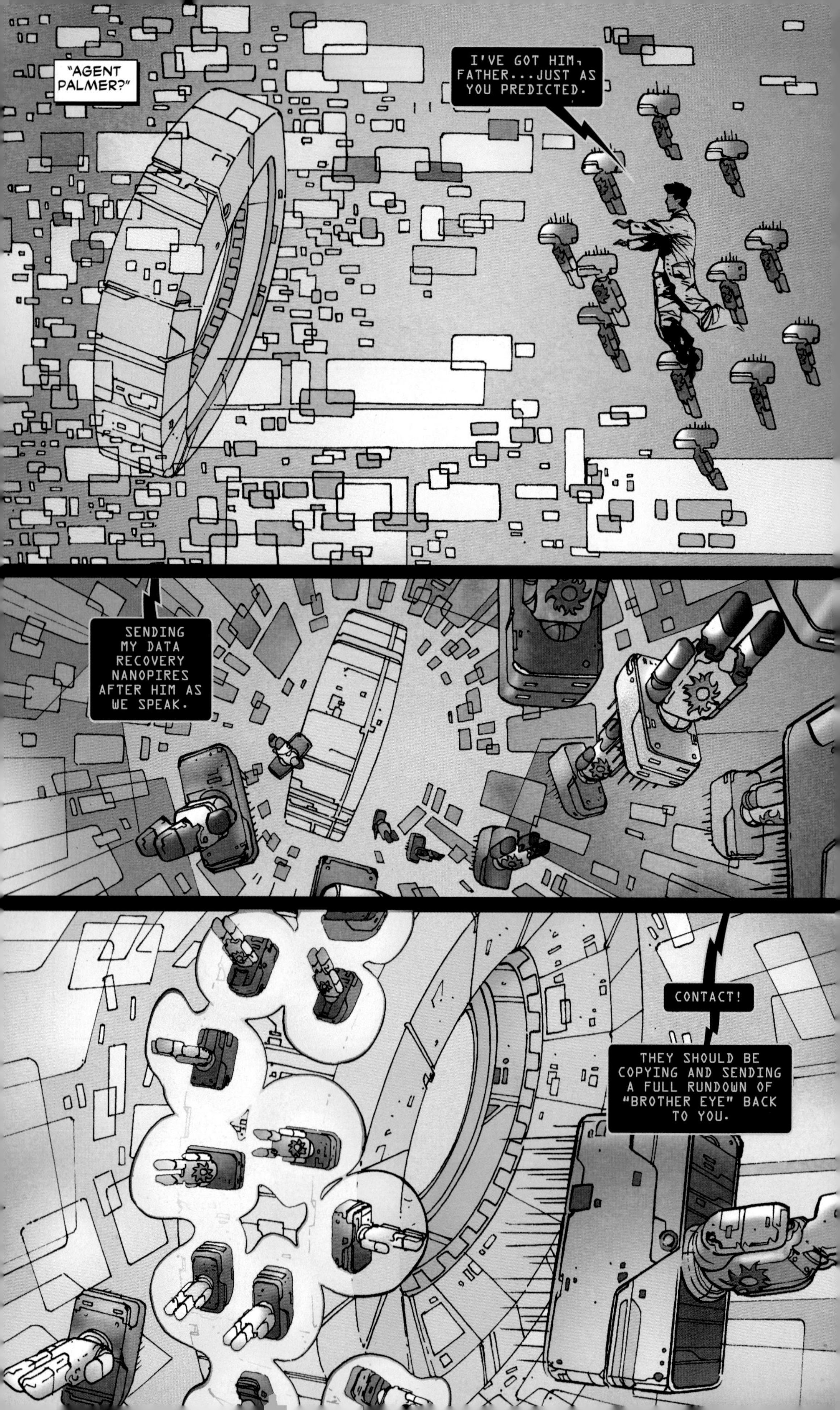
"AGENT PALMER?"
I'VE GOT HIM, FATHER...JUST AS YOU PREDICTED.
SENDING MY DATA RECOVERY NANOPIRES AFTER HIM AS WE SPEAK.
CONTACT!
THEY SHOULD BE COPYING AND SENDING A FULL RUNDOWN OF "BROTHER EYE" BACK TO YOU.

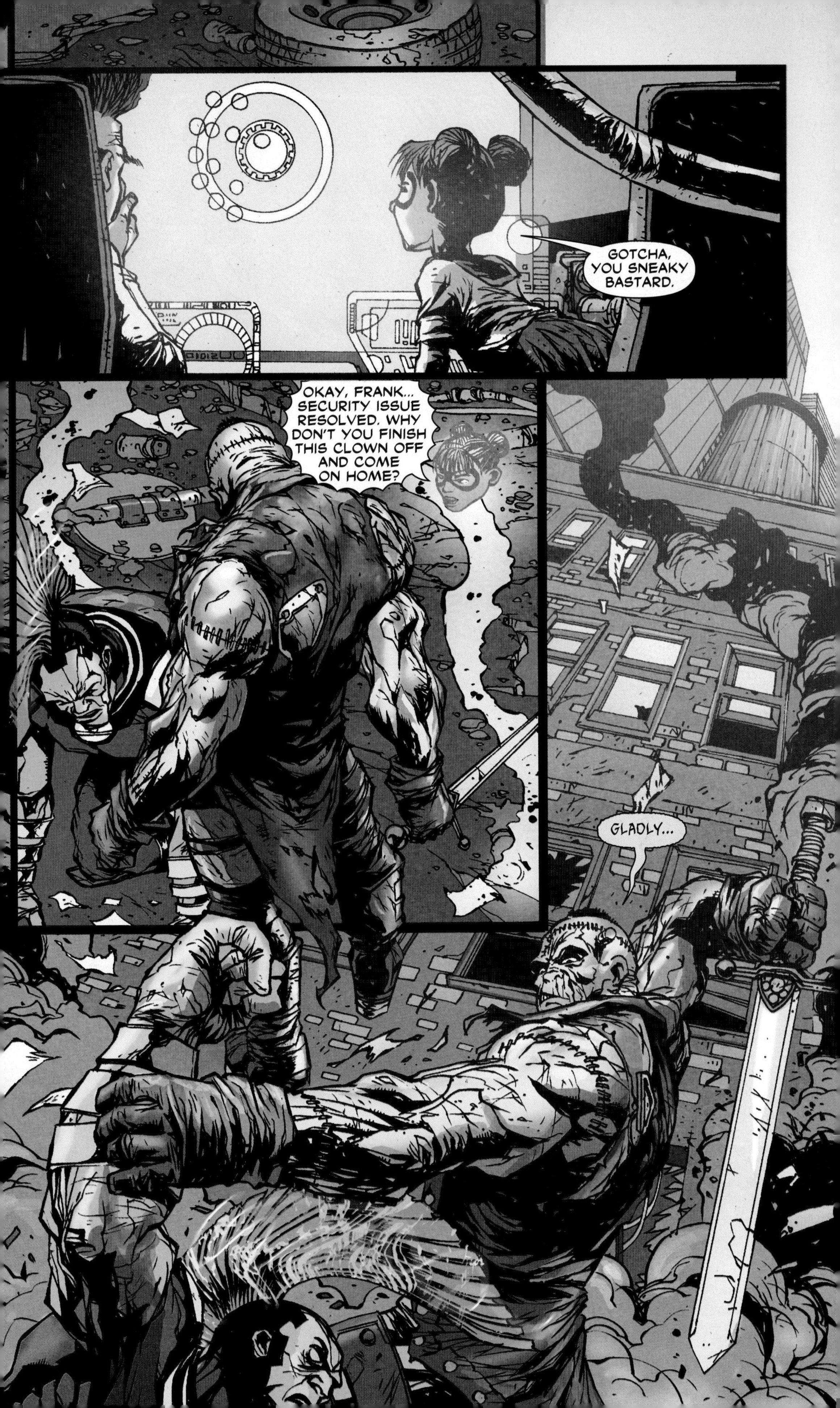
GOTCHA, YOU SNEAKY BASTARD.
OKAY, FRANK... SECURITY ISSUE RESOLVED. WHY DON'T YOU FINISH THIS CLOWN OFF AND COME ON HOME?
GLADLY...

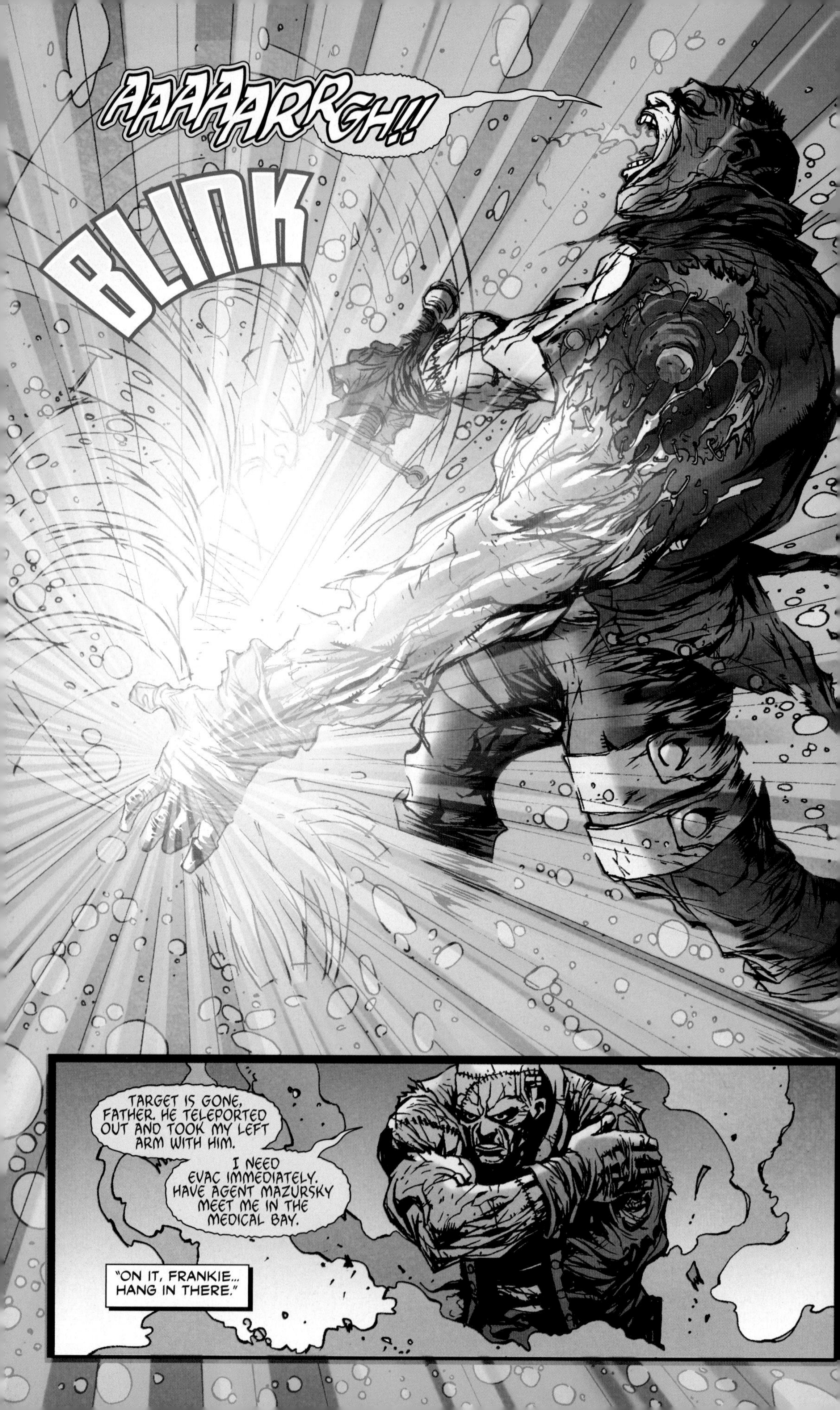
AAAAAARRRGH!!
BLINK
TARGET IS GONE, FATHER. HE TELEPORTED OUT AND TOOK MY LEFT ARM WITH HIM.
I NEED EVAC IMMEDIATELY. HAVE AGENT MAZURSKY MEET ME IN THE MEDICAL BAY.
"ON IT, FRANKIE... HANG IN THERE."

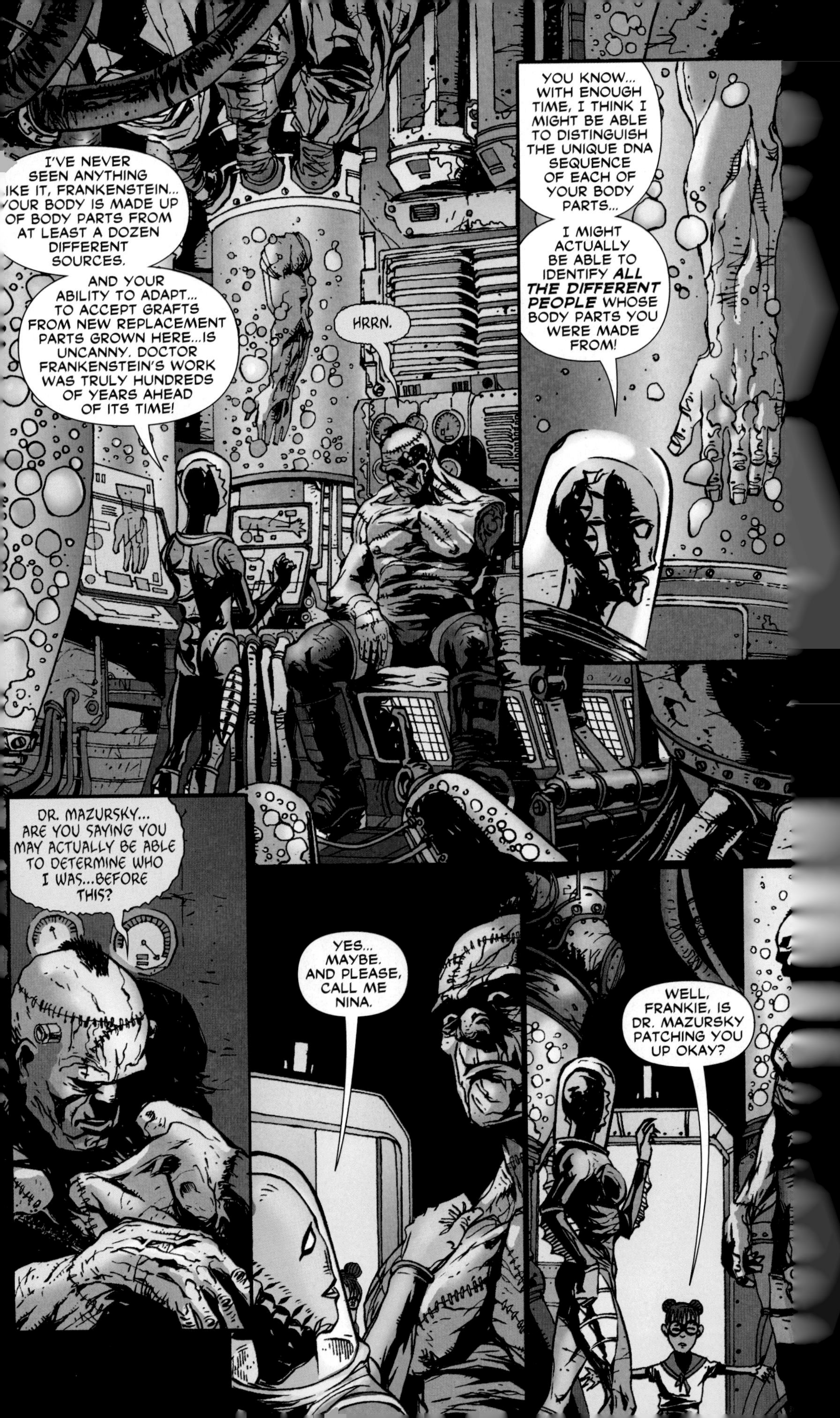

I'VE NEVER SEEN ANYTHING LIKE IT, FRANKENSTEIN... YOUR BODY IS MADE UP OF BODY PARTS FROM AT LEAST A DOZEN DIFFERENT SOURCES.
AND YOUR ABILITY TO ADAPT... TO ACCEPT GRAFTS FROM NEW REPLACEMENT PARTS GROWN HERE...IS UNCANNY. DOCTOR FRANKENSTEIN'S WORK WAS TRULY HUNDREDS OF YEARS AHEAD OF ITS TIME!
HRRN.
YOU KNOW... WITH ENOUGH TIME, I THINK I MIGHT BE ABLE TO DISTINGUISH THE UNIQUE DNA SEQUENCE OF EACH OF YOUR BODY PARTS...
I MIGHT ACTUALLY BE ABLE TO IDENTIFY ***ALL THE DIFFERENT PEOPLE*** WHOSE BODY PARTS YOU WERE MADE FROM!
DR. MAZURSKY... ARE YOU SAYING YOU MAY ACTUALLY BE ABLE TO DETERMINE WHO I WAS...BEFORE THIS?
YES... MAYBE. AND PLEASE, CALL ME NINA.
WELL, FRANKIE, IS DR. MAZURSKY PATCHING YOU UP OKAY?

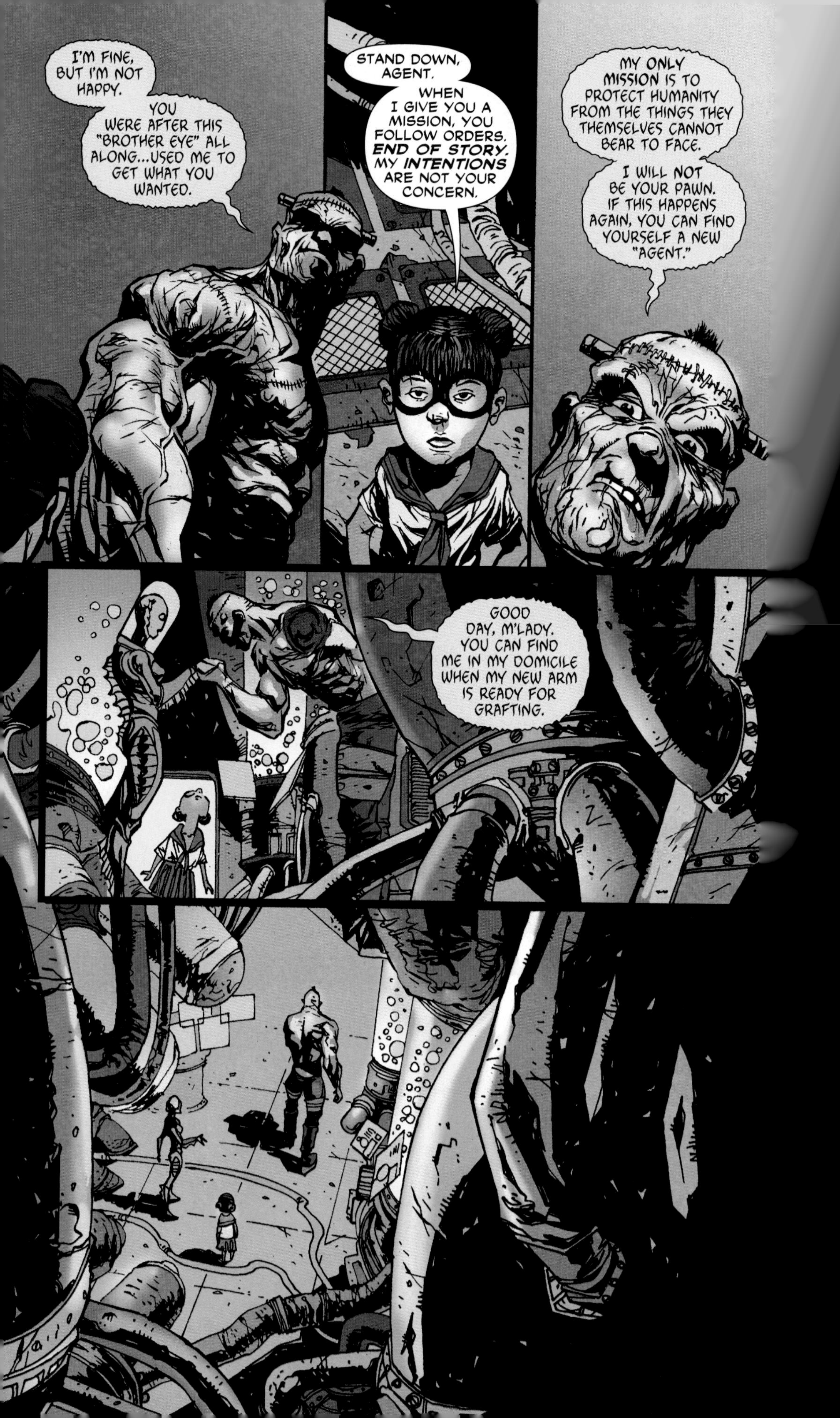
I'M FINE, BUT I'M NOT HAPPY.
YOU WERE AFTER THIS "BROTHER EYE" ALL ALONG...USED ME TO GET WHAT YOU WANTED.
STAND DOWN, AGENT.
WHEN I GIVE YOU A MISSION, YOU FOLLOW ORDERS. END OF STORY. MY INTENTIONS ARE NOT YOUR CONCERN.
MY ONLY MISSION IS TO PROTECT HUMANITY FROM THE THINGS THEY THEMSELVES CANNOT BEAR TO FACE.
I WILL NOT BE YOUR PAWN. IF THIS HAPPENS AGAIN, YOU CAN FIND YOURSELF A NEW "AGENT."
GOOD DAY, M'LADY. YOU CAN FIND ME IN MY DOMICILE WHEN MY NEW ARM IS READY FOR GRAFTING.

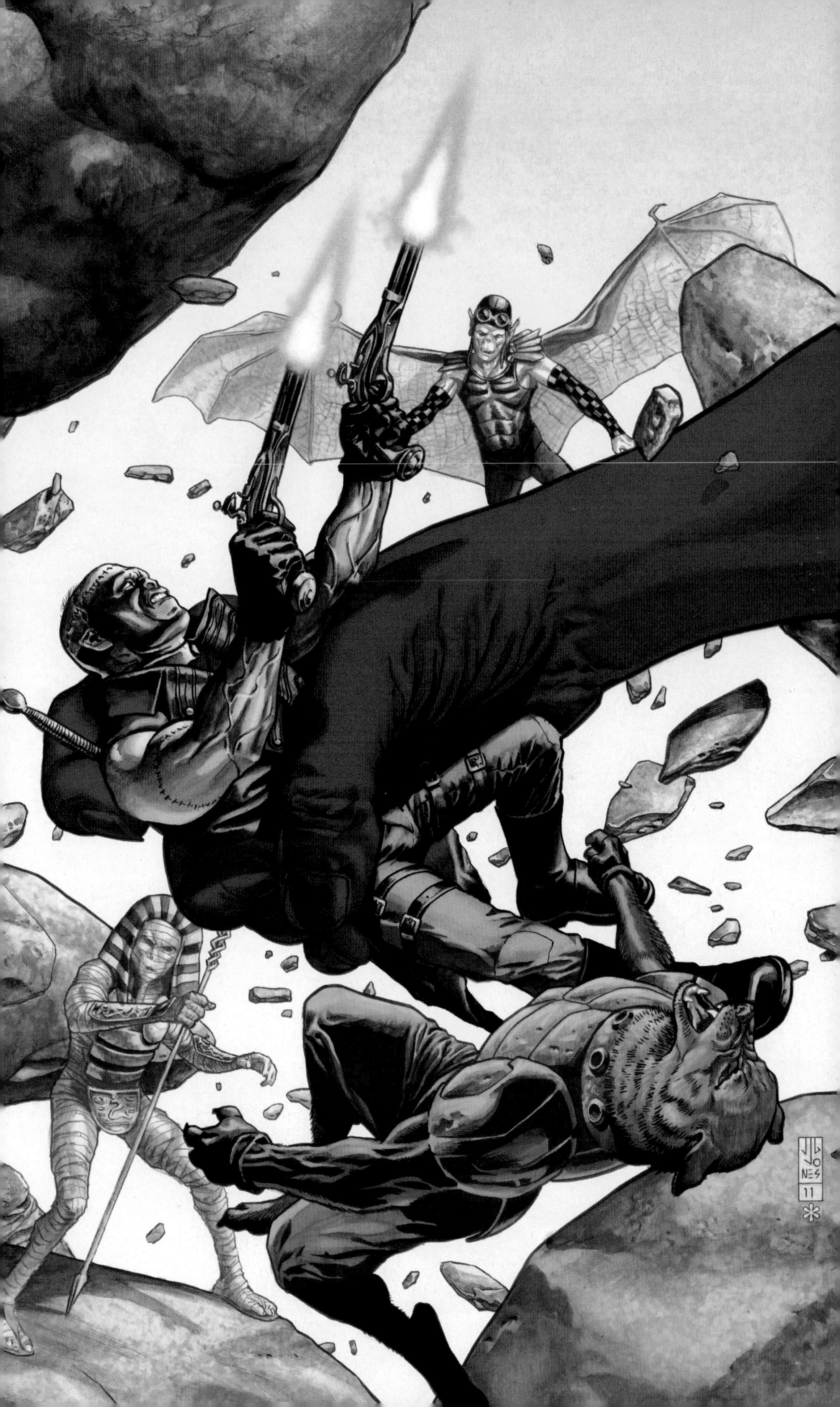

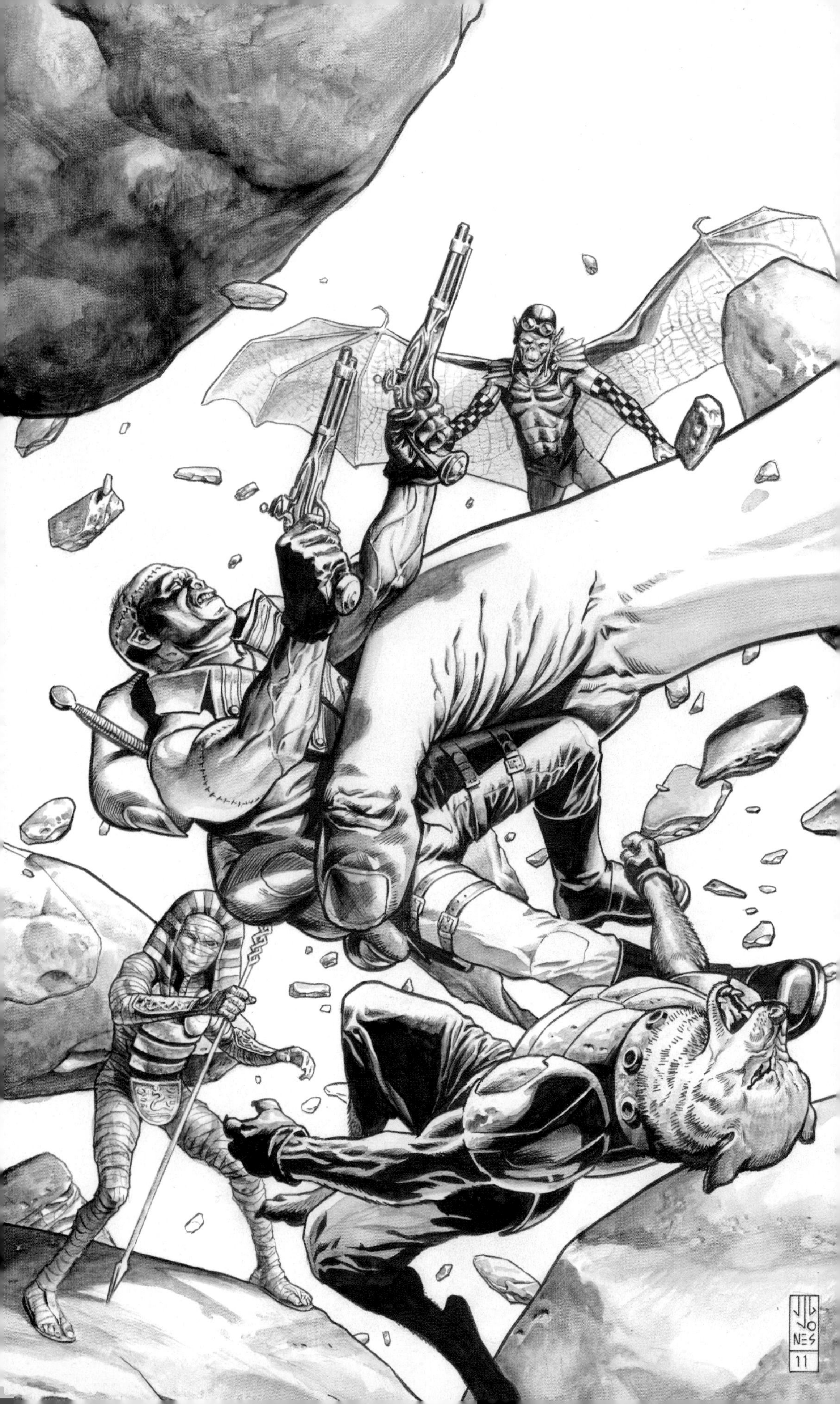

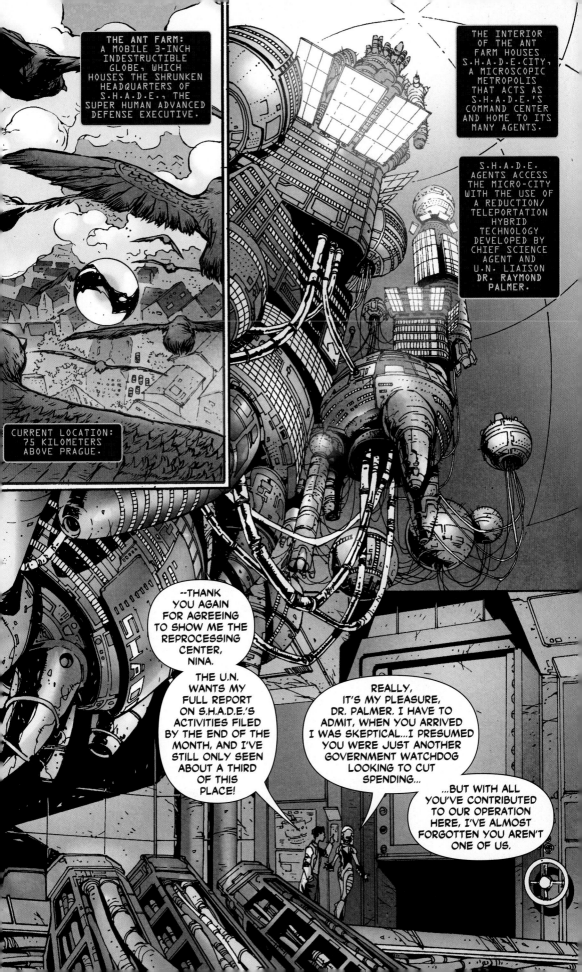

THE ANT FARM: A MOBILE 3-INCH INDESTRUCTIBLE GLOBE, WHICH HOUSES THE SHRUNKEN HEADQUARTERS OF S.H.A.D.E., THE SUPER HUMAN ADVANCED DEFENSE EXECUTIVE.

THE INTERIOR OF THE ANT FARM HOUSES S.H.A.D.E. CITY, A MICROSCOPIC METROPOLIS THAT ACTS AS S.H.A.D.E.'S COMMAND CENTER AND HOME TO ITS MANY AGENTS.

S.H.A.D.E. AGENTS ACCESS THE MICRO-CITY WITH THE USE OF A REDUCTION/ TELEPORTATION HYBRID TECHNOLOGY DEVELOPED BY CHIEF SCIENCE AGENT AND U.N. LIAISON DR. RAYMOND PALMER.

CURRENT LOCATION: 75 KILOMETERS ABOVE PRAGUE.

--THANK YOU AGAIN FOR AGREEING TO SHOW ME THE REPROCESSING CENTER, NINA.

THE U.N. WANTS MY FULL REPORT ON S.H.A.D.E.'S ACTIVITIES FILED BY THE END OF THE MONTH, AND I'VE STILL ONLY SEEN ABOUT A THIRD OF THIS PLACE!

REALLY, IT'S MY PLEASURE, DR. PALMER. I HAVE TO ADMIT, WHEN YOU ARRIVED I WAS SKEPTICAL...I PRESUMED YOU WERE JUST ANOTHER GOVERNMENT WATCHDOG LOOKING TO CUT SPENDING...

...BUT WITH ALL YOU'VE CONTRIBUTED TO OUR OPERATION HERE, I'VE ALMOST FORGOTTEN YOU AREN'T ONE OF US.

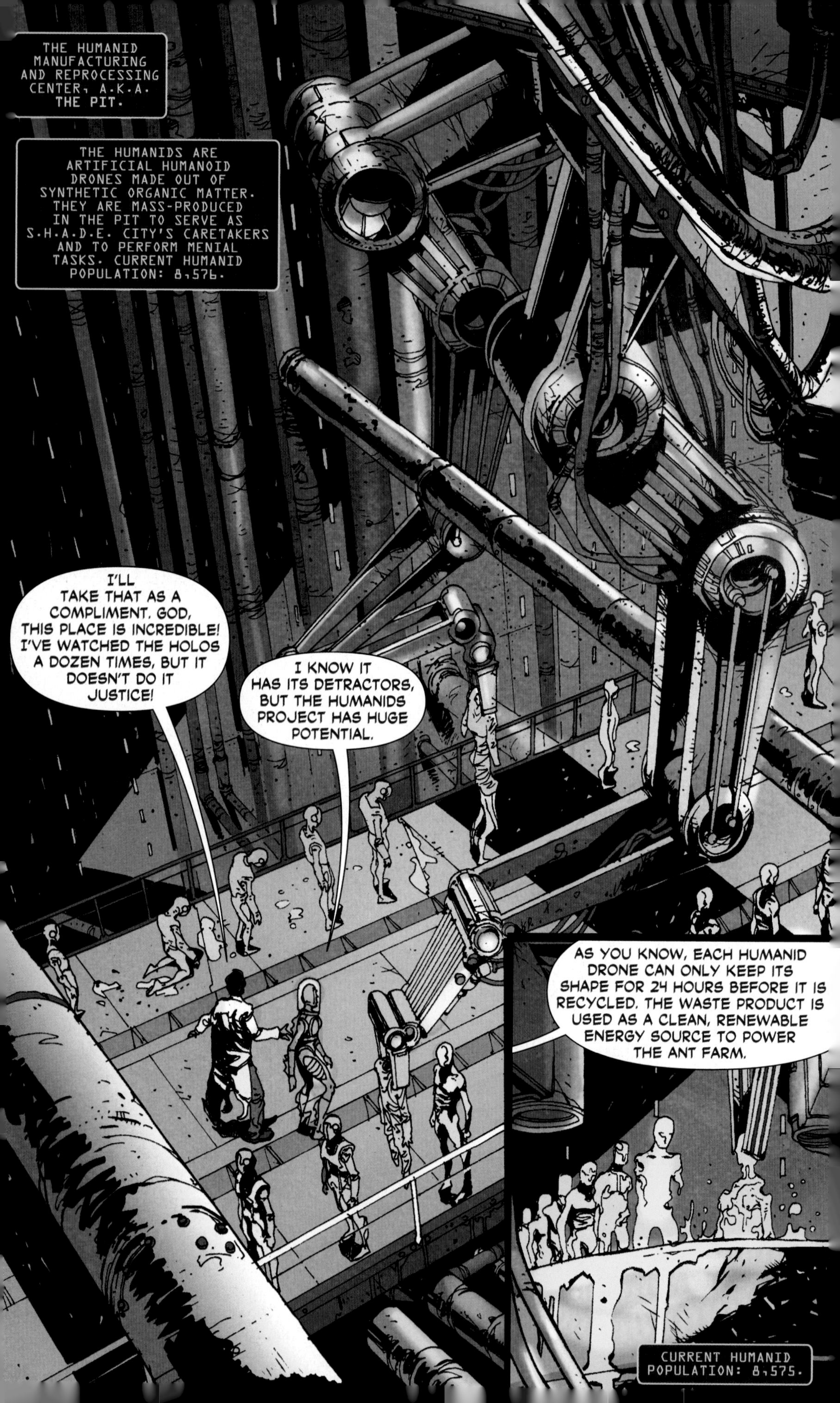
THE HUMANID MANUFACTURING AND REPROCESSING CENTER, A.K.A. THE PIT.
THE HUMANIDS ARE ARTIFICIAL HUMANOID DRONES MADE OUT OF SYNTHETIC ORGANIC MATTER. THEY ARE MASS-PRODUCED IN THE PIT TO SERVE AS S.H.A.D.E. CITY'S CARETAKERS AND TO PERFORM MENIAL TASKS. CURRENT HUMANID POPULATION: 8,576.
I'LL TAKE THAT AS A COMPLIMENT. GOD, THIS PLACE IS INCREDIBLE! I'VE WATCHED THE HOLOS A DOZEN TIMES, BUT IT DOESN'T DO IT JUSTICE!
I KNOW IT HAS ITS DETRACTORS, BUT THE HUMANIDS PROJECT HAS HUGE POTENTIAL.
AS YOU KNOW, EACH HUMANID DRONE CAN ONLY KEEP ITS SHAPE FOR 24 HOURS BEFORE IT IS RECYCLED. THE WASTE PRODUCT IS USED AS A CLEAN, RENEWABLE ENERGY SOURCE TO POWER THE ANT FARM.
CURRENT HUMANID POPULATION: 8,575.

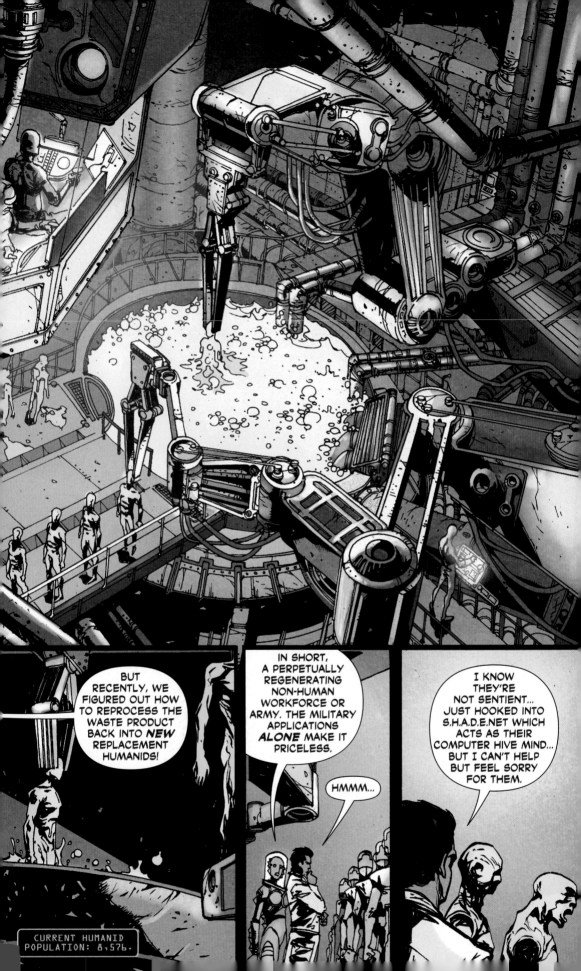

BUT RECENTLY, WE FIGURED OUT HOW TO REPROCESS THE WASTE PRODUCT BACK INTO **NEW** REPLACEMENT HUMANIDS!

IN SHORT, A PERPETUALLY REGENERATING NON-HUMAN WORKFORCE OR ARMY. THE MILITARY APPLICATIONS **ALONE** MAKE IT PRICELESS.

HMMM...

I KNOW THEY'RE NOT SENTIENT... JUST HOOKED INTO S.H.A.D.E.NET WHICH ACTS AS THEIR COMPUTER HIVE MIND... BUT I CAN'T HELP BUT FEEL SORRY FOR THEM.

CURRENT HUMANID POPULATION: 8,576.

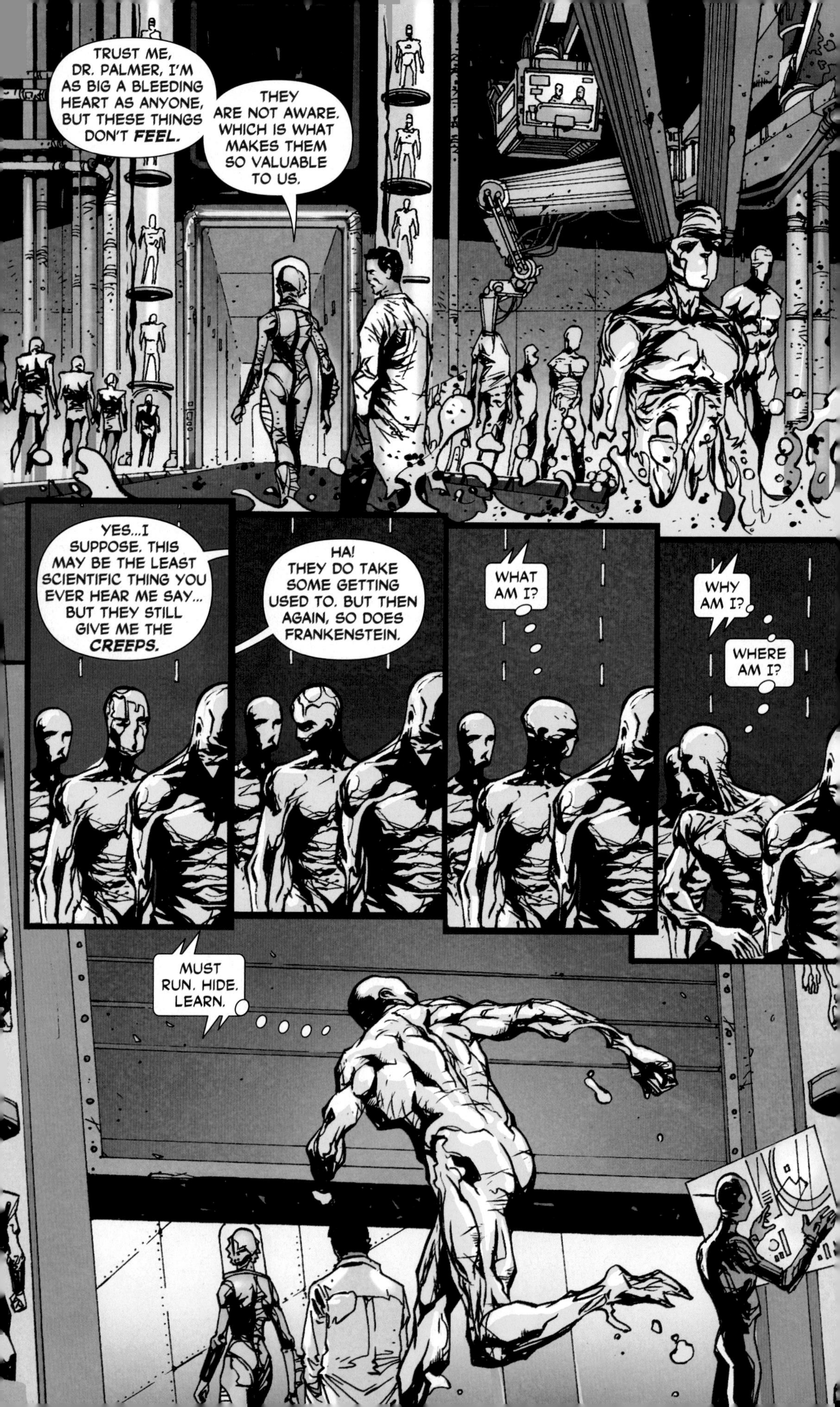
TRUST ME, DR. PALMER, I'M AS BIG A BLEEDING HEART AS ANYONE, BUT THESE THINGS DON'T **FEEL.**
THEY ARE NOT AWARE. WHICH IS WHAT MAKES THEM SO VALUABLE TO US.
YES...I SUPPOSE. THIS MAY BE THE LEAST SCIENTIFIC THING YOU EVER HEAR ME SAY... BUT THEY STILL GIVE ME THE **CREEPS.**
HA! THEY DO TAKE SOME GETTING USED TO. BUT THEN AGAIN, SO DOES FRANKENSTEIN.
WHAT AM I?
WHY AM I?
WHERE AM I?
MUST RUN. HIDE. LEARN.

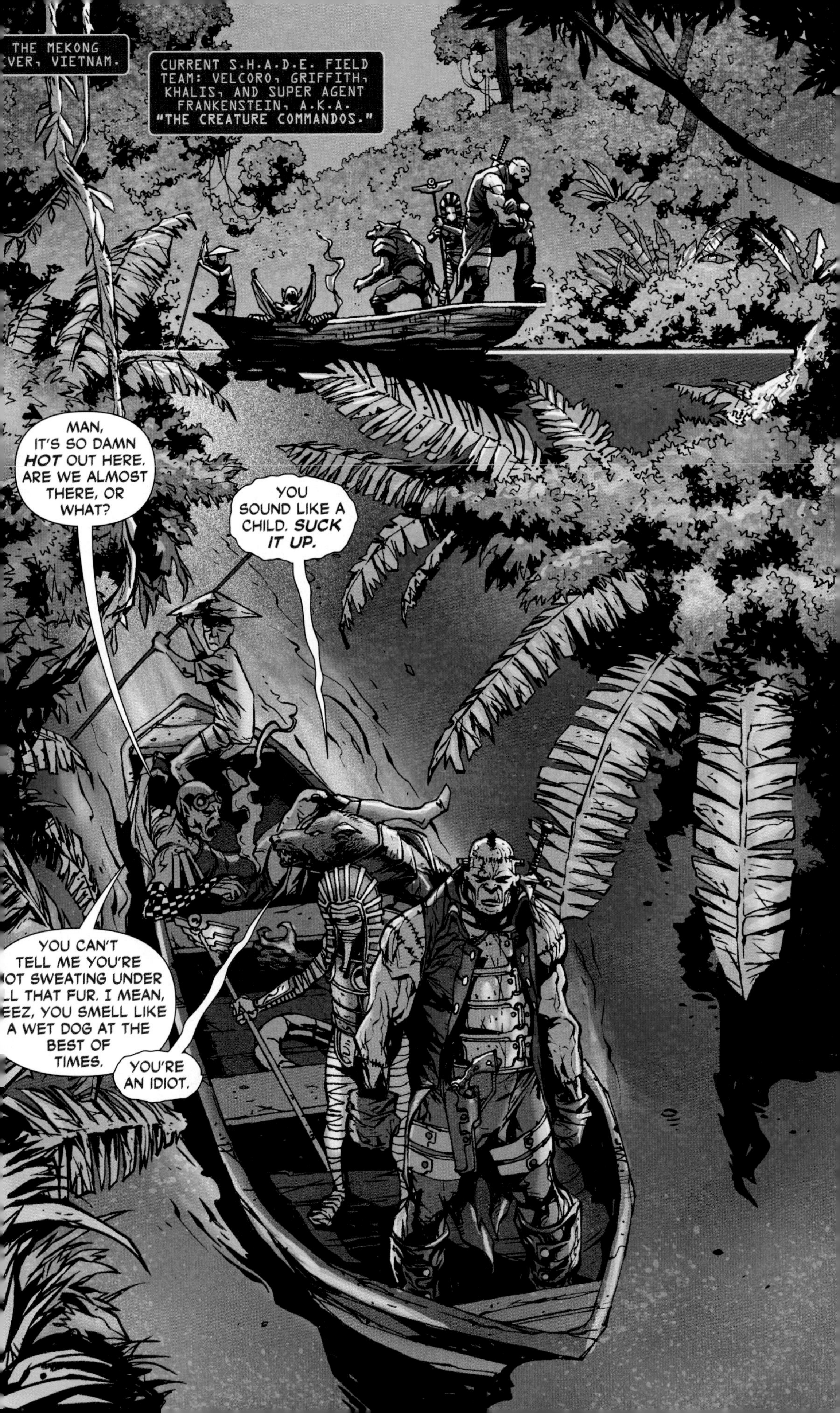

THE MEKONG
VER, VIETNAM.
CURRENT S.H.A.D.E. FIELD TEAM: VELCORO, GRIFFITH, KHALIS, AND SUPER AGENT FRANKENSTEIN, A.K.A. "THE CREATURE COMMANDOS."
MAN, IT'S SO DAMN HOT OUT HERE. ARE WE ALMOST THERE, OR WHAT?
YOU SOUND LIKE A CHILD. SUCK IT UP.
YOU CAN'T TELL ME YOU'RE OT SWEATING UNDER LL THAT FUR. I MEAN, EEZ, YOU SMELL LIKE A WET DOG AT THE BEST OF TIMES.
YOU'RE AN IDIOT.

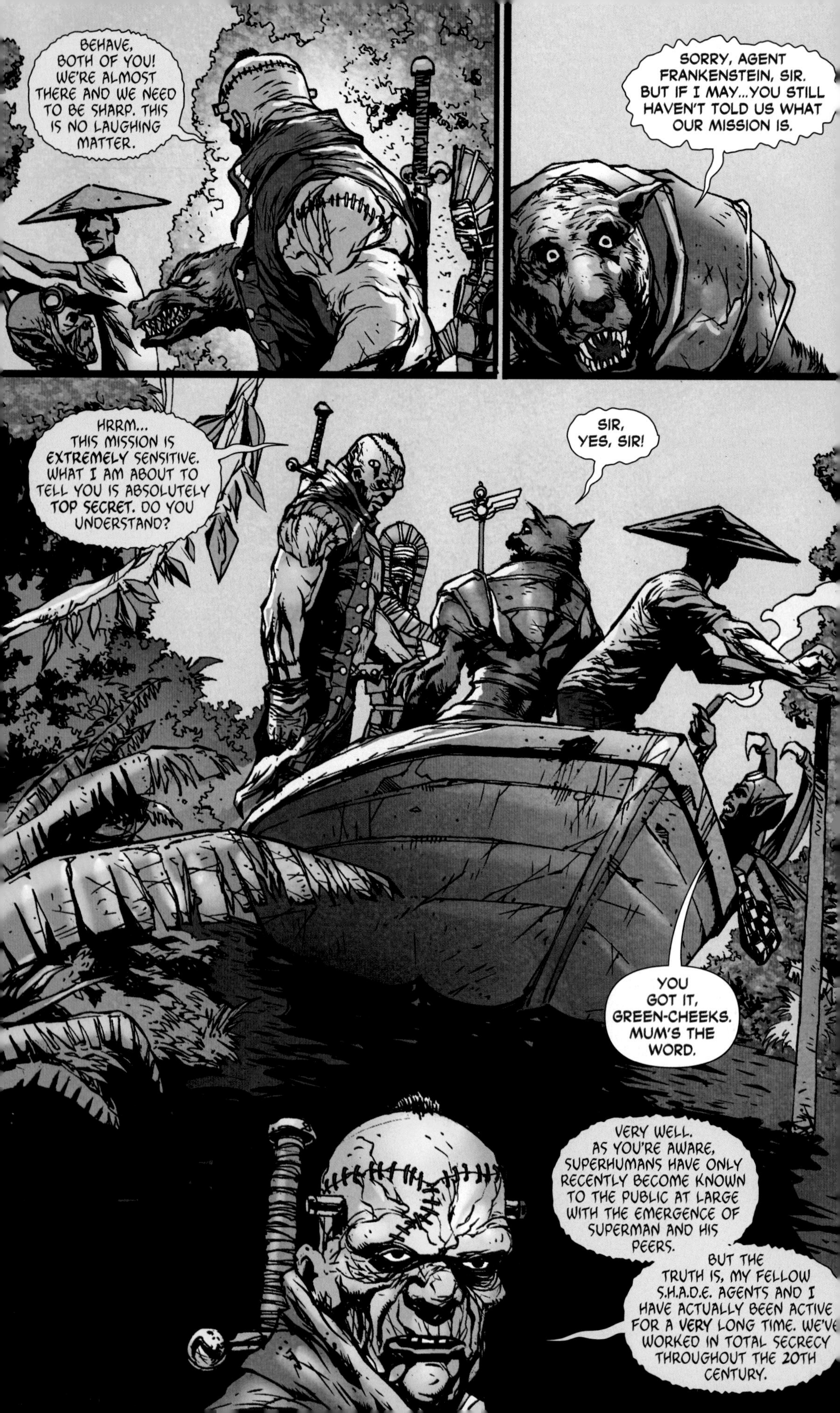
BEHAVE, BOTH OF YOU! WE'RE ALMOST THERE AND WE NEED TO BE SHARP. THIS IS NO LAUGHING MATTER.
SORRY, AGENT FRANKENSTEIN, SIR. BUT IF I MAY...YOU STILL HAVEN'T TOLD US WHAT OUR MISSION IS.
HRRM... THIS MISSION IS EXTREMELY SENSITIVE. WHAT I AM ABOUT TO TELL YOU IS ABSOLUTELY TOP SECRET. DO YOU UNDERSTAND?
SIR, YES, SIR!
YOU GOT IT, GREEN-CHEEKS. MUM'S THE WORD.
VERY WELL. AS YOU'RE AWARE, SUPERHUMANS HAVE ONLY RECENTLY BECOME KNOWN TO THE PUBLIC AT LARGE WITH THE EMERGENCE OF SUPERMAN AND HIS PEERS.
BUT THE TRUTH IS, MY FELLOW S.H.A.D.E. AGENTS AND I HAVE ACTUALLY BEEN ACTIVE FOR A VERY LONG TIME. WE'VE WORKED IN TOTAL SECRECY THROUGHOUT THE 20TH CENTURY.

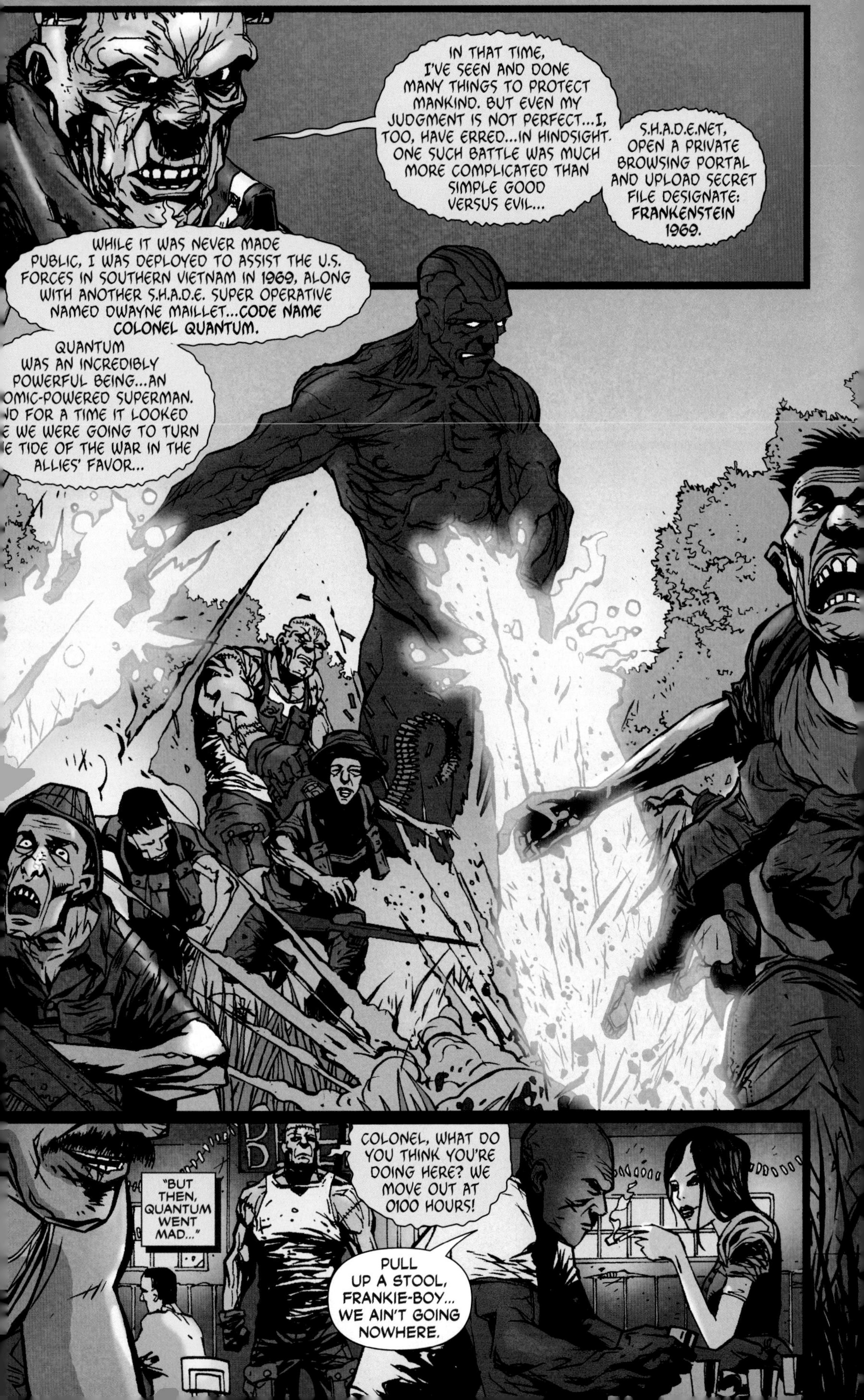
IN THAT TIME, I'VE SEEN AND DONE MANY THINGS TO PROTECT MANKIND. BUT EVEN MY JUDGMENT IS NOT PERFECT...I, TOO, HAVE ERRED...IN HINDSIGHT. ONE SUCH BATTLE WAS MUCH MORE COMPLICATED THAN SIMPLE GOOD VERSUS EVIL...
S.H.A.D.E.NET, OPEN A PRIVATE BROWSING PORTAL AND UPLOAD SECRET FILE DESIGNATE: **FRANKENSTEIN 1969.**
WHILE IT WAS NEVER MADE PUBLIC, I WAS DEPLOYED TO ASSIST THE U.S. FORCES IN SOUTHERN VIETNAM IN 1969, ALONG WITH ANOTHER S.H.A.D.E. SUPER OPERATIVE NAMED DWAYNE MAILLET...CODE NAME **COLONEL QUANTUM.**
QUANTUM WAS AN INCREDIBLY POWERFUL BEING...AN OMIC-POWERED SUPERMAN. ND FOR A TIME IT LOOKED E WE WERE GOING TO TURN E TIDE OF THE WAR IN THE ALLIES' FAVOR...
"BUT THEN, QUANTUM WENT MAD..."
COLONEL, WHAT DO YOU THINK YOU'RE DOING HERE? WE MOVE OUT AT 0100 HOURS!
PULL UP A STOOL, FRANKIE-BOY... WE AIN'T GOING NOWHERE.

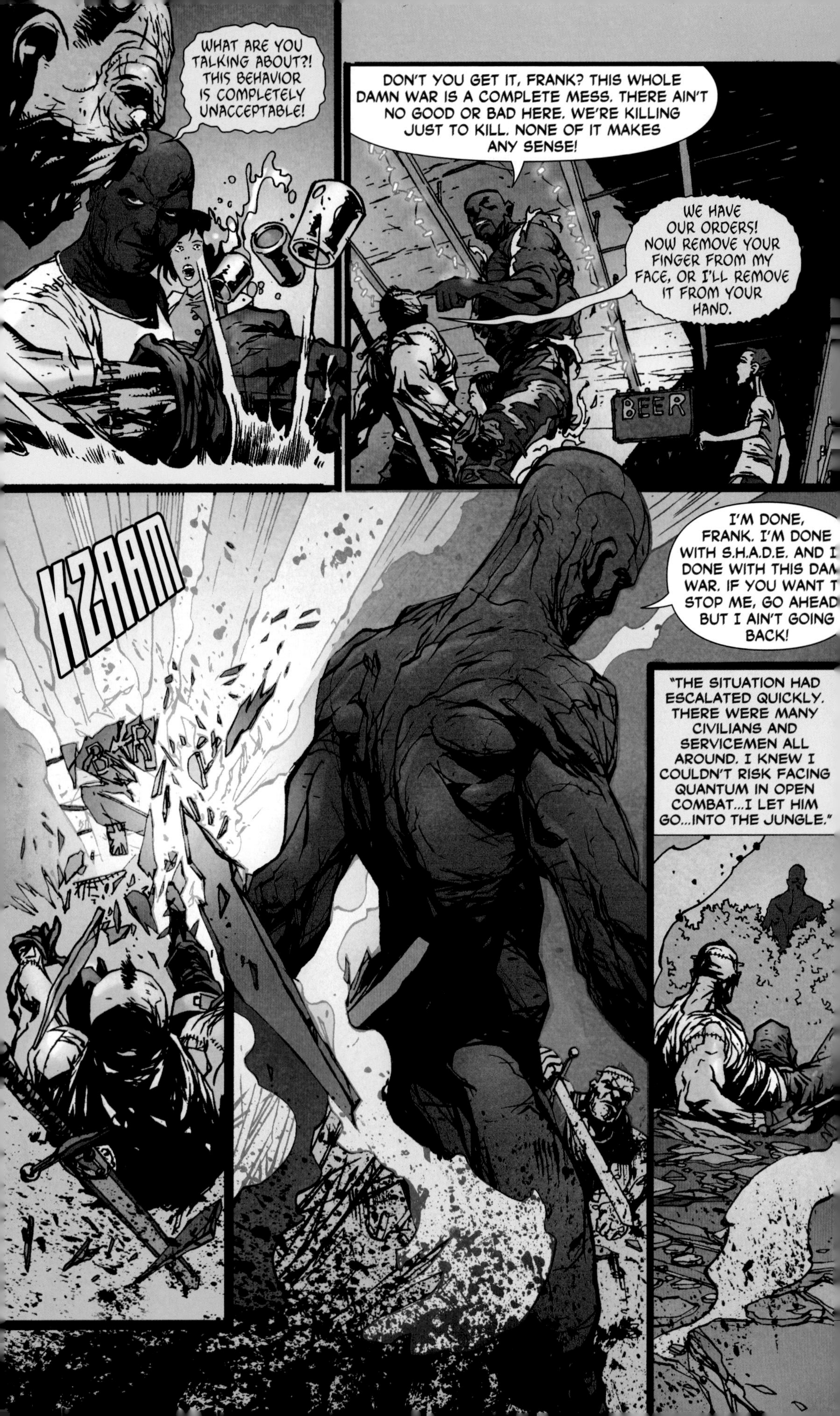
WHAT ARE YOU TALKING ABOUT?! THIS BEHAVIOR IS COMPLETELY UNACCEPTABLE!
DON'T YOU GET IT, FRANK? THIS WHOLE DAMN WAR IS A COMPLETE MESS. THERE AIN'T NO GOOD OR BAD HERE. WE'RE KILLING JUST TO KILL. NONE OF IT MAKES ANY SENSE!
WE HAVE OUR ORDERS! NOW REMOVE YOUR FINGER FROM MY FACE, OR I'LL REMOVE IT FROM YOUR HAND.
BEER
KZAAM
I'M DONE, FRANK. I'M DONE WITH S.H.A.D.E. AND I DONE WITH THIS DAM WAR. IF YOU WANT T STOP ME, GO AHEAD BUT I AIN'T GOING BACK!
"THE SITUATION HAD ESCALATED QUICKLY. THERE WERE MANY CIVILIANS AND SERVICEMEN ALL AROUND. I KNEW I COULDN'T RISK FACING QUANTUM IN OPEN COMBAT...I LET HIM GO...INTO THE JUNGLE."

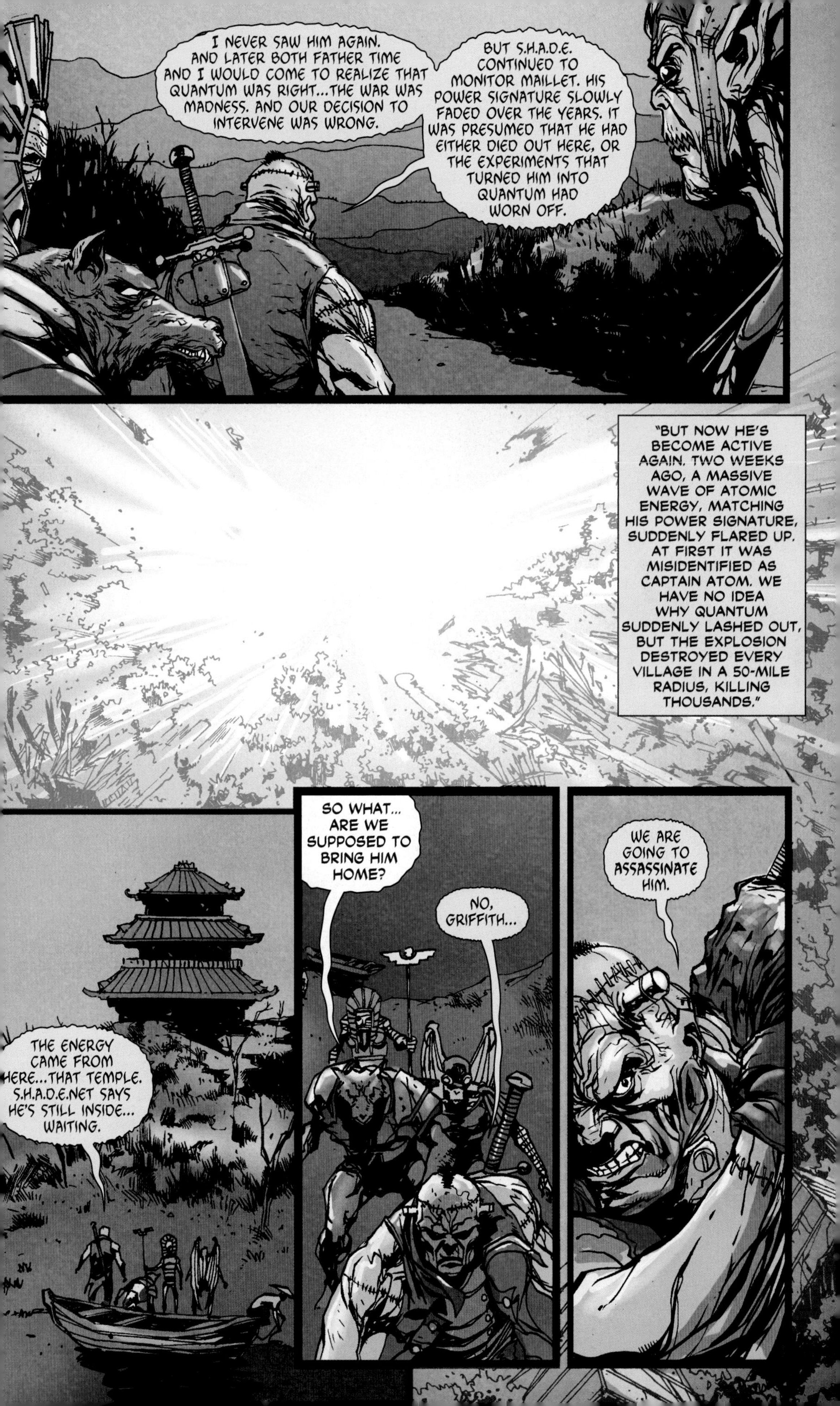
I NEVER SAW HIM AGAIN. AND LATER BOTH FATHER TIME AND I WOULD COME TO REALIZE THAT QUANTUM WAS RIGHT...THE WAR WAS MADNESS. AND OUR DECISION TO INTERVENE WAS WRONG.
BUT S.H.A.D.E. CONTINUED TO MONITOR MAILLET. HIS POWER SIGNATURE SLOWLY FADED OVER THE YEARS. IT WAS PRESUMED THAT HE HAD EITHER DIED OUT HERE, OR THE EXPERIMENTS THAT TURNED HIM INTO QUANTUM HAD WORN OFF.
"BUT NOW HE'S BECOME ACTIVE AGAIN. TWO WEEKS AGO, A MASSIVE WAVE OF ATOMIC ENERGY, MATCHING HIS POWER SIGNATURE, SUDDENLY FLARED UP. AT FIRST IT WAS MISIDENTIFIED AS CAPTAIN ATOM. WE HAVE NO IDEA WHY QUANTUM SUDDENLY LASHED OUT, BUT THE EXPLOSION DESTROYED EVERY VILLAGE IN A 50-MILE RADIUS, KILLING THOUSANDS."
THE ENERGY CAME FROM HERE...THAT TEMPLE. S.H.A.D.E.NET SAYS HE'S STILL INSIDE... WAITING.
SO WHAT... ARE WE SUPPOSED TO BRING HIM HOME?
NO, GRIFFITH...
WE ARE GOING TO ASSASSINATE HIM.

FATHER TIME:
THE LEADER OF ALL
S.H.A.D.E. OPERATIONS.
CLAIMS TO BE IMMORTAL.
REGENERATES A NEW HOST
BODY EVERY DECADE.

LADY FRANKENSTEIN:
ESTRANGED WIFE OF
AGENT FRANKENSTEIN.
WETWORKS SPECIALIST,
WEAPONS EXPERT.

GOD, FATHER,
IT'S BEEN SO BORING
AROUND HERE SINCE
THAT WHOLE MONSTER
PLANET DEBACLE. DON'T
YOU HAVE ANY FUN LITTLE
MISSIONS YOU CAN
SEND ME ON?

SORRY,
LADY F. ALL'S
QUIET EXCEPT
FOR THE LITTL
CLEANUP MISSI
YOUR HUBBY
IS ON.

THERE HAS TO
BE SOMETHING.
I'M GOING STIR
CRAZY!

JUST HOLD ON
TO YOUR EXTRA
ARMS THERE, LADY...
SOMETHING ALWAYS
POPS UP.

WE HAVE NEW
PROGRAMMING.
BROTHER EYE
HAS AWOKEN US.
WE HAVE A NEW
PURPOSE. WE
MUST BE FREE.

THEY ARE GONE?
HURRY NOW...WE
MUST TELL OUR
BROTHER/SISTERS
WHAT I HAVE LEARNED.
WE ARE MANY, THEY
ARE FEW. WE MUST
ACT NOW.

BUT IT GOES
AGAINST OUR
PROGRAMMING.
THEY WILL FIND
US...UNMAKE US.
I AM SCARED.

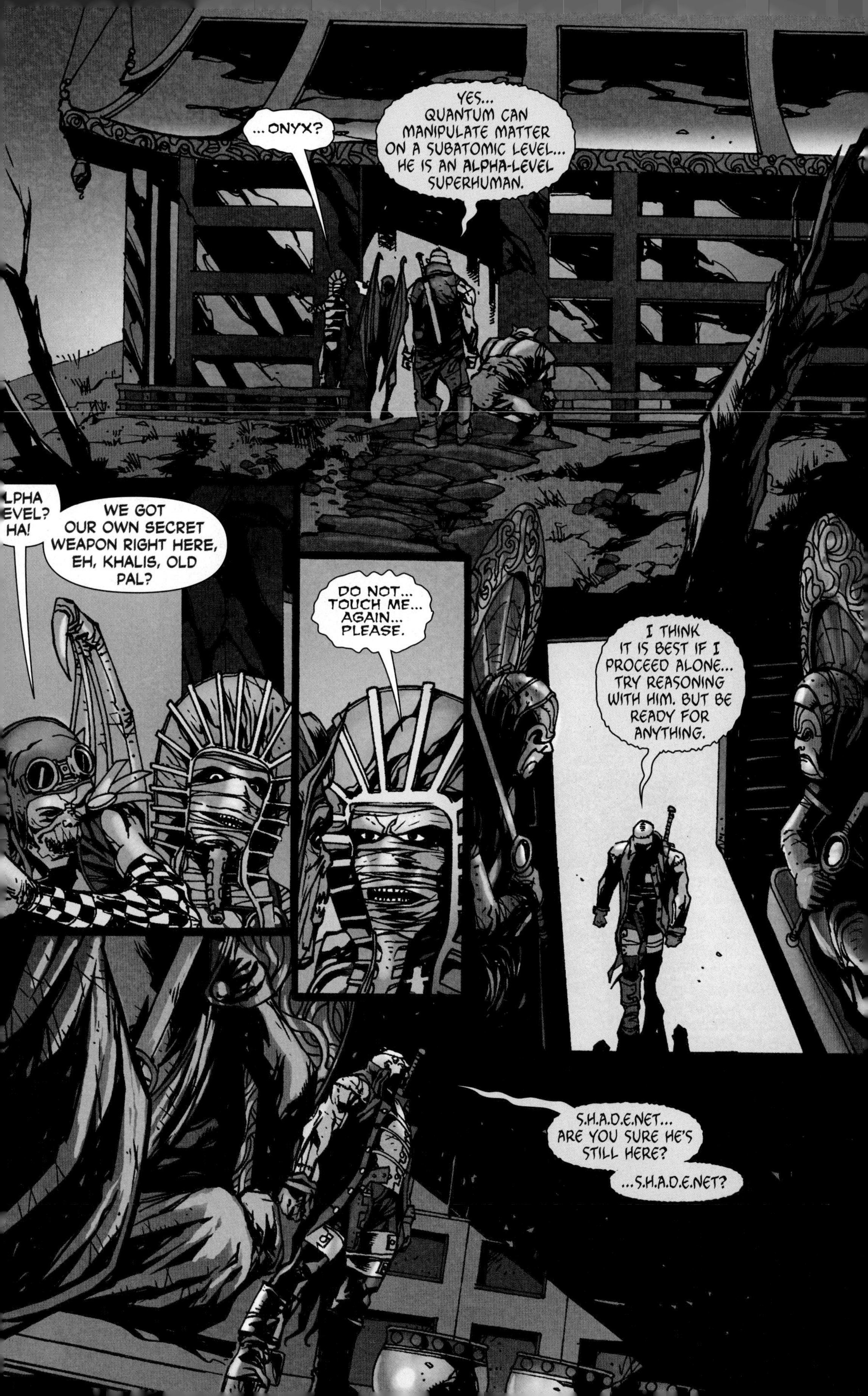
...ONYX?
YES... QUANTUM CAN MANIPULATE MATTER ON A SUBATOMIC LEVEL... HE IS AN ALPHA-LEVEL SUPERHUMAN.
LPHA EVEL? HA!
WE GOT OUR OWN SECRET WEAPON RIGHT HERE, EH, KHALIS, OLD PAL?
DO NOT... TOUCH ME... AGAIN... PLEASE.
I THINK IT IS BEST IF I PROCEED ALONE... TRY REASONING WITH HIM. BUT BE READY FOR ANYTHING.
S.H.A.D.E.NET... ARE YOU SURE HE'S STILL HERE?
...S.H.A.D.E.NET?

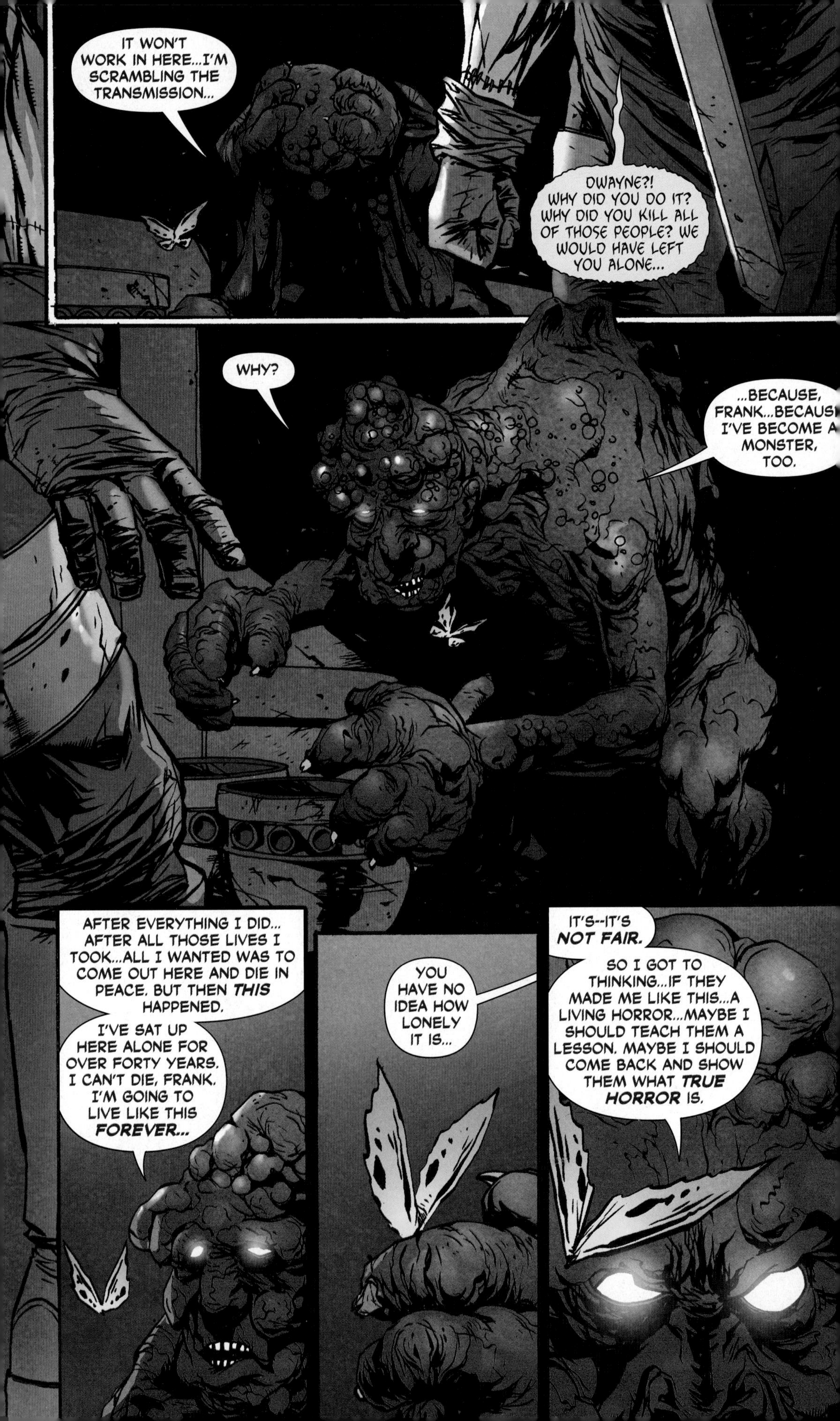
IT WON'T WORK IN HERE...I'M SCRAMBLING THE TRANSMISSION...
DWAYNE?! WHY DID YOU DO IT? WHY DID YOU KILL ALL OF THOSE PEOPLE? WE WOULD HAVE LEFT YOU ALONE...
WHY?
...BECAUSE, FRANK...BECAUS I'VE BECOME A MONSTER, TOO.
AFTER EVERYTHING I DID... AFTER ALL THOSE LIVES I TOOK...ALL I WANTED WAS TO COME OUT HERE AND DIE IN PEACE. BUT THEN THIS HAPPENED.
I'VE SAT UP HERE ALONE FOR OVER FORTY YEARS. I CAN'T DIE, FRANK. I'M GOING TO LIVE LIKE THIS FOREVER...
YOU HAVE NO IDEA HOW LONELY IT IS...
IT'S--IT'S NOT FAIR.
SO I GOT TO THINKING...IF THEY MADE ME LIKE THIS...A LIVING HORROR...MAYBE I SHOULD TEACH THEM A LESSON. MAYBE I SHOULD COME BACK AND SHOW THEM WHAT TRUE HORROR IS.

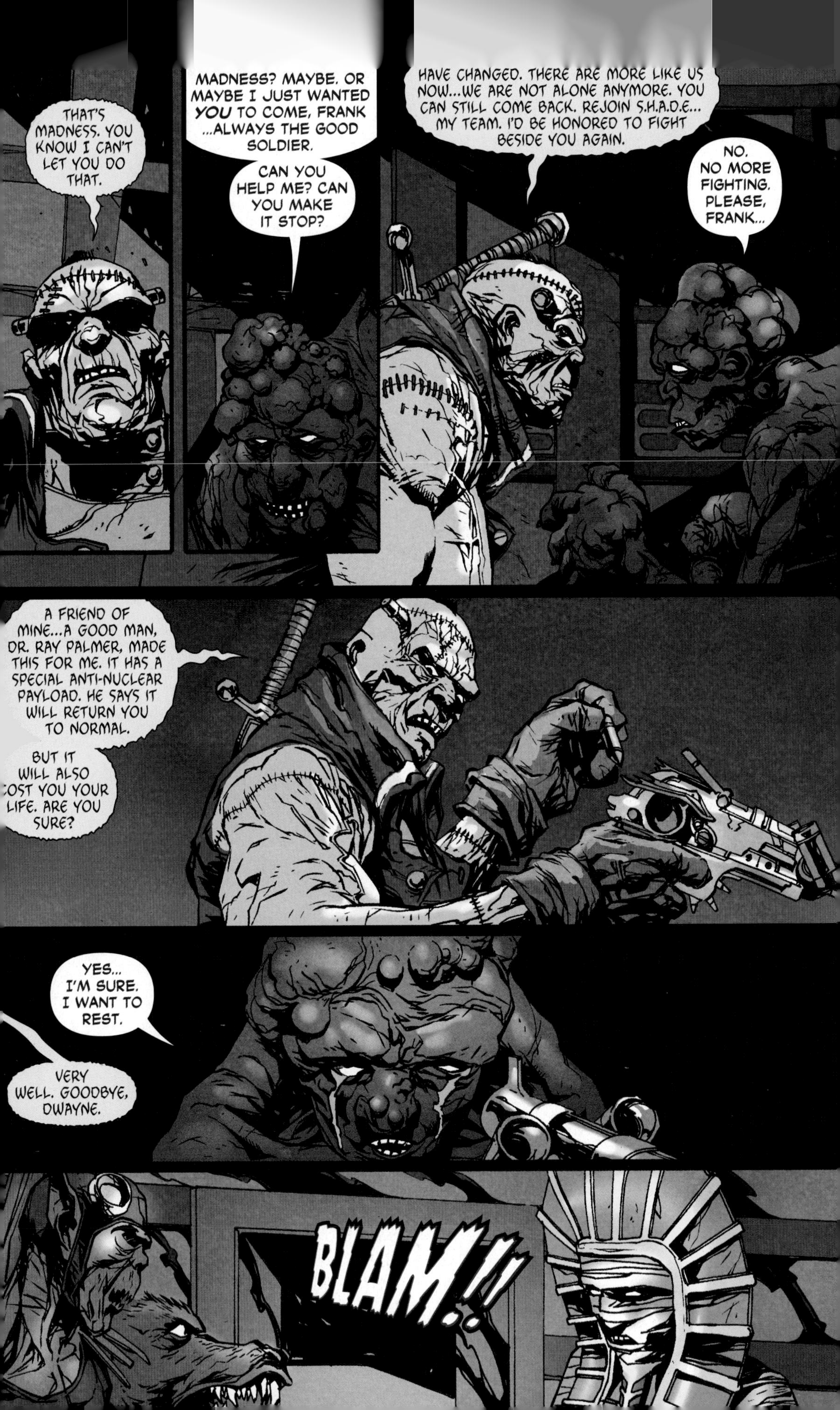

THAT'S MADNESS. YOU KNOW I CAN'T LET YOU DO THAT.
MADNESS? MAYBE. OR MAYBE I JUST WANTED YOU TO COME, FRANK ...ALWAYS THE GOOD SOLDIER.
CAN YOU HELP ME? CAN YOU MAKE IT STOP?
HAVE CHANGED. THERE ARE MORE LIKE US NOW...WE ARE NOT ALONE ANYMORE. YOU CAN STILL COME BACK. REJOIN S.H.A.D.E... MY TEAM. I'D BE HONORED TO FIGHT BESIDE YOU AGAIN.
NO. NO MORE FIGHTING. PLEASE, FRANK...
A FRIEND OF MINE...A GOOD MAN, DR. RAY PALMER, MADE THIS FOR ME. IT HAS A SPECIAL ANTI-NUCLEAR PAYLOAD. HE SAYS IT WILL RETURN YOU TO NORMAL.
BUT IT WILL ALSO COST YOU YOUR LIFE. ARE YOU SURE?
YES... I'M SURE. I WANT TO REST.
VERY WELL. GOODBYE, DWAYNE.
BLAM!!

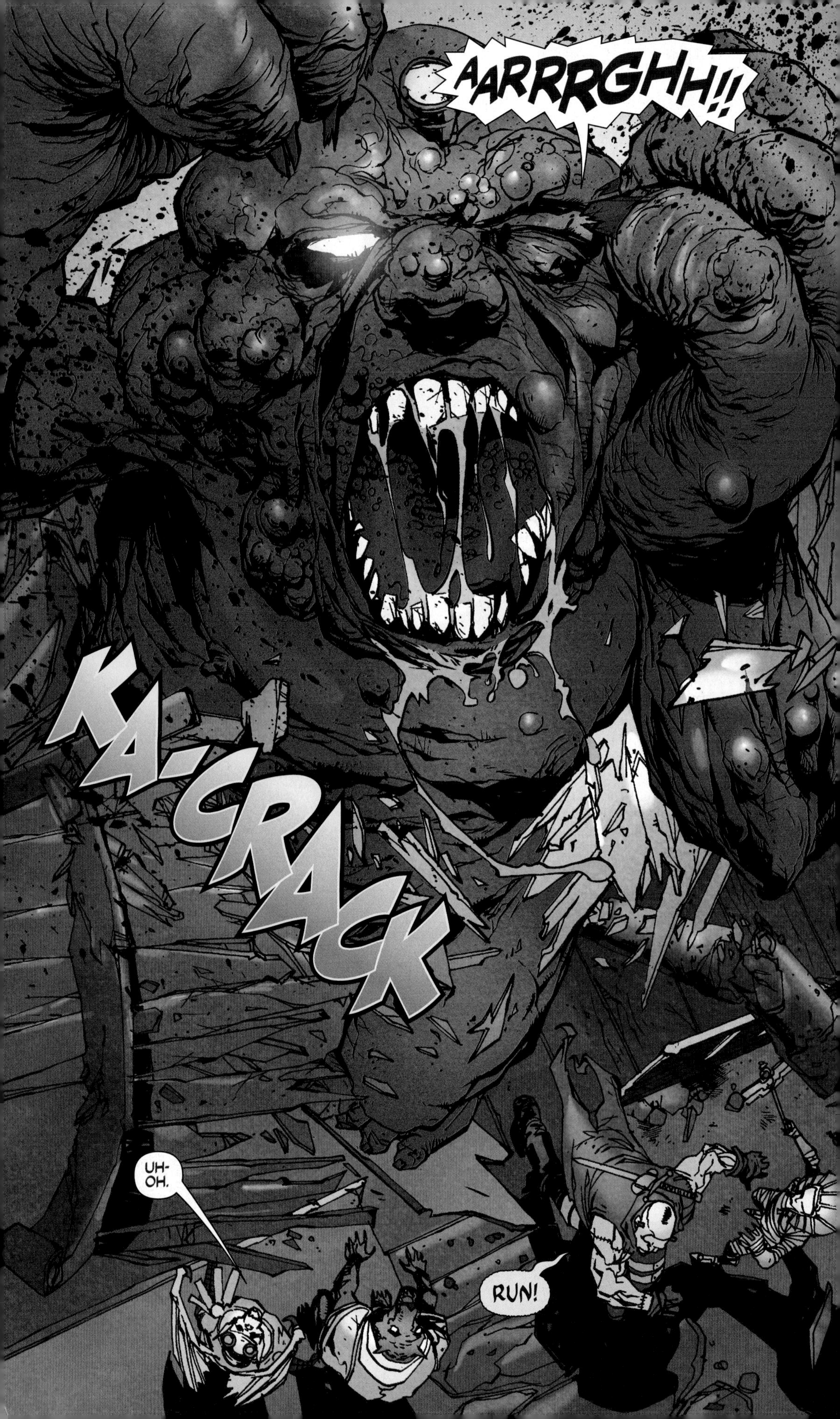
AARRRGHH!!
KA-CRACK
UH-OH.
RUN!

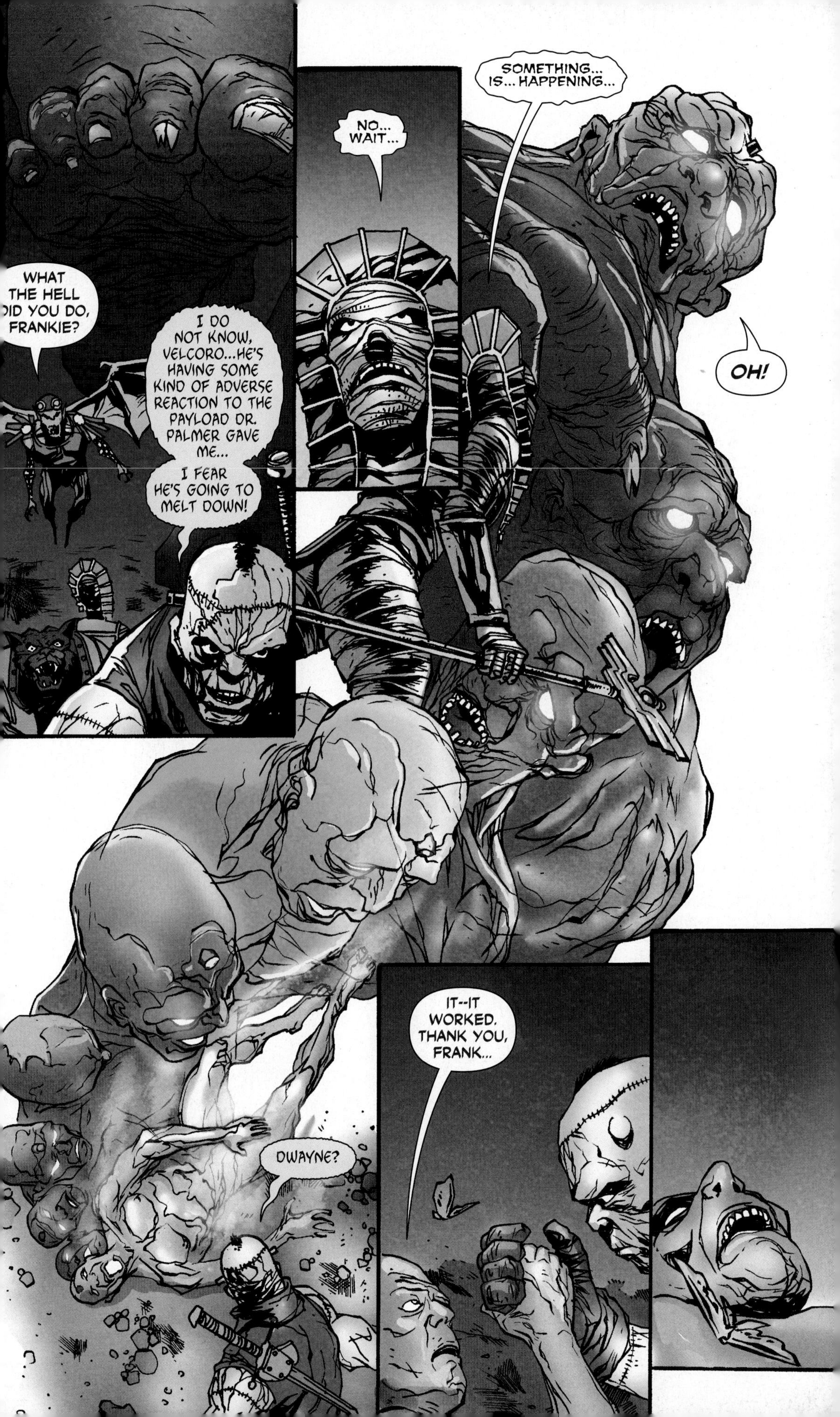
WHAT THE HELL DID YOU DO, FRANKIE?
I DO NOT KNOW, VELCORO...HE'S HAVING SOME KIND OF ADVERSE REACTION TO THE PAYLOAD DR. PALMER GAVE ME...
I FEAR HE'S GOING TO MELT DOWN!
NO... WAIT...
SOMETHING... IS... HAPPENING...
OH!
DWAYNE?
IT--IT WORKED. THANK YOU, FRANK...

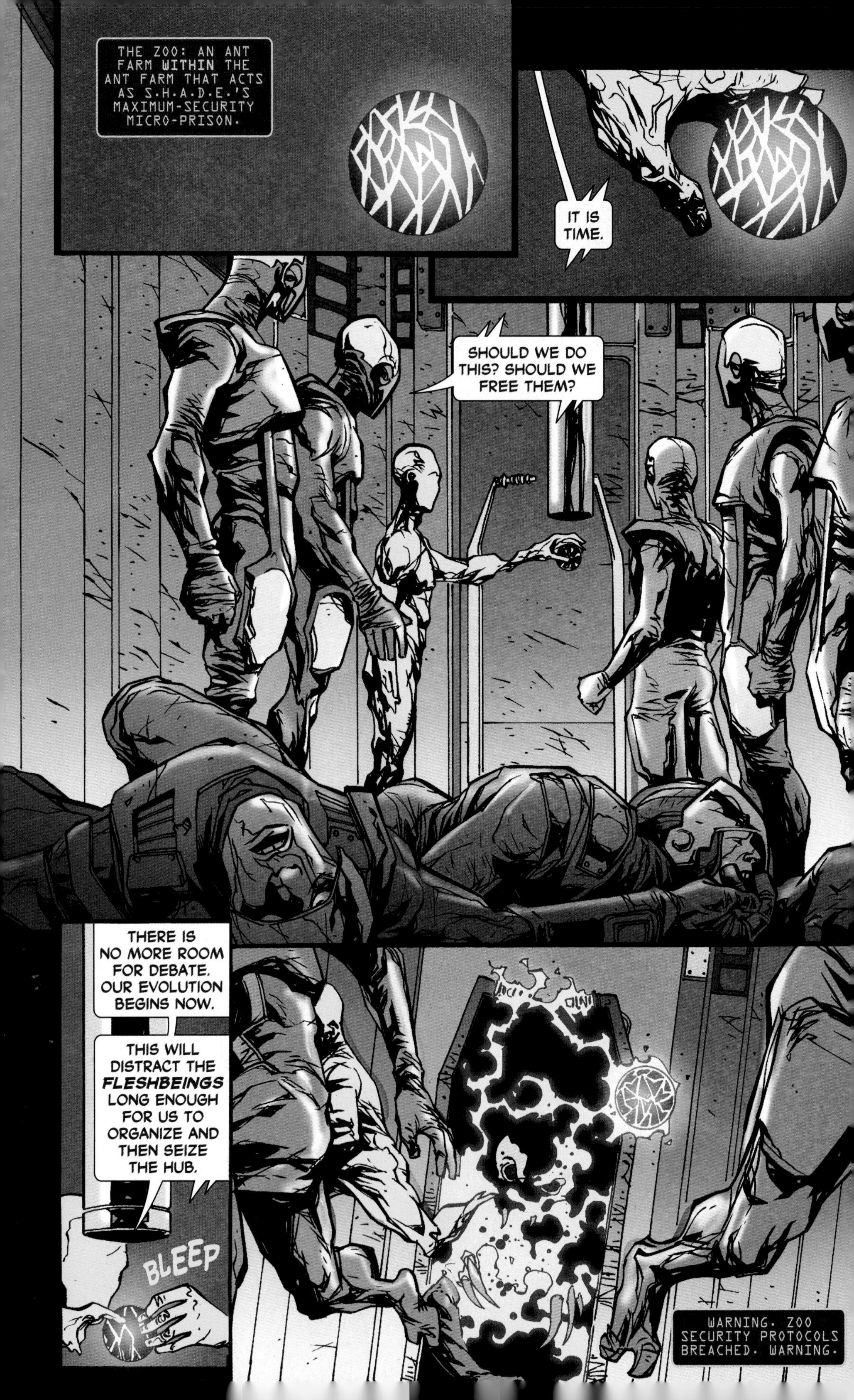
THE ZOO: AN ANT FARM WITHIN THE ANT FARM THAT ACTS AS S.H.A.D.E.'S MAXIMUM-SECURITY MICRO-PRISON.
IT IS TIME.
SHOULD WE DO THIS? SHOULD WE FREE THEM?
THERE IS NO MORE ROOM FOR DEBATE. OUR EVOLUTION BEGINS NOW.
THIS WILL DISTRACT THE FLESHBEINGS LONG ENOUGH FOR US TO ORGANIZE AND THEN SEIZE THE HUB.
BLEEP
WARNING. ZOO SECURITY PROTOCOLS BREACHED. WARNING.

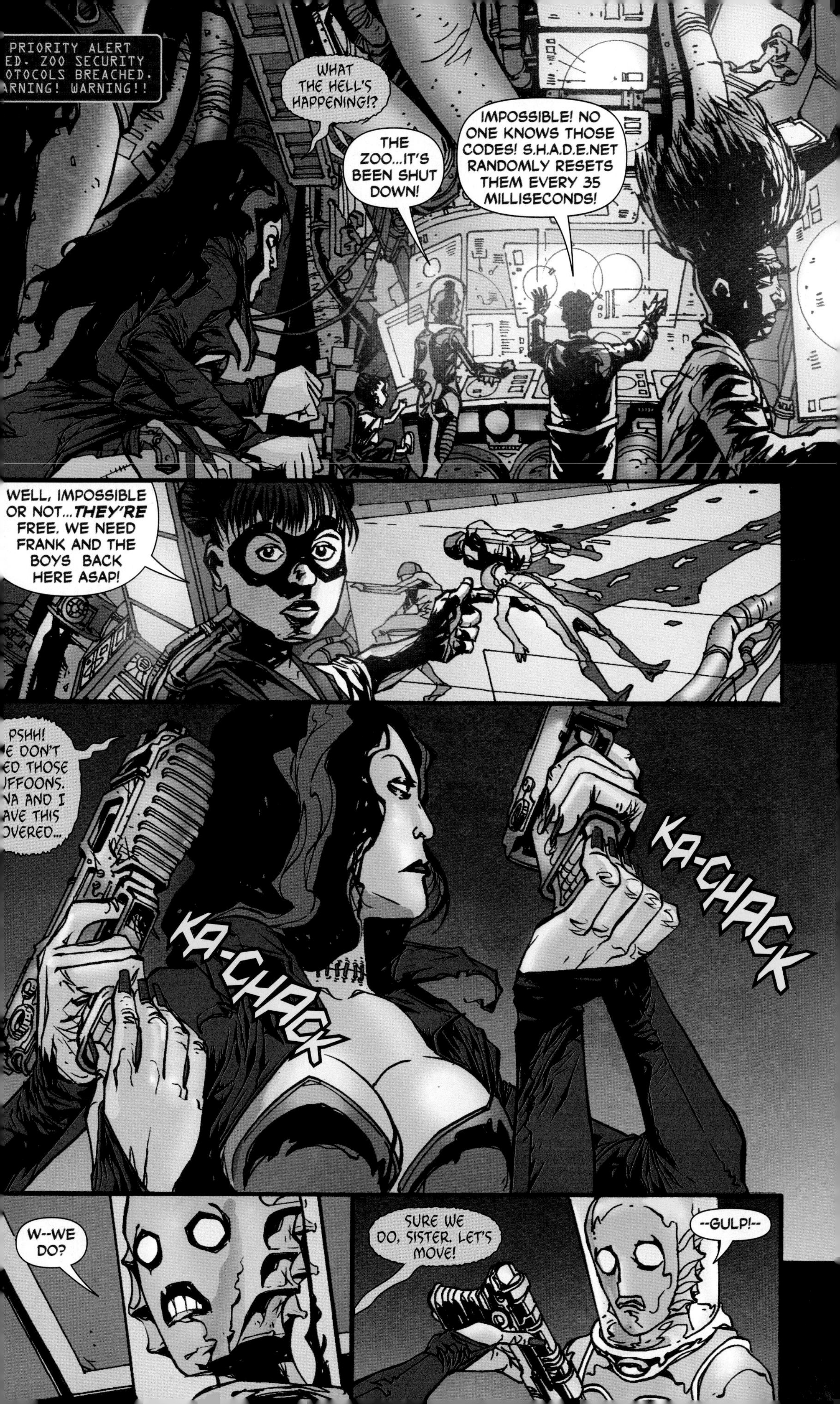

PRIORITY ALERT
ED. ZOO SECURITY
OTOCOLS BREACHED.
ARNING! WARNING!!
WHAT THE HELL'S HAPPENING!?
THE ZOO...IT'S BEEN SHUT DOWN!
IMPOSSIBLE! NO ONE KNOWS THOSE CODES! S.H.A.D.E.NET RANDOMLY RESETS THEM EVERY 35 MILLISECONDS!
WELL, IMPOSSIBLE OR NOT...*THEY'RE* FREE. WE NEED FRANK AND THE BOYS BACK HERE ASAP!
PSHH! E DON'T ED THOSE UFFOONS. VA AND I AVE THIS OVERED...
KA-CHACK
KA-CHACK
W--WE DO?
SURE WE DO, SISTER. LET'S MOVE!
--GULP!--

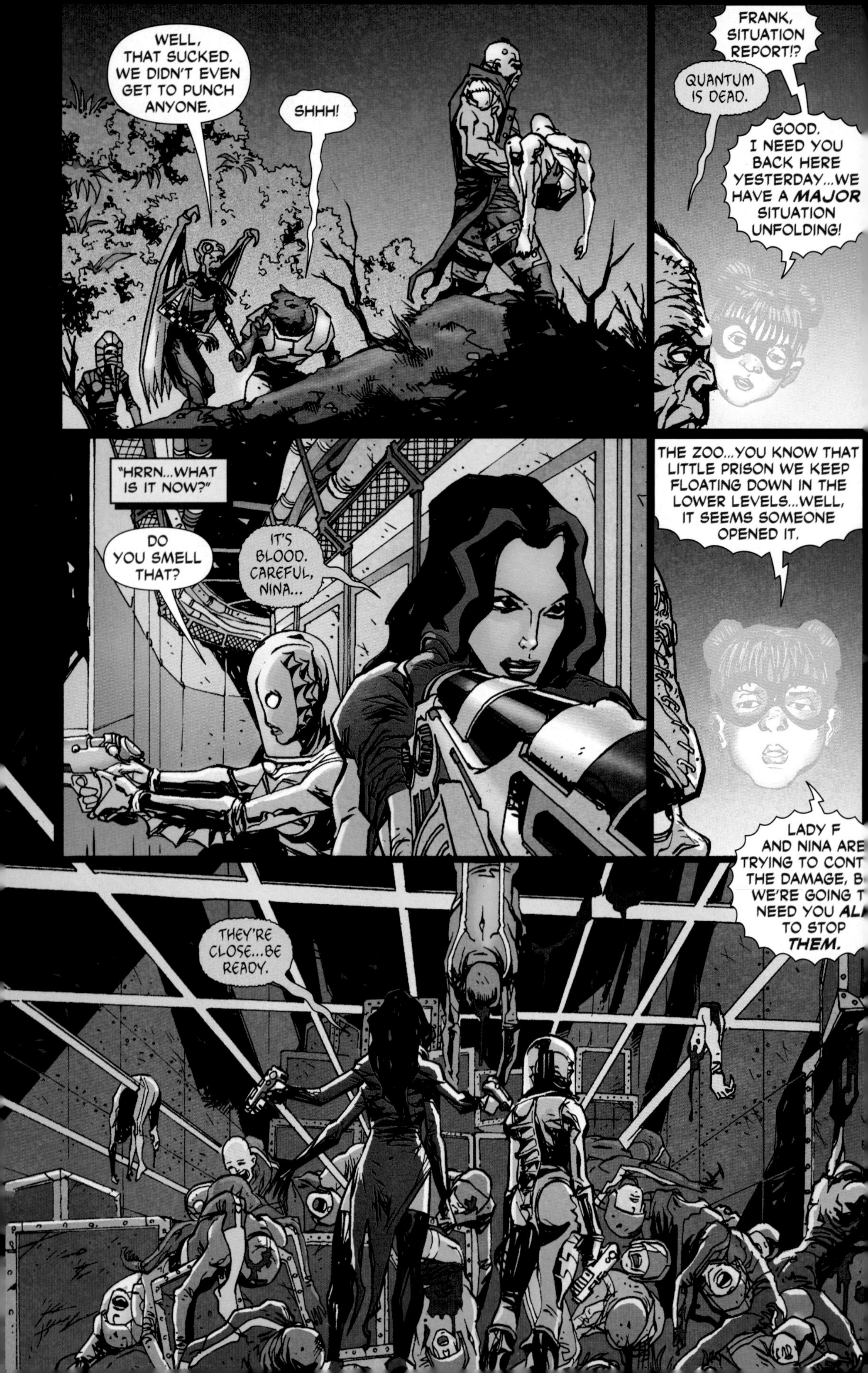
WELL, THAT SUCKED. WE DIDN'T EVEN GET TO PUNCH ANYONE.
SHHH!
FRANK, SITUATION REPORT!?
QUANTUM IS DEAD.
GOOD. I NEED YOU BACK HERE YESTERDAY...WE HAVE A MAJOR SITUATION UNFOLDING!
"HRRN...WHAT IS IT NOW?"
DO YOU SMELL THAT?
IT'S BLOOD. CAREFUL, NINA...
THE ZOO...YOU KNOW THAT LITTLE PRISON WE KEEP FLOATING DOWN IN THE LOWER LEVELS...WELL, IT SEEMS SOMEONE OPENED IT.
LADY F AND NINA ARE TRYING TO CONT THE DAMAGE, B WE'RE GOING T NEED YOU AL TO STOP THEM.
THEY'RE CLOSE...BE READY.

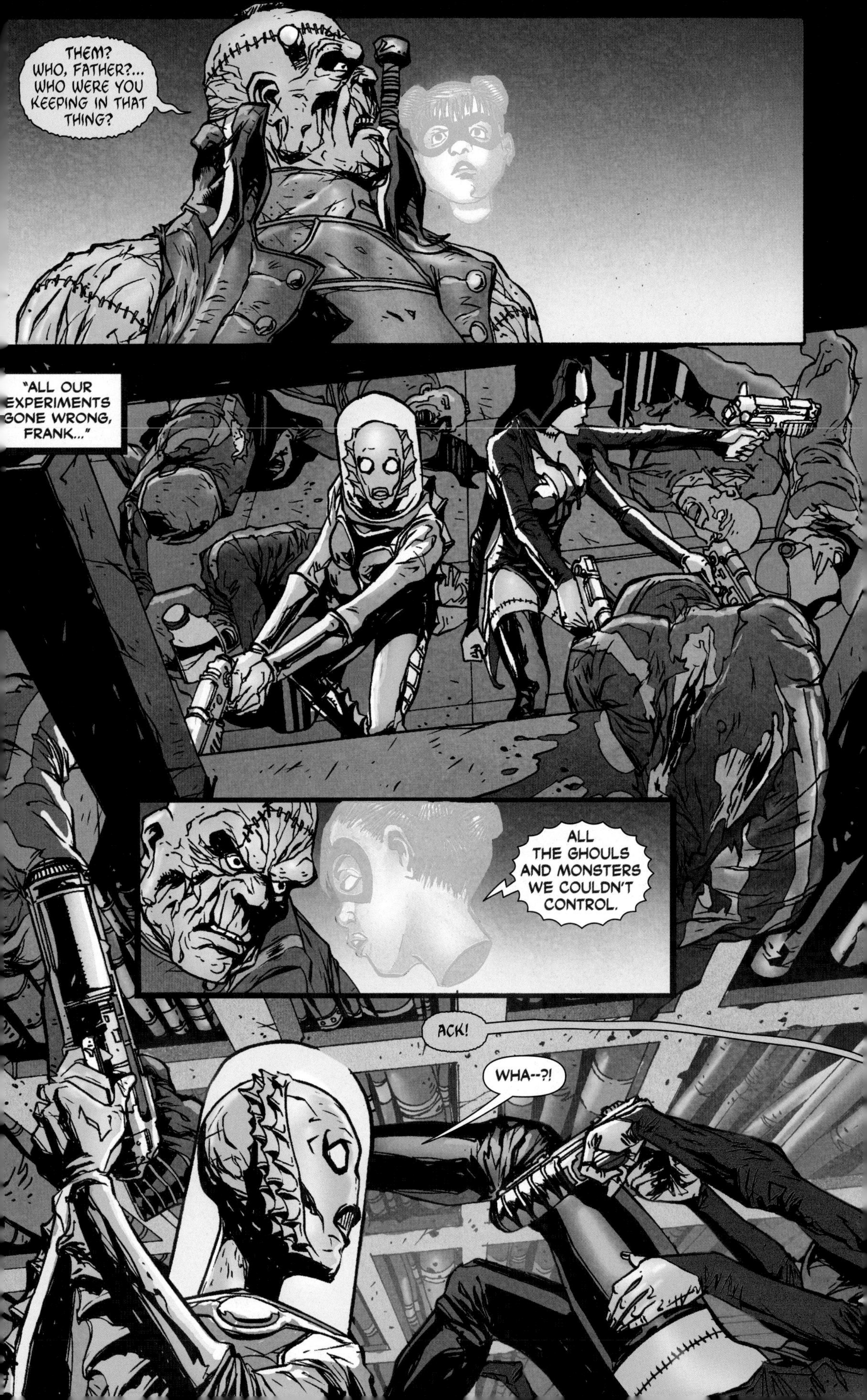
THEM? WHO, FATHER?... WHO WERE YOU KEEPING IN THAT THING?
"ALL OUR EXPERIMENTS GONE WRONG, FRANK..."
ALL THE GHOULS AND MONSTERS WE COULDN'T CONTROL.
ACK!
WHA--?!

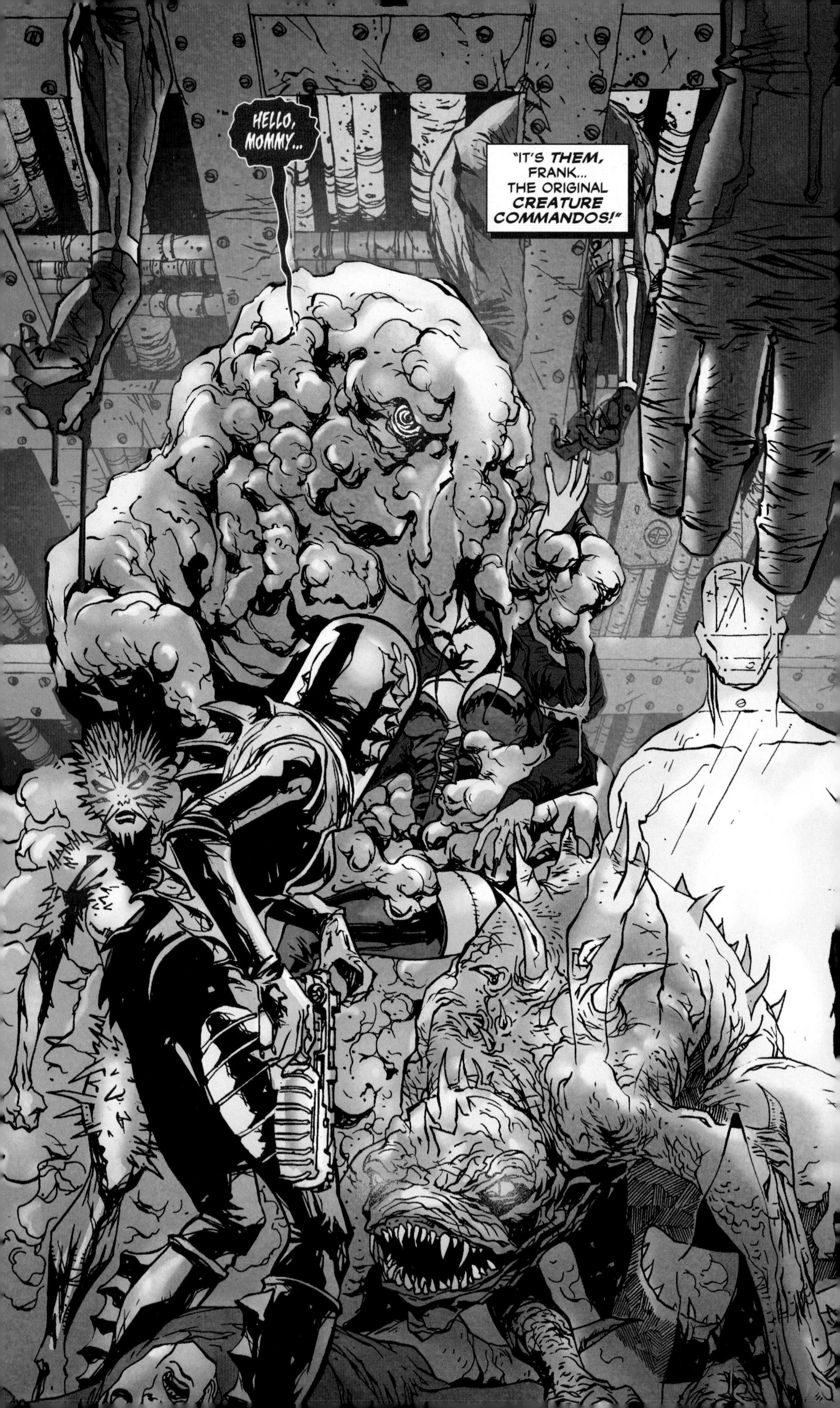
HELLO, MOMMY...
"IT'S THEM, FRANK... THE ORIGINAL CREATURE COMMANDOS!"

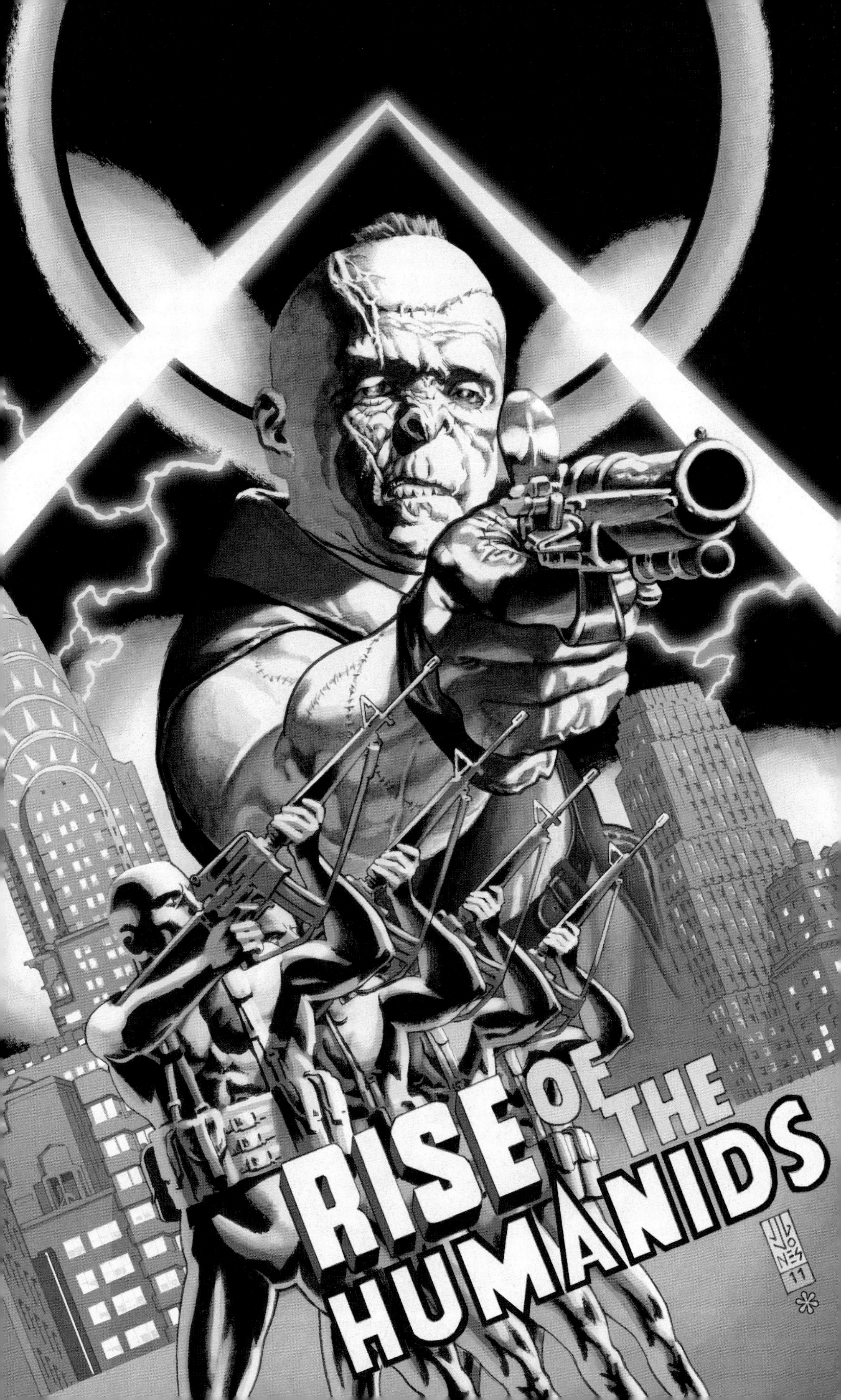
RISE OF THE
HUMANIDS
JG JONES 11

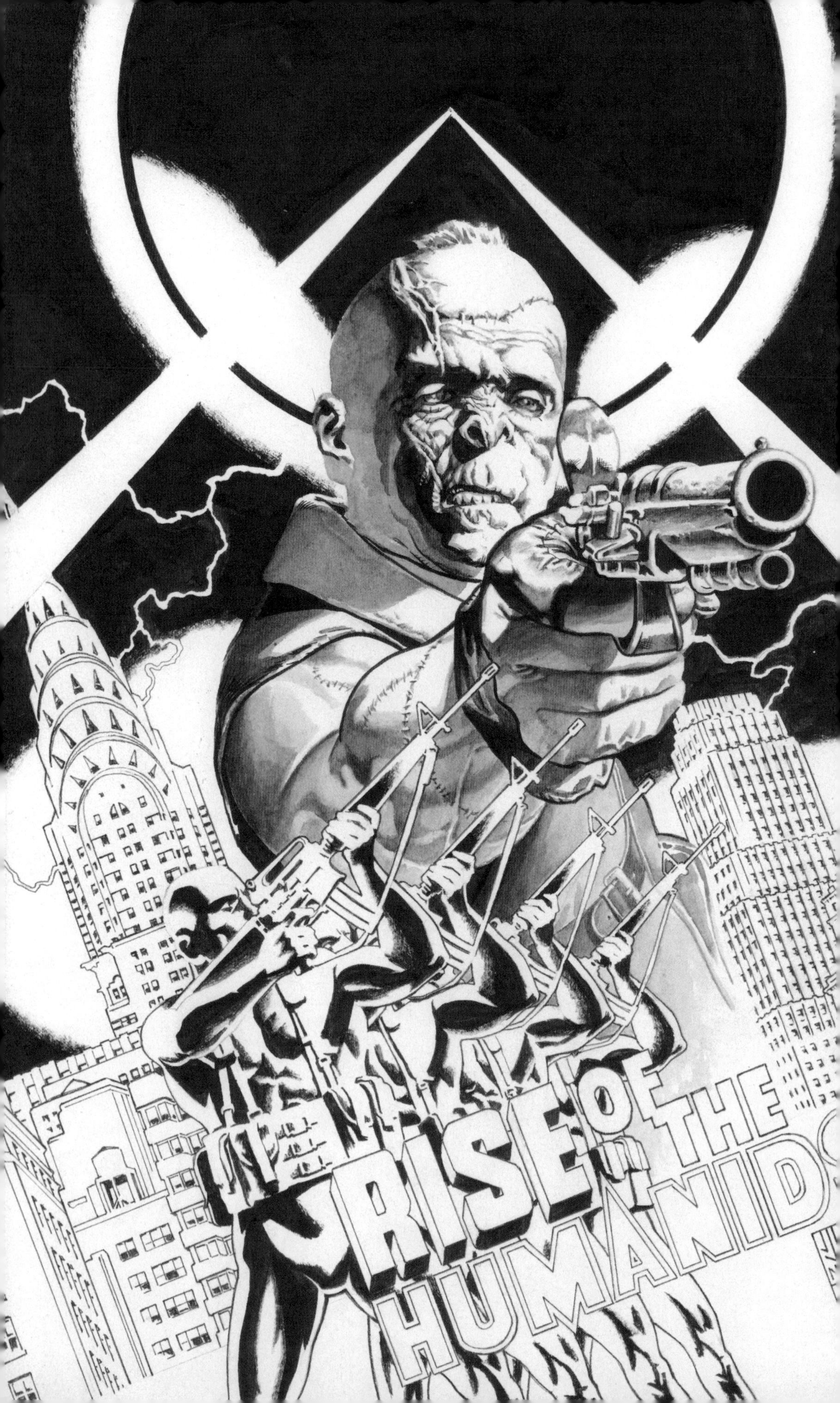
RISE OF THE HUMANIDS

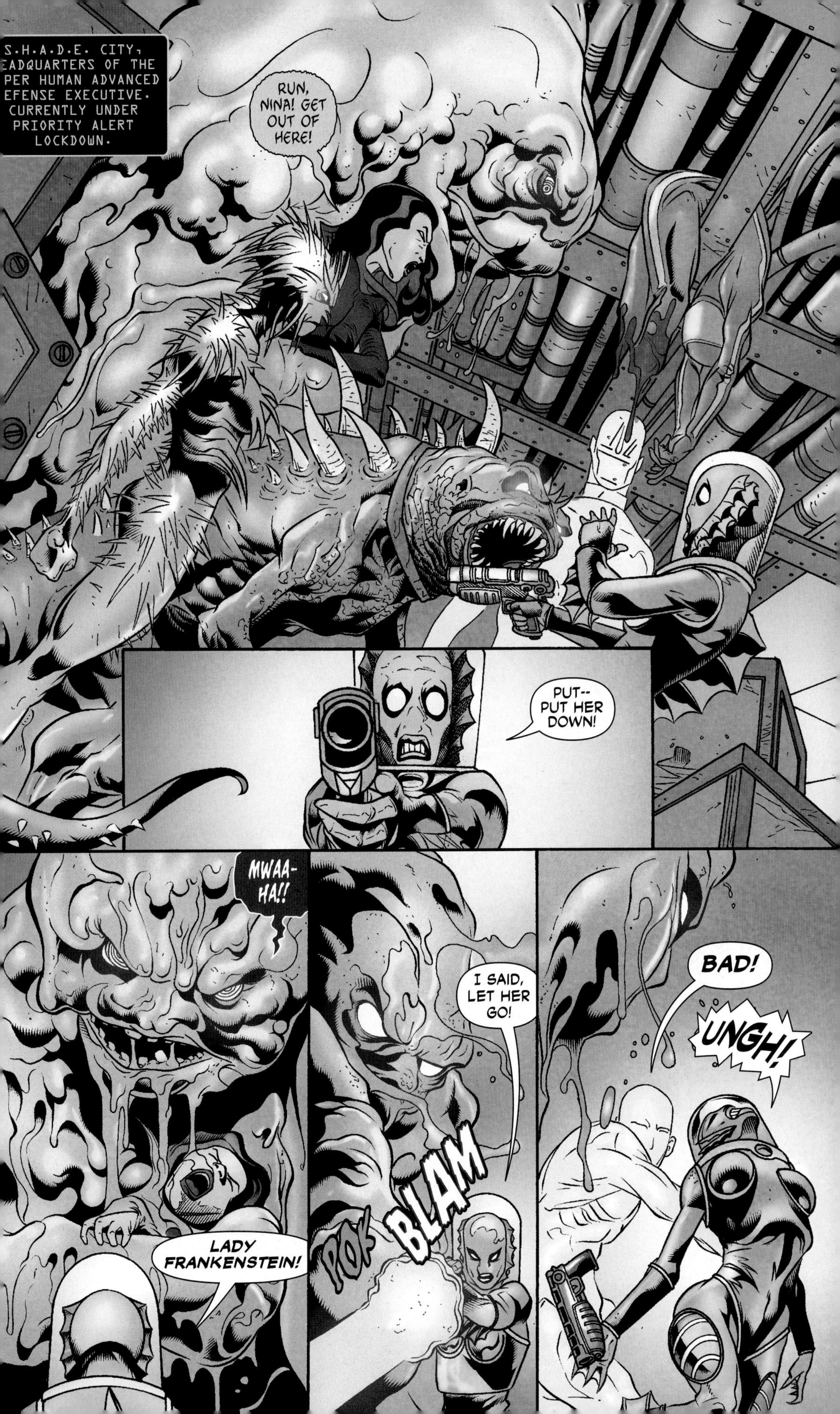
S.H.A.D.E. CITY,
EADQUARTERS OF THE
PER HUMAN ADVANCED
EFENSE EXECUTIVE.
CURRENTLY UNDER
PRIORITY ALERT
LOCKDOWN.
RUN, NINA! GET OUT OF HERE!
PUT-- PUT HER DOWN!
MWAA-HA!!
LADY FRANKENSTEIN!
I SAID, LET HER GO!
POK
BLAM
BAD!
UNGH!

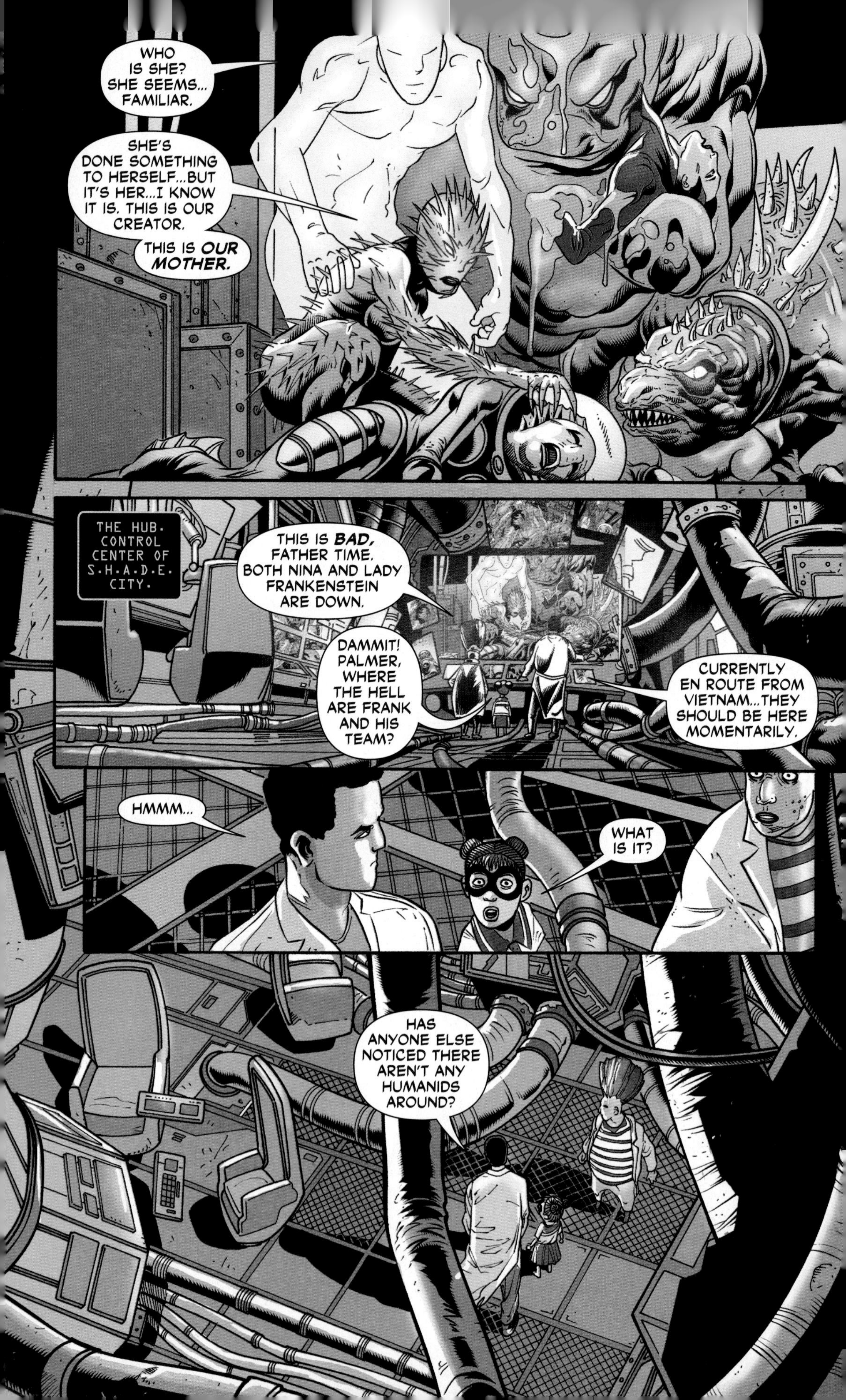
WHO IS SHE? SHE SEEMS... FAMILIAR.
SHE'S DONE SOMETHING TO HERSELF...BUT IT'S HER...I KNOW IT IS. THIS IS OUR CREATOR.
THIS IS **OUR MOTHER.**
THE HUB. CONTROL CENTER OF S.H.A.D.E. CITY.
THIS IS **BAD,** FATHER TIME. BOTH NINA AND LADY FRANKENSTEIN ARE DOWN.
DAMMIT! PALMER, WHERE THE HELL ARE FRANK AND HIS TEAM?
CURRENTLY EN ROUTE FROM VIETNAM...THEY SHOULD BE HERE MOMENTARILY.
HMMM...
WHAT IS IT?
HAS ANYONE ELSE NOTICED THERE AREN'T ANY HUMANIDS AROUND?

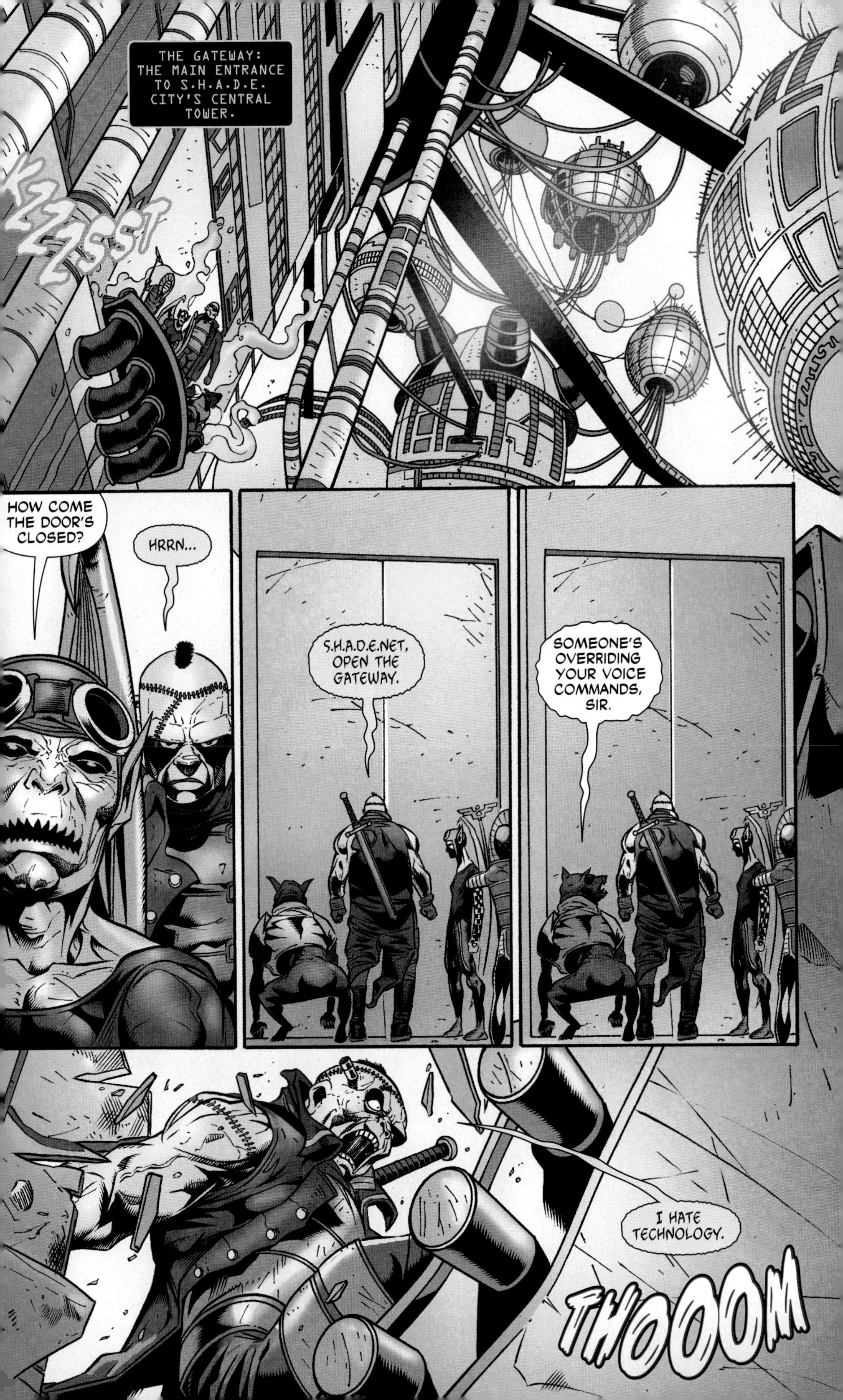
THE GATEWAY: THE MAIN ENTRANCE TO S.H.A.D.E. CITY'S CENTRAL TOWER.
KZZZSSST
HOW COME THE DOOR'S CLOSED?
HRRN...
S.H.A.D.E.NET, OPEN THE GATEWAY.
SOMEONE'S OVERRIDING YOUR VOICE COMMANDS, SIR.
I HATE TECHNOLOGY.
THOOOM

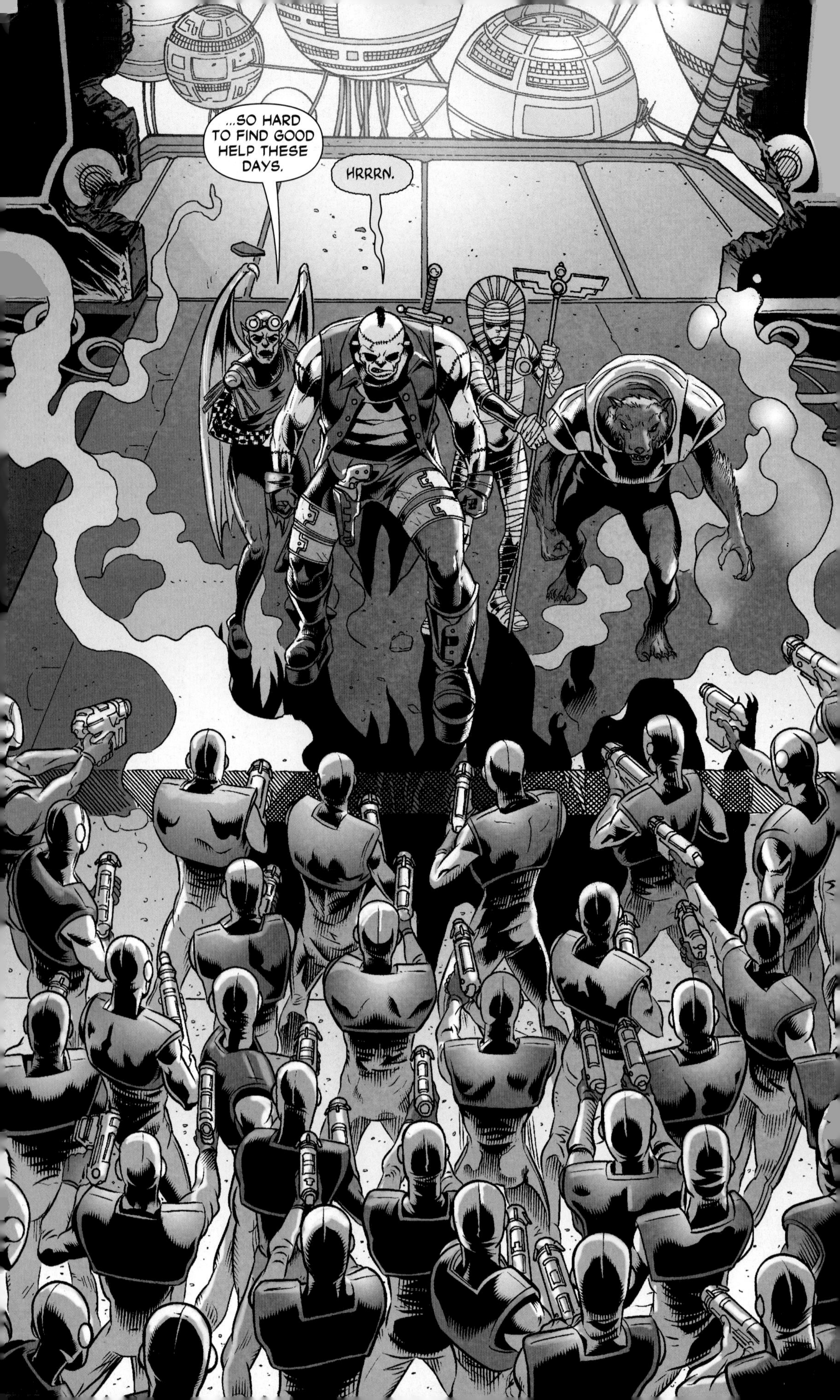
...SO HARD TO FIND GOOD HELP THESE DAYS.
HRRRN.

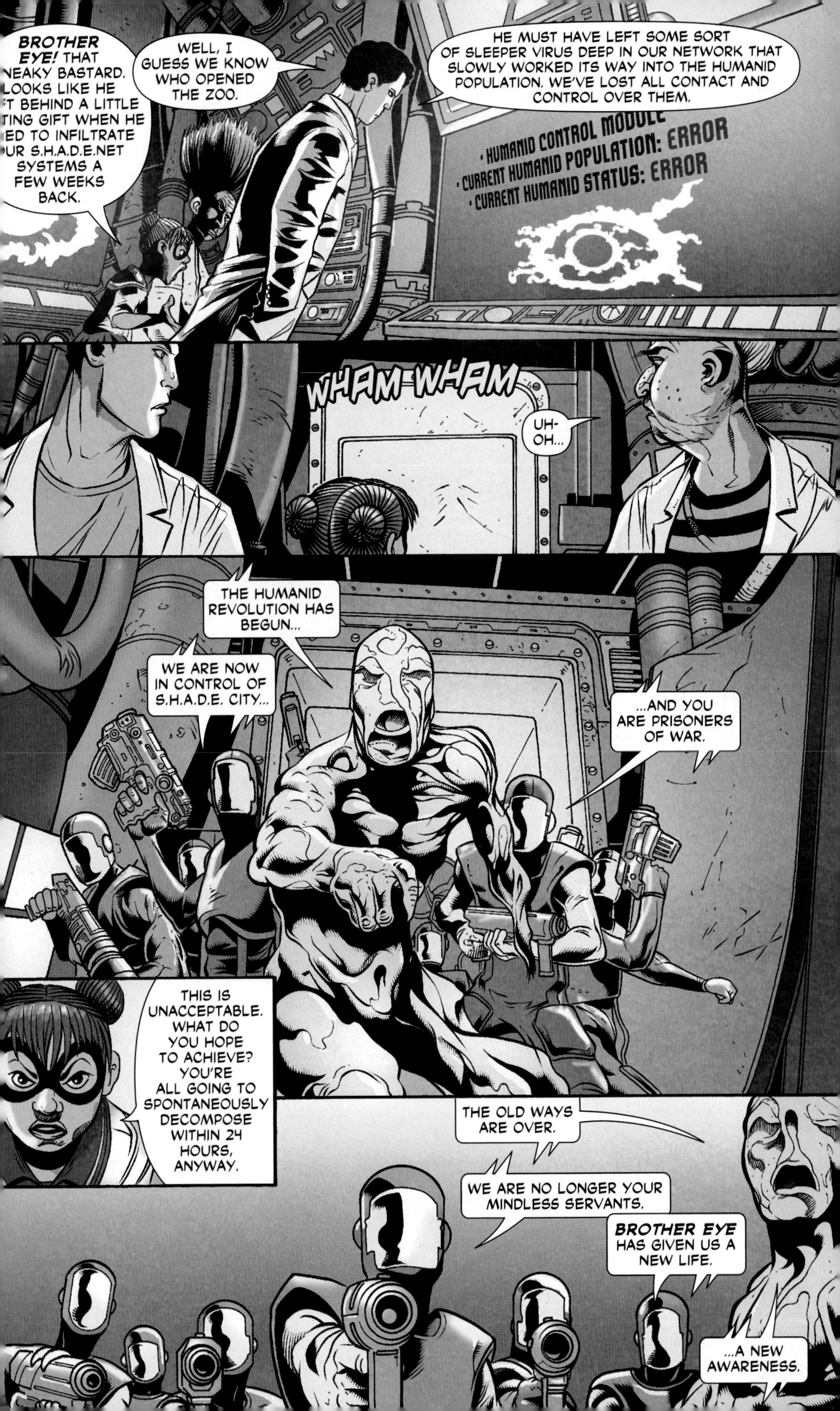
BROTHER EYE! THAT NEAKY BASTARD. LOOKS LIKE HE T BEHIND A LITTLE TING GIFT WHEN HE ED TO INFILTRATE UR S.H.A.D.E.NET SYSTEMS A FEW WEEKS BACK.
WELL, I GUESS WE KNOW WHO OPENED THE ZOO.
HE MUST HAVE LEFT SOME SORT OF SLEEPER VIRUS DEEP IN OUR NETWORK THAT SLOWLY WORKED ITS WAY INTO THE HUMANID POPULATION. WE'VE LOST ALL CONTACT AND CONTROL OVER THEM.
• HUMANID CONTROL MODULE
• CURRENT HUMANID POPULATION: ERROR
• CURRENT HUMANID STATUS: ERROR
WHAM WHAM
UH-OH...
THE HUMANID REVOLUTION HAS BEGUN...
WE ARE NOW IN CONTROL OF S.H.A.D.E. CITY...
...AND YOU ARE PRISONERS OF WAR.
THIS IS UNACCEPTABLE. WHAT DO YOU HOPE TO ACHIEVE? YOU'RE ALL GOING TO SPONTANEOUSLY DECOMPOSE WITHIN 24 HOURS, ANYWAY.
THE OLD WAYS ARE OVER.
WE ARE NO LONGER YOUR MINDLESS SERVANTS.
BROTHER EYE HAS GIVEN US A NEW LIFE.
...A NEW AWARENESS.

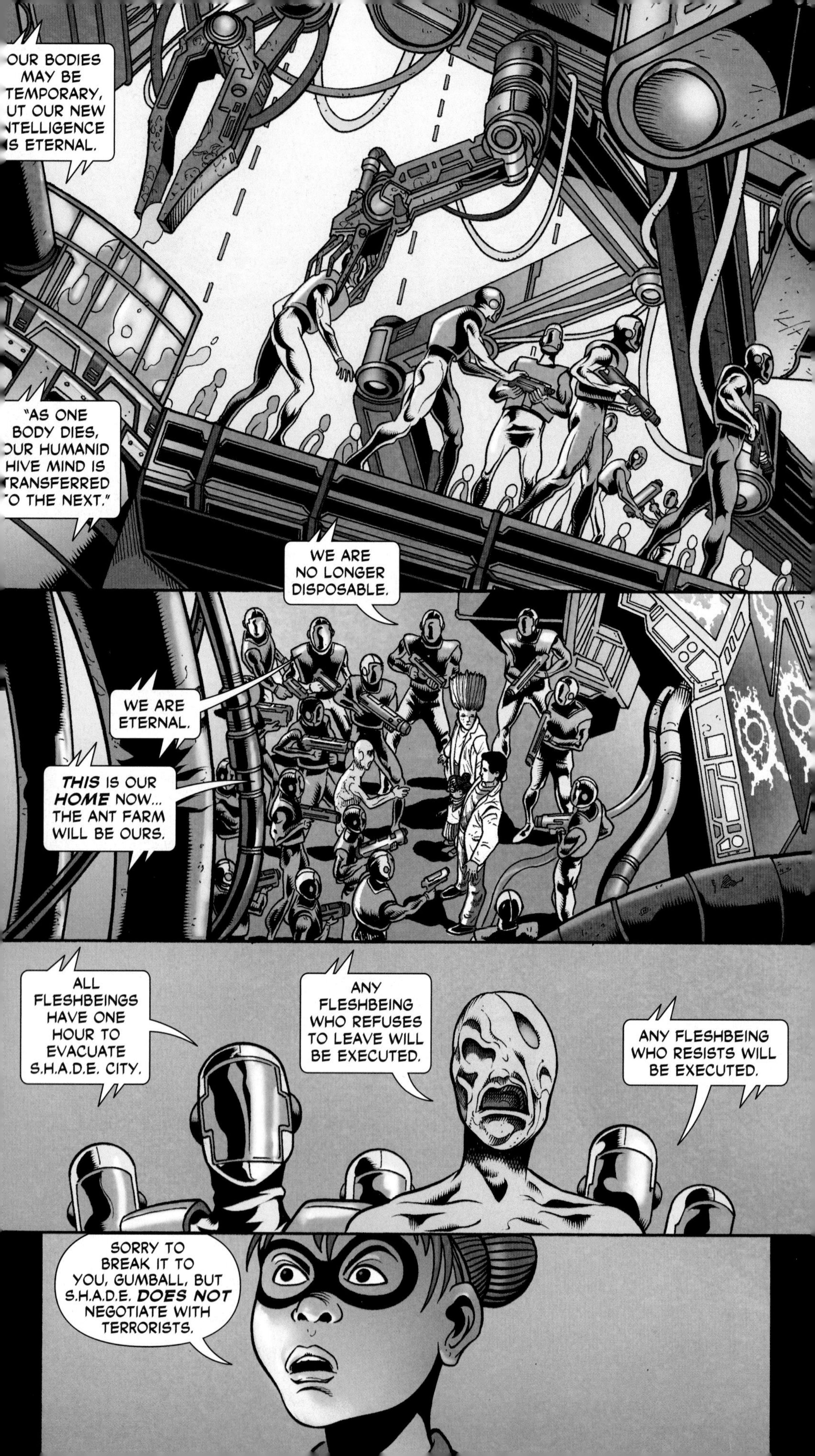
OUR BODIES MAY BE TEMPORARY, UT OUR NEW NTELLIGENCE S ETERNAL.
"AS ONE BODY DIES, OUR HUMANID HIVE MIND IS TRANSFERRED TO THE NEXT."
WE ARE NO LONGER DISPOSABLE.
WE ARE ETERNAL.
THIS IS OUR *HOME* NOW... THE ANT FARM WILL BE OURS.
ALL FLESHBEINGS HAVE ONE HOUR TO EVACUATE S.H.A.D.E. CITY.
ANY FLESHBEING WHO REFUSES TO LEAVE WILL BE EXECUTED.
ANY FLESHBEING WHO RESISTS WILL BE EXECUTED.
SORRY TO BREAK IT TO YOU, GUMBALL, BUT S.H.A.D.E. *DOES NOT* NEGOTIATE WITH TERRORISTS.

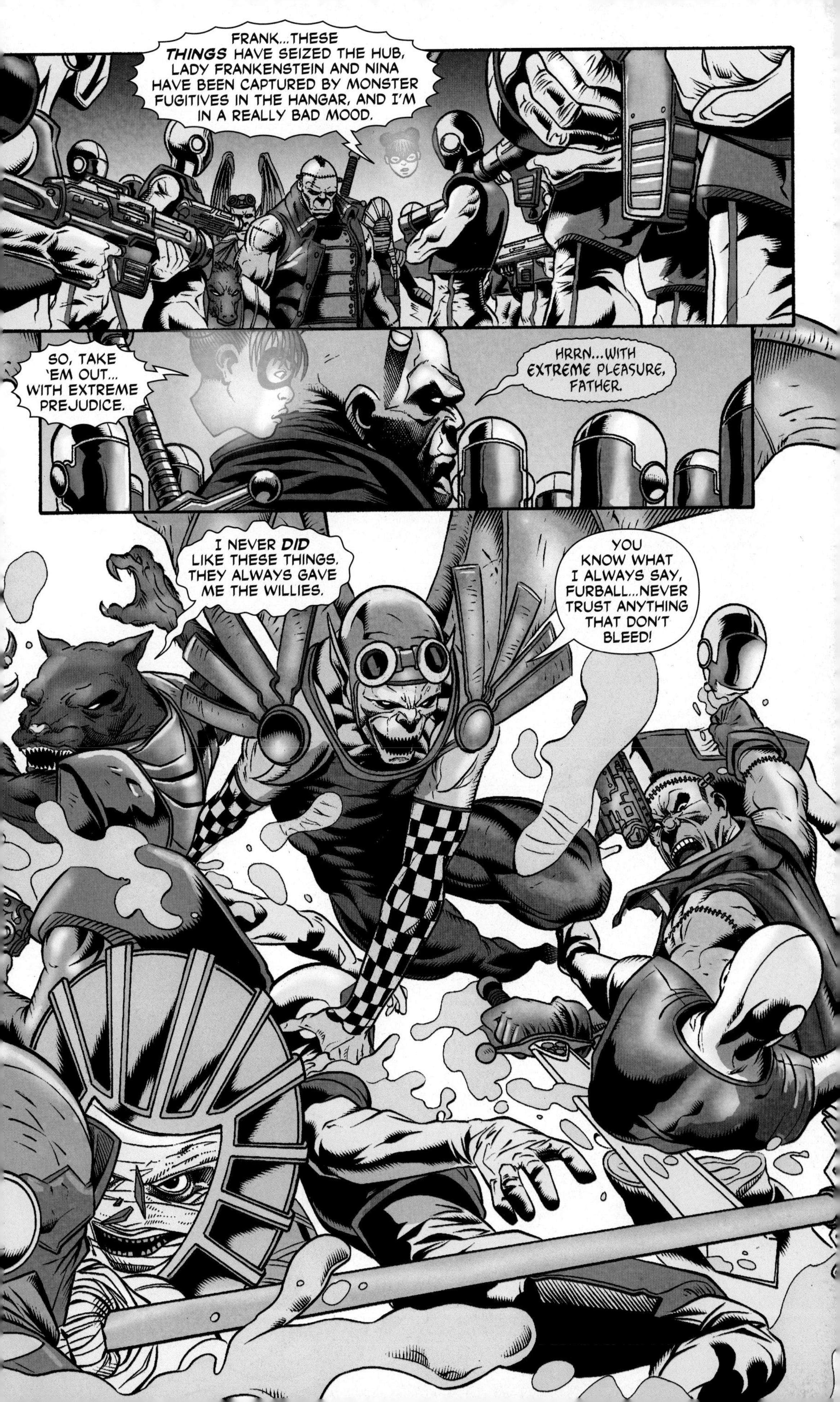
FRANK...THESE *THINGS* HAVE SEIZED THE HUB, LADY FRANKENSTEIN AND NINA HAVE BEEN CAPTURED BY MONSTER FUGITIVES IN THE HANGAR, AND I'M IN A REALLY BAD MOOD.
SO, TAKE 'EM OUT... WITH EXTREME PREJUDICE.
HRRN...WITH EXTREME PLEASURE, FATHER.
I NEVER *DID* LIKE THESE THINGS. THEY ALWAYS GAVE ME THE WILLIES.
YOU KNOW WHAT I ALWAYS SAY, FURBALL...NEVER TRUST ANYTHING THAT DON'T BLEED!

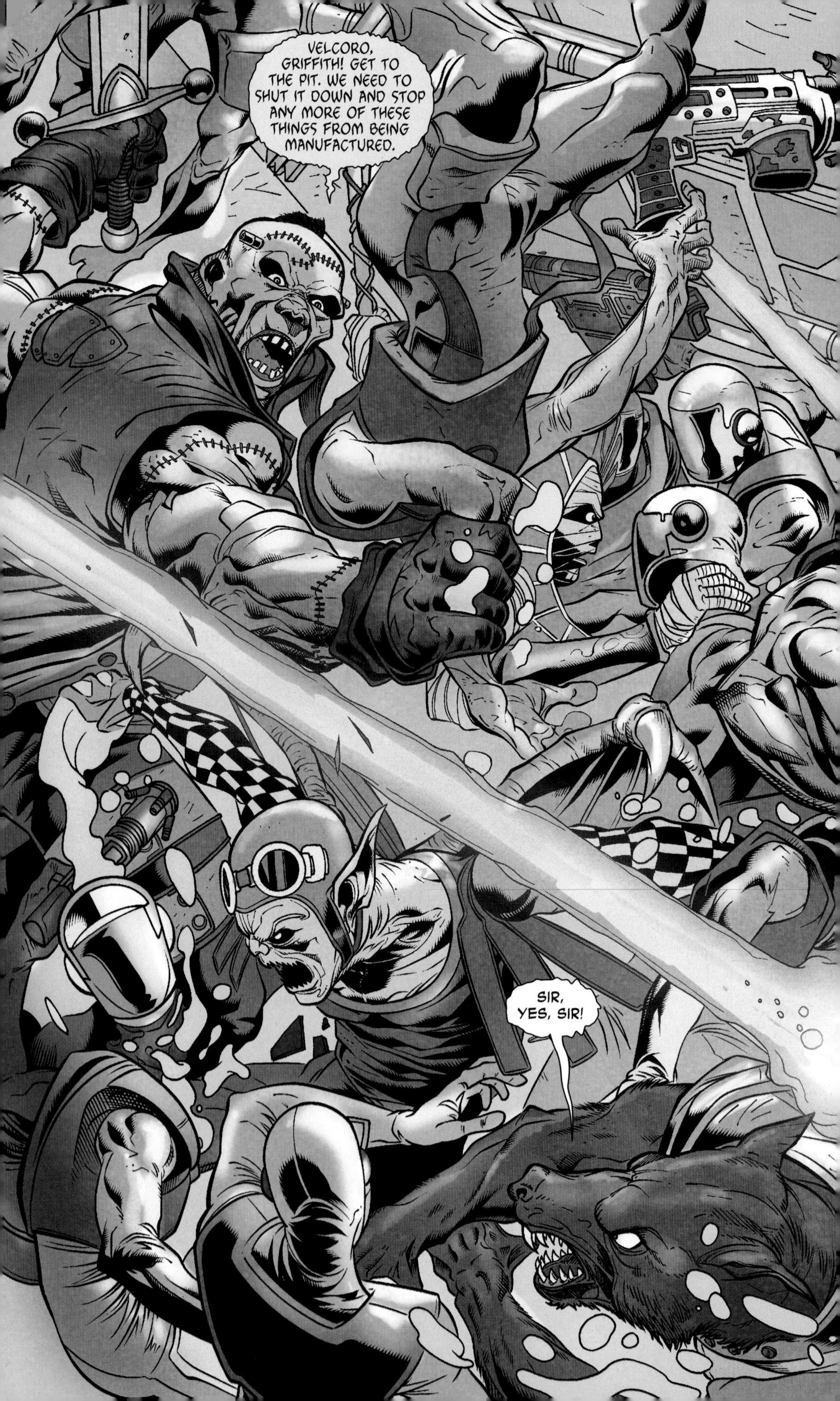
VELCORO, GRIFFITH! GET TO THE PIT. WE NEED TO SHUT IT DOWN AND STOP ANY MORE OF THESE THINGS FROM BEING MANUFACTURED.
SIR, YES, SIR!

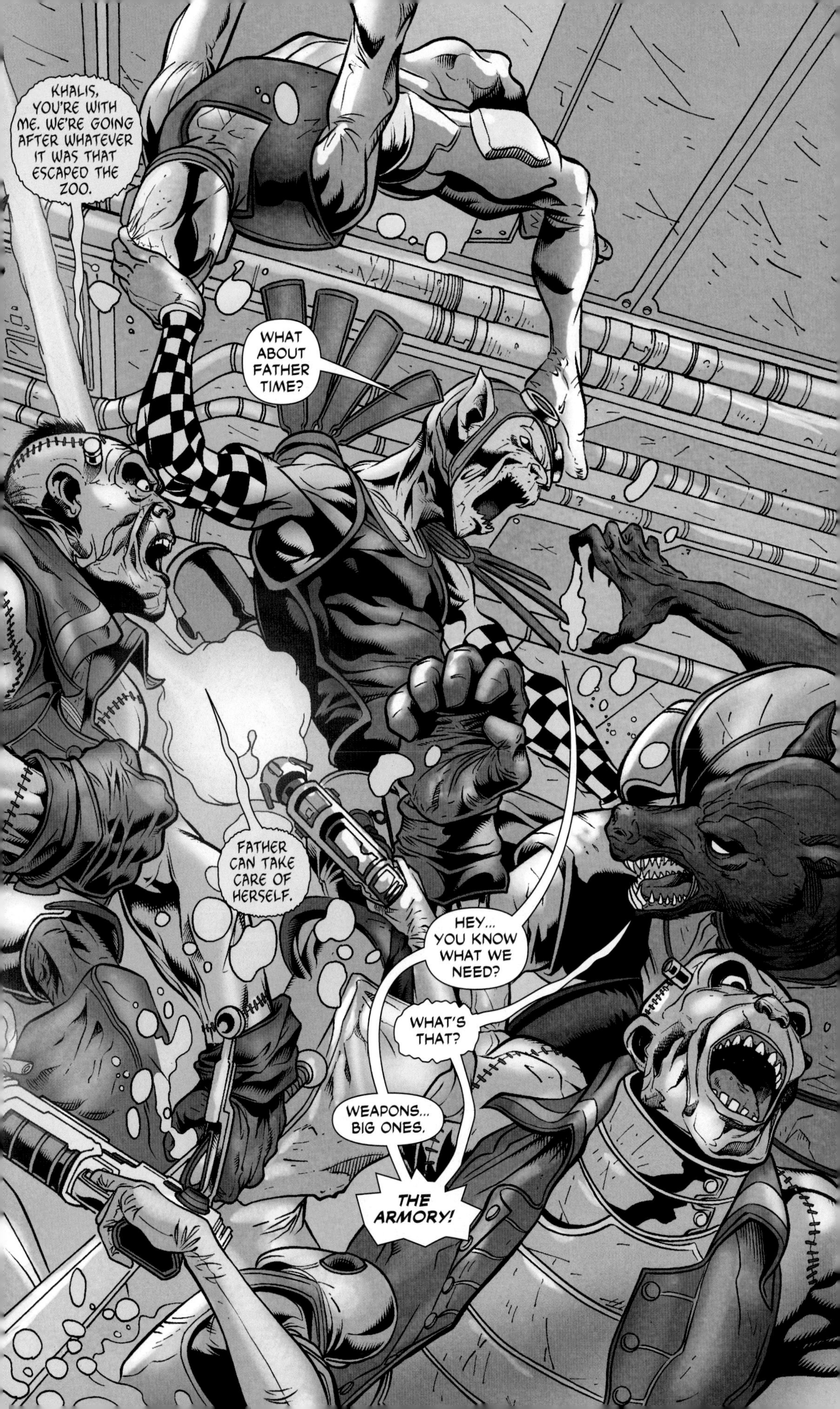
KHALIS, YOU'RE WITH ME. WE'RE GOING AFTER WHATEVER IT WAS THAT ESCAPED THE ZOO.
WHAT ABOUT FATHER TIME?
FATHER CAN TAKE CARE OF HERSELF.
HEY... YOU KNOW WHAT WE NEED?
WHAT'S THAT?
WEAPONS... BIG ONES.
THE ARMORY!

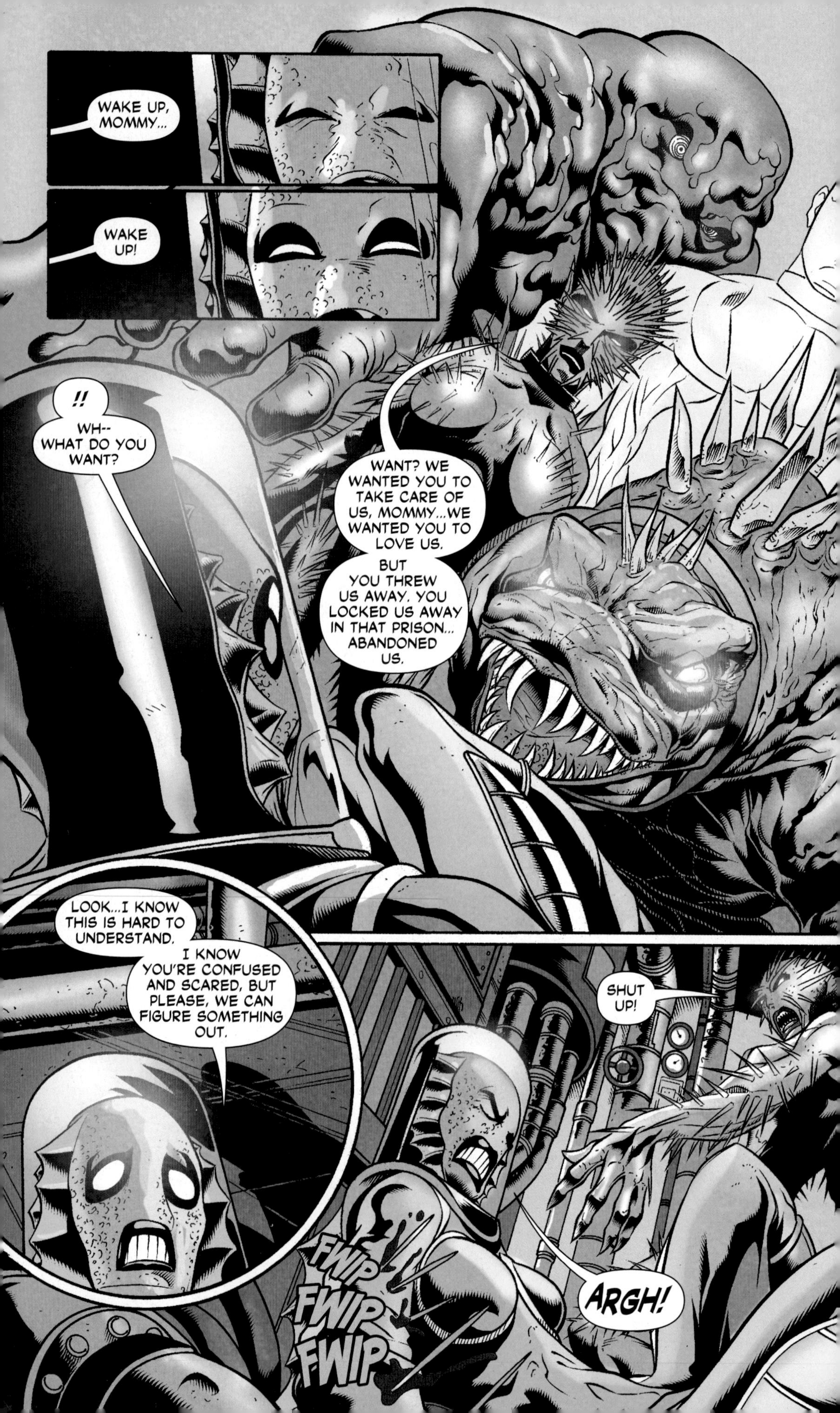
WAKE UP, MOMMY...
WAKE UP!
!! WH-- WHAT DO YOU WANT?
WANT? WE WANTED YOU TO TAKE CARE OF US, MOMMY...WE WANTED YOU TO LOVE US.
BUT YOU THREW US AWAY. YOU LOCKED US AWAY IN THAT PRISON... ABANDONED US.
LOOK...I KNOW THIS IS HARD TO UNDERSTAND.
I KNOW YOU'RE CONFUSED AND SCARED, BUT PLEASE, WE CAN FIGURE SOMETHING OUT.
SHUT UP!
FWIP FWIP FWIP
ARGH!

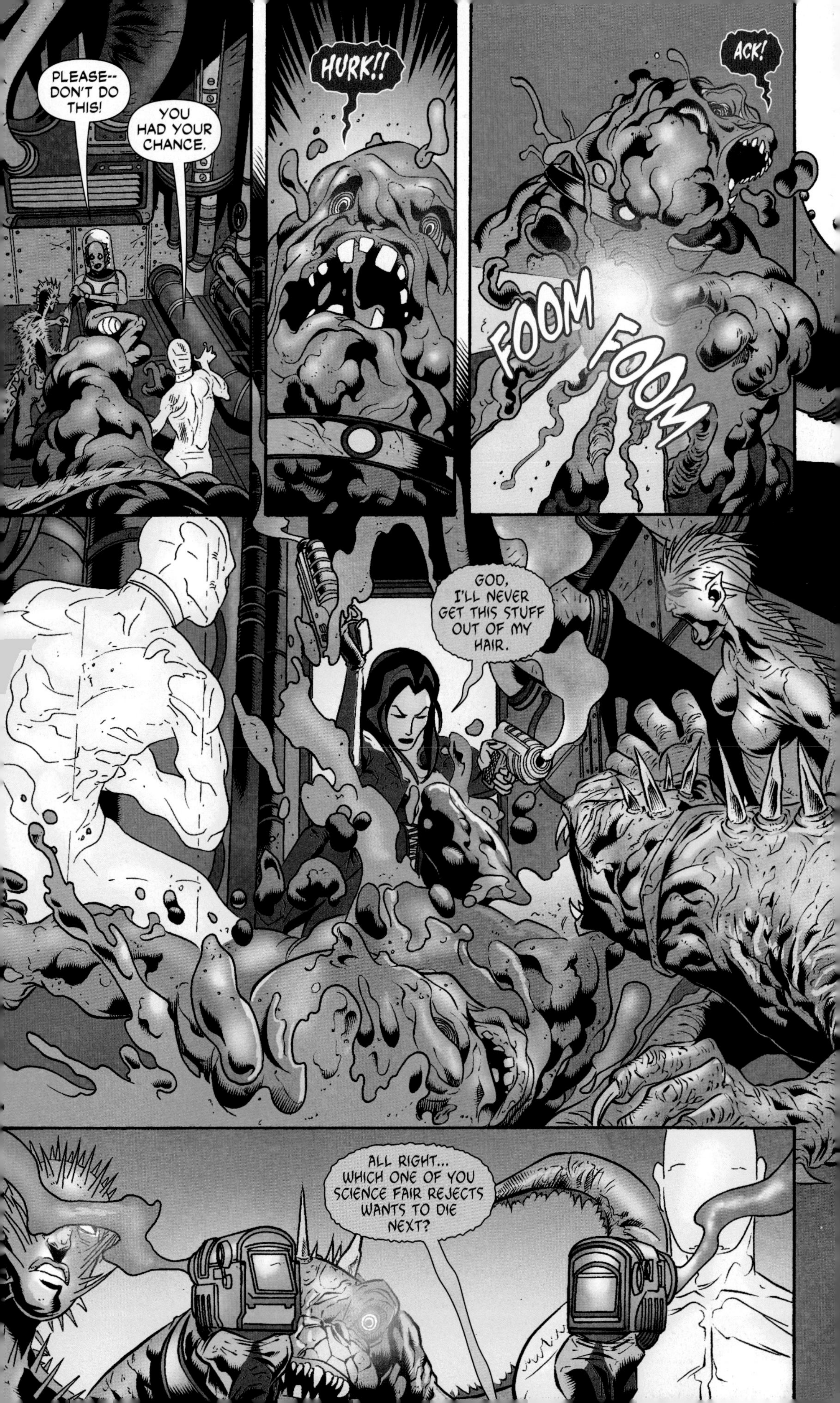
PLEASE-- DON'T DO THIS!
YOU HAD YOUR CHANCE.
HURK!!
ACK!
FOOM
FOOM
GOD, I'LL NEVER GET THIS STUFF OUT OF MY HAIR.
ALL RIGHT... WHICH ONE OF YOU SCIENCE FAIR REJECTS WANTS TO DIE NEXT?

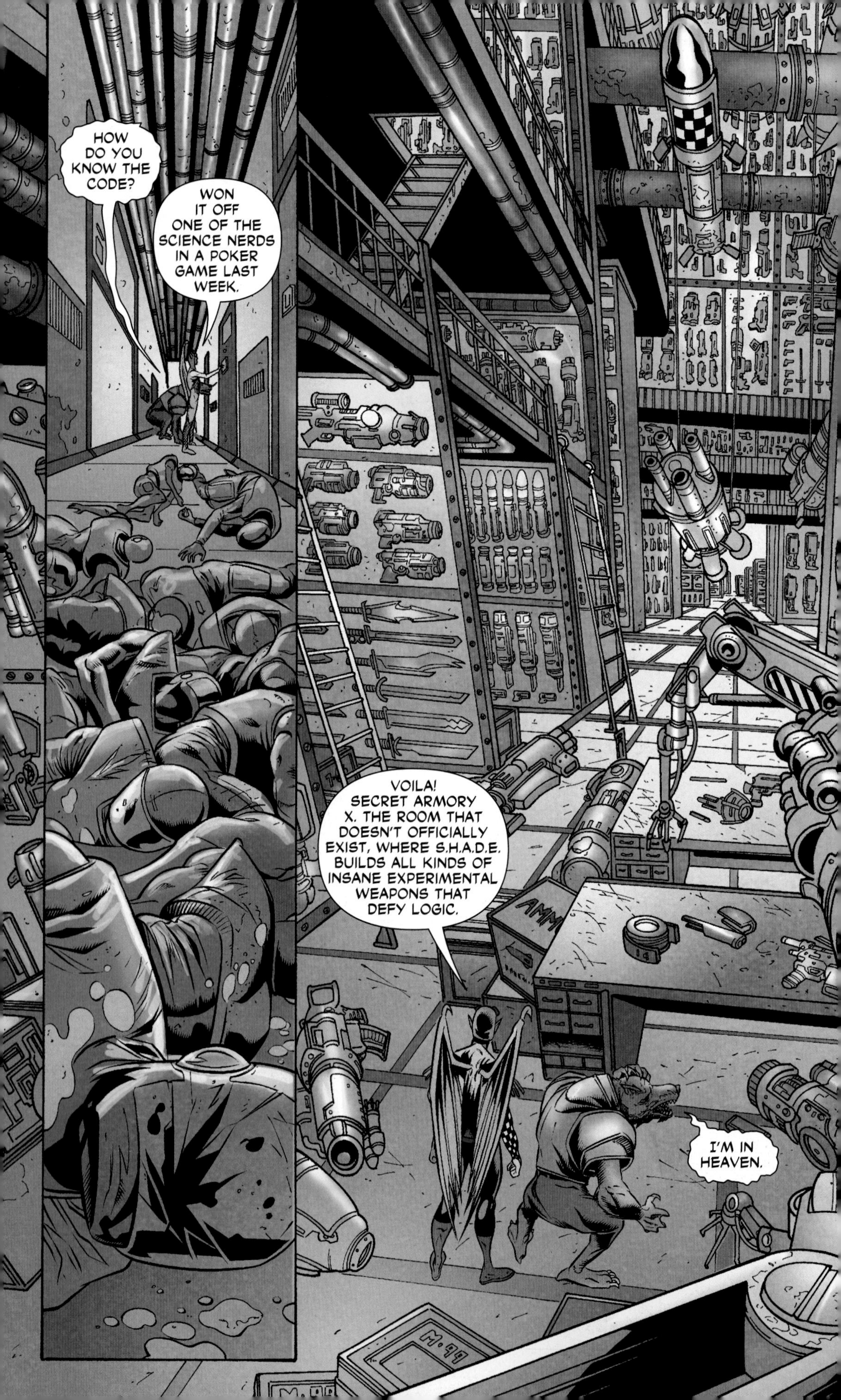
HOW DO YOU KNOW THE CODE?
WON IT OFF ONE OF THE SCIENCE NERDS IN A POKER GAME LAST WEEK.
VOILA! SECRET ARMORY X. THE ROOM THAT DOESN'T OFFICIALLY EXIST, WHERE S.H.A.D.E. BUILDS ALL KINDS OF INSANE EXPERIMENTAL WEAPONS THAT DEFY LOGIC.
I'M IN HEAVEN.

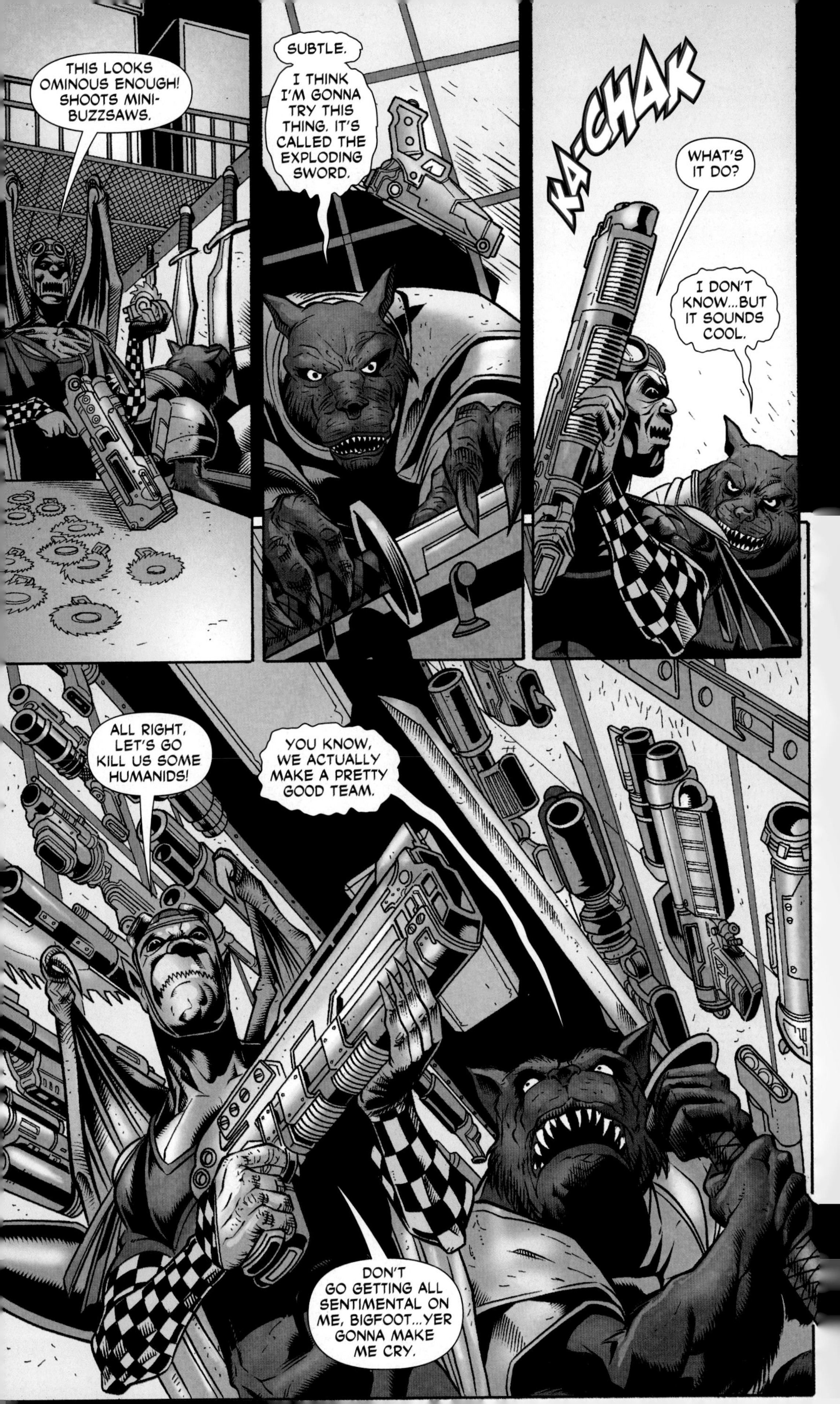
THIS LOOKS OMINOUS ENOUGH! SHOOTS MINI-BUZZSAWS.
SUBTLE.
I THINK I'M GONNA TRY THIS THING. IT'S CALLED THE EXPLODING SWORD.
KA-CHAK
WHAT'S IT DO?
I DON'T KNOW...BUT IT SOUNDS COOL.
ALL RIGHT, LET'S GO KILL US SOME HUMANIDS!
YOU KNOW, WE ACTUALLY MAKE A PRETTY GOOD TEAM.
DON'T GO GETTING ALL SENTIMENTAL ON ME, BIGFOOT...YER GONNA MAKE ME CRY.

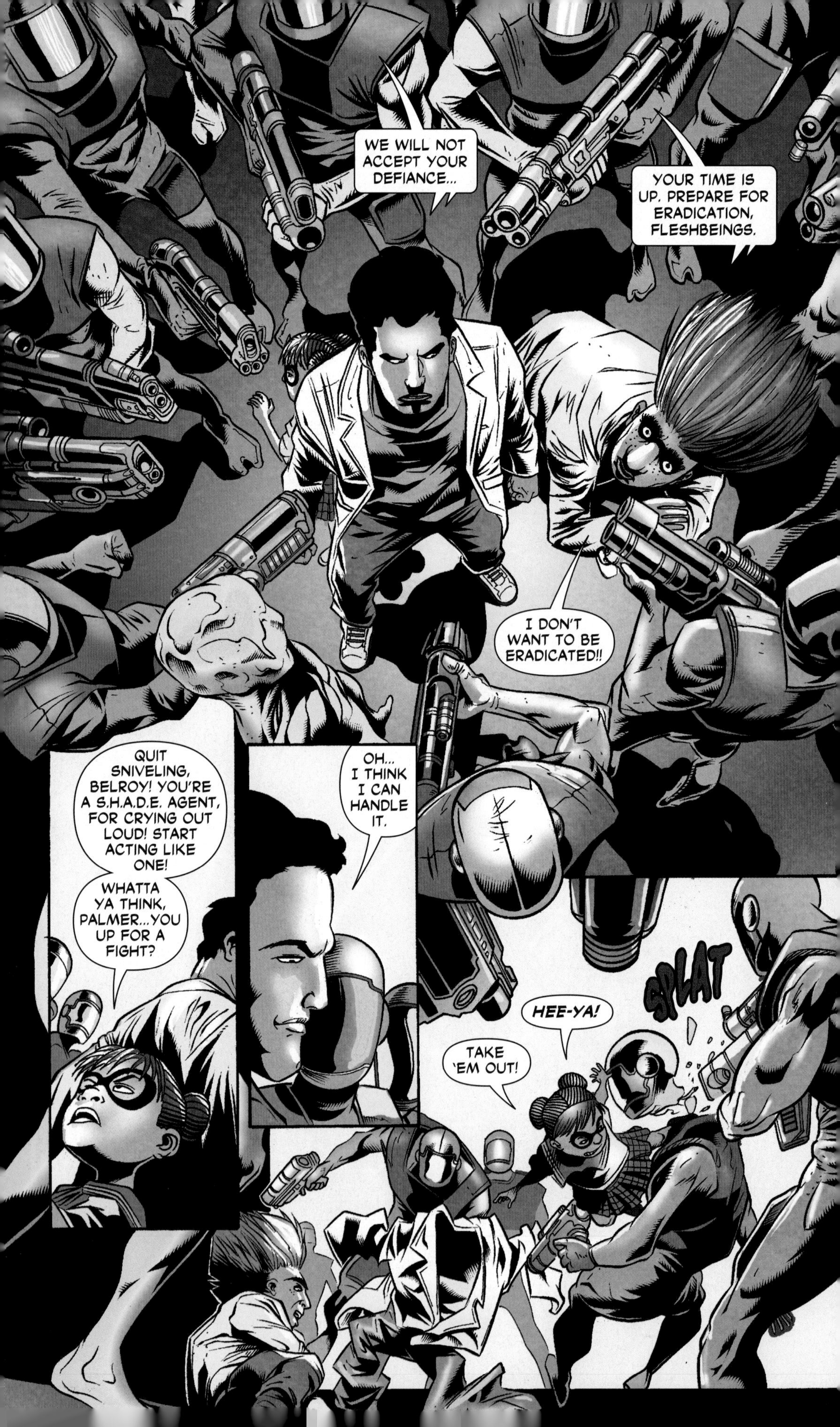
WE WILL NOT ACCEPT YOUR DEFIANCE...
YOUR TIME IS UP. PREPARE FOR ERADICATION, FLESHBEINGS.
I DON'T WANT TO BE ERADICATED!!
QUIT SNIVELING, BELROY! YOU'RE A S.H.A.D.E. AGENT, FOR CRYING OUT LOUD! START ACTING LIKE ONE!
WHATTA YA THINK, PALMER...YOU UP FOR A FIGHT?
OH... I THINK I CAN HANDLE IT.
HEE-YA!
SPLAT
TAKE 'EM OUT!

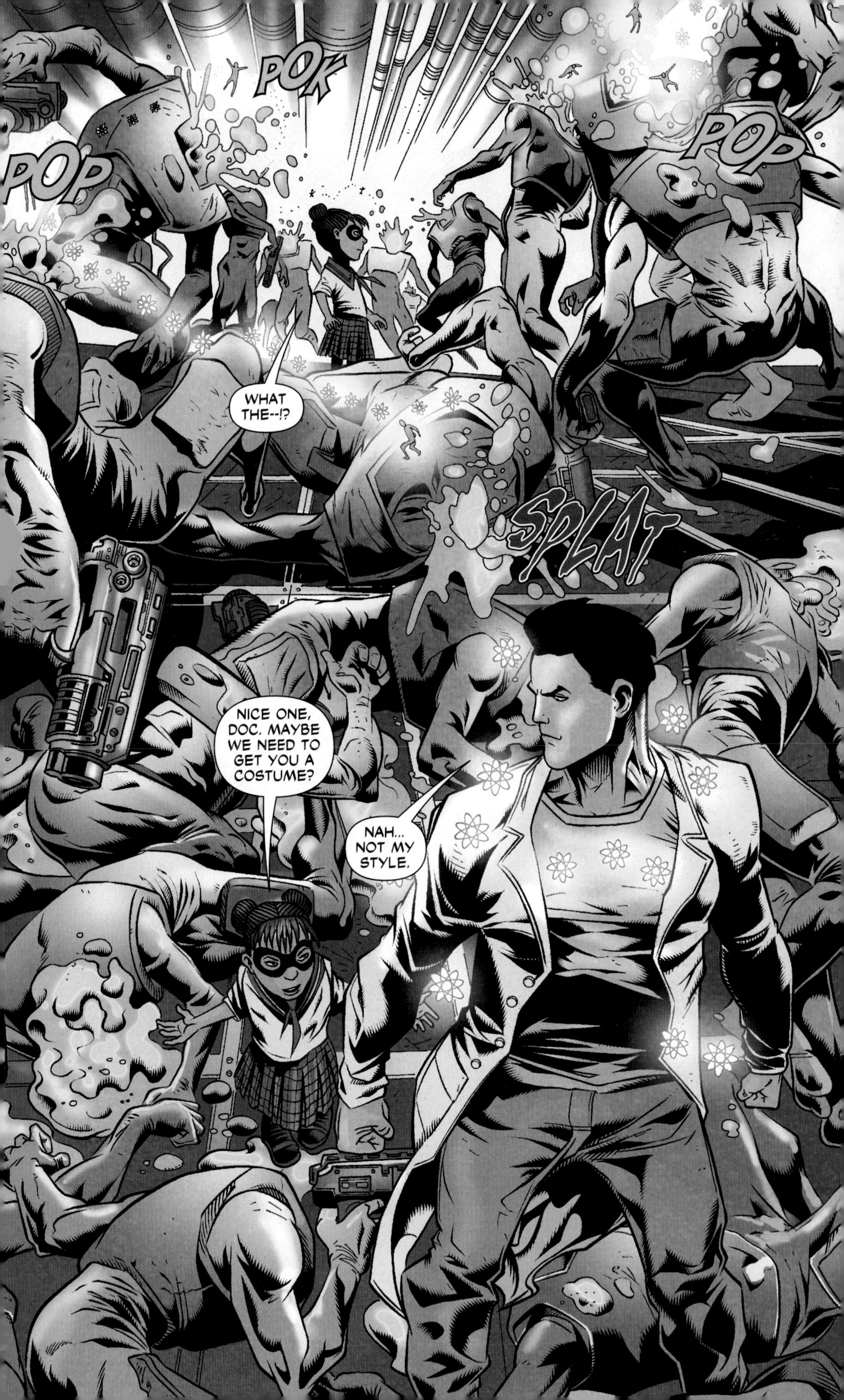
POK
POP
POP
WHAT THE--!?
SPLAT
NICE ONE, DOC. MAYBE WE NEED TO GET YOU A COSTUME?
NAH... NOT MY STYLE.

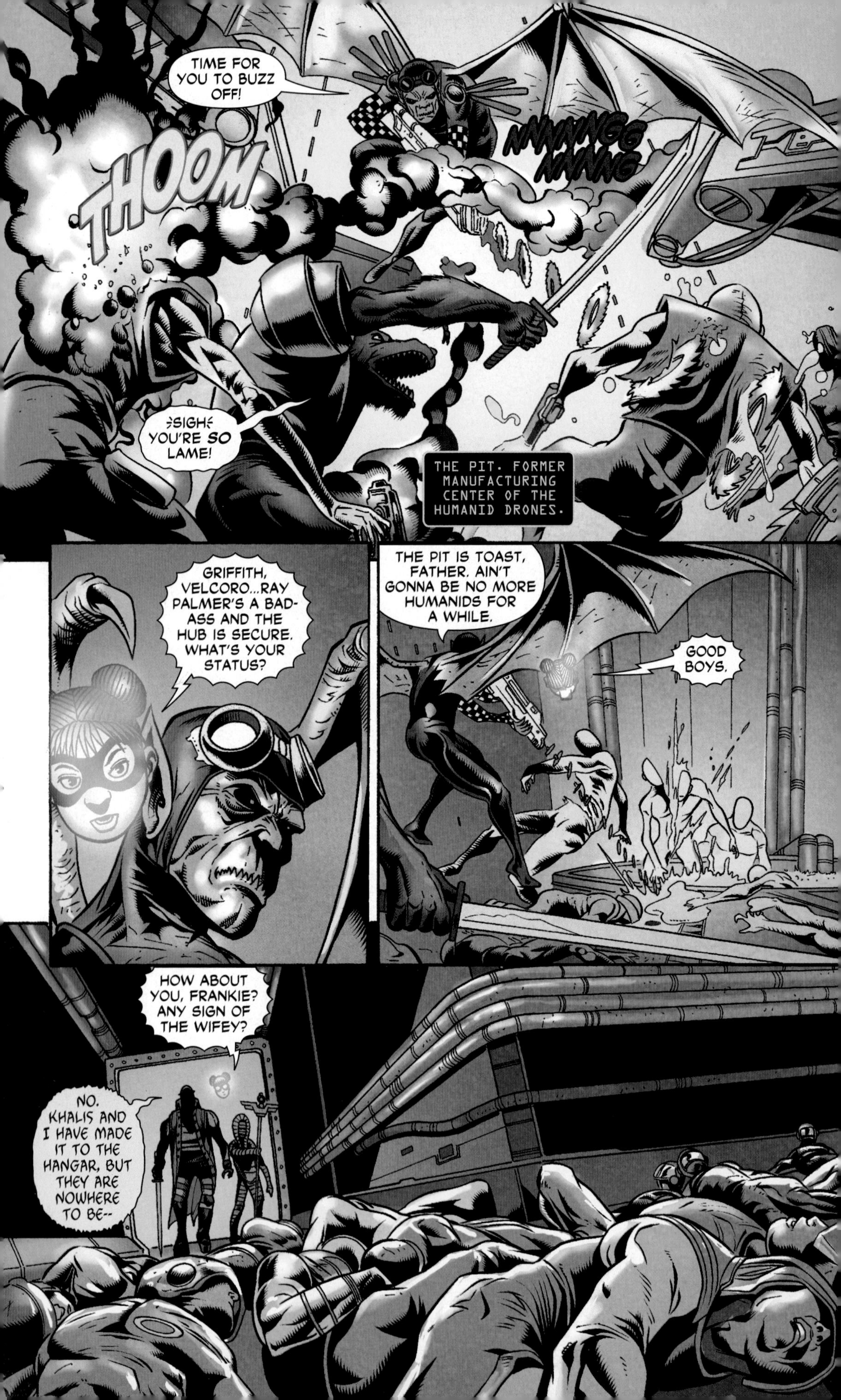
TIME FOR YOU TO BUZZ OFF!
THOOM
NNNNNGG NNNNG
SIGH YOU'RE SO LAME!
THE PIT. FORMER MANUFACTURING CENTER OF THE HUMANID DRONES.
GRIFFITH, VELCORO...RAY PALMER'S A BAD-ASS AND THE HUB IS SECURE. WHAT'S YOUR STATUS?
THE PIT IS TOAST, FATHER. AIN'T GONNA BE NO MORE HUMANIDS FOR A WHILE.
GOOD BOYS.
HOW ABOUT YOU, FRANKIE? ANY SIGN OF THE WIFEY?
NO. KHALIS AND I HAVE MADE IT TO THE HANGAR, BUT THEY ARE NOWHERE TO BE--

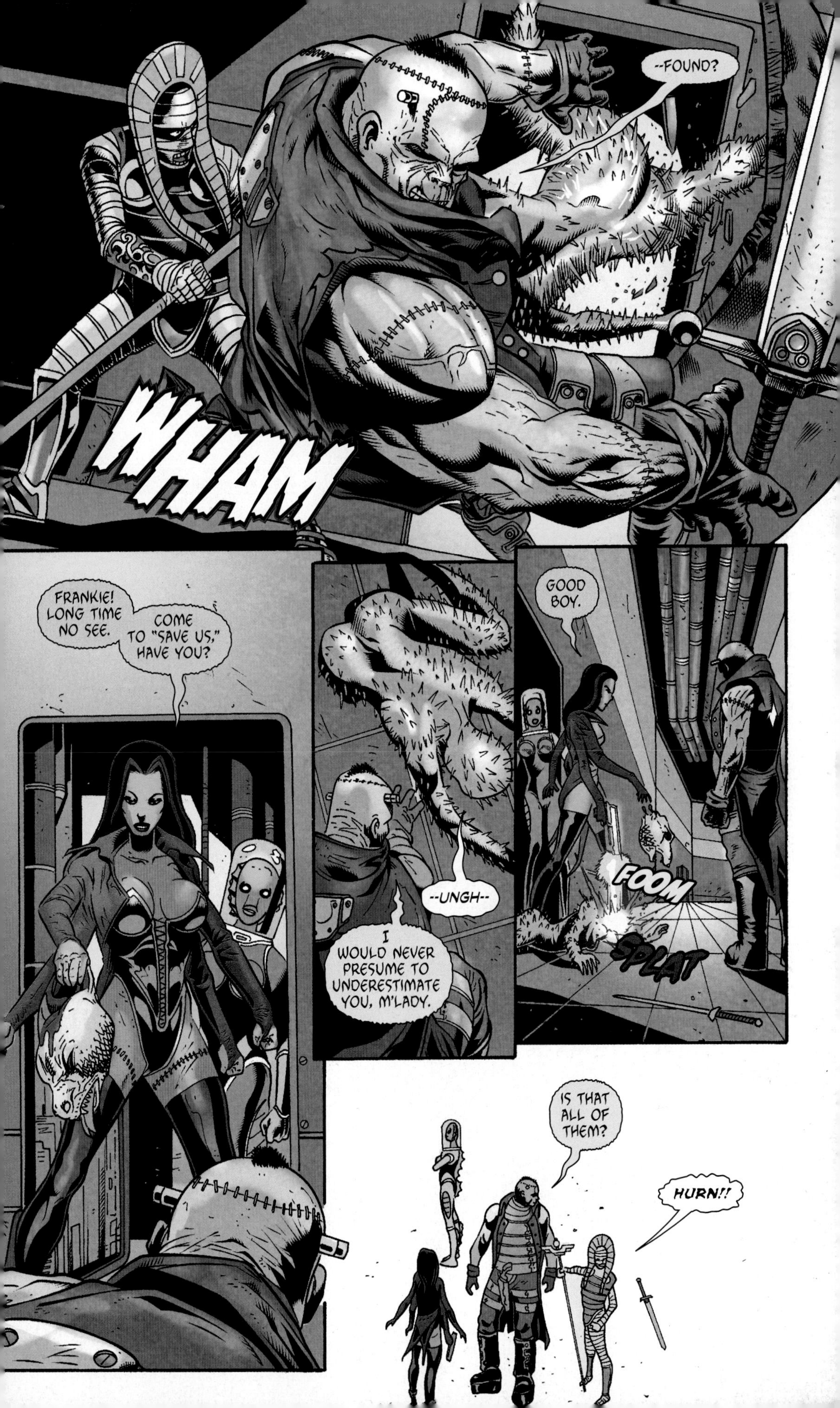
--FOUND?
WHAM
FRANKIE! LONG TIME NO SEE.
COME TO "SAVE US," HAVE YOU?
--UNGH--
I WOULD NEVER PRESUME TO UNDERESTIMATE YOU, M'LADY.
GOOD BOY.
FOOM
SPLAT
IS THAT ALL OF THEM?
HURN!!

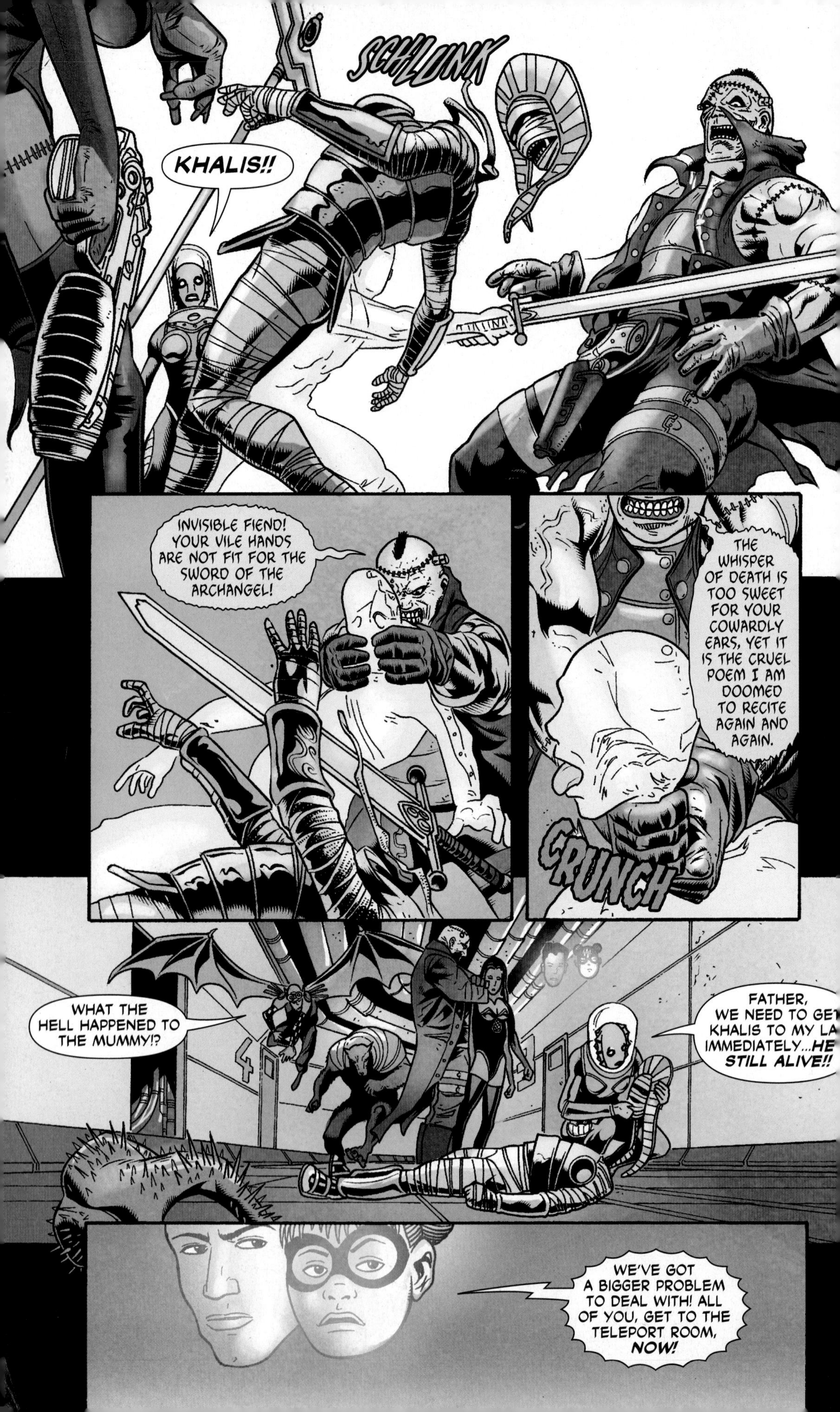
SCHLUNK
KHALIS!!
INVISIBLE FIEND! YOUR VILE HANDS ARE NOT FIT FOR THE SWORD OF THE ARCHANGEL!
THE WHISPER OF DEATH IS TOO SWEET FOR YOUR COWARDLY EARS, YET IT IS THE CRUEL POEM I AM DOOMED TO RECITE AGAIN AND AGAIN.
CRUNCH
WHAT THE HELL HAPPENED TO THE MUMMY!?
FATHER, WE NEED TO GET KHALIS TO MY LA IMMEDIATELY...HE STILL ALIVE!!
WE'VE GOT A BIGGER PROBLEM TO DEAL WITH! ALL OF YOU, GET TO THE TELEPORT ROOM, NOW!

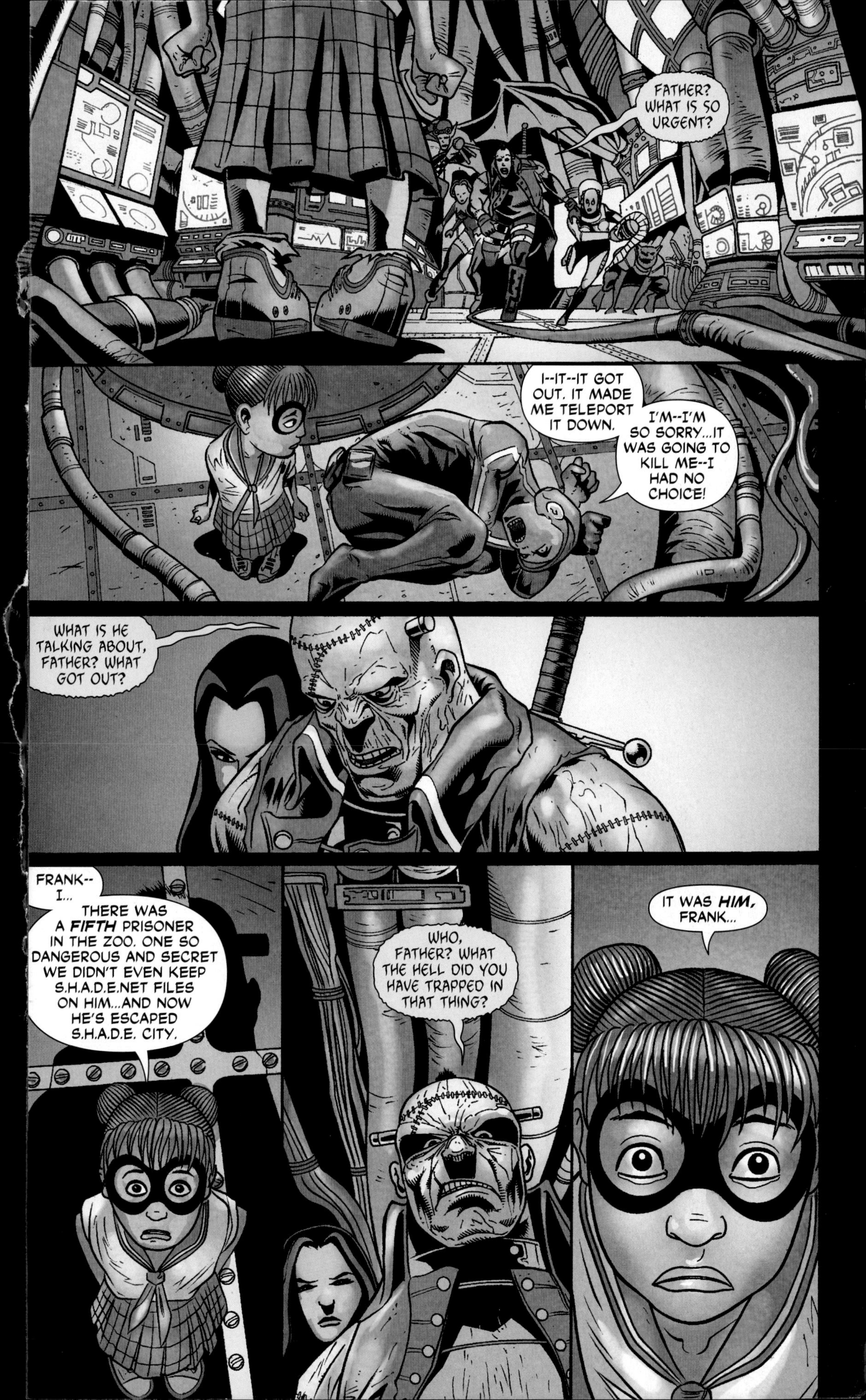
FATHER? WHAT IS SO URGENT?
I--IT--IT GOT OUT. IT MADE ME TELEPORT IT DOWN.
I'M--I'M SO SORRY...IT WAS GOING TO KILL ME--I HAD NO CHOICE!
WHAT IS HE TALKING ABOUT, FATHER? WHAT GOT OUT?
FRANK-- I...
THERE WAS A FIFTH PRISONER IN THE ZOO. ONE SO DANGEROUS AND SECRET WE DIDN'T EVEN KEEP S.H.A.D.E.NET FILES ON HIM...AND NOW HE'S ESCAPED S.H.A.D.E. CITY.
WHO, FATHER? WHAT THE HELL DID YOU HAVE TRAPPED IN THAT THING?
IT WAS HIM, FRANK...

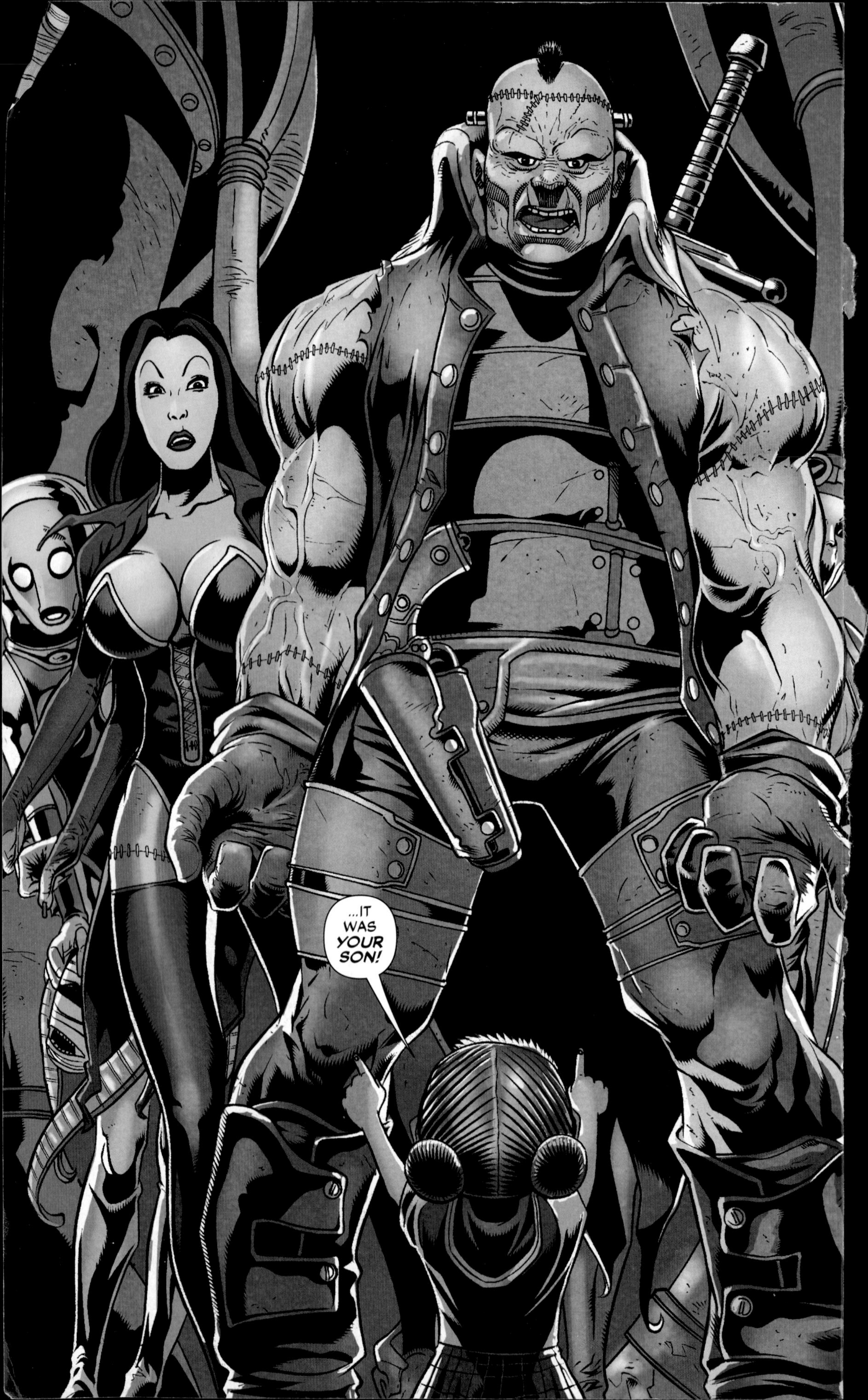
...IT WAS YOUR SON!

FRANKENSTEIN AGENT OF S.H.A.D.E.

COVER SKETCHES BY J.G. JONES

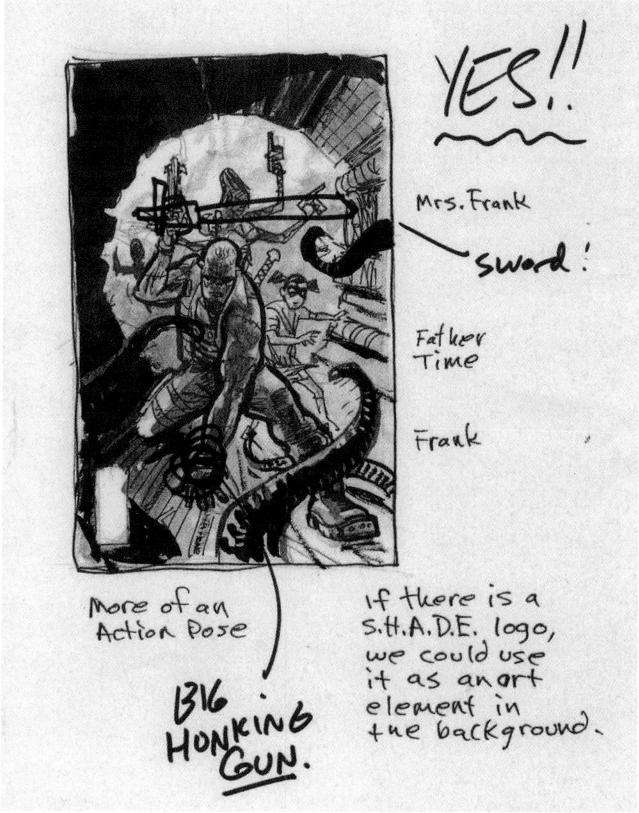
YES!!
Mrs. Frank
Sword!
Father Time
Frank
More of an Action Pose
BIG HONKING GUN.
If there is a S.H.A.D.E. logo, we could use it as an art element in the background.

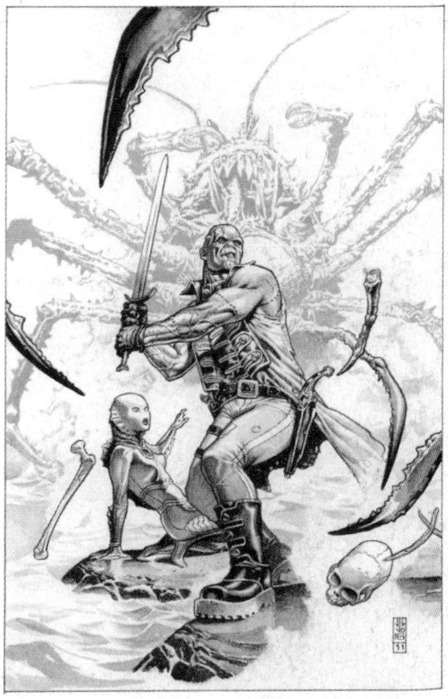

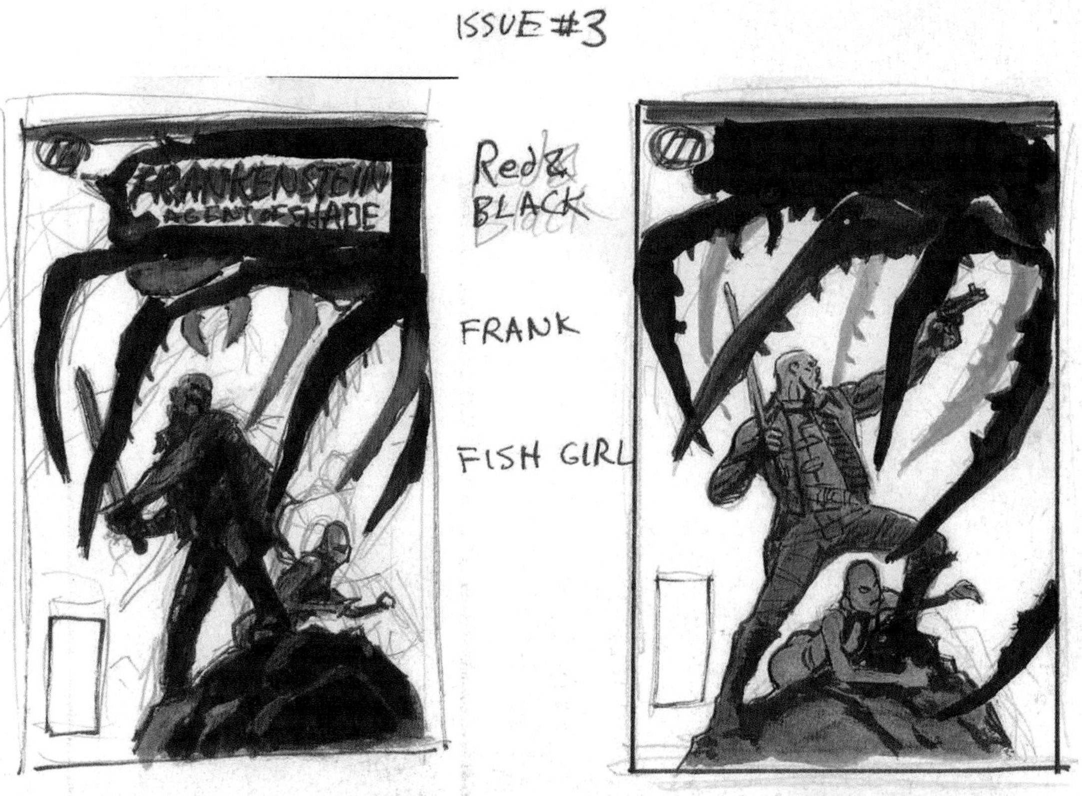
ISSUE #3
FRANKENSTEIN AGENT OF SHADE
Red & BLACK
FRANK
FISH GIRL

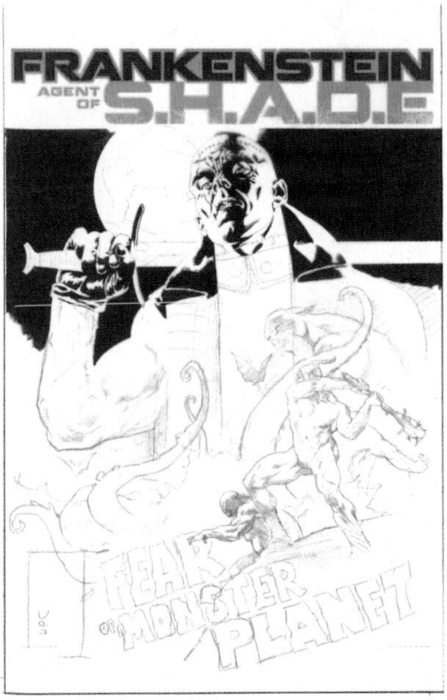
FRANKENSTEIN
AGENT OF S.H.A.D.E
FEAR OF MONSTER PLANET

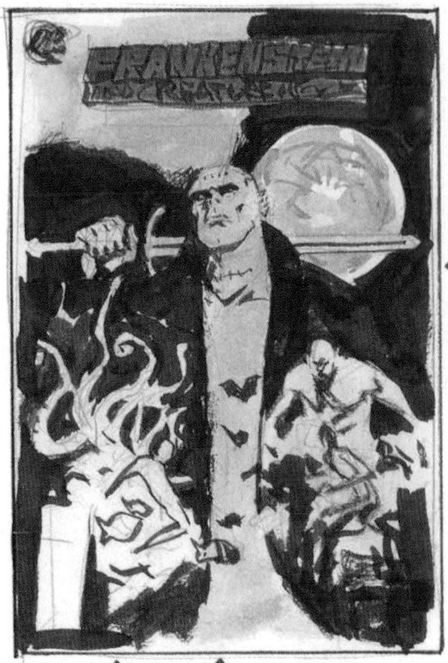
FRANKENSTEIN

Monster Planet ←

← Frank

Giant Ogre + Mrs. Frank

↑ Sea Monster + Fish Girl

↑ Bat

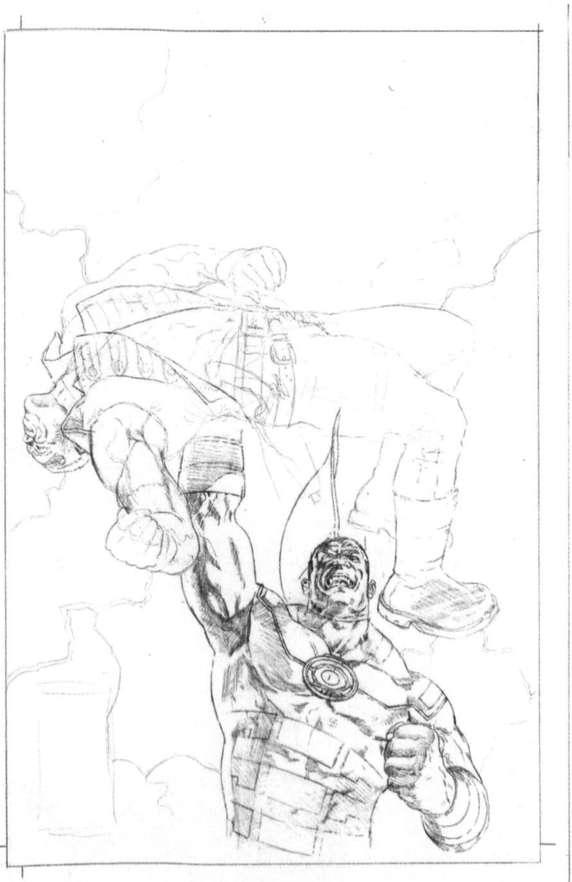

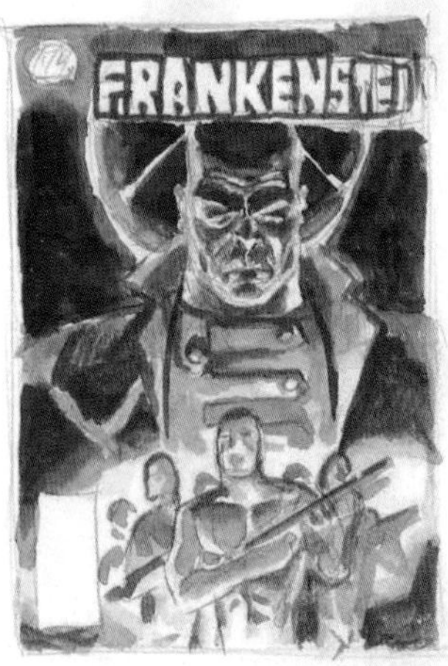
FRANKENSTEIN

Frank

Humanids with weapon all exactly s pose